SOCIAL CHANGE
ECONOMIC LIFE IN

C000147599

Series Editor: Duncan Gallie

SKILL AND OCCUPATIONAL CHANGE

SOCIAL CHANGE AND
ECONOMIC LIFE INITIATIVE

This volume is part of a series arising from the Social Change and Economic Life Initiative—a major interdisciplinary programme of research funded by the Economic and Social Research Council. The programme focused on the impact of the dramatic economic restructuring of the 1980s on employers' labour force strategies, workers' experiences of employment and unemployment, and the changing dynamics of household relations.

ALSO PUBLISHED IN THIS SERIES

Social Change and the Experience of Unemployment
Edited by Duncan Gallie, Catherine Marsh, and Carolyn Vogler

Employer Strategy and the Labour Market
Edited by Jill Rubery and Frank Wilkinson

Gender Segregation and Social Change
Edited by Alison MacEwan Scott

The Social and Political Economy of the Household
Edited by Michael Anderson, Frank Bechhofer, and
Jonathan Gershuny

Trade Unionism in Recession
Edited by Duncan Gallie, Roger Penn, and Michael Rose

SKILL AND OCCUPATIONAL CHANGE

Edited by

ROGER PENN, MICHAEL ROSE
and

JILL RUBERY

OXFORD UNIVERSITY PRESS
1994

Oxford University Press, Walton Street, Oxford OX2 6DP

Oxford New York Toronto
Delhi Bombay Calcutta Madras Karachi
Kuala Lumpur Singapore Hong Kong Tokyo
Nairobi Dar es Salaam Cape Town
Melbourne Auckland Madrid
and associated companies in
Berlin Ibadan

Oxford is a trade mark of Oxford University Press

Published in the United States
by Oxford University Press Inc., New York

British Library Cataloguing in Publication Data
Data available
ISBN 0-19-827914-0
ISBN 0-19-827928-0 (pbk.)

Library of Congress Cataloging in Publication Data
Skill and Occupational Change | edited by
Roger Penn, Michael Rose, and Jill Rubery.—
(The Social change and economic life initiative)
1. Unemployment—Great Britain—Psychological aspects.
2. Unemployed—Great Britain—Psychology. 3. Great Britain—
Social conditions—1945- . 4. Great Britain—Social conditions—1945-
5. Social change. I. Gallie, Duncan. II. Marsh, Catherine.
III. Vogler, Carolyn M., 1950- . IV. Series.
HD5708.S65 1994 331.13'7941—dc20 93-14377
ISBN 0-19-827914-0
ISBN 0-19-827928-0 (pbk.)

Set by Hope Services (Abingdon) Ltd.
Printed in Great Britain
on acid-free paper by
Biddles Ltd., Guildford and King's Lynn

FOREWORD

This volume is part of a series of publications arising from the Social Change and Economic Life Initiative—a programme of research funded by the Economic and Social Research Council. The major objectives of the programme were to study the nature and determinants of employer labour force policies, worker experiences of employment and the labour market, the changing dynamics of household relations and the impact of changes in the employment structure on social integration and social stratification in the community.

The research programme focused on six local labour markets: Aberdeen, Coventry, Kirkcaldy, Northampton, Rochdale, and Swindon. These were selected to provide contrasting patterns of recent and past economic change. Three of the localities— Coventry, Kirkcaldy, and Rochdale—had relatively high levels of unemployment in the early and mid-1980s, whereas the other three experienced relatively low levels of unemployment.

The data collected by the Initiative give an exceptionally rich picture of the lives of people and of the operation of the labour market in the different localities. Three representative surveys were carried out between 1986 and 1987, providing fully comparable data across the localities. The first—the Work Attitudes/ Histories survey—was a random survey of the non-institutional population aged between 20 and 60, involving interviews with about 1,000 people in each locality. It provides information on work histories, current experiences of employment or unemployment, and attitudes to work. This was taken as the point of departure for the other two surveys, focusing respectively on the household circumstances of respondents and on the policies of their employers. In the Household and Community Survey approximately a third of the original respondents were reinterviewed to develop a picture of their household strategies, their organization of domestic work, their leisure activities, their friendship networks, and their attitudes towards welfare provision. Where people had partners, interviews were carried out both with the original respondents and with their partners. The Employers' survey was based on telephone interviews with senior management in the establishments for which respondents in the original Work Attitudes/Histories survey worked. A further non-random follow-up survey was carried out involving 180 of the establishments that had taken part in the initial survey. The details of the research design and sampling for the different phases of the programme are provided in an Appendix at the end of this volume.

In addition, related studies were carried out in individual localities, focusing in greater depth on issues that had been covered in the common surveys. These included studies of the historical context of employment practices, current processes of technical change, managerial employee relations policies, industrial relations, gender segregation, the relationship between employer and employee perceptions of employment conditions, and household strategies with respect to labour market decisions and the organization of work within the household.

The team that implemented the programme consisted of thirty-five researchers drawn from fourteen different institutions. It brought together sociologists, economists, geographers, social historians, and social psychologists. The major common research instruments were collectively constructed through a series of working groups responsible for particular aspects of the study. The programme involved, then, a co-operative interdisciplinary research effort for which there are few precedents in British social science.

DUNCAN GALLIE
National Co-ordinator and Series Editor

ACKNOWLEDGEMENTS

THIS book forms part of the Social Change and Economic Life Initiative (SCELI) series. The SCELI programme of research was initiated and supported by the Economic and Social Research Council. Fieldwork for the Work Attitudes/Histories survey and for the Household and Community survey was undertaken by Public Attitude Surveys (High Wycombe) Ltd. The authors and editors wish to thank the many colleagues and others who commented on earlier drafts of the chapters. Chapters 2 and 7 were originally published in *Work, Employment and Society*, and Chapter 6 in the *British Journal of Sociology*; we thank the Editors of both journals for permitting us to republish them here.

CONTENTS

List of Figures   xi

List of Tables   xii

Notes on the Contributors   xvii

1. Introduction: The SCELI Skill Findings   1
   Michael Rose, Roger Penn, and Jill Rubery

   Part I: Patterns of Skill Change

2. Patterns of Skill Change: Upskilling, Deskilling, or
   Polarization?   41
   Duncan Gallie

3. Occupational Change in a Working-Life Perspective:
   Internal and External Views   77
   Peter Elias

4. Technical Change and Skilled Manual Work in
   Contemporary Rochdale   107
   Roger Penn

5. Technical Change and the Division of Labour in
   Rochdale and Aberdeen   130
   *Roger Penn, Ann Gasteen, Hilda Scattergood, and
   John Sewel*

   Part II: Subjective Dimensions of Skill

6. Management and Employee Perceptions of Skill   159
   *Brendan Burchell, Jane Elliott, Jill Rubery, and
   Frank Wilkinson*

7. Gender and Skills   189
   Sara Horrell, Jill Rubery, and Brendan Burchell

8. Towards a Phenomenology of Skill   223
   Brian Francis and Roger Penn

9. Job Satisfaction, Job Skills, and Personal Skills   244
   Michael Rose

10. Skill and Samuel Smiles: Changing the British
    Work Ethic   281
    Michael Rose

Methodological Appendix   336
Bibliography   346
Index   357

LIST OF FIGURES

3.1 Changes in occupational employment, 1971–1989   82
3.2 Cohort analysis of employed persons in 'complex' occupations: 30 to 34 year-olds, 40 to 44 year-olds, and 55 to 60 year-olds at time of survey, by gender   86
3.3 Employed men and women with children: distribution between simple and complex occupations, five years before and five years after the first or second birth, for births after 1971   89
3.4 A stylized view of male occupational change   104
3.5 A stylized view of female occupational change   105
5.1 Unemployment 1960–1988 in Rochdale and Aberdeen   131
6.1 Perceptions of job content   176
7.1 Cumulative frequency distributions by index of skill   209
8.1 Perceptions of a skilled job   229
8.2 Fitted probabilities of defining skill as trade or apprenticeship   232
8.3 Fitted probabilities of defining skill as requiring training   234
8.4 Fitted probabilities of defining skill as qualifications   235
8.5 Fitted probabilities of defining skill as requiring experience   236
8.6 Fitted probabilities of defining skill as high ability   237
8.7 First two dimensions of correspondence analysis of perceptions of skill   239
9.1 Levels of skill-matching and mean scores for composite job satisfaction, by sex and type of work contract   264
10.1 Relative influence of skill and other major independent variables on the composite scores for the Expressive Work Ethic variable   311
10.2 Combination of mean scores for Expressive Work Ethic and for Economic individualism in selected occupational groups   319

LIST OF TABLES

2.1 Class distribution: respondents and parents and
    by areas   46
2.2 Skill characteristics by class   48
2.3 Changes in skill and responsibility   52–3
2.4 Class composition of sectors   58
2.5 Increase in skill and responsibility by sector   60
2.6 Qualifications required and own qualifications   61
2.7 Advanced technology and skill levels by class   64
2.8 Advanced technology and skill change by class   66
2.9 Qualifications and training of men and women employees   67
2.10 Increase in skill and responsibility by sex   69
2.11 Skill and impact of advanced technology by sex   70
2.12 Increasing skill and responsibility by occupational
    segregation   71
2.13 Comparison of women in full-time and part-time work   72
2.14 Increasing skill and responsibility by occupational
    segregation: women full-time and part-time employees   74
3.1 Examples of the type of occupations labelled 'simple'
    or 'complex'   84
3.2 Trends in employment in 'complex' occupations by
    gender, 1971–1989   85
3.3 The relationship between employment in 'complex'
    occupations, personal characteristics, job
    characteristics, and economic change   92–4
3.4 Proportion of respondents who stated that their current
    or most recent occupation was their most skilled   99
3.5 The relationship between subjective deskilling, personal
    characteristics, and current employment   102–3
4.1 Microelectronics-based technologies installed in the
    Rochdale engineering industry by 1986   114
4.2 National origins of microelectronics-based machinery
    in the Rochdale engineering industry   115

4.3   The relationship between the implementation of
      microelectronics-based machines and the changing size
      of the workforce, 1980–1986   116
4.4   The relationship between sector of employment and
      the changing proportion of skilled workers within the
      overall workforces in Rochdale, 1980–1986   120
4.5   The relationship between the implementation of micro-
      electronics-based machinery and the overall propor-
      tion of skilled workers in Rochdale, 1980–1986   121
4.6   The relationship between the changing proportion of
      skilled workers and the recognition of trade unions
      within plants   121
4.7   Technician and craft apprentices in Rochdale   124
4.8   The relationship between industrial sector and the
      changing proportion of apprentices in Rochdale,
      1980–1986   124
4.9   The relationship between the implementation of
      microelectronics-based new technologies and the
      changing proportion of apprentices in Rochdale,
      1980–1986   125
4.10 The relationship between the changing size of plant
      and the changing proportion of apprentices in
      Rochdale, 1980–1986   125
4.11 The relationship between trade union recognition and
      the changing proportion of apprentices in Rochdale,
      1980–1986   126
4.12 The relationship between whether a plant is a sub-
      sidiary of the larger corporate unit or is independent
      and the changing proportion of apprentices in
      Rochdale, 1980–1986   126
5.1   Introduction of new equipment in the preceding two
      years (percentage saying 'Yes')   137
5.2   Technological changes and changes in the number
      employed (larger establishments only)   138
5.3   Technological change and the levels of skill for jobs
      (larger establishments only)   138
5.4   Technical change and further training needs in
      Rochdale and Aberdeen (larger establishments only)   139
5.5   Technical change in manufacturing plants in
      Rochdale and Aberdeen since 1980   142–3

5.6   Technical change in service-sector establishments in
      Rochdale and Aberdeen since 1980   144–5
5.7   Change in production and clerical/administrative
      areas in relation to technical change in manufacturing
      plants in Rochdale and Aberdeen   146–7
5.8   Change in production and clerical/administrative
      areas in relation to technical change in
      manufacturing plants in Rochdale and Aberdeen   150–1
5.9   Technical change and levels of skill in manufacturing
      plants in Rochdale and Aberdeen   152–3
5.10 Technical change and levels of skill in service-sector
      establishments in Rochdale and Aberdeen   152–3
6.1   Employees' and managers' perceptions of job
      content: all jobs   171
6.2   Perceptions of job content by job category: average
      of employees' and managers' ratings as a percentage of
      ratings of lower-skilled production and service
      employees   173
6.3   The relative valuation of job content: managers'
      ratings of job content as percentages of employees'
      rating of job content   174
6.4   Perceptions of job content: employees' and managers'
      scores   187
7.1   Conventional classifications of skill, employees and
      self-employed   194–5
7.2   Factors important in doing the job well, employees
      and self-employed   200
7.3   Responsibilities involved in the job, employees and
      self-employed   203
7.4   Scope for discretion or choice at work, employees
      and self-employed   206
7.5   Index of skill, employees   210
7.6   Perceptions of own job as skilled, controlling for
      index of skill, for component variables in the index
      of skill, and for social class, employees and self-
      employed   214–15
7.7   Why respondents consider their jobs to be 'skilled'
      or not 'skilled'   218
8.1   Responses to the question 'What is a skilled
      job   224

8.2	Parameter estimates and standard errors of final logistic models for the given dependent variables	238
8.3	Explanatory variables used in the preliminary cross-tabulations and in the logistic regression analyses	242–3
9.1	Correspondence between scores for skill of job and skill of individual in the employee sample	248
9.2	Skills-matching and skills-mismatching: distribution of employees between main subgroups	249
9.3	Differences in levels of job satisfaction between particular job aspects in the employee sample	253
9.4	Types of skill-matching and satisfaction with the intrinsic aspects of present job	254
9.5	Types of skill-matching and satisfaction with the extrinsic aspects of present job	256
9.6	Types of skill-matching and satisfaction with the authority aspects of present job	258
9.7	Types of skill-matching and overall satisfaction with present job	261
9.8	Levels of skill-matching by sex and type of work contract	262
9.9	Banded composite scores for job satisfaction, by sex and type of work contract	263
9.10	Relative influence of the skill variables and other workplace and individual variables on scores for composite job satisfaction	266–7
10.1	Normative commitment to paid work in the major labour market groups, all active subgroups	291
10.2	Support for four rationales of paid work in the major labour-market groups, derived from combined and weighted reasons for working	294
10.3	Support for economic individualism (self-reliance ideology) in the major labour market groups	296
10.4	Effect of seeing one's job as skilled on support for the main aspects of the work ethic	298
10.5	Effect of degree of control in the work process on support for the main aspects of the work ethic	300
10.6	Effect of qualifications now required to do current job on support for the main aspects of the work ethic	304

10.7   Effect of training, work-learning experience, and
       qualifications actually held on support for the main
       aspects of the work ethic   307
10.8   Effect of composite variables for job-skill and own-
       skill on support for the main aspects of the work
       ethic   309
10.9   Levels of skill and support for the main aspects of
       the work ethic in selected occupational groups   317
10.10 Method for computing index-figures and scores for
       normative commitment to paid work in subgroups   326
10.11 Method for computing index figures and scores for
       economic individualism (self-reliance ideology) in
       subgroups, illustrated by favourability to trade
       unions   327
10.12 Effect of weighting reasons for having paid work in
       subgroups, illustrated by dummy data   330
10.13 Method for calculating scores for expressive work
       rationale in subgroups, illustrated by reference to
       qualifications actually held   331

A.1   The Work Attitudes/Histories Survey, 1986   337
A.2   The Household and Community Survey, 1989:
       achieved sample by characteristics at time of Work
       Attitudes/ Histories Survey   341
A.3   The Baseline Employer sample   343

CONTRIBUTORS

BRENDAN BURCHELL, Lecturer in Social Psychology, Faculty of Social and Political Sciences, University of Cambridge.

PETER ELIAS, Research Fellow, Institute for Employment Research, University of Warwick.

JANE ELLIOTT, Fellow, Newnham College, Cambridge.

BRIAN FRANCIS, Lecturer in Statistics, Centre for Applied Statistics, University of Lancaster.

DUNCAN GALLIE, Foundation Fellow in Sociology, Nuffield College, Oxford.

ANN GASTEEN, Lecturer, Department of Economics, University of Aberdeen.

SARA HORRELL, Assistant Lecturer, Faculty of Economics and Politics, Cambridge.

ROGER PENN, Reader in Economic Sociology, Department of Sociology, Cartmel College, Lancaster.

MICHAEL ROSE, Visiting Fellow in Economic Sociology, School of Management, University of Bath.

JILL RUBERY, Senior Lecturer, Manchester School of Management, University of Manchester Institute of Science and Technology.

HILDA SCATTERGOOD, Department of Sociology, Cartmel College, Lancaster.

JOHN SEWEL, Professor, Department of Sociology, University of Aberdeen.

FRANK WILKINSON, Senior Research Officer, Department of Applied Economics, University of Cambridge.

1

Introduction: The SCELI Skill Findings

MICHAEL ROSE, ROGER PENN, AND JILL RUBERY

DEBATES ON SKILL IN BRITAIN

The chapters of this book are based on the research carried out for the Social Change and Economic Life Initiative (SCELI) supported by the Economic and Social Research Council. SCELI was launched in 1985, just over a decade after Braverman's (1974) influential publication on the degradation of work. This book had led to a continuing and intense debate over the direction and nature of change in the skill level of jobs, and perhaps more fundamentally over the meaning or social significance of the terms 'skill' and 'skilled work'. Developing alongside this debate over deskilling was a second, over flexibility in work tasks and pressures for new systems of work to meet changing competitive conditions and new (especially electronic) technologies. Intermingling with both these debates, but always retaining its own dynamic, was yet another, over gender and the relationships between social and gender divisions and the meaning and concept of skill.

All three strands of social analysis had already (Knights, Willmott, and Collinson, 1985; Crompton and Jones, 1984; Warner, 1984; Cockburn, 1983; Thompson, 1983; Wood, 1982; Wilkinson, 1981; Zimbalast, 1979) done much to expand and deepen our understanding of the processes of occupational and skill change by the time the SCELI programme was launched. Analysis and debate in each of them has continued steadily since, fed by regular additions to the case-study and even the survey evidence, as well as by new theoretical contributions (Knights and Willmott, 1990, 1987, 1986a; Pollert, 1989; Thompson, 1989; West, 1990; Wood, 1989; Clark et al., 1988). On the other hand, and despite this rapidly expanding literature, there had never been an opportunity to develop a large-scale survey—one informed by all three perspectives on the factors influencing the development and perception of skills. SCELI aimed to fill this gap.

Changes in skill have been recognized to result from three separate, if interrelated, processes: (i) changes in the functions carried out by the working population; (ii) changes in the methods of performing various functions; (iii) changes in the division of labour which influence what share of the working population is engaged in skilled tasks. Changes in products, in services, in technology, in management strategy, and in work design all necessarily impinge on the development of skills within the labour force. Much of the debate around the deskilling hypothesis has thus been concerned with disentangling these various influences, and with debating the extent to which Braverman was correct in hypothesizing that there is (indeed, must be) an underlying tendency towards degradation of labour which will be disclosed in the historical development of technology and management strategy—even though, here and there, pockets of worker resistance, and the necessarily uneven development of capitalism, 'allow' apparently perverse and contradictory trends towards upskilling.

While this debate about the existence, or otherwise, of an 'imperative' within capitalist production to exert managerial control through deskilling was occupying the research agendas of sociologists, including many with a theoretical and materialist approach, and others concerned with historical method and the assimilation of detailed case-study material, a quite separate debate was emerging amongst economists. Yet it had equal significance for the analysis of occupational and skill change.

The 1970s and 1980s witnessed the destablilization of markets and an apparent waning of the post-1945 system of Fordism and mass production. Saturation of mass-consumption markets in advanced countries, the development of a new international division of labour, and the greater availability of flexible technologies all seemed to require a radical reassessment of the potential for industrial development in developed countries—or at least in 'the West'. Competition based on labour costs, which had favoured a tightly controlled, skill-degraded, and low-paid labour force, it was strongly argued, was being displaced by new market conditions requiring a different, more supple—and more subtle—form of competition based on flexibility (Piore and Sabel, 1984). Product diversity, design excellence, high quality, and reliability were becoming the new criteria for market success; and, to compete, firms needed flexible production systems, flexible labour costs, and flexibly skilled labour.

The change in the nature of competition could also be seen as relaxing the formerly accepted imperatives in the organization of production. The possibility was raised that the main trend would be towards upskilling; or, perhaps more likely, towards a polarization of skills. While new employer strategies would create flexible, highly skilled workers in secure employment at one end of the spectrum, they would produce flexible, low-skilled, and highly disposable workers at the other. This scenario thus raised the thorny question of whether an increase in the flexibility of labour can be equated with an increase in skill. How far could multi-skilling and task versatility ('polyvalence') be regarded as a genuine form of upskilling, rather than simply as a different permutation of the existing division of labour? (To multiply the number of semi-skilled or unskilled component tasks of a job, and then to relabel it as 'skilled', seemed more like an exercise in repackaging than a true new departure.) Yet Adam Smith's example of task division in pin manufacture, based on the transition from initial multi-skilling to a detailed division of labour, had often been taken as synonymous with deskilling; the smaller the range of tasks, the lower the degree of discretion afforded to the worker in determining the order or the method of production.

The relevance of the gender debate to understanding processes of occupational and skill change has been manifested in several ways. First, it was the critique of Braverman based on analyses of gender divisions in the labour force that highlighted the distinction between the attribution and recognition of skill, thanks to social power, and the skill and discretion actually deployed at work. Case study after case study found examples of women's work which was arguably—even evidently—skilled in terms of job content but which was neither perceived, graded, nor rewarded as skilled work. (See, for example, Walby 1986; Knights and Willmott, 1986*a*; Craig, Garnsey, and Rubery, 1985; Cockburn, 1983; Armstrong, 1982; Phillips and Taylor, 1980.)

These analyses also highlighted the limited range of factors that might in practice be thought of as contributing to the skill level of a job. Yet factors associated with women's work were often omitted from job-evaluation schemes; and skills learned informally, particularly in the home, were treated as 'natural' and not in need of any special financial premium. The need to distinguish clearly between the perceptions of skill held by employees or managers, actual job content, and the formally ascribed status of skill, has been further highlighted in the flexibility debate. The designation of workers as 'peripheral', for example, may have more to do with the status of the workers within the labour market than with the type of work they do or its centrality to an employer's work process. These undervaluations of skill by no means apply only to women; but it has been the feminist strand in the debate that has brought the issue to the fore and given it urgency.

RESEARCH STRATEGIES AND SCOPE OF THE DATA

In developing their questionnaires for the SCELI surveys, the research teams were thus faced with both a requirement and the opportunity to draw on the very extensive and multi-faceted debate on skill in the ten preceding years. Space limitations restricted the extent to which some skill issues could be examined within the core surveys; but several teams took up the 'subsidiary' questions in their own 'team-specific' sections of the survey questionnaire,[1] or in parallel enquiries (see Methodological Appendix). Some of these Related Studies made use of case-study or qualitative techniques of enquiry. Most authors in this volume would recognize how this supplementary material repeatedly helped their own interpretations of many quantitative findings.

It is worth stressing here that *both* survey and qualitative data were collected for five central skill issues: (i) employers' handling of work reorganization following technical and product-market change; (ii) the impact of technical change on occupations and skills viewed from both employers' and employees' perspectives; (iii) individual views of skill levels, job content, discretion, and recent changes in jobs; (iv) qualifications currently needed to do jobs as well as those held by people doing them; and (v) length of formal training-times as well as estimates for the period needed by respondents to learn to do their current work well. It was possible to analyse all the data separately by gender and by type of employment (full-time, part-time, self-employed), and to relate aspects of skill and job content to a wide range of information about individual work-histories, the characteristics of workplaces, and broader social and work attitudes.

Not all these approaches and data sources are explicitly utilized in the chapters that follow, though often they are present by implication, from preliminary analyses of data that were not followed up, papers prepared for the seminars held for disseminating results, discussions between co-authors, and editorial planning for the main reports. Likewise, the subject-matter overlaps with that of several other volumes to be published in the SCELI series, especially those on continuity and change in gender segregation (A. MacEwen Scott, 1994), on employer strategies (Rubery and Wilkinson, 1994), and on trade unionism (Gallie, Penn, and Rose, forthcoming). It was decided that the present volume should focus clearly upon the issue of skill and occupational change as experienced by individuals, with questions of work flexibility and employer strategy being given more detailed treatment elsewhere. However, the interrelationships and intermeshing between the themes explored within the SCELI data-sets can be considered a major feature of the research programme as a whole. Readers are referred to these other volumes in the series for complementary findings on the theme of skill, occupation, and technical change presented here.[2]

It is believed that the chapters presented here also show how closely various aspects of the skills problematic interpenetrated in the analyses of the data most relevant to the essential theme. Each one examines a special skill issue and presents distinct sets of results, some of them drawn from Related Studies and team-specific questions as well as from the commonly shared 'core' material. Several chapters present specially developed measures or offer what are believed to be original concepts or methods of analysis. Yet many findings and conclusions are closely complementary, and it is hoped that this multiple linkage of findings will be further brought out by the specific cross-references provided in the text of chapters.

The chapters could have been grouped in more than one way.

It was finally decided that the order of the chapters should reflect two relatively distinct themes, though most chapters deal in some way with both: (i) patterns of skill change and development in the recent past; and (ii) the subjective and individual aspects of skill. The volume makes a special contribution, it is believed, to each of these two themes; but the second is a little less familiar than the first and, logically speaking, seems to follow on from it. The remainder of this chapter will attempt to bring out the overall structure of findings that results from adopting this organization, while providing an initial guide to individual chapters, and highlighting what appear to be the more interesting areas of complementarity between them.

It is probable that the data to be presented have important implications for the threefold debate on skill outlined above. The deskilling thesis has, as noted, been by far the best-known and most influential overall interpretation of historic skills change. While 'fundamentalist' degradation theory has lost the very strong support it enjoyed in the 1970s, it has hitherto proved impossible to arrive at a firmly grounded final verdict on it. A constant problem has been the lack and unevenness of much of the evidence on trends in skill in Britain, and in other industrial countries. The preference, especially in Britain, for case studies based on occupations has exposed both sides to the objection that, consciously or not, they always select those occupations that best suit their personal hunches, tastes, or convictions. It is thought that the evidence presented here does allow a more decisive verdict because of its scope and detail. The variety of disciplines and perspectives present in the research teams also reduced the risk of unconscious bias. But the material does have some limitations which should be mentioned at the outset.

The main data source used in the following chapters is the Work Attitudes/Histories sample of just over 6,000 adults. It should be stressed that, technically speaking, this sample is *not* a random national sample of British employees; it is a random sample of economically active people aged 20 to 60 years drawn from six localities deliberately targeted on theoretical and practical grounds. (Readers are referred the Methodological Appendix for further explanation of sampling procedures and the selection of local labour markets.) It excluded very young recent entrants to the labour market; it also excluded people close to the official retirement age for males (65 years). These parameters should be noted.

On the other hand, the employee sub-sample here is a large one, not far short of 4,000 cases (that is, almost 20 times larger than the sample in the landmark *Affluent Worker* study (Goldthorpe *et al.*, 1969)). Some skill data are also available for further large labour-market segments (the unemployed, the self-employed, full-time home-makers, students, and trainees) in the full sample of just over 6,000 persons. The skill data are varied and detailed, covering all occupations of any size in the real working population. The results that emerge separately from the Work Attitudes/Histories survey, the Employers Baseline survey (just under 1,000 larger workplaces) and Employers 30 surveys (case studies of 191 establishments), and from case studies of firms undertaken for Related Studies, are strikingly consistent in their overall pattern, and nowhere more so than in their findings on changes in skill. (Chapters 4 and 5, which examine skill and technical change data collected from employers, bring this out clearly.) It is therefore very difficult not to conclude that the SCELI findings do provide a very good guide to real trends in skill in Great Britain as a whole in the 1980s.

THE DOUBLE DIRECTION OF SKILL CHANGE

If this is agreed, the findings remove any uncertainty over the main skill trends in these years. The data suggest, and they do so compellingly, that the direction of change was running against any *general* process of deskilling. In SCELI, about half of those employees who had held jobs five years earlier said they had experienced some skill gains in the five years preceding the survey. When those who had moved from one job to another (possibly higher-skilled) job, or had received some significant pro-motion in a job they had held for the whole of this period were excluded, the picture remained equally clear.

On the other hand, this essential finding does leave open many questions about the scale of these skill gains, and the exact pat-tern of change where gains were offset by some loss. The case-study material obtained in Related Studies suggests that some gains were of a minor or even trivial kind, at least from an observer perspective. (By the same token, however, others were clearly substantial.) In many cases, it should be remembered, any change to work tasks—a minor adjustment of content, a marginal gain in variety, or a trifling increase in responsibility—might even have been *experienced* as an increase in skill by the people doing the work. (In Chapter 2, Elias discusses 'experience' effects more generally.) Moreover, a large minority of employee respondents said they had experienced no change in skill over the previous five years. It might be asked whether there is in practice a kind of zero-point to the skill of some work: it may be the case that some low-skill jobs cannot be further deskilled simply because they already call for so little skill. Yet a minority—though admittedly a small one—did indeed report a fall in the skill of a job they had held over the five-year reference period. Nor can there be any doubt that many newly created jobs were low in the skill they called for, especially those offering part-time work. (A broadly similar pattern emerges for changes in levels of responsibility at work, as Gallie shows in detail in Chapter 2.)

It may also be unwise to make statements about the possible dynamics of change, on the basis of these results alone, without careful qualification. They cannot be used to settle, once and for all as it were, arguments about long-term processes, towards either deskilling or upskilling, that are supposedly 'inherent' in the British economy or capitalism as a whole: clear as they are, the results do not show, and ought not to be taken to show, that the changes were occurring in obedience to some underlying 'law' or other. True enough, the work-history data (see below) do point to processes of *long-term* incremental change in skills in *this* employee sample. However, they are a quite insufficient basis for concluding that overall gains have continued to occur, at a comparable rate, since the fieldwork was undertaken.

On the other hand, with all these provisos, one thing can be said with absolute confidence: the data run counter to most claims made in the 'strong' versions of the deskilling and 'degradation of work' theses, whilst seriously discrediting most assumptions those interpretations have made about the way larger employers handle technical change. The chapters in this book, dealing with distinct aspects of the skill problematic, *all* support the view that skill is undergoing a complex change which the original deskilling thesis—and, for that matter, any simplistic 'human capital' scenario of upskilling—cannot satisfactorily encompass. To repeat: the overall findings were of a tendency towards modest increases in the skill and responsibility of the largest block of jobs, with serious deskilling processes affecting very few existing jobs, though many newly created jobs called for little skill. Variations on this theme recur constantly in individual chapters. There seems to be no way of squaring the original degradation thesis with such overwhelming contrary evidence. It ought not to be rejected, along with most of its milder derivatives.

Certainly, as Gallie stresses in Chapter 2, the upskilling processes have been highly skewed. The main beneficiaries of skill gains, Gallie shows, were respondents in service-class occupations; that is to say, those fortunate employees who already had jobs embodying technical challenge, appreciable responsibility, and the exercise of authority. In service-class groups men, and those women who worked full-time, had experienced a gain in skill more frequently than members of intermediate or working-class occupations. Any claim that automation or computerization has reduced skill amongst such already advantaged groups seems to be quite simply wrong; in fact, for these groups especially, 'subjection' to such technologies can even be taken as a proxy measure of relatively high skill.

Gallie also provides a clear answer to the question of who has benefited *least* from trends towards upskilling. As the foregoing remarks suggest, for example, those employees whose work did not call for use of the new electronic technologies had experienced skill gains less often. This pattern is overlaid more strongly with a second one, related to gender. Women fared worse overall than men. But women who worked part-time in non-skilled manual tasks fared worst of all. SCELI confirms that part-time women cleaners, shop-workers and catering staff especially, now more than ever, make up an underclass in the 'objective' skills hierarchy. (In hierarchies of what might be called 'attributed' skill, their relative position may even have worsened, as the Cambridge team argue in Chapter 7.)

These findings are reinforced by those of Elias in Chapter 3. Here a different technique for measuring skills change is adopted. Elias divides jobs into two categories, 'complex' and 'simple', tracing the pattern of occupational change over time using data from the work histories of employees. The work histories covered all main employment events since the respondent first entered the labour market (up to 45 years earlier), recording pay, size of workplace, any supervisory duties, union membership, etc., besides every job title and brief details of the work done. The findings point clearly to an increasing trend towards the emergence of 'complex' jobs, with men as its main beneficiaries. While women employees also benefited from the underlying trend *at the start of their careers*, the effect of a period of family formation was to remove almost all of the upgrading effects. Most women rejoining the labour force after child bearing had re-entered it in low-level occupations, despite a higher occupational attainment in earlier stages of their work history, when they formed part of younger age-cohorts.

Was this by necessity or choice? After all, one simple explanation might seem to be that many women re-entrants, perhaps seeking to limit demands on their time and energy, *deliberately avoided* jobs at the level for which they were qualified by experience. Yet Elias's findings for men who had experienced unemployment are strikingly similar: this other form of career-break had often been followed by acceptance of some downgrading in the re-entry occupation.

In terms of the overall findings of the Work Attitudes/Histories survey, then, the nature of the change seems to have been twofold. An essential movement in the direction of upskilling was offset by some 'absolute' deskilling; more significantly still, many newly created jobs were already low in skill, and these were precisely the jobs that were least likely to experience significant upskilling. It is thus possible to argue a good case for a process of relative polarization in skills. To simplify, the already more skilled employees, and those occupying more skilled posts, were more likely to acquire skill and to gain more challenge in their work; those with least skill stood most at risk of losing it and, though they more often gained skill than lost it, they thereby gained relatively less skill and challenge. In other words, a process roughly analogous to that affecting income distribution in Britain in the 1980s can be discerned in the SCELI employee sample. At least in *relative* terms, the position of those who were already disadvantaged in their skill deteriorated, while with each main step up the occupational hierarchy, the scale of gains increased.

THE PROBLEM OF SKILL OFFSETS

Researchers who favour a case-study or other qualitative method for examining skill change may accept this overall picture of a double movement in skill levels but still feel uneasy about the foregoing findings. This is understandable. Survey research may have the advantage of large numbers for plotting overall changes in skill in a group of occupations or employers. Its results may well permit broadly reliable conclusions about the overall degree of change, and enable broadly valid comparisons between the extent of change in differing occupations and industries. However, surveys have limitations for examining processes of skill change. Real changes in given task assignments and responsibilities are sometimes extremely intricate, as are changes modifying skills possessed by individuals. This fact is easily overlooked through a failure to consider the full effect of in-service training, of unevenness in exposure to 'experience effects', or of the tendency for old 'tacit skills' to die out, with new ones gradually replacing them in some cases but not in others. (For a detailed illustration, see Clark *et al.*, 1988: 115–28.)

The complexity of changes to task skills may be 'washed out' in survey work in three obvious ways. Firstly, survey questions have usually to be of a simple, standardized kind, excluding much detail for any given job or occupation. Secondly, the period covered by enquiries usually has to be standardized too, on the necessary but shaky assumption that differing rates of change average out 'across the board'. Finally, interviewers have to ask for assessments from informants; when the latter are employees, they may overlook or exaggerate changes; when they are workplace managers or employee representatives, individuals may have very differing ideas about what constitutes a significant change in skill—or indeed, about what skill itself consists of.

There is a further worrying problem, which particularly affects the study of skill change by means of sample survey interviews. Even in the case of less-skilled manual work, very few tasks comprise just one significant work operation or responsibility; most consist of several, or many. With every step upwards on the occupational ladder, further aspects or types of skill—of an intellectual, organizational or social kind—are added. Once again, even for less skilled employees, one element of overall skill may expand while another contracts. A further difficulty is that these processes usually occur at different rates and may simultaneously affect a large number of different job elements.

The complexity of most jobs creates the risk, when examining processes of longer-term change, that unwary observers may notice areas of loss but discount areas of gain or, conversely, count gains but overlook losses. When either loss or gain is actually *expected* on theoretical grounds, such risks are maximized. The debate about the alleged long-term degradation of manual work was from the start marked by such difficulties: proponents of degradation seldom had trouble providing impressive examples of the loss or contraction of one, or of several, prominent skill elements in a given occupation; their opponents could often just as readily point to what appeared to be gains. In so far as both parties insisted upon the priority of the data that most impressed them, or that their expectations had led them to select, the debate was bound to reach an impasse.

It was well recognized at the planning stage of the Work Attitudes/Histories survey that skill losses might counteract or offset skill gains, while some skill gains might compensate skill losses. ('Compensate', in this context, should not be taken to imply 'compensate *fully*'.) A case could have been made for at least trying to examine the extent of such offset processes, however incompletely, in the core survey employee interviews. But it has to be accepted that time constraints were such as to have ruled out the additional enquiries that would have been necessary to produce dependable information about such 'compensatory' effects. It seems likely that many respondents would indeed have reported both gains and losses; but very little, or nothing, could have been asked about the technical content of each offset process. Instead, then, respondents were asked to provide an *overall* assessment of the movement of the level of skill in their current job.[3] Research teams still had the option of adding further enquiries about skill offsets in their 'team-specific' section of the questionnaire; but the results would have applied to a smaller sample without obviating the inherent drawbacks of the survey method for studying skill offsets.

Arguably on many grounds, then, the best way to deal with the problem was to take it up in a Related Study of a more qualitative kind. However, it was essential in this case to select for such intensive study types of skill that were particularly important for theoretical reasons. Fortunately for both these purposes, it was possible to extend already substantial fieldwork on the question of skills compensation processes that had been undertaken in the Rochdale locality by members of the Lancaster team, outside SCELI, among skilled male manual employees (Penn, 1982*a*, 1983*b*, 1985; Penn and Scattergood, 1985). (Teams will be referred to by the institution co-ordinating local work.)

In considering the overall link between occupation, class, and skill in a historical perspective, skilled (male) manual workers constitute an especially important point of reference, because the focus of the classic discussions of alienated work (Blauner, 1964) and work degradation (Braverman, 1974) was in each case upon this layer of the occupational structure. Previous case-study work, for example by Sorge and Warner (1986), Jones (1982), or Senker *et al.* (1981), into the effect of automation on engineering crafts, had shown a net balance of skill-gains while recognizing some offset processes. Penn's earlier work (1985) also began developing a theory of skill compensation to give such findings about skill change amongst craft workers in engineering an integrated explanatory framework and theoretical coherence. The theory can, perhaps, be most appropriately applied to long-standing skilled occupations such as these. Some problems obviously occur in extending it to cover some newer types of work which have been affected by constant technical change since their appearance. (In particular, some still lack a 'history' to be studied, because of their recent appearance or lack of stability.) Most newer manual occupations, after all, have never achieved the technical and *social* coherence which, from an early point, characterized the traditional engineering crafts. For the latter, as Penn argues, a more explicit theory of compensation seems to have special applicability.

Chapters 4 and 5 show how the theory developed, extending earlier empirical research concerned with technological change and skill in the paper-manufacturing industry in Britain since 1970 (Penn and Scattergood, 1985). No 'middle-range' theory was yet available to explicate the interdependence of computerization and changes to skilled work in this industry. The theory was also put forward as a way of furthering research on trends in skill among other important groups of manual workers, at a time when the debate set off by Braverman (1974) twelve years earlier was showing many signs of becoming stultifyingly abstract. Chapter 5 was written jointly by the Lancaster and Aberdeen teams and involved an extension of the theory to include not only manual work in manufacturing plants but also in the service sector, and in clerical work. The two teams constructed a larger set of hypotheses, derived from the theory, to guide data collection at a series of establishments in the two localities.[4]

Taken together, then, Chapters 4 and 5 show two phases in the emergence of a new theoretical approach to skills change. Indeed, Chapter 4 points to the new areas of enquiry that were to guide design of the second study. In this sense, it can be seen as 'freestanding' from the point of view of its theoretical contribution. However, it also illustrates one important way in which new interpretations develop in the light of research findings. Quite apart from their attempt to move theory forward, moreover, the two chapters provide much additional field data, from the Employer Baseline survey, the Employer 30 survey, and from the Rochdale Related Study using intensive case studies. These findings, for employers that had experienced often far-reaching technical change, complement and confirm many of the findings about trends in skill from the employee interviews of the Work Attitudes/Histories survey.

Yet again, these findings from Aberdeen and Rochdale cannot be reconciled with degradation theory of almost any kind, and least of all as originally formulated. Indeed, between them, Chapters 2, 3, 4, and 5 show how three quite different types of method and evidence—employee reports in survey interviews, personal life and work histories, and case studies of establishments—produce a consistent and increasingly detailed view of skills change. The issues confronted directly in them are often raised less explicitly in the remaining five chapters. However, the latter share more closely a distinct problematic concerned with the subjectively experienced dimensions of skill, its personal meaning, and its effects on work attitudes and values.

DIFFERING PERCEPTIONS OF SKILL

Sociologists of work have long, though perhaps incompletely, recognized the subjective dimensions of skill deriving from socially constructed images and scales of value, and the resulting tension between *technical* and *social* definitions of skill. Much of previous investigation, however, has been concerned with what might be called the micropolitics and the microeconomics of socially defined skill, in particular the capacity of strategically situated groups of manual workers to bargain successfully for an 'inflated' skill status as well as a premium on their money rewards. More recently, in labour process theory, increased attention has been paid to the role of subjectivity (Knights and Willmott, 1990; Sturdy, Knights, and Willmott, 1992); and this follows on from the early work of Burawoy (1979) on 'manufacturing consent' in the workplace, and from the gender literature on the impact of social identity on the creation and maintenance of *gendered* skill and job statuses.

Chapters 6 and 7 by the Cambridge team consider two further aspects of the subjective dimension of skill. The first is the perception by employers and employees of the skill level of specific jobs. The second is the interaction of gender and part-time work in perceptions of job content and skills. After all, the expansion of occupations depending on part-timers seems to imply, for the foreseeable future, a built-in continuation of massive skill deficits in the work performed by about two-fifths of women employees in Britain. And it seems to do so in more than the 'obvious' sense shown by the primary SCELI findings on the break between full-time and part-time work. This is because the measurable skill deficits in work done by part-timers are often amplified by socially constructed and socially perpetuated definitions of skill itself, which may then be considered 'objective' by those holding them. In the everyday world these definitions can heavily condition the experience of their personal skills situation by groups of employees and by individuals, in some cases unwarrantably emphasizing a sense of possessing high skill, perhaps more often confirming an unjustified sense of lacking it.

Burchell, Elliott, Rubery, and Wilkinson examine the technical content of a wide range of jobs in Chapter 6, to answer the question of how far managers and employees in the same workplace agreed on the level and types of skill called for in the jobs done by the employees concerned, making use of a set of questions used in their Related Study in the Northampton Travel to Work Area.[5] As the Cambridge team point out, managers may leave some job descriptions loose in order to allow piecemeal adjustments to work organization as technology or markets change. Workers, too, may seek to discover or to create areas of discretion over their work methods, pace of work, and other job features. Both sides thus have an interest in building areas of indeterminacy in the technical features of a job; and it would be surprising if employees and managers agreed over all, or even most, of the skill requirements of many jobs.

The Cambridge team begin, however, by showing that there *was* relatively close overall agreement over *some* job requirements, in particular those relating to levels of responsibility for handling resources, to access to and use of information, to handling other people, and even to output (or standards of service). There was also fairly close agreement over what physical and clerical skills were called for in respondents' jobs. Yet sharp and widespread disagreement arose over three crucial areas in the actual jobs held by respondents: (i) the degree of *social skill* they embodied; (ii) the *organizing ability* they called for; and (iii) the *degree of discretion* they allowed in practice.

Burchell, Elliott, Rubery, and Wilkinson show that there were in fact even wider discrepancies in perceptions of job content when the data were classified according to seven major job types. For example, managers, in comparison with the employees doing them, 'underrated' the need for clerical abilities, social and organizing skills, and responsibility for handling people, in jobs classified as low-skilled production or service work. On the other hand, the managers 'overrated' the responsibility for using information, for applying resources, and for handling other people in the lower-graded administrative and managerial jobs. For *all* employee grades, except for middle management itself, managers undervalued the degree of discretion exercised in the work; in the case of manual worker and routine white-collar grades, their estimation of responsibility was strikingly low.

It is possible to object that some employees in the lower-skilled jobs examined by the team somewhat overstated the need for 'non-manual' activities in their work, as part of a strategy to upgrade its status and rewards: the authors acknowledge and deal with this 'rodent operative syndrome' (as they term it). Yet, the Cambridge team maintain, it can hardly explain such *wide* discrepancies. And why should people in lower management jobs have 'understated' their own requirement for *managerial* skills? The most plausible conclusion seems to be that managers in these workplaces often did not know, so well as they might have, the real content of many jobs in their own work processes. It might be noted, incidentally, that if these findings apply generally in Britain, they weaken the argument that deskilling or upskilling are normally produced by management strategies—how correct is it to speak of managers having a *strategy* for skills in those workplaces where management knowledge of the skills actually needed or deployed is so incomplete as this?

Many factors may account for such incomplete knowledge of the skills that jobs demand. Two seem particularly important. First, objective information about the work, when it existed, was often incomplete. Secondly, the gaps in such information were evidently *systematic*; above all, there was least awareness of the organizing and social skills exercised by less skilled manual workers, and underestimation of the degree of job discretion experienced by nearly all employees.

The Cambridge team go on to provide examples from case-study work of specific inaccuracies in management perceptions of the skills used in low-graded occupations. (These findings on skill perceptions should be interesting to both managers and union bargainers, as well as to social scientists.) They also underline further weaknesses in the degradation version of the deskilling thesis: first, its bias towards a 'traditional male craftsman' model of worker skill, which overlooks the social and organizing elements of skill; and secondly, its overstatement of the success of managers in applying scientific management to eliminate discretion in routine work. (As Rose in Chapter 9 shows, incidentally, satisfaction with 'using one's own initiative' was by far the highest of the eight specific aspects of job satisfaction examined in the Work Attitudes/Histories survey, and a majority of employees even in the lowest-skilled jobs expressed high satisfaction with this aspect of their work.) There is, then, some real justification for the later wry comment of the Cambridge team that 'the workforce as a whole does not appear to be convinced by either the deskilling argument or by the argument that the qualities and attributes of the worker make little difference to the productivity of the job'.

SKILL PERCEPTIONS AND GENDER

Both Gallie in Chapter 2 and Elias in Chapter 3 show that gender intervenes sharply in the processes of enskilling (acquiring skill) and upskilling (experiencing gains in skill), in the wake of technical change. As Gallie points out, however, these processes are affected by the concentration of women in certain jobs, especially part-time work. In Chapter 7, Horrell, Rubery, and Burchell examine how gender conditions the subjective definition of skills. The Cambridge team asked additional questions of their sample about specific areas of skill and responsibility required in their own jobs.[6] Once again, these questions added important data about the 'non-technical' or 'social' components of jobs, such as responsibility for checking the work of others or the necessity for knowing one's way around an organization, which are often overlooked in the debate on skill.

Confirming Gallie's findings in Chapter 2 on the link between gender and selection for skilled work, the Cambridge team show that, even where there was parity of overall skill levels between the sexes, the detailed content of skill nevertheless varied significantly. For example, at the general level, women who worked full-time were more likely than women part-timers to have jobs with skill levels comparable to those of men. But they were more likely than men to list social skills such as handling clients as a key skill component of their work. For all employees, however, the Cambridge team found that individuals required *special* skill components—and quite often too, a greater degree of autonomy—in many more types of job than they themselves had expected.

The team's additional measures showed there to be less overall difference than might have been expected in some aspects of jobs often thought indicative of skill, with more overlap between the sexes in these areas than might be supposed. However, the position was very different at the subjective level. Those respondents who scored highly for overall skill on the team's composite variable, which embodied the extra skill indicators available, not surprisingly, also claimed that their jobs were skilled, irrespective of sex, and even of part-time employment. Yet over half those male employees, and almost half those *full-time* women employees, whose jobs scored *low* on the skill index, nevertheless defined their work as 'a skilled job'. Far fewer low-scoring women part-timers did so.

An obvious explanation might seem that the measures used were defective, operating so as to exaggerate the 'real' skill of jobs—or at least doing so more often when respondents were part-timer women. Regrettably, observational data were not available to test for such a distortion, or to validate the rather more likely explanation advanced by the authors that the skills of part-time jobs are systematically underrated by the people doing them, as well as by others. (A corollary is that full-timers may sometimes have additional, 'non-technical' reasons for considering their jobs as 'skilled'.) The problem was handled by asking respondents to explain further what they meant when they said their jobs were 'skilled'. The opportunity to do so was taken in a follow-up study of almost 200 respondents two years after the Work Attitudes/Histories survey. Those still in the same jobs were asked once again whether they considered their jobs skilled or not: almost all gave the same answer. (This finding itself suggests the original question worked reliably.) They were then asked to say by which main criteria they considered their job skilled. Over half (54 per cent) the respondents who considered their work skilled explained that they did so because the tasks and responsibilities called for special training, technical qualifications, or expertise of some kind. This is perhaps reassuring. Yet a large minority (26 per cent) of the respondents gave a tautological answer such as 'the job itself is skilled'.

While indicating that, in the main, employees in the Work Attitudes/Histories survey as a whole probably adopted a *technical* frame of reference rather more often than a socially established one, this result points to the influence of social definitions amongst a minority of them. But the Cambridge team are cautious in drawing further conclusions since the sample obtained for this reinterview exercise was relatively small. (In particular—and it is a possibly significant 'finding' in itself—relatively few people who had said their job was *not* skilled in the Work Attitudes/Histories survey came forward for the second interview.)

Fortunately, however, additional evidence about the role of social definitions of skill was collected by Elias, and by the Lancaster team. Elias in Chapter 3 shows a fairly high degree of correlation between the objective and some subjective aspects of skill. He does so by setting results obtained by using indicators accepted as broadly objective measures of skill (in this case, derived from the occupational codings on the work histories) beside judgements made by respondents about the 'most skilled' of all jobs they had listed. The level of skill of a currently held job can certainly distort such comparisons, but Elias controls for this effect; older women, he shows, and men who had experienced a period of unemployment, were the least likely to describe their current job as skilled. Amongst these employees also, perceptions of skill were, it seems, essentially based on technical realities.

EMPLOYEE DEFINITIONS OF SKILL

In Chapter 8, Francis and Penn extend Elias's, and the Cambridge team's, analysis of the subjective meaning of a 'skilled job' in a further direction and in far more detail. The Lancaster team obtained a definition of a 'skilled job' from every member of the Rochdale locality sample who currently had a job, or who had ever had a job. Respondents were able to list, in order of importance, all features of a job which they personally regarded as essential criteria of skill. This chapter confirms the main findings of the Cambridge team, and of Elias, on this issue: 'technical' explanations clearly predominated. Francis and Penn then distinguished individuals who insisted on a *single* technical criterion such as 'training', 'apprenticeship', or 'qualifications' in particular, and those giving specific combinations of technical criteria. They go on to show how these answer patterns were linked *systematically* to structural variables, but above all to occupational membership and position.

As Francis and Penn point out, sociologists and social psychologists of work have always known that employed people do not agree upon any single definition of skill. Yet, surprisingly, the question of which employees use which criteria seems never to have been followed up in the field. As they show, rich material can be obtained simply by asking people to say what a skilled job means and requesting an explanation. It is worth noting, Francis and Penn suggest, that ordinary people show much less hesitation when answering this question than do many social scientists. Of those answering, about 40 per cent gave multiple replies, perhaps suggesting some uncertainty, though otherwise confirming the real everyday complexities of skill; but fewer than 5 per cent of the Rochdale sample were unable to give an answer, including those people who had limited experience of employment.

For over three-quarters of the sample, answers mentioned some kind of training or special learning period, such as apprenticeship in particular. This finding counts heavily against the view that social definitions of skill, even of a 'negotiated' kind, are the most common or influential in the everyday world. It challenges in particular any view that skill is frequently defined in a more or less arbitrary way, or thanks simply to bargaining power or raw gender advantages, in the absence of *any* adequate or even plausible technical grounds whatsoever. For the majority of these Rochdale employees, skilled work designated tasks or responsibilities for which people must have had systematic or at least some 'serious' technical preparation.

On the other hand, this finding strongly supports one feminist variant of the 'social definition of skills' approach. If skill is seen as the product of training, work that relies on (for example) caring and domestic skills that have been acquired *without* any formal training is very much less likely to be seen by most people as skilled, irrespective of its real technical content or its demands on initiative and ingenuity; a criterion of 'training required'—and here the Rochdale findings again recall those of the Cambridge team—necessarily ignores or plays down social skills, everyday *tacit skills* (Jones and Wood, 1984), or other forms of 'folk expertise', as components of skill, though those required in some 'non-skilled' jobs are of a high order.

Yet again, a minority of respondents defined a skilled job *solely* by reference to factors such as qualifications, experience, or high personal ability, and many more mentioned one or more of these criteria as an adjunct to trained competence. Indeed, factors other than, or in addition to, technical training were listed by 55 per cent of the Rochdale sample, though not always in first place. Some of these criteria refer to personal characteristics such as 'ability' that strictly speaking are individual. Yet they were put forward as the criteria of a skilled *job*, not of the person performing it. The Rochdale data thus show that many employees themselves have a tendency to confuse the two modes of skill which Rose calls *job-skill* and *own-skill* in Chapters 9 and 10. No less important, they partly support a 'credentialist' (Berg, 1970) version of the 'social definitions' approach to skill; that is to say, the claim that often, and possibly increasingly, qualifications are demanded less as a warrant of technical ability than as a screening device to weed out 'undesirable' candidates, or—more positively—as a sign of personal character traits such as persistence that may be relevant to performing well in actual job assignments.

The Lancaster team's findings in Rochdale also threw light on one final question. Definitions of skill, as might be expected, varied with the age and sex of respondents; and, since they possibly point to important social trends, the authors are surely justified in stressing how much they did so. However, Francis and Penn consider it more instructive to examine in detail how a current occupation affected definitions of skilled work. As the occupational structure is changing in broadly known ways, it thus becomes possible to suggest how support for various interpretations of skill may alter in coming years. Francis and Penn in fact refrain from doing so at length, but their chapter will be valuable to those interested in such forecasting.

Stressing the advantage of comparing several occupational groups that have been targeted on theoretical grounds—an approach Rose also adopts in Chapter 10—they proceed with an examination of the subjective meaning of skill most often held in these groups, contrasting it with observer definitions of skill based on a broadly known location on the 'skills ladder' embodied in the occupational structure, on a position in an organizational hierarchy, or on a personal stock of skill acquired through training, improvement, and work experience. These results provide a further confirmation of the intense interest most employees take in definitions of their own and of other employees' skill; as noted above, this is a matter on which nearly all employees appear to have definite and, in their own terms, extremely lucid opinions.

MATCHING OF PERSONAL AND JOB SKILLS

While the tension between subjective definitions of skill and the skills possessed or exercised by individuals is explored both by the Cambridge and by the Lancaster teams, Gallie in Chapter 2 and Elias in Chapter 3 also point to another kind of tension at the individual level. Elias does so in the course of examining a specific subgroup: those people re-entering the labour market (typically after a period of child-rearing or unemployment); Elias shows that such re-entrants often suffer a drop in the skill level of their re-entry job, in comparison with an earlier job, for which the individual may have had training, or have acquired skill through experience. In doing so, Elias is also drawing attention not just to a drop in the skill levels between *jobs*, but to a mismatch between the skill level of the *person* and that of the re-entry job. Gallie deals with skill mismatches at the individual level too, taking a close look at the technical and educational qualifications of the people doing low-skilled manual work, concluding that the skill of jobs, and the formal competence of individuals doing them, appears often to have been out of balance, and sometimes as seriously as Elias shows it to have been for re-entrants to the labour market.

Two of the measures used by Gallie as indicators of the *skill of the work done* by people—length of training, and time taken to learn to do the work well—can also be regarded as variables that throw light on a different aspect or mode of skill. This is the *skill possessed by individuals*. The length of a learning time is a pointer (a good if imperfect one) to the range and challenge of the tasks or responsibilities a given job calls for; that is to say, to its *structural* features as a work role. For sociologists, the structural properties of roles have usually been considered of prior importance to the personal characteristics of the individuals occupying the roles. Yet the skill acquired by an individual can result in changes to his or her sense of identity as an economic agent, with possible consequences for job attitudes, for example by creating closer personal identification with an occupation, or by building a sense of following a career. These subjective effects of skill, like others, are not randomly distributed.

In Chapter 9, Rose develops the conceptual distinction under-lying Gallie's analysis, which has been present by implication in much of the debate on skill and on occasion (Cockburn, 1983; Spenner, 1983; Kallenberg and Berg, 1987; Clark *et al.*, 1988) confronted in full.[7] To build his measures of *job-skill* (the skill of work roles) and *own-skill* (the skill of workers as individuals), Rose combined two sets of separate skill variables, creating com-posite variables for *own-skill* and *job-skill* respectively. The result-ing measures necessarily overlap, because of the element of ambiguity, noted above, that seems inherent in variables such as training time. The composite skill variables may thus understate the full incidence of skills mismatching in the Work Attitudes/Histories sample.

But they are distinct enough to suggest serious mismatching between *own-skill* and *job-skill* for around 40 per cent of the SCELI employees. Where *own-skill* was 'in surplus' (that is, where it seemed appreciably higher than *job-skill*), Rose labels the mismatching 'underutilization'; and where there was a 'deficit' of *own-skill* in relation to *job-skill*, he labels the mismatch 'under-qualification'. It seems reasonable, on intuitive or common-sense grounds, that a 'surplus' of *own-skill* will affect job attitudes in rather different ways from a 'deficit'. 'Underutilization', by definition, implies that some acquired skill or competence is 'wasted' (and most probably unrewarded), and the likely effect on job satisfaction is evidently negative; equally clearly, 'under-qualification' should increase overall job satisfaction, through a sense of overcoming obstacles, or of possessing personal abilities that outweigh formal training or accreditation. (As noted, Francis and Penn found that a number of their Rochdale respon-dents put particular stress on personal 'ability' as the defining characteristic of a skilled job itself.)

SKILLS AND JOB SATISFACTION

First, however, Rose briefly examines levels of satisfaction with particular features of the job currently held by employees, dividing them into *extrinsic, intrinsic,* and *authority* aspects. Levels of satisfaction varied very sharply between the three aspects, being generally lower for *extrinsic* factors, and in particular with 'Total Pay' and with 'Hours Worked'. A perhaps surprising finding was the very high level of satisfaction with the *intrinsic* job factors, and notably with the degree of challenge in the work. As noted earlier in this chapter, satisfaction with 'Ability to Use Own Initiative' was highest of all, by a clear margin; though falling in relative terms, it still remained high in groups with very low-skilled jobs, and was slightly higher amongst those experiencing technical and organizational change. This is obviously not what would be expected if any process of general work degradation were occurring, even given the complication of poorly esteemed tacit skills examined by the Cambridge team.

For examining the effects of skill-matching, however, Rose concentrated upon overall levels of job satisfaction. Mismatching produced the effects that seem reasonable in terms of the subjective logic attributed to 'underutilized' and 'underqualified' individuals. (In a sense this provided a necessary test of Rose's skill measures: if they had been duplicates, no effects would have appeared; if they had been invalid, the findings would have been contradictory or lacked any pattern.) With wider skills-mismatching the effects were sharper still: those respondents who were very greatly 'underqualified' for their present jobs expressed far higher than average general job satisfaction; those who were greatly 'underutilized', on the other hand, were the least satisfied of all. A more interesting finding, perhaps, is that, other things being equal, and *whatever the degree of skills-matching*, overall job satisfaction grew with the level of skill required by the work done, irrespective of the individual's qualifications, formal job training, and relevant work experience. On the other hand, *own-skill* tended to operate in the opposite direction, 'pulling against' the effect of increasing *job-skill*. (Higher *job-skill*, however, did itself reduce satisfaction with *particular* aspects of a job, notably with Hours Worked.) Rose then presents a more general model of the workplace and individual factors affecting overall job satisfaction in the employee sample, and discusses his skill variables in relation to them.

Workplace variables were, as would be expected, the most influential; but both the skill measures had significant *independent* effects on general job satisfaction. The level of *job-skill* operated the more strongly of the two; and, as noted, it did so in a positive direction. Though operating less strongly, the level of *own-skill* pulled in a *negative* direction. An interesting finding here, in the light of the Cambridge team's discussion of the skill position of women, was that women part-timers, *after workplace factors were fully controlled,* expressed higher overall job satisfaction than both men and women full-timers. This strengthens the suggestion of the Cambridge team that many part-timers may evaluate their jobs by *different* criteria (which are not necessarily their own). Combining both findings, it therefore appears that many part-timers—at least in comparison with full-timers—may not only understate the skill of their work, but may also overstate its rewards.

SKILL AND WORK INVOLVEMENT

Though such a conclusion may not come as a surprise to some employers of 'grateful slaves' (Hakim, 1991) who are part-timers, it raises more fundamental questions about the distribution of work orientations and forms of work commitment in relation to skill and the working-time contract. Rose's examination of skill and work commitment in Chapter 10 confirms that many women part-timers in the sample had a characteristic Secondary Economic orientation to employment. Such an involvement may also help to account for *some* of their high levels of job satisfaction and *some* of their reluctance to view their work as skilled. It none the less remains consistent with the Cambridge analysis: part-timers' satisfaction with their current jobs was in fact closer to levels to be expected for jobs that are *indeed* more highly skilled.

Many debates of the 1960s and 1970s, Rose argues in Chapter 10, whether on the effect of technology on jobs or on the alienation of industrial workers, were all concerned in one way or another with the interaction between work attitudes, broader economic perspectives, and workers' social consciousness on the one hand, and skill levels on the other. In Britain in particular, semi-skilled, assembly-line work had been seen as a major source of economically instrumental *orientations to work*. Social psychologists and reformist management thinkers found much in this sociological work that converged with their own analysis (O'Brien, 1992; Trist, 1981), and its implications for the design of industrial work were recognized from an early date (Hulin and Blood, 1968). A critique of fragmented work based on it helped dynamize the so-called revolt against work (Sheppard and Herrick, 1972) and intense industrial conflict of the early 1970s, as well as the Quality of Working Life (QWL) movement that followed this unrest (Rose, 1985). However, the landmark British sociological study of the 'affluent workers' of the early 1960s itself put more stress on influences 'beyond the factory gates' than on levels of skill in forming an instrumental orientation to work (Goldthorpe *et al.*, 1969).

The arrival of an increasingly 'post-industrial' (or, less contentiously, post-Fordist) economy from the later 1970s onwards coincided in Britain with a government campaign to alter cultural attitudes about economic life, at the same time as rendering economic behaviour itself more competitive and self-reliant. Theorists of post-industrialism (there is at times no avoiding this possible misnomer for a 'post-*factory*' world) had long been arguing (Bell, 1974) that the decline of smokestack industry and rise of service occupations would erode social respect for paid employment. The Thatcher Governments, on the other hand, believed such values were produced by misgovernment. Thus they sought to restore Victorian economic values 'of the Samuel Smiles self-help variety' (Lawson, 1992: 64 ff.; Gilmour, 1992: 139 ff.). Workers would rediscover respect for work as they learned to live without 'nannying' employment protection or 'excessive' social welfare; the establishment of an *enterprise culture* implied freeing economic agents—*morally* no less than financially—from *dependency culture*.[8]

The Work Histories/Attitudes data, Rose finds, provide scant support for simpler versions of the post-industrial view of work values, in particular the view that the work ethic is in sharp decline thanks—so to speak—to the triumph of the shopping mall over the factory floor as the place where the serious business of life will occur. Nor are the SCELI findings consistent with the belief that a stiff dose of economic liberalism can of itself create *moral involvement* (Etzioni, 1975) in work. If 'work ethic' is taken to mean normative commitment to paid work, Rose argues, the work ethic probably has stronger support nowadays than it ever did have. The sources of this support, he argues, can largely be attributed to an upward shift in skill levels in many work tasks, in a comparable rise in personal qualifications, and in the expansion of the higher-skilled technical and service occupations.

Skill, Rose claims, plays a major role in determining the strength of the work ethic. Both the skill of jobs and the skill of individuals were amongst the five or six most important influences on the work ethic of SCELI employees. The spread of service-class employment, especially, provides more tasks with a high skill content, as do most forms of technical change, above all those associated with the electronic technologies. These changes reinforce the work ethic in the essential sense of commitment to paid work.

One of the clearest expressions of the link between skill and work commitment is a growing career orientation of women who work full-time (or wish to do so), and who (albeit slowly) have been gaining greater access to higher-skilled, more responsible jobs, propelled in large part by growing levels of education, technical qualification, and job-related training. There was no real difference between the strength of work commitment among such women and that among men with equivalent levels of job-skill and own-skill.

But work commitment is many-sided. Part-timer women, as noted, were far more likely to have a strong Secondary Economic orientation to work, and to view their jobs as a means of supplementing a family income rather than as a *central life-interest* (Dubin, 1956, 1958). This partly 'opportunist' work involvement no doubt reflects still strong traditional values about the male role as family breadwinner, as well as constraints upon full-time employment such as the scarcity of affordable child-care provision. However, most part-timer women not only work at jobs on the very bottom rungs of the occupational and organizational ladders but also have very low personal skill attainments, even when some allowance is made for their possession of poorly esteemed domestic, social, and tacit skills. Their very low stocks of recognized own-skill reduce the incentive of part-timers to seek full-time employment or to redefine employment, in their overall scheme of social values, as a central life-interest. To simplify somewhat, they perhaps have insufficient (recognized) own-skill to 'market' more strategically, or to provide them with a trigger for a critical review of their social and economic roles.

Women with a high level of own-skill are in precisely the opposite position. This is not to suggest that the strong work ethic of highly qualified women is the product of a simple, economically determinist process, or is characterized solely by economic calculation. Their work commitment, Rose maintains, is also *normative* in the elementary sense; that is, sustained by social values and attitudes that more strongly support a lifetime commitment to work on the part of women than they did two decades ago. Longer periods of education, or the experience of professional training, have simultaneously provided them with models of action, reference groups, and even a rhetoric of values, that broadly reinforce normative change. However, the values and norms making high employment commitment an expression of a new social role for women, and which validate new economic identities for them, gain in relevance as own-skill increases. Besides sharpening the *motive* to adopt a career perspective on employment, a high stock of human capital provides greater employment opportunities that yield the *means* to realize a lifetime commitment to employment.

Chapter 10 ends by examining how an Economic Individualist labour-market ideology is affected by skill and relates to the work ethic. There appears to have been no necessary relationship between strong Economic Individualism and a strong work ethic in the employee sample. This suggests that the political drive of the 1980s to support the work ethic by strengthening Economic Individualism was misconceived; furthermore, support for an ideology of assertive self-reliance was itself affected by levels of both *own-skill* and *job-skill*, but negatively; though these 'skill effects' are less strong than for the work ethic, endorsement of Economic Individualism fell off in the employee sample as skill levels rose. It seems that occupation is the key intervening variable for understanding the link between these two strands of employment values.

Economic Individualism, indeed, was particularly high amongst some groups with very high own-skill and job-skill that *also* had a strong work ethic. Examining targeted occupational groups very similar to those used by the Lancaster team, Rose shows that the work ethic and Economic Individualism are combined in characteristic ways. Thus Teachers and Line Managers have a comparably strong work ethic, but differ dramatically in terms of Economic Individualism. This might perhaps have been expected. However, Staff and Specialist Managers (such as those employed in personnel departments or computer units) had a combination of employment values much closer to that of Teachers than to that of their Line Manager colleagues. Such blends of employment values might be explained in many ways. Differences in the technical content of personal qualifications and training of an equally high level, in the special types of skill called upon in the work process of different occupations, in processes of self-selection, or in the experience of technical training and socialization into occupations, may also be important. Here are still more questions for further research, to be added to the many others suggested throughout the book.

SKILLS FORMATION

Chapter 10 does not examine the relationship between skill and individual *work effort*. But team-specific evidence on this question suggests clearly that strengthening the work ethic by improving skills training may also reinforce work effort as a behavioural trait.[9] Especially if increases in skill encourage commitment to a higher *quality* of work performance, as well as increasing the competence to achieve it, then a greater training effort seems doubly justified.

Before concluding, it may thus be appropriate to comment briefly on the relation between skills change in the 1980s and training provision, as shown by SCELI, since the themes of inequalities in job-skill, and by implication of inequalities in access to own-skill, recur throughout this volume. Though the available data would repay further analysis, the essential situation is a simple one. On the other hand, large majorities of employees at all levels in the Work Attitudes/Histories survey could report increases in the skills and responsibilities of their work, and a comparably large majority of employers in the Employers 30 case studies could also report increased demands for skill in all main grades of work done in their establishments. Yet for the same period (the five years preceding the enquiry) there was no commensurate increase in the training provision reported by employees, or, perhaps more tellingly, reported by employers themselves. (Substantial minorities of employees even reported an actual reduction.) Some occupational groups with a traditionally poor level of formal training reported hardly any increase in the training provided for them by their employers.[10]

This contrast provides a further, sobering reminder of the unevenness of change in Britain in the 1980s in the key area of skill and the labour market. Efforts to improve training at all levels have certainly occurred in the years since the research. It remains to be seen what effect they will have on the persistent imbalance in skills acquisition and improvement in Britain (Lee, 1989), as well as on the design of jobs. It is hoped that the work reported in this book will provide a useful set of benchmarks for future studies of such questions as well as feeding the continuing theoretical debate on skill.

It is appropriate, however, to conclude by drawing attention once again to the consistency, and to the complementarity, of the main findings presented here on changes in skill, in its distribution, in its subjective aspects, and in its place in socio-economic and wider cultural change in Britain the 1980s. This convergence seems remarkable, and is reassuring, given that the writers were drawn from varying disciplines: Labour Economics, and the Sociology of Work in the main, but with a strong contribution from Social Psychology. (Several of the writers have also made previous contributions to Social and Economic History, or to Industrial Relations.) Methods, and techniques of analysis, varied as much as disciplinary specialism, and the treatment of themes in the chapters certainly reflects this methodological pluralism. Yet, as noted at the outset, there have been few serious difficulties in reconciling the findings or conclusions of the different teams or authors. Particular findings or interpretations put forward here will no doubt be challenged, perhaps sharply, in the light of later research; but it is hoped that the general terrain on which the major skill issues are debated in future will look more open, more varied, and in that sense less familiar, as a result of the general contribution made by the research reported here.

NOTES

1. The final version of the Attitudes/Histories questionnaire was planned to run for an average time of around 90 minutes per respondent. Of this, an hour or so was budgeted for 'core' questions (those asked in all localities); but up to 25 minutes were available for 'team-specific' enquiries, in which each of the six main teams could follow up special interests using their locality sample (still around 1,000 cases). It was open to teams to share some of their team-specific questions, thus obtaining larger samples.

2. The following chapters in other volumes of the SCELI series also have substantial sections examining skill issues, and can be regarded as complementary to the chapters by their authors in the present volume. In *Employer Strategy and the Labour Market* (Rubery and Wilkinson, 1994): (i) 'Employer Strategy and Change in the Employment Relationship' (Michael Rose) shows that the more strategic SCELI employers had achieved more functional flexibility and skill change, but without adopting Human Resources Management, 'Japanization', or anti-union policies; (ii) 'Internal and External Labour Markets: Towards an Integrated Analysis' (Jill Rubery) looks at the way external labour market opportunities for types of labour can affect the way jobs are graded and paid. In *Trade Unions in Recession* (Gallie, Penn, and Rose, forthcoming): (i) 'The Experience of Trade Unions in Rochdale in the 1980s' (Roger Penn) considers the continuing role of craft skill in workplace industrial relations; (ii) 'Still Life in Swindon' (Michael Rose) presents detailed case studies of employees in 'sunrise' industries in Swindon, where qualitative methods confirmed and threw light on the increases in job skills found in the Work Histories/Attitudes survey. In *Gender Segregation in British Labour Markets* (A. Scott, 1994), 'Part-Time Work and Gender Inequality in the Labour Market' (Jill Rubery, Sara Horrell, and Brendan Burchell) extends the analysis of differences in skills and pay related to gender, and in attitudes related to full-time and part-time work.

3. Employees were asked: 'I'd like you to compare your current job with what you were doing five years ago. For each of the following things, would you say whether there has been a significant *increase* between then and now, a significant *decrease*, or little or no change?' A list of nine job features was then dealt with in turn. Three directly related to skill (Level of Skill You Use in your Job; Responsibility Involved in your Job; Provision of Training), and a fourth (Variety of Tasks You Perform) did so indirectly. Three (How Fast You Work; Effort You

Have to Put into your Work; Tightness of Supervision over your Work) related to work intensity (Elger, 1990). The remaining two (Job Security; Chances of Promotion) related to the organizational situation in general. Statistical analysis shows close intercorrelation between the 'skill' aspects (including variety of tasks) at the individual level. Results apply to a reduced sample since some respondents had not held a job five years earlier and were thus not asked the question; more importantly, a minority had held a *different* job five years earlier. These respondents had to be excluded when analysing changes of skill affecting a given job. In the Employers 30 case studies of 191 establishments, employers were asked to assess the overall pattern of skill change over the previous five years in up to seven main skill groups. Their replies were coded for one of the following categories by the research teams: Large Decrease/Decrease/No Change/Increase/ Large Increase/Gains and Losses Equal. Here, then, an attempt to allow for skill offsets was made, though it only caters for the limiting (and, in the event, relatively infrequent) case where gains and losses exactly 'compensated' each other.

4. This provided a good example of two teams working closely together on the collection and interpretation of team-specific comparative data within the overall SCELI research framework. The field research was greatly facilitated by the main Rochdale fieldworker (Hilda Scattergood) moving to Aberdeen to lecture at Aberdeen University.

5. Travel to Work Areas (TTWAs) are defined by the Department of Employment, usually centre on a large 'core' town, but extend considerably beyond it, to include small towns which are in effect satellites of its labour market. The SCELI Travel-to-Work Areas varied considerably in geographical and spatial terms. Aberdeen, for example, included a large hinterland of very sparsely populated Scottish countryside stretching into the Highlands. The Swindon TTWA embraced small but substantial towns such as Wotton Bassett, Hungerford, Marlborough, and Shrivenham. The 'conurbation' localities (Rochdale and Coventry) were far more concentrated spatially. The TTWA localities were *not* selected for reasons of demography or urban geography, but for their historic and contemporary differences in industrial structure and employment levels; any important 'locality effects' would presumably reflect such variations. In the event, surprisingly few significant variations between locality samples were found, even *before* controlling for occupational and industrial structures. Locality effects can, it is believed, be safely disregarded in most analyses of changing skills once such variables are controlled.

6. For a full explanation and listing of the team-specific questions on skill asked by the Cambridge team in Northampton, see Ch. 7. Two

main sorts of enquiries were used: (i) a rating of seven *factors impor-tant in doing the job well* (such as lengthy experience of the work, knowing one's way around the organization, having a particular knack or talent); (ii) a listing of *responsibilities involved in the job* (such as for the safety and health of others, for checking work, or for keeping confidential information).

7. The authors of the main report on the 'Southampton' studies of tech-nological change undertaken in the mid-1980s (Clark, McLoughlin, Rose, and King, 1988) in fact developed a *threefold* conceptual divi-sion of skill (see esp. Chs. 4 and 6) for their detailed case-study work on skills change amongst telephone exchange maintenance techni-cians. Acknowledging Cockburn's (1983) work on printers, they write: 'Our initial aim will be to present a task-centred analysis, based on the view that skill is rooted in the content of work-tasks. We will refer to this dimension of skill as *skill in the task*. We will then distin-guish two further dimensions of skill. These are *skill in the person*, that is the skills possessed by individuals accumulated from a variety of sources (training, experience, and so on), and the political or *occu-pational* definition of skill by workgroups, trade unions and manage-ments, who ascribe skilled status to jobs and seek to influence the way they are distributed' (Clark *et al.*, 90). *Skill of the task* here is conceptually very close to that of *job-skill* as used in Chs. 9 and 10; *skill in the person* also approximates to *own-skill*. The *occupational* dimension of skill, however, is closer to what is more often called *socially defined* skill, which is not examined at any length in this vol-ume in the sense implied. The Southampton team rightly point out that this aspect of skill is the product of often complex workplace and labour-market dynamics. The organizational situation of work-groups, as well as external labour-market conditions, is important for understanding the limits of such negotiation. The best comparative examination of such processes is still perhaps to be found in Sayles's *Behaviour of Industrial Work Groups: Prediction and Control* (1958). One way of interpreting Sayles's conclusions is that there may be a 'status price' (or even a 'status rent') to be arrived at by bargaining from an advantaged position in the establishment division of labour. However, this is easier to win in some situations than others, thanks among other things to technological factors. More generally, it seems improbable that a high 'status price' (as opposed to a high *wage-price*) can be defined and imposed arbitrarily, however great a group's advantages, irrespective of all real levels of job-skill or own-skill. Real job-skill and own-skill levels may enable an inflated 'status price' to be set, but the reverse cannot happen. To be designated a 'high-skilled' group will usually require some at least plausible 'evidence' of

skill. If there is none, award of high-skilled status thanks to bargaining power obviously cannot, of itself, produce real job-skill or own-skill. The case-study material available to the Southampton researchers enabled them to explore in some detail the '*political*' aspect of the total skill situation of the groups of technicians studied, and the empirical priority of the other two aspects seems clear from this. (As they point out, a key variable was real change in the technology itself, with effects on tasks, and on the former tacit skills used in fault diagnosis in particular, that were not to be evaded.) The questionnaire data available from the Work Attitudes/Histories survey did not enable proper exploration of socially defined skills. Related studies by the Lancaster team (see Chs. 4 and 5) the Cambridge team (see Chs. 6 and 7) did, however, produce material relevant to the issue, as did the Lancaster team's investigation, using team-specific material for Rochdale, of the meaning to individuals of 'a skilled job' (see Ch. 8).

8. Nigel Lawson, as Financial Secretary to the Treasury in the early years of the Thatcher Governments, was well placed to observe and to shape these policies. In ch. 6 ('Sterling and Recession, 1979–81') of his memoir *The View from No. 11* the late Chancellor of the Exchequer explains this mission succinctly and with great candour, claiming sole credit for coining and popularizing the term *enterprise culture* and joint credit (together with Martin Jacques, then editor of the journal *Marxism Today*) for the term 'Thatcherism'. He states that to his best knowledge it was Margaret Thatcher herself who coined the term *dependency culture*, though he also often made free use of it as a minister. Lord Lawson continues: 'Be that as it may, the point here was that we were seeking not simply to remove various controls and impositions, but by so doing to *change the entire culture of a nation*' (Lawson, 1992: 64–5; emphasis added). Many other passages in the book leave no doubt about the priority given to this cultural aim in practice.

9. The Work Attitudes/Histories core survey provided some data on the expenditure of greater effort ('working harder'). For the employee sample as a whole, the proportions reporting an increase in the variety of tasks (61%), the responsibility of work (58%), and skill required (50%) are close to the proportion reporting an overall increase in effort required (55%); but the proportions reporting an increase in the pace of work (38%) and closer supervision (20%) were rather lower. This suggests that increases in effort were linked more closely to increased task flexibility than to crude work intensification (Elger, 1990). Further analysis of the data for occupational groups might shed more light on the upskilling versus intensification issue. The core survey, however, provides no evidence relating to any

subjective readiness to expend greater effort. Team-specific data for the Swindon labour market nevertheless permit a passing comment on this matter. The 615 current employees in the Swindon sample were asked whether they worked unpaid overtime in their current job, or had done so in any previous job, and about their feelings about doing so. (Those who had never worked unpaid overtime were asked their opinions about employees who did.) The findings are clear. Respondents with a strong work ethic were far more likely to have worked unpaid overtime, and the great majority said they were happy to do at least some unpaid work. Those who had never worked unpaid overtime were also far more likely to approve of people who did when they scored highly for work ethic. On the other hand, there was no such link between Economic Individualism and approval for unpaid overtime work. To encourage the working of unpaid overtime is evidently a highly dubious policy aim. Some occupations or organizations already seem to promote a 'norm of overwork' whose link with productivity is open to question, though its link with stress illnesses is not. 'Workaholics' may reduce the motivation of co-workers or otherwise undermine their capacity to work effectively. There is a case for restraining 'conspicuous over-work' by imposing stricter limits on working hours. Improved effort in relation to the flow and quality of work are a quite different matter; and in this regard the SCELI evidence strongly supports the view that improvements in training and in the challenge of jobs— that is, changes resulting in real skill increases—did produce at least some important gains in the *effectiveness* of work.

10. For the Work Attitudes/Histories employee sample, the proportion reporting increased training over the last five years, at 27% was almost half that reporting an increase in the skill demanded by the job. The highest increases in training provision were amongst service-class groups such as Staff and Specialist Managers (44%) and Line Managers (40%); the lowest were amongst working-class groups, in particular Domestic Staff (15%), Catering Workers (9%), and Caretakers and Cleaners (4%). In the Employers 30 case studies, employers were asked if they had achieved 'major efficiency changes' in the previous five years amongst seven main employee groups. For each job group, around half those employers who had such workers said they had achieved such gains in the group. They were then asked to say what they considered to have been the main reason for these gains in efficiency. For all job groups, the most important reason cited was technical change, followed by better deployment of labour. For most job groups, only 6% of employers cited improved training as the most important reason; however, this rose to 8% for

lower-level managers and 12% for middle and upper managers. No data were collected about *second* most important reasons; this might have shown higher proportions since much technical change necessitates at least some increase in training. Even with this proviso, the figures seem to confirm the findings amongst employees themselves.

PART I
Patterns of Skill Change

2

Patterns of Skill Change: Upskilling, Deskilling, or Polarization?

DUNCAN GALLIE

A central concern of social scientific analysis of work and work organization has been with the way in which economic change affects the level of skill and the distribution of skills within the working population. We can distinguish three broad lines of argument in the literature. The first, which might be described as the 'optimistic perspective', postulates that the technological development of the advanced industrial societies implies steadily more complex types of work task and therefore higher levels of skill (e.g. Kerr *et al.*, 1960; Blauner, 1964). This change both results in an upward shift in the overall occupational structure of the workforce (marked in particular by the relative growth of non-manual occupations and the decline of manual) and leads to skill increases within occupational categories. These changes in the character of work tasks and work skills, it is argued, have major implications for patterns of work organization. With higher levels of skill, employers become increasingly dependent upon the willingness of employees to use their initiative. As a result, it becomes counter-productive to manage work organizations in an authoritarian way. Rather, to be effective, they must be designed in a way that allows employees greater discretion at work, thereby increasing their motivation and making the best use of their knowledge and skill.

A second perspective, however, suggests a very different scenario of long-term change. A number of writers have built upon the theories of 'scientific management', initially propounded by Frederick Taylor, to argue that the dominant tendency is towards a decline in the real skill content of jobs (e.g. Braverman, 1974; Crompton and Jones, 1984). These authors do not ignore the

striking expansion of non-manual work, nor do they deny that
formal skill gradings might suggest rising levels of skills. Where
they differ is in their interpretation of these phenomena. The
growth of non-manual occupations, they argue, has been accompanied by a profound internal transformation of their character.
As non-manual work has become more central to production, it
has been increasingly routinized and mechanized—a tendency
accelerated by the rapid diffusion of office automation. As a
result, non-manual employees lose their relatively privileged work
situation and become broadly similar in their skill levels to manual employees. At the same time, mechanization and automation
undercut traditional skills among manual employees, a process
reflected in the decline of pre-job training times. In introducing
organizational change, employers may well find it useful to relabel posts in a way that sweetens the pill of a declining quality of
work, offering employees increased organizational status and
even the appearance of promotion. But this expansion of higher
grades is deceptive: it reflects an industrial relations strategy
rather than any real increase in skill levels. The underlying
dynamic behind the process of deskilling is thought to be an
increased concern by management to tighten control over the
work process. A high level of employee discretion decreases predictability and gives the workforce power to resist managerial
efforts to achieve higher productivity and higher levels of profit.
By routinizing work, predictability is increased and the capacity
of employees to resist is weakened through the greater substi-
tutability of labour.

A third position combines elements of the first two. Rather
than postulating some general tendency towards either upskilling
or the lowering of skill levels, the central development is seen to
be an increasing polarization of the workforce between those
who benefit from economic change through an improvement in
their work situation and career chances and those who are
trapped in low-skilled and generally disadvantaged forms of
employment. There are a number of different versions of the
argument. Some maintain that there is a growing division
between a primary labour market for the higher-skilled, with
work systems based on high levels of employee autonomy backed
up by training and career incentives, and a secondary labour
market, where management makes little effort to maintain skills

through training but relies on intensifying work effort through deskilling and direct supervisory control (Edwards, 1979; Edwards *et al.*, 1975). The primary sector is sometimes identified with large firms in near-monopolisitc product-market situations, and the secondary sector with smaller companies in competitive market situations. Another version of the thesis lays the explanatory emphasis for the growth of the primary sector on the implications of advanced technologies for the growth of firm specific skills (Doeringer and Piore, 1971). This, it is suggested, places pressure on firms to provide adequate training and to create a work environment that encourages employees to remain in the firm, thus minimizing lost training investment. This effective conversion of part of the workforce into a fixed cost is accompanied by the development of another sector of insecure secondary labour that can be easily disposed of if there is a fall in demand (Berger and Piore, 1981). Yet other versions of the polarization argument stress the difference between developments in manufacturing industry, where employment is predominantly full-time and the unions are well rooted, and those in the service sector where a higher proportion of employment is part-time, casual, and low-quality.

This chapter seeks to address some of the issues raised by this debate. First, using a number of different indicators of skill, it examines whether changes in the occupational structure do reflect an expansion of higher-skilled jobs. Secondly, it considers the extent to which people experienced upskilling or deskilling within occupational classes in the early 1980s. Finally, it looks at the implications of the growth of the service sector, of technological change and of gender for the distribution of skills and for the experience of skill change.

The data are drawn from the ESRC's Social Change and Economic Life Initiative. This was based on six urban labour markets selected to provide contrasting labour-market conditions. Three of the labour markets—Swindon, Aberdeen, and Northampton—had known relatively buoyant employment conditions for the better part of the 1980s, although more recently there had been a sharp deterioration in the economic situation in Aberdeen. The other three labour markets—Coventry, Rochdale, and Kirkcaldy—had experienced prolonged recession through the 1980s, although there were some signs of the emergence of a new and more dynamic sector in Kirkcaldy. In each of the six localities interviews were carried out in 1986 with 1,000 people. Respondents for the survey were randomly selected from the overall non-institutional population aged between 20 and 60.[1]

OCCUPATIONAL CHANGE AND SKILL

There is general agreement that there has been a long-term rise in non-manual employment. Routh (1987), for example, has traced this across the century through a detailed comparison of the census data. In 1911 clerical workers, for instance, constituted only 4.8% of the occupied population in Britain. By 1981, they had risen to 14.8%. Similarly, there has been a striking growth in the professional strata. In 1931 professionals represented around 4.6% of the working population, whereas by 1981 this had increased to 14.7%. While the non-manual categories were rapidly expanding, the manual workforce was declining in both relative and absolute terms. Over the longer term, this has produced a major shift in the overall occupational structure. On the eve of the First World War, nearly 80% of the occupied population were manual workers; by 1987, the workforce was roughly evenly divided between manual and non-manual (48% non-manual, 52% manual).

A major problem in making rigorous comparisons across time is the lack of commensurability of the different occupational classification systems used in different censuses. A very similar picture of the general trends, however, emerges if we compare in our own data the distribution of occupations of parents and children coded to a common classification system. While the original coding was in terms of a very much more detailed register of occupational titles (Prandy classification) than is provided by the Registrar-General's classification, the most convenient way to study the general pattern is to look at the data aggregated into the Goldthorpe occupational class schema which is increasingly being accepted as the most robust of the more aggregated classification systems (Goldthorpe, 1987; Marshall *et al.*, 1988). Given the sample numbers, we have adopted a version of the class schema that groups classes 1 and 2 into a single service class of professionals, administrators, managers, higher technicians, and non-manual supervisors. We have also put together semi-skilled and unskilled manual workers and routine sales and service workers into a single category of the non-skilled manual class. This type of comparison between parents and children does not give an accurate snapshot of the social structure for some specific point in the past, but it is likely to be a good indication of general trends of change. Table 2.1*a* shows clearly that, for both men and women, there has been a marked shift towards non-manual work between the types of jobs that the parents were engaged in when the children were 14 years old and the types of jobs that the members of our sample currently held. Whereas 37% of the fathers had had non-manual jobs, this was the case for 49% of the sons. Similarly, the proportion of women in non-manual work has risen from 31% to 51%. There has been a particularly sharp rise in the proportion in the Goldthorpe 'service class'. On the other hand, there has been a fairly steep decline in both the skilled and non-skilled working classes.

Further confirmation of the pattern of change can be found if the more prosperous local labour markets are compared with those that had suffered more profoundly from economic recession. If we look at those currently in employment, the more prosperous labour markets had the highest proportion of non-manual workers and the lowest proportion of manual (Table 2.1*b*). The difference ranged from Aberdeen at one end of the spectrum, where 59% of employees were in non-manual work, to Kirkcaldy at the other, where less than half of employees (45%) were non-manual. Even at locality level, then, economic growth would appear to be clearly related to change in the occupational structure.

However, while this general pattern of occupational change is difficult to contest, what has been much more controversial is the significance that should be attached to such changes. The optimistic scenario relies heavily on the view that the growth of non-manual work in terms of such classifications represents a real increase in the skill content of jobs. Defenders of the pessimistic scenario argue that such classification systems are often arbitrarily arrived at or are based on wholly outdated conceptions of the skill involved in particular types of job. It has to be said that the relationships between such classifications and skill is problematic. The definition of the Registrar-General's class schema has gone

TABLE 2.1. *Class distribution: respondents and parents and by areas* (%)

	Service	Lower non-manual	S'visory/ technical	Skilled manual	Non-skilled manual	All non-manual	N
(a) Class of respondents/class of their parents							
Men's own class	34	7	8	22	30	49	
Father's class	23	6	8	30	36	37	
Women's own class	21	27	3	7	42	51	
Mother's class	8	21	2	17	51	31	
(b) Classes by area, current employees							
Aberdeen	34	19	6	13	28	59	727
Coventry	27	18	5	18	33	50	606
Kirkcaldy	27	12	6	18	36	45	596
Northampton	33	19	6	16	27	58	660
Rochdale	31	16	6	13	33	53	634
Swindon	34	15	7	10	32	54	649
TOTAL	31	17	6	15	31	54	3,872

Note: The data for this and following tables have been drawn from the Work Attitudes/Histories Survey 1986.

through some bewildering changes. At one stage presented as a measure of the social standing of occupations, it was converted into a measure of skill ranking with curiously little reorganization of its constituent categories. Certainly, we have little information about the criteria on which decisions about skill ranking were reached. The Goldthorpe class schema does not claim to provide a hierarchical ranking of skills. It seeks to classify people in terms of the different types of employment relations in which they are involved. This leaves open the precise linkages between such categories and skill criteria *per se*. Similarly, the analysis of social change through the use of such schemas raises the issue of the extent to which changes in class distribution reflect changes in general skill levels, as distinct from mere changes in the distribution of occupational titles or changes in other aspects of people's employment situation.

To examine this, we clearly need to compare occupational classes in terms of more specific criteria of skill. This, however, is easier said than done, given that one aspect of the controversy between optimists and pessimists involves the meaning of skill and hence what constitutes an appropriate indicator of skill. Very broadly, the pessimists have tended to adhere to what might be termed a 'craft definition' of skill, in which skill content is most effectively measured by the amount of task-specific training that someone requires. The optimists, on the other hand, have argued that one of the most fundamental characteristics of social change is precisely a change in the nature of skill. Increasingly, it is suggested, effective work performance depends upon the use of more general educational skills. At the same time, technical change is leading to an increased dependence upon people's ability to exercise responsibility and judgement in the face of rapidly changing environments and high levels of unpredictability. Given our current, very inadequate, state of knowledge about such issues, the most prudent course is to take into account a variety of rather different indicators of skill. In particular, we have focused upon five indicators: first, people's reports about the qualifications that somebody would need to get their type of job if they were applying for it now; secondly, the length of training that people received for their kind of work after completing full-time education; thirdly, the amount of time that it had taken them, after they first started the type of job, to learn to do it well; fourthly, whether or not they had direct responsibility for supervising the work of others, and fifthly, whether they themselves considered their work to be skilled. (As Francis and Penn argue in Chapter 8, definitions of a 'skilled job' usually do require an adequate technical justification.) Together, these various measures cover both the 'craft' and the 'general education/responsibility' conceptions of skill.

To what extent do the class categories represent different levels or types of skill? If we take the Goldthorpe classes, a first point to note is that the service class is quite clearly differentiated from all others. For instance, if we take the qualification levels that are currently required, some 85% of service-class employees report that at least O level or its equivalent would be required, whereas in the class that comes closest to this—the lower non-manual workers—the proportion was only 61% (Table 2.2). Those in the service class were also quite clearly the most likely to have received training for their work, they were the least likely to think that they could learn to do the job well in a short period of time, and they were the most likely to think of their job as skilled.

However, when we turn to the lower non-manual, the technician/supervisory and the skilled manual categories, there are few grounds for asserting any clear skill ranking between classes. Rather, we appear to be dealing with different types of skills. For

TABLE 2.2. *Skill characteristics by class* (%)

	Service	Lower non-manual	S'visory/ technical	Skilled manual	Non-skilled manual
O level equivalent currently required	85	61	50	51	12
No training	34	52	49	43	76
Learnt to do the job in less than a month	10	21	24	17	52
Responsible for work of others	65	22	64	27	13
Consider job skilled	91	68	70	86	40

instance, lower non-manual workers were substantially more likely than employees in the other two classes to be in jobs where at least O level or its equivalent would be required. On the other hand, they were less likely than skilled manual workers to have had training for their type of job or to think of their own work as skilled. Those in the technician/supervisory class were much akin to skilled manual workers in terms of qualifications needed and they were rather less likely to be trained or to feel that they needed experience before being able to do the job well. Where of course they rank much higher is in the responsibility their work carries. With the exception of responsibility, these three classes are closer to each other on the various skill dimensions than they are to other classes. In so far as there are differences, we are dealing with quite distinct dimensions of skill and any simple ranking would be misleading.

What does, however, emerge quite clearly from the data is the sharp break between these three intermediary classes and the non-skilled manual workers. The latter come at the bottom of the skill hierarchy on every one of our indicators and the gap between them and the class closest to them is usually very large. For instance, only 12% of non-skilled manual workers were in jobs where employers were requiring at least O level or its equivalent, whereas in the next lowest class on this dimension—the technician/supervisory class—the figure was 50%. As much as 76% of non-skilled manual workers were in jobs that required no training at all, whereas even among the lower non-manual employees the figure was only 52%. Non-skilled manual employees were twice as likely as those in any other class to say that they could learn to do their job well in less than a month. Finally, this was the only class in which a majority of employees regarded their work as unskilled. Whereas 68% of lower non-manual workers, 70% of those in the technician/supervisory class, and 86% of skilled manual workers thought their work was skilled, the figure for non-skilled manual workers falls to 40%.

It is, then, the respective sizes of the service and non-skilled manual classes (rather than of the non-manual and manual categories) that must be viewed as the key indicators of general skill levels. In these terms, it is still clear that the general trend has been towards the expansion of more skilled occupations. Taking the service class, for instance, 23% of fathers but 34% of sons were in this category, while the proportions among women had increased from 8% to 21% (Table 2.1*a*). Similarly, there has been a clear decline in the proportion of the workforce in non-skilled manual work. Whereas 36% of fathers had been non-skilled manual workers, this was the case for only 30% of sons; 51% of mothers had been in this type of work, compared with 42% of daughters. Similarly, if the current class structures of the more prosperous and more recessionary labour markets are compared, there is a consistent pattern in which the size of the service class is larger in the more prosperous labour markets and the size of the non-skilled manual class is smaller. The more prosperous labour markets reveal an upward shift in the skill distribution, which cannot be dismissed easily as a mere artefact of labelling procedures.

PATTERNS OF CHANGE IN SKILL WITHIN OCCUPATIONAL CLASSES

An increase in skill levels due to the expansion of higher-skilled occupational classes may be offset by a sharp deterioration of skill levels within classes. To investigate this, it is necessary to examine directly whether or not people have experienced skill changes. Again, given the variety of conceptualizations of skill, it is important to examine patterns of change using more than one measure. People were first asked about whether they felt that the level of skill that they used in their job had increased, decreased, or stayed the same over the previous five years, and then whether there had been changes in the level of responsibility involved in their job.[2]

The first point to note is that, on each of these indicators, a much higher proportion of employees report an increase in the skill level of their jobs than report a decrease. Overall, as can be seen in Table 2.3, 52% of employees indicated that the level of skill they used in their job had increased over the five years, whereas it had decreased for only 9%. An even higher proportion—60%—said that the responsibility involved in their job had increased, while only 7% said that there had been a decrease. The frequency with which people reported skill increases varied considerably, however, by class. Among service-class employees, some two-thirds (67%) reported that the skills involved in their job had increased over the last five years. The fiercest controversy in the literature has centred on the experiences of lower non-manual and skilled manual workers. Our evidence here is quite unambiguous. While workers in these classes were less likely than service-class workers to have experienced a skill increase, it was still the case that about half felt that the level of skill that they used in their job had become greater, and people were very much more likely to have experienced an increase in skill than a decrease. Whereas 55% of lower non-manual employees and 50% of skilled manual felt that their jobs now demanded a higher level of skill, not more than 8% in either category felt that the skill level of their work had decreased.

The real break in employment experiences would again appear to be between the intermediate classes and the non-skilled manual workers. While even among the latter the proportion that reported a decline in their skills was a mere 15%, it is notable, none the less, that the experience of a skill increase was very much rarer than in any other class. Only 33% felt that the skill level of their work had increased during the previous five years, while the majority (53%) felt that it had remained unchanged. Similarly, the non-skilled manual class was the only one in which a majority of employees (58%) felt that the responsibility involved in their work had either stayed the same or decreased.

The experience of an increase in the level of skills that people use in their job might reflect two rather different processes. It might be the result of upward occupational mobility or of changes in work at the same broad occupational level. We can explore this by constructing mobility profiles for the period 1981 to 1986. Those who remained within the same Goldthorpe class over this period are classified as immobile, while those who moved up from the intermediate or manual into the service class, or from the manual working class into one of the intermediate classes, are classified as upwardly mobile. Conversely those who moved from a service-class position to an intermediate class or to the working class are taken as downwardly mobile, and the same holds for those who moved from an intermediate class to the working class. How did the subjective experience of skill change vary with these different patterns of mobility?

A first point to note is that the great majority of employees

TABLE 2.3. *Changes in skill and responsibility* (%)

	Service	Lower non-manual	S'visory technical	Skilled manual	Non-skilled manual	All
SKILL						
All Employees 1986						
Increase	67	55	56	50	33	52
Decrease	4	7	9	8	15	9
						(N = 3,101)
Employees in same class 1981–6						
Increase	65	52	50	49	33	50
Decrease	3	5	5	8	12	7
						(N = 2,609)
Employees in same OUG 1981–6						
Increase	64	51	48	47	33	49
Decrease	2	5	4	6	5	4
						(N = 2,059)
Employees with no 'job' change 1981–6						
Increase	59	43	47	38	27	42
Decrease	1	2	3	7	4	3
						(N = 1,238)

RESPONSIBILITY

All employees 1986						
Increase	72	60	75	59	42	60
Decrease	4	8	4	6	10	7
						(N = 3,100)
Employees in same class 1981–6						
Increase	70	58	72	59	43	58
Decrease	4	6	1	5	7	5
						(N = 2,604)
Employees in same OUG 1981–6						
Increase	68	57	71	58	40	57
Decrease	3	4	1	3	2	3
						(N = 2,055)
Employees with no 'job' change 1981–6						
Increase	62	48	67	51	33	49
Decrease	1	1	2	2	2	2
						(N = 1,238)

had not experienced any significant class mobility over this period. Overall 84% were in the same class position in 1986 as they had been in 1981. Some 6% had been upwardly mobile into the service class and a further 4% from the manual working class into one of the intermediate classes. Downward mobility was less frequent than upward mobility over this period, with some 2% moving from the service class to an intermediate-class position and 4% being downwardly mobile into the manual working class.

It is clear that those that had been upwardly mobile were considerably more likely to have experienced an increase in their skill levels. The greatest increase in skills (78%) was among those that had moved from the manual working class to the service class, followed by people who had changed from an intermediate class to the service class. Mobility between the manual and the technical/supervisory or lower non-manual classes was also accompanied for the great majority (68%) by an increase in skill levels. The picture when one turns to the indicator of responsibility in work is similar. Those that have been upwardly mobile in terms of their class position have overwhelmingly taken up work requiring greater responsibility. On the other hand, the downwardly mobile in class terms were also distinctive in that they are the only category in which we find substantial levels of deskilling. For instance, 33% of people who had moved from a service-class position to the manual working class felt that their work involved a lower level of skill than before, and this was the case for a similar proportion of those that had moved from an intermediate class to the working class. Similarly, with the experience of changes in responsibility, it is those that have been downwardly mobile in class terms that had had the sharpest experience of the degradation of work. Overall, 32% of those that had been downwardly mobile had moved to work involving less responsibility. This primarily reflected the experiences of those that had moved from non-manual to manual work.

The inclusion of the upwardly mobile, then, is certainly likely to raise the proportions that have experienced skill increases, while the inclusion of the downwardly mobile reduces them. If we focus on those that had remained in the same class over the five years, however, it is striking how little difference the exclusion of the mobile categories makes (Table 2.3). We still find that only a very small proportion of employees (7%), felt that their work had been deskilled. At the same time, there remain very considerable variations in people's experiences by class. Whereas 65% of service-class employees had experienced a skill increase over the period, the proportion among non-skilled manual workers falls to 33%. Similarly, 70% of service-class employees had seen the responsibility involved in their job increase, while this was the case for only 43% of the non-skilled manual workers.

It might be that there is still mobility, albeit of a limited kind, within classes and that it is the experiences of those that have benefited from such career moves that accounts for the generally low level of deskilling. Similarly, classes may differ in the extent to which they provide opportunities for upward mobility and this may explain the wide discrepancies in experiences by class. We examined this by focusing down first on those that had remained within the same occupational group between 1981 and 1986 and second, most stringently, on those that had experienced no change either in their employer or in the type of work they were doing over these years. The pattern among those that had remained within the same occupational group is virtually indistinguishable from that of employees that had remained in the same class: we find very similar overall proportions that had experienced upskilling and very similar inter-class differences. If we turn to the wholly immobile group—those for whom we can be sure that there has been no element of career mobility—there is some decline in the proportions that had seen their skills increase over the period, but the broad picture remains the same (Table 2.3). The likelihood of having experienced a skill increase remains very much higher than that of having been deskilled. Indeed, those that have experienced no mobility at all are also the least likely to have been deskilled (3%). This confirms that deskilling, in so far as it occurs, is very rarely experienced by people that remain at the same job; rather it is connected with changes between jobs.

Finally, the sharply diverging experiences of service-class and non-skilled manual employees cannot be accounted for in terms of differential patterns of intra-class mobility. One might have expected career moves to have been a particularly important source of the experience of upskilling within the service class, but in practice the difference between service-class and non-skilled manual workers remains every bit as sharp when career movers are eliminated. It is clear that the experience of upskilling has been widespread in the service class even among those who remained in the same jobs (59%), while among non-skilled manual workers it has been very rare (27%).

In short, even if one discounts the effects of significant upward mobility through the occupational structure, there is very little evidence of substantial deskilling. For the great majority that have remained in the same general position in the occupational structure, the experience has been either an increase in, or a continuity of, the skills and responsibility involved in their work. In so far as people have experienced deskilling, this flows from a significant change in their location in the occupational structure. It is only among those that had been downwardly mobile that we find really significant levels of deskilling. At the same time, our evidence does provide some support for the view that a polarization of skills is occurring. This does not take the form of a contrast between a sector where skills are rising and a sector where they are declining. Rather the contrast is between those in higher occupational classes that have experienced an enrichment of their skills and those in non-skilled manual work whose position has remained static. In general, recent changes appear to be aggravating past differences in skill levels in that those in more skilled work were more likely to have increased their skills, while those in less skilled work were overwhelmingly likely to have remained at the same skill level.

THE IMPLICATIONS FOR SKILL OF THE GROWTH OF THE SERVICE SECTOR

What are the processes underlying these patterns of skill differentiation? To begin with, the conflicting arguments about skill have frequently been linked to rather different views about the implications of the growth of the service sector. For the optimists, this represents the expansion of knowledge-based occupations and leads to an increase in the qualifications and skill required in work (Bell, 1974). For the pessimists, the expansion of the service sector is characterized by the growth of a cheap, poorly qualified workforce that is confined to routine, repetitive work (Braverman, 1974).

If we compare, in Table 2.4, the overall occupational class distributions between manufacturing and services, we find little evidence of a clear trend towards lower-level jobs. Rather, the service class is larger in the service sector than in manufacturing (35% compared with 23%), while the proportion of employees in non-skilled manual work is similar. The other major difference is the much higher proportion of skilled manual workers in manufacturing and of lower non-manual workers in services. However, we have seen earlier that it would be misleading to regard such differences as constituting a skill shift in any particular direction.

For the purposes of these debates the manufacturing and service sectors are often discussed as though they were internally homogeneous. Yet it seems more probable that there are very important lines of internal differentiation and one of these is likely to be the distinction between the public and private subsectors. In fact our data shows that, while the class compositions in public and private manufacturing are broadly similar, they differ substantially between the public and private services. The service class is very much larger in the public than in the private services, while the non-skilled manual class is considerably bigger in the private services. In the private services, the service class is roughly the same size as in manufacturing, while the non-skilled manual class is larger than in any other subsector (36%). To the extent, then, that the growth of the services is based on private-sector growth, there is some support for the view that it is generating a particularly high proportion of low-level jobs.

We have examined more closely the nature of intersectoral differences by comparing classes in manufacturing and services in terms of our earlier skill criteria.[3] Overall, the service and lower non-manual classes are fairly similar in the two sectors, while there are some indications that skilled manual workers may have higher skill levels in the service sector. The two classes for which service-sector work does appear to be associated with lower skill levels are the technician/supervisory class and the non-skilled manual class. This was the case in both the public and the private services. The exceptionally high proportion of non-skilled manual workers in private services is then compounded by the fact that jobs in this category are of an even lower skill level than their equivalents in manufacturing.

Finally, how do people's experiences of skill change compare

TABLE 2.4. *Class composition of sectors* (%)

	Service	Lower non-manual	S'visory/ technical	Skilled manual	Non-skilled manual	% of all employees	N
Nationalized industries	27	11	9	24	29	4	151
Private manufacturing	23	10	5	30	32	29	1,077
Public services	45	17	6	5	27	31	1,162
Private services	25	25	6	8	36	30	1,099
All manufacturing	23	10	6	29	32	33	1,236
All services	35	21	6	6	32	61	2,292

in the two sectors? The basic pattern found earlier in which the experience of upskilling was very much more frequent than that of deskilling holds for both manufacturing and the services (Table 2.5). Overall, 53% of employees in manufacturing and 50% in services had experienced a skill increase over the last five years, while only 9% in either sector felt that their skill level had declined. We also find again in each sector the very wide disparities in experience by class. However, there is one striking contrast between sectors—namely, in the degree of disadvantage experienced by non-skilled manual workers in the services compared with manufacturing. Whereas in manufacturing 40% of non-skilled manual workers had increased skill, in the services this was the case for only 26%. The pattern is the same in both the public and the private parts of the service sector. Non-skilled manual workers in the services were also less likely to have increased the responsibility in their jobs, although the difference between manufacturing and services was less substantial (40% in services, compared with 45% in manufacturing).

Overall, then, the transition from a manufacturing to a service-based economy does not of itself have major implications for patterns of skill. The general distribution of skills in services is if anything higher. What is clear, however, is that there is a deep fissure within the service sector. The private sector is characterized by a particularly high proportion of low-skilled jobs. Furthermore, as with the public services, these jobs are lower-skilled than in manufacturing and they have given employees much less chance for increasing their skills in recent years. The structure of work in the service sector, then, aggravates the general tendency towards a polarization in skill experiences.

It might be argued that this simply reflects the type of workers that are available for work in this sector. To examine this we can compare the qualifications that employees have actually obtained with those that are currently required for their jobs (Table 2.6). This reveals a very interesting pattern. Taking the proportions for at least O level or its equivalent, we find that overall there is a broad matching of requirements and qualifications in the service class and among skilled manual workers. For the technician/supervisory class, there is some suggestion that in manufacturing industry there is a shortfall of employees with the requisite qualifications, while in the service sector a proportion of

Duncan Gallie

TABLE 2.5. *Increase in skill and responsibility by sector* (%)

	Service	Lower non-manual	S'visory technical	Skilled manual	Non-skilled manual	All
SKILL						
Nationalized industries	75	63	46	40	44	54
Private manufacturing	71	60	60	50	40	53
Public services	66	44	48	43	26	50
Private services	65	61	63	56	26	50
All manufacturing	72	60	57	49	40	53
All services	66	53	55	51	26	50
RESPONSIBILITY						
Nationalized industries	74	40	90	63	46	62
Private manufacturing	80	59	83	59	45	61
Public services	69	55	59	57	38	57
Private services	77	65	79	60	42	61
All manufacturing	79	57	85	60	45	61
All services	71	61	68	58	40	59

TABLE 2.6 *Qualifications required and own qualifications (% O level equiv.)*

	Nationalized industries	Private manuf.	Public services	Private services	All manuf.	All services
Service						
Required	90	80	92	76	82	86
Own	91	78	91	77	80	86
O–R	+1	–2	–1	+1	–2	0
Lower non-manual						
Required	75	59	66	55	61	59
Own	58	61	67	66	61	67
O–R	–6	+2	+1	+11	0	+8
Technical/supervisory						
Required	70	57	44	40	60	43
Own	64	54	57	59	56	59
O–R	–6	–3	+13	+19	–4	+16
Skilled manual						
Required	43	48	68	45	47	53
Own	36	48	53	53	47	53
O–R	–7	0	–15	+8	0	0
Non-skilled manual						
Required	15	13	10	12	13	11
Own	30	25	34	39	25	36
O–R	+15	+12	+24	+27	+12	+25

employees have higher qualifications than they need. It is, however, in the non-skilled manual class that the really major discrepancies emerge between employee qualifications and job requirements. A substantial number of employees in both manufacturing and services have higher qualifications than required, but the tendency to overqualification is particularly marked in the services (and especially in the private services). Indeed, it is notable that, while non-skilled manual work in the services requires similar and possibly lower qualification levels than in manufacturing, the actual qualification levels of employees are significantly higher. It seems likely, then, that it is the way that jobs are structured, rather than the capacities of the individuals that fill them, that accounts for the exceptionally low levels of skill in the service sector.

AUTOMATION AND SKILL

What was the impact of advanced technology on people's experience of skill change? One of the most contentious debates in the literature has focused on the implications of technical change for skill levels (Wood, 1982; Lane, 1988; Martin, 1988). In general this debate has suffered from a heavy reliance on case studies, of unknown typicality, that have provided very diverse pictures of the pattern of change. This has been the case both for studies of manual work (see, *inter alia*, Braverman, 1974; Wilson, 1988; Clark *et al.*, 1988) and for studies of non-manual work (see, *inter alia*, West, 1982a; Wainwright and Francis, 1984; Webster, 1986). The one more representative survey of the relationship between technical change and skill (Daniel, 1987) concluded strongly in favour of the view that technical change tended to raise the skill level of jobs. This, however, was based entirely on the views of managers. Employees are likely to be closer to the cutting edge of such change, yet there is currently little satisfactory data about the overall trends in their experiences.

Overall 39% of employees in our localities were working with automated or computerized equipment. It might have been expected that the use of advanced equipment would be less prevalent in the recessionary labour markets. However, while it was certainly the case that it was less common in Kirkcaldy

(34%), and Rochdale (32%), it is notable that Coventry is very comparable with the more prosperous labour markets. This may partly reflect the processes of automation occurring in car-manufacturing, since Coventry was distinct for the high proportion of its non-skilled manual workers using advanced technology.

If we now look at the way in which the use of automated equipment relates to our skill measures, the picture that emerges is a very clear one. On each indicator, work with advanced technology was associated with higher skill levels (Table 2.7). For instance, of those in jobs involving the use of automated or computerized equipment, 73% of employees reported that at least O level or its equivalent was required for new recruits, whereas this was the case for only 37% of those that did not use advanced technology. Only 39% of people using automated equipment said that they had not received training for the type of work that they were doing, as against 62% of those not using automated equipment. Further, people reported substantially longer on-the-job learning times with automated equipment. Where such equipment was not used, 35% felt that it had taken a month or less to learn to do the job well, whereas this was the case with only 15% of those using advanced equipment. Conversely, 40% of employees working with advanced technology, as against 30% of others, thought that it required a year or more experience. Finally, 82% of those using automated equipment regarded their jobs as skilled, compared to 60% of those not using it.

An important point to note is that the use of automated or computerized equipment varies considerably by class. For instance, 57% of service class and 51% of lower non-manual employees used it, compared with only 29% of skilled and 19% of non-skilled manual workers. Technicians and supervisors formed an intermediary group (40%). In every category, the use of automated equipment was associated with higher skill demands. However, this was least marked with respect to service-class work and it was generally of fairly moderate importance for skilled manual work. It was particularly in the technician, supervisory, and lower non-manual categories that advanced technology was related to a higher level of qualifications required for new recruits.

The conclusion that the use of advanced technology is generally associated with a rise in skill levels is reinforced when we

Table 2.7. *Advanced technology and skill levels by class* (%)

	Service	Lower non-manual	S'visory/ technical	Skilled manual	Non-skilled manual	All
USING ADVANCED TECHNOLOGY						
With O level	87	73	62	59	48	72
O Level+ currently required	90	74	71	61	32	73
No training	30	47	29	36	54	39
Experience needed less than 1 month	7	17	14	13	35	15
Consider job skilled	94	75	80	88	59	82
Responsible for supervising others	67	27	83	44	22	49
NOT USING ADVANCED TECHNOLOGY						
With O level	82	56	55	46	28	49
O level+ currently required	80	44	35	47	7	37
No training	39	59	61	47	81	62
Experience needed less than 1 month	15	25	29	18	56	35
Consider job skilled	86	60	63	85	36	60
Responsible for supervising others	62	15	50	21	11	27

examine people's experience of changes in the skill requirements of their work. Whereas 67% of those using automated equipment felt that the skill they used in their job had increased over the previous five years, this was the case for only 39% of others. The pattern was consistent across each of the localities and at each class level. However, it was particularly marked with respect to non-skilled manual, lower non-manual, and skilled manual work (Table 2.8). Further, the argument that advanced technology is related to a higher level of responsibility for employees appears well supported: 74% of those using technologically advanced equipment had experienced an increase in responsibility, compared with 49% of those doing other types of work. The pattern is again very similar across classes.

These results are entirely consistent with the picture that has emerged from interviews with employers (Daniel, 1987). The concordance between the two sets of data strongly suggests that the skill changes that have been examined are changes in the requirements of the job, rather than changes in the knowledge and experience that people bring to the same job. This is reinforced by the earlier evidence that there is a difference on the various skill-*level* measures between those who were working with advanced technology and those who were not. It is unlikely, however, that these trends reflect a deterministic impact of new technology. Technology *per se* has been shown to be relatively neutral in its implications for work organization (Jones, 1982; Hartmann *et al.*, 1984; Giordano, 1988; Kelly, 1989) and, indeed, automation may widen the scope for managerial choice. The general association between technical change and higher skill levels is likely to reflect factors such as the prevailing nature of managerial views about effective ways of enhancing employee motivation and the bargaining power of employee work groups (Gallie, 1988*a*). The introduction of new forms of technology is primarily important in accelerating organizational change, since it gives such issues greater immediacy and it generates greater social structural fluidity.

GENDER AND SKILL

A third factor strongly related to the level of skill is gender. As can be seen in Table 2.9, men were more likely to be in jobs

Duncan Gallie

TABLE 2.8. *Advanced technology and skill change by class* (%)

	Service	Lower non-manual	S'visory/ technical	Skilled manual	Non-skilled manual
USING ADVANCED TECHNOLOGY					
Experiencing increases in:					
Skill	74	66	66	66	53
Responsibility	78	68	88	71	59
NOT USING ADVANCED TECHNOLOGY					
Experiencing increases in:					
Skill	57	41	48	44	27
Responsibility	65	50	65	53	37

where at least O level or its equivalent was required (59% compared with 43%). Conversely, women were far more likely to be in jobs where no qualifications were currently required: 50% of women were in such jobs, whereas among men the proportion fell to 32%. There were also striking differences in training between men and women. Less than half of male employees (44%), but nearly two-thirds of women employees (63%) had received no training at all for the type of work that they were currently doing. Finally, 38% of women were in jobs that required less than a month to learn to do well, compared with 18% of men. In short, on the basis of these indicators, the skill requirements of women's jobs would appear to be substantially lower than those of men. It should be noted that these indicators do not take account of arguments about the importance of tacit skills in women's work (Dex, 1988). The differences they suggest, however, are reflected in people's subjective perceptions of their jobs. Overall 79% of men, but only 57% of women, regard their work as skilled. The difference emerges very clearly in each locality.

The pervasive character of gender segregation in the occupational structure is now well established. In each of the localities, women were less likely than men to be in service-class occupations and very much more likely to be in lower non-manual occupations. Similarly, in the manual categories women were predominantly in the non-skilled manual class while men were more evenly divided between skilled and non-skilled manual work. This raises the possibility that the differences between men and women

Table 2.9. *Qualifications and training of men and women employees*

	Service	Lower non-manual	S'visory/ technical	Skilled manual	Non-skilled manual	All
O level+ currently required	87	70	60	55	14	59
Without training	32	40	41	41	66	44
Experience needed less than 1 month	9	15	16	12	36	18
Responsible for supervising others	70	35	72	29	18	45
Consider job skilled	93	70	75	89	54	79
WOMEN						
O level+ currently required	82	58	22	27	10	43
Without training	37	56	71	57	84	63
Experience needed less than 1 month	13	23	49	39	65	38
Responsible for supervising others	56	17	38	16	8	24
Consider job skilled	85	68	54	68	29	57

in terms of qualifications required, training, and experience needed are another way of expressing these major differences in allocation between broad occupational classes.

However, our data suggest that differences by gender are even more pervasive than this. What is notable is that within each occupational category women come out lower on each of the skill indicators than men. The consistency of the pattern is altogether remarkable. For instance, among lower non-manual employees, 70% of the men, but only 58% of the women, are in jobs where new recruits would be expected to have the equivalent of O level or higher levels of qualification, while 40% of the men but 56% of the women are without training. Further, 15% of men but 23% of women in lower non-manual jobs said that it had taken less than a month to be able to do the job well. The differences are less marked with respect to service-class occupations, but otherwise they are of a similar order of magnitude across classes. This indicates that, even when similarly classified, women are in fact in very different types of work from men.

Has there been a difference in the extent to which men and women have experienced changes in their skill levels in recent years? Our evidence would suggest that men have benefited to a considerably greater extent than women from the process of upskilling. For both men and women, an increase in skills was substantially more likely than a decrease (Table 2.10). However, whereas a majority of men (56%) had increased their skills in the previous five years, this was the case for only 45% of women. There is also a substantial difference by gender in experiences of change in responsibility: 66% of men as against 50% of women considered that their responsibility had increased. There is some indication, then, that differences in skill levels between men and women may have been widening in the course of the 1980s.

How are we to account for such significant gender differences in skill experience? We have seen that a major factor associated with both skill levels and skill change has been whether or not people were working with advanced forms of technology. At least part of the difference in recent experiences between men and women may be related to the fact that women are substantially less likely to be working with such equipment. Whereas 46% of men were in jobs that involved the use of computerized or automated equipment, this was the case for only 33% of women.

TABLE 2.10. *Increase in skill and responsibility by sex* (%)

	Service	Lower non-manual	S'visory/ technical	Skilled manual	Non-skilled manual	All
SKILL						
Men	68	56	61	52	40	56
Women	64	55	38	42	24	45
RESPONSIBILITY						
Men	75	66	79	63	51	66
Women	67	58	59	28	33	50

There remain substantial differences in qualifications required, training and on-the-job experience needed even between men and women working with advanced technology. However, as can be seen in Table 2.11, it is striking that, if technology is controlled for, men and women would appear to have had very similar experiences of skill change: 70% of men working with technically advanced equipment had increased their skills compared with 64% of women. Where people were not working with advanced equipment, a minority of both men and women had experienced a skill increase (44% and 35% respectively).

There was also a clear association between women's experiences of skill change and the degree of gender segregation. As an indicator of gender segregation, we asked people: 'In general, is your type of work done exclusively by men, mainly by men, by a fairly equal mixture of men and women, mainly by women, or almost exclusively by women?'[4] Of women employees 6% were in types of work primarily carried out by men, while just over a quarter (26%) were in occupations that were seen as having a fairly equal mixture of men and women. The majority of women were in 'feminized' occupations, with 46% in work mainly done by women and 22% in work exclusively done by women. As can be seen in Table 2.12, women in male occupations were twice as likely as women in exclusively female occupations to have experienced an increase in their skills (66% compared with 37%). Indeed women in male occupations were more likely to have had a skill increase than men in this situation. However, men retain their advantage in the mixed-sex occupations—with some 66% of

Duncan Gallie

TABLE 2.11. *Skill and impact of advanced technology by sex (%)*

	Using adv. technology		Not using adv. technology	
	Men	Women	Men	Women
O level equivalent+ currently required	76	67	44	31
No training	33	48	54	70
Learnt to do job in less than 1 month	11	22	23	46
Responsible for work of others	59	31	33	20
Considers job skilled	87	73	72	49
Increase in skills	70	64	44	35
Increase in responsibility	77	65	57	42

TABLE 2.12. *Increasing skill and responsibility by occupational segregation*

Job is done:	Men increasing skill (%)	Men increasing responsibility (%)	Women increasing skill (%)	Women increasing responsibility (%)
Almost exclusively by men	51 (920)	62 (922)	66 (11)	75 (11)
Mainly by Men	57 (756)	67 (758)	67 (60)	76 (60)
Equal men/women	66 (285)	74 (285)	49 (322)	57 (322)
Mainly by women	61 (17)	64 (17)	44 (584)	48 (580)
Exclusively by women	— (1)	— (1)	37 (280)	40 (279)

Note: Parenthetic figures give N; cells left blank have very low N.

men as against 49% of women being upskilled. A virtually identical pattern emerges for changes in responsibility.

Finally, a third factor that would appear to be of major importance is the prevalence of part-time employment. It is particularly women in part-time employment that are in jobs with lower skill requirements than those of men (Table 2.13). Women in full-time work are closer to the pattern of male employees than they are to that of female part-timers. For instance, women in full-time work are almost as likely to be in jobs requiring at least O level or its equivalent as men (58% compared with 59% among men). In contrast, only 24% of part-timers were in this type of work. Similarly, women in full-time employment are only marginally more likely to be in jobs not requiring qualifications than the average for male employees (34% compared with 32%), while a majority of women in part-time work (70%) were in jobs requiring no qualifications. The same pattern emerges with training and with the need for on-the-job experience. Moreover, if we turn to the changes that people have experienced in their skills over the last five years, it is notable that, once part-time workers are excluded, the gender difference disappears entirely: 58% of women in full-time employment experienced an increase in their skill levels compared with five years earlier, whereas this was the case for 56% of men. On the other hand, among women in part-

TABLE 2.13. *Comparison of women in full-time and part-time work* (%)

	Women in part-time	Women in full-time	All men
No qualifications required	70	34	32
O level equivalent+ required	24	58	59
No training	78	51	44
1 year+ training	9	24	35
Under 1 month experience needed	58	23	18
1 year+ experience needed	10	27	45
Consider job skilled	38	72	79
Responsible for supervising others	10	35	45
Experience increase in skills	26	58	56
Experience increase in responsibility	34	61	66
Using advanced technology	19	45	46

time work, a mere 26% had experienced an increase in the skill required of their job.

We have seen that the chances of women increasing their skill varies powerfully by the degree of occupational gender segregation. But why should this be the case? Given the importance of the full-time/part-time divide for women's employment experiences, one possibility is that gender segregation is important because of the way in which it is linked to different types of employment contract. This is indeed an important part of the explanation. The proportion of women in full-time employment grows as one moves from segregated to desegregated jobs. It is clear that a considerable part of the effect of gender segregation can be attributed to the greater prevalence of part-time work in the more highly segregated settings (Table 2.14). Full-timers in mainly 'female' work are actually more likely to have experienced an increase in skills than those in non-gendered occupations and they are only a little behind women employed in predominantly male occupations. While women full-timers in a predominantly male occupation have an advantage over other women full-timers in their likelihood of experiencing an increase in responsibility, there remain striking differences when we compare full-timers and part-timers within each category. For instance, where occupations were non-gendered, 64% of women in full-time employment but only 40% of part-timers had experienced an increase in responsibility. Where occupations were mainly 'female', 62% of full-timers compared with 29% of part-timers had seen their responsibility increase. The main persisting disadvantage for women full-timers was in the lower responsibility in work of those in exclusively female settings. But, overall, it seems clear that women's skill experiences are more decisively affected by the prevalence of part-time work than they are by gender segregation. (Furthermore, as Horrell, Rubery, and Burchell show in Chapter 7, the type of 'tacit' skills required in much part-time work may also be those most likely to be undervalued for broader social reasons.)

CONCLUSION

The central concern of this chapter has been to assess a number of conflicting arguments in the literature about the direction of

TABLE 2.14. *Increasing skill and responsibility by occupational segregation: women full-time and part-time employees*

Job is done:	Increasing skill (%)		Increasing responsibility (%)	
	Full-timers	Part-timers	Full-timers	Part-timers
Almost exclusively by men	72	—	83	—
	(10)		(10)	
Mainly by Men	65	59	77	59
	(49)	(8)	(49)	(8)
Equal Men/Women	54	30	64	40
	(221)	(87)	(221)	(87)
Mainly by Women	59	25	62	29
	(303)	(258)	(300)	(256)
Exclusively by women	52	21	41	36
	(122)	(140)	(121)	(140)

Note: Parenthetic figures give N; cells left blank have very low N.

skill change. It has focused in particular on three theses: the 'optimistic' perspective that there has been a generalized upskilling of the workforce; the 'pessimistic' perspective that there has been extensive deskilling; and, finally, the view that there has been a growing polarization in the distribution of skills and in the experience of skill change.

Overall, our evidence suggests strongly that those that have argued that there is some pervasive tendency to deskilling either throughout the occupational structure, or in particular occupational classes within it, are mistaken. (Using a different method, Elias reaches similar conclusions in the next chapter.) We found that the experience of deskilling was very rare and this was true for all occupational classes. It was only among those that had been downwardly mobile between social classes that deskilling occurred with any frequency. The evidence was more favourable to the optimistic perspective. It showed that the upward shift in the occupational structure did indeed reflect the expansion of higher-skilled jobs, even when a range of different indicators of skill were used. Further, in most occupational classes, the commonest experience has been that of upskilling. This was true not only for the higher-level service-class positions, but also for lower non-manual workers, technicians, and skilled manual workers.

However, a closer examination of the data shows that the argument that is best supported is that of a polarization of skill experiences between classes. The already major skill differentials between the intermediary (let alone the service class) and the non-skilled manual class appear to have been accentuated in the 1980s. Those that already had relatively high levels of skill witnessed an increase in their skill levels, while those with low levels of skill saw their skills stagnate. The growth of the service sector has clearly been one of the structural factors that has contributed to this. Its public sector has been a major source of the growth of the service class, while the expansion of its private sector has been associated with the presence of a particularly large and exceptionally low-skilled category of non-skilled manual work. The polarization of skills is also closely associated with technological change. Those that have been in a position to use advanced technology in their work have seen their skills increase; those that have not had this possibility have been much more likely to see their skills remain unchanged. Finally, the evidence points to a deep gender divide in skill experiences. It is men above all that have benefited from the progress of skills in the 1980s, while women are much less likely to have seen their skills increase. The central factor connected with this would appear to be the existence of a major sector of part-time female work, in which the existing levels of skill are typically low and which has remained untouched by the processes that have elsewhere contributed to skill enrichment.

NOTES

1. The Initiative is an inter-university research programme in which all of the major research instruments were collectively constructed. The fieldwork was conducted by the Public Attitude Surveys Research Ltd.
2. The question wording was: I'd like to compare your current job with what you were doing five years ago. For each of the following things, would you say there had been a significant *increase* between then and now, a significant decrease, or little or no change: the level of skill you use in your job; the responsibility involved in your job.
3. The relevant tables can be found in D. Gallie, 1988*c*.
4. The aspect of gender segregation considered here is that of 'occupational' segregation by gender. The same analyses were repeated for 'workplace' segregation (the extent to which, at their place of work, women worked primarily with other women). The results were virtually identical. The relevant tables are available in a working paper (see n. 3).

3

Occupational Change in a Working-Life Perspective: Internal and External Views

PETER ELIAS

INTRODUCTION

At issue in the debate on the development of a 'post-industrial' society is the changing nature of paid work and its centrality within the sphere of human activities. The continuing gains in labour productivity, the reduction in the annual average amount of time spent in paid employment, and the growth of women's participation in the labour force indicate that paid work has become both more *intensive* and more *extensive*.[1] In other words, when people work, they are more productive than their predecessors and, for women, their involvement in paid work is spread more evenly through the potential working life.

Other strands to this debate concern the changing organization of work. Some commentators have proposed the view that paid work can be identified in terms of 'core' or 'peripheral' activities, with 'core' jobs placing greater demands upon the time, degree of commitment, and required knowledge of the job holder than for 'peripheral' jobs (Atkinson, 1984, 1985*b*). Others stress the impact of technical change which reduces the requirement for less skilled labour (via automation, information processing, etc.) and increases the demand for those familiar with the development and application of such technologies (Blauner, 1964; R. A. Wilson, 1989).

A further element in these arguments examines the implications of increasing disposable income and its impact upon the demand for labour-intensive leisure services. The growth of low-paid part-time jobs in the hotel and catering sector is indicative of such trends. The high level of personal service involved in such jobs gives little scope for productivity gains, reorganization of such work is constrained by the nature of the service which is provided, and it is often the case that such jobs offer little by way of job satisfaction (Elias, 1988). (Chapters 7 and 9 examine the subjective expectations and job-satisfaction levels of people doing such work.[2])

Thus, a confusing picture is presented. 'Post-industrialization' is not so much a phenomenon as a catch-phrase which encompasses these aspects of the changing nature of paid work. This chapter examines one element in this debate, the impact of changes in occupational structure on the skill requirements of jobs and the skills and work experience of those working in such jobs. It presents results from a modest attempt to determine the effect which recent changes in occupational structure have had on the relative economic position of those who held such jobs.

The study presented in this chapter also addresses an important methodological issue which arises when attempting to understand the impact of wider structural changes on the experience of the individual. Longitudinal or retrospective enquiries frequently make use of an individual's changing evaluation of his or her job at different times, or on a retrospective evaluation. It is important in such studies to control for the accumulated work experience of the individual. It may be the case that the knowledge and work experience gained by individuals over a period of time causes them to describe their work as becoming 'more skilled', but this 'work experience' effect is specific to the individual in a particular job and is not necessarily a feature of the job. Francis and Penn's examination in Chapter 8 of employees' own definitions of a skilled job seems to provide some further evidence of this effect. Studies which utilize such techniques but do not take account of this effect are likely to overestimate the extent to which work appears 'more skilled' at the time of the enquiry than at some earlier date.

The study approaches this problem in two ways. First, a series of occupational histories are examined for movements into and out of 'complex' occupations. This approach is termed an *external* view of occupational mobility in that it abstracts from an individuals' personal assessment of whether or not their work has become more complex or more skilled. A group of occupations is defined to include skilled manual occupations, non-manual jobs which have a significant training or qualification requirement, professional, technical, and managerial jobs. This group is labelled 'complex' occupations in that it consists of all jobs for which there is some prerequisite in terms of the skills/training/ qualifications and/or prior work experience for competent performance. All remaining occupations as defined within the 1980 *Classification of Occupations* (OPCS, 1980) are termed 'simple' occupations, reflecting the fact that for such jobs there is a minimal requirement for associated skills, training, qualification, or work experience. The analysis presented in this chapter looks at the movement of persons between these two broad occupational groups. Graphical and multivariate techniques are used to portray and explore the general nature of such changes and their covariates. Although this approach yields interesting findings, it can be criticized for its dependence upon an externally imposed classification of jobs into 'complex' and 'simple' occupations. Critics of this approach would argue that the results are more informative of the changing nomenclature of occupational description and the quirks of occupational classification than of any substantive changes in work content. For this reason, the chapter also presents the results of an analysis of an *internal* view of occupational movement. This relies upon a personal evaluation of the 'most skilled job' held throughout an individual's working life, without attempting to define the meaning of the work 'skill'. To overcome the objection that can be levelled at such studies, that they often fail to take account of 'work-experience' effects, the analysis presented in this section distinguishes between those people who evaluate their current job as their 'most skilled' compared with those who designated some earlier job in their working life as 'most skilled'. For a latter group any potential 'work experience' effects are obviously subsumed by the impact of occupational change. The analysis proceeds by examining for systematic relationships between membership of these two groups, lifecycle events, and economic change.

OCCUPATIONAL CHANGE, 1971–1989

At the aggregate level, occupational change must be indicative of changes in the organization of work. The growing importance of managerial jobs, for example, derives from the creation of wider (and possibly looser) organizational and control structures in firms and institutions. But occupational change also represents a barometer of technological change. The growth of computing occupations and scientific and engineering occupations, for example, has arisen out of a direct relationship between technical innovation and development and the type of work related to new technologies. Most importantly, however, occupational change is driven by the expansion or contraction of particular sectors in the economy. The decline in craft and skilled manual occupations is predominantly a function of the decline of the manufacturing sector, particularly so for skilled engineering occupations. The growth of catering and cleaning occupations derives from the rapid and continued expansion of leisure services.

Attempts to measure the extent of occupational change have raised more questions than the answers that have been sought. Occupational change can be measured only if occupational descriptions have been codified and classified within some structure. Occupational descriptions may reflect more the changing nature of work organization than the changing content of work itself. Occupational classification are altered to reflect changes in the language used to convey information about work. Misclassification is commonplace in the inexact environment of occupational coding, lending an additional degree of uncertainty to the interpretation and understanding of changes in occupational structure. None the less, some of the changes in occupational structure recorded in the 1970s and 1980s are so profound that they must be indicative of major changes in the type of work people perform. For example, the level of employment in the category of occupations defined as 'craft and skilled manual occupations' (machine tool setter-operators, plumbers, electricians, plasterers, carpenters, welders, auto mechanics, etc.) is estimated to have fallen from 4.7 million to 4.0 million by 1988 (from 19.3 per cent to 15.5 per cent of total employment). The level of employment in 'plant and machine operative' occupations fell from 3.5 million to 2.6 million (14.7 per cent to 10.2 per cent of total employment in the same period). Employment in 'professional' occupations (those jobs for which entry is usually restricted to persons holding a degree or equivalent) rose from 1.5 million to 2.4 million and the category of 'managerial' occupations grew from 2.7 million to 3.5 million. Overall, the 'white-collar' occupational group (managers, professionals, technicians, clerical, and sales occupations) grew by 3.1 million between 1971 and 1981, whereas the 'blue-collar' occupations (craft and skilled manual, plant and machine operatives, and labourers) declined by 2.1 million.

These changes were felt unevenly across different sectors of the economy. The manufacturing sector has been the location of much of the decline in 'blue-collar' work, offset to some extent by the rise in professional, managerial and technical occupations in this sector. Certain sectors, notably those which are associated with leisure services (hotels, restaurants, bars, etc.), have seen significant increases in the demand for labour, most of which has been organized on a part-time basis and consists of fairly low-status, low-paid occupations (food handling, cleaning, etc.).

The extent and diversity of these trends, together with the increase in the labour force participation of women, suggests that many people may have experienced major occupational changes at some stage in their working life and that such changes will be recorded in their work histories. The next section in this chapter describes how such data were processed to study the extent of such major occupational moves, distinguishing between moves into 'complex' jobs versus movement into 'simple' jobs. Figure 3.1 summarizes these changes, distinguishing between the occupational changes experienced by men and women and comparing the period 1971–81 with 1981–9.

In the 1970s, the predominant feature of occupational change was the dramatic decline in craft and related occupations and plant and machine operatives. As mentioned earlier, the dominant factor behind these trends was the general decline of the manufacturing sector. These changes were experienced predominantly by males, with women benefiting from the expansion of clerical, secretarial, and associate professional/technical occupations in this same period. This growth of female employment in associate professional/technical and clerical occupations continued in the 1980s. The latter period (1981–9) saw much less change in male occupational structure, given the more stable situation in the manufacturing sector in the 1980s.

Changes in occupational employment, 1971–1981

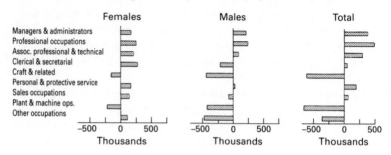

Changes in occupational employment, 1981–1989

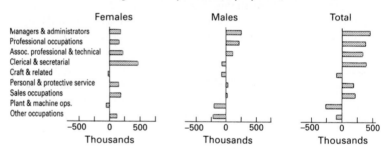

Figure 3.1. Changes in occupational employment, 1971–1989

'COMPLEX' VERSUS 'SIMPLE' OCCUPATIONS

Traditionally, occupational mobility has been studied in terms of changes in the status ranking or labour market relationships of particular groups (for example skilled/semi-skilled/unskilled, manual/non-manual, middle class/working class, 'service'/'non-service' class or white collar/blue collar). For the current purpose, a classification is adopted which focuses more upon the complexity of work and the length of the period of training usually associated with it. Through this schema, jobs can be classified as providing either a 'simple' or 'complicated' work environment. This was achieved by questioning respondents in detail about the nature of their jobs and the subsequent classification of such jobs to a detailed code frame. All such occupations were reclassified into 'complex' or 'simple' categories. In this classification, all jobs which are managerial, professional, or technical are deemed 'complex'. In other areas of work, the distinction depends upon the nature of the tasks which typically constitute the duties of a job holder. All jobs which have foreman or supervisory status are, by default, 'complex'. Table 3.1 gives a sample of jobs in a variety of occupational areas and distinguishes various job titles common to that area in terms of whether or not the job is labelled 'simple' or 'complex'. This is a categorization of work that is somewhat different from the usual 'manual/non-manual' distinction which is used to dichotomize the structure of occupations. The purpose is to explore the notion that technical and organizational changes have had different impacts upon various groups in the labour market, 'deskilling' work in some areas and creating jobs which are more demanding in terms of their performance requirements in other areas. The definition has been operationalized by coding occupations to the 1980 *Classification of Occupations* (OPCS, 1980), at the level of 1980 Social Classes. All occupations allocated to Social Classes I, II, III(M), and III(N) are classed as 'complex'. All occupations allocated to Social Classes IV and V are classed as consisting of 'simple' tasks.[3]

Using this broad division of occupational structure, the information given in the preceding section can be reinterpreted as shown in Table 3.2. This indicates the percentage of employment in 'complex', as opposed to 'simple' jobs in three years: 1971, 1981, and 1989. For males, the changes in occupational structure which took place over the decade 1971 to 1981 led to a significant rise in the proportion of male employment in 'complex' jobs, a trend which continued through the 1980s. For women, a lower proportion are found in occupations which have been deemed 'complex' and there has been no growth in the proportion of women in such jobs over these two decades.

In summary, it is evident that there have been major changes in occupational structure over the last 20 years. These have been driven by the scale of industrial change in the late 1970s and early 1980s, particularly the decline of employment in the manufacturing sector and the growth in the service sector. In terms of the gender structure of occupational change, men and women have experienced quite different influences. For men, the predominant force has been the decline in craft and skilled manual

TABLE 3.1 *Examples of the type of occupations labelled 'simple' or 'complex'*

Category of occupation	'Simple'	'Complex'
Agricultural occupations	Farm worker	Farmer, farm manager
Materials-processing occupations	Grader, sorter	Vehicle body builder
Craft occupations	Sewer, metal hardener	Tailor, carpenter
Materials-handling occupations	Warehouseman	Fork-lift truck operator
	Goods porter	Crane driver
Transport occupations	Bus conductor	Signalman
Construction occupations	Roofer, general building worker	Bricklayer, plasterer
Clerical occupations	Telephone operator, mail sorter	Receptionist, typist
Caring occupations	Hospital porter, ward orderly	Nurse, nursery nurse
Catering occupations	Waiter, kitchen hand	Chef, cook
Cleaning occupations	Cleaner, road sweeper	Foreman (cleaners)
Sales occupations	Shelf filler	Sales representative, sales assistant

Source: OPCS (1980).

TABLE 3.2. *Trends in employment in 'complex' occupations by gender, 1971–1989* (%)

	Employment in 'complex' jobs		
	1971	1981	1989
All employed	82	83	84
Males	85	88	90
Females	76	76	76

Source: R. A. Wilson (1990).

occupations, and in plant and machine operative occupations. Additional to these changes has been a strong growth in male employment at the managerial, professional, and technical level. As far as the 'complexity' of work is concerned, defined in terms of the number of 'complex' as opposed to 'simple' jobs, these two main changes in occupations have counterbalanced each other. In general the occupational structure of male employment has moved slowly towards a higher proportion of 'complex' jobs.

For women, two countervailing factors are at work. On the one hand, women have benefited considerably from the growth of professional and associate professional/technical jobs. On the other, the major growth of employment in low-status jobs in the sector 'miscellaneous services' has countered the tendency towards any increase in female employment in complex occupations. In 1971, 76 per cent of women were employed in 'complex' jobs, compared with 85 per cent of men. By 1989, this proportion had risen for men but not for women. The gap between the proportion of men and women in 'complex' jobs had climbed from 9 percentage points to 14 percentage points.

OCCUPATIONAL CHANGE AND OCCUPATIONAL MOBILITY

This section examines the relationship between the major occupational changes which have been taking place within the wider

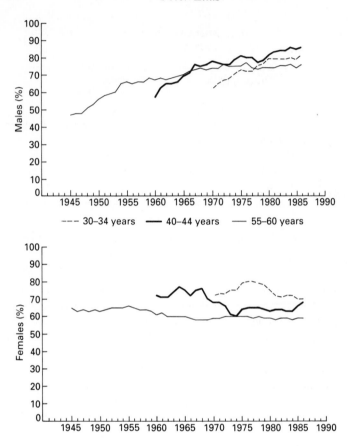

Figure 3.2. Cohort analysis of employed persons in 'complex' occupations: 30 to 34 year-olds, 40 to 44 year-olds, and 55 to 60 year-olds at time of survey, by gender.

Source: Social Change and Economic Life Initiative, Work Attitudes/Histories Survey, 1986.

economy, referenced in the preceding sections, and the broad occupational movements which are registered within the work histories of respondents to the 1986 Work Attitudes/Histories survey conducted as a part of the Social Change and Economic Life Initiative.

To develop a picture of the occupational changes that are recorded in these work histories, it is necessary to group survey respondents together into a series of age bands comparing the evolution of occupational histories of different age groups in each year before the survey data and since completion of their full-time education. Through this technique, termed 'cohort' analysis, the average occupational structure of the employed member of the cohort can be portrayed graphically in terms of the percentage employed in 'complex' occupations in each year of their working lives.

Figure 3.2 examines the occupational histories of men and women in the six SCELI localities. Three age groups (defined in terms of age at the time of the survey) are indicated; 30–34 years, 40–44 years, with those aged 55–60 years shown on each graph for comparison. In each case, the graph shows the percentage of those in employment in each earlier year of their work history who are employed in an occupation classified as 'complex'.

Studying the graphs for males first, it can be seen that the evolution of occupational changes is quite noticeable and unidirectional. For the three age groups shown, advancing age is associated with an increasing proportion of the age group in 'complex' jobs. Upon joining the workforce after completion of their full-time education, about 50–60 per cent of men are employed in such occupations. This rises by about 5 percentage points every five years. In other words, the net effect of occupational changes over the last 20 years upon the occupational environment of men is that a higher proportion work in jobs which are more demanding in terms of their constituent tasks.

For women, it appears that a higher proportion start their working lives in 'complex' jobs (each of the graphs shown in Figure 3.2 commences at a higher percentage than does the corresponding graph for men), but the trend thereafter is completely different. After an initial upward movement, each age group moves downward, indicating that an increasing proportion of women are moving into occupations which have 'simple' task requirements.

Previous work on occupational mobility over the lifecycle of the individual (as opposed to intergenerational mobility) has focused upon the relationship between family formation, part-time work, and the occupational work histories of women. These studies, reviewed in Elias (1988), together with the accompanying analysis of information on women's work histories from the 1980

Women and Employment survey, indicated that women experience a significant amount of downward occupational mobility and
that such occupational movements are associated with the transition into part-time jobs following the return to work after a
period of family formation. The information shown in Figure 3.2
reconfirms these findings, using a more up-to-date source of information and, importantly, shows that men experience an average
upward trend in terms of their movement into complex jobs.

OCCUPATIONAL MOBILITY AND FAMILY FORMATION

Figure 3.2 indicates that, on average, men tend to move out of
'simple' occupations and into 'complex' occupations as they
spend more of their working lives gaining work experience. Also,
higher proportions of young men start work in 'complex' occupations than for the older age cohorts. For women, there appears
to be an equivalent increase in the proportion of jobs in their
work histories categorized as 'complex', but this effect is concentrated among the younger age cohorts of women and only for a
short period of time during their working lives. On the basis of
earlier work, it is hypothesized that family formation is an
important intervening event for women. This section pursues the
issue further, elaborating the graphical technique used in the preceding section, then recasting the analysis within a multivariate
statistical framework.

The chart for women in Figure 3.2 indicates that their work
histories include, on average, a decreasing proportion of 'complex' occupations and this downward trend commences approximately six to eight years after first entry into the labour market,
at or around ages 22–24 years. This coincides with the approximate mean age of women returning to work after the birth of a
first child. Thus, it may be more instructive to examine the work
histories of women (and men) with reference to a particular event
in their work history (childbirth) rather than with reference to a
particular year.

Figure 3.3 examines the occupational histories of men and
women who had had at least one child (histograms *a* and *c*) or at
least two children (histograms *b* and *d*). The occupational histories are restricted to men or women who are in the age range

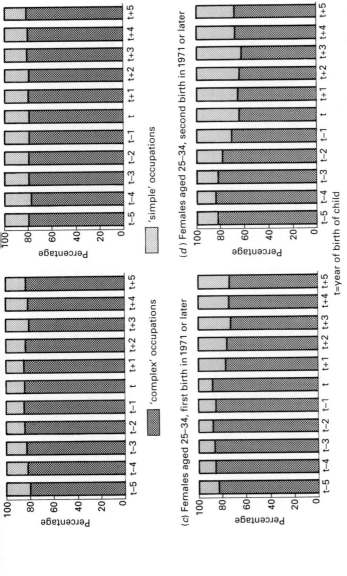

Figure 3.3. Employed men and women with children: distribution between simple and complex occupations, five years before and five years after the first or second birth, for births after 1971

Source: Social Change and Economic Life Initiative Work Attitudes/Histories survey, 1986.

25–34 years and focus exclusively on births which took place between 1971 and 1986, the data of the survey. Each set of histograms contrasts the occupational histories of men and women for the period five years before and five years after the birth of their first child.

Histogram *a* shows the average occupational position for men aged 25–34 in 1986 whose partner had her first child in 1971 or later. It can be seen that there is a slight upward trend in the proportion employed in 'complex' jobs, consistent with the information portrayed in the previous section. There is no indication of any significant break in this trend at or around the year in which his partner gave birth to her first child (shown as year 't' in the diagrams).

For women, the position is quite different, especially for younger women (or those who postponed their first child until their late twenties). Histogram *c* reveals that up until the year in which her first child was born, these women were, on average, moving into 'complex' occupations. However, the return to work after first childbirth is accompanied by a sizeable fall in the proportion of employed women who are working in occupations designated as 'complex'.

Histograms *b* and *d* Figure 3.3 show the same information for men and women with at least two children. Again, the picture for men is one of gradual movement out of occupations classified as 'simple' to those classified as 'complex'. The situation for women is somewhat different than for the first birth, showing a gradual decline in the proportion employed in 'complex' occupations up to the year in which the second birth took place, followed by little movement back into 'complex' occupations in the five year period following the birth. The gradual decline is in evidence because those who have experienced a second birth have, by definition, had their first birth in some earlier period. Birth intervals between first and second children are in the order of 2 years. Thus, histogram *d* of Figure 3.3 confounds the occupational impact of both first and second births.

This new evidence confirms that, for men, childbirth has little impact upon their worklife occupational mobility, measured in terms of their progression from relatively undemanding to more complex types of jobs. For women, the evidence indicates that family formation has a profound impact upon their occupational histories, that the impact is cumulative in terms of the number of children a woman has, that the contrast between occupations before and after family formation is becoming more marked among younger women (or those who have postponed family formation) and that there is little indication that such net occupational movement out of the more demanding jobs into 'simple' jobs is a temporary phenomenon, confined to a one- or two-year period after family formation.

The next stage in this examination of occupational change and its impact upon individual work histories is to place these various influences within a multivariate framework. This is achieved by classifying the occupational characteristics of each of the employment years in a person's working life with a dichotomous variable. The value 'zero' is assigned to those occupations designated as 'simple' and the value 'one' is assigned to those occupations allocated to the 'complex' category. The resulting occupational history for each individual is then represented by a string of zeros and ones, recording their movement into an out of 'complex' jobs. Because of the scale of the resulting data, the analysis is restricted to one of the SCELI localities which has experienced a sharp decline in manufacturing sector employment, high levels of unemployment among men in the early 1980s, and a tradition of high levels of female labour force participation, the Coventry locality.

Table 3.3 shows results from a linear regression model in which the dependent variable is a dichotomous variable having a value of 'one' if an individual is employed in a 'complex' job, zero otherwise, and a set of 'explanatory' variables which describe the relationship between the allocation to a 'complex' category of employment, personal characteristics of the individual, employment characteristics, and indicators of economic change. Some of these characteristics are fixed for each individual, in that they represent characteristics which cannot, or are assumed not to, change through time. Others vary through time and are individual specific (such as the industry sector in which a person works).

This type of analysis appears complicated at first sight, but it can be interpreted in a fairly intuitive way. The numbers in the columns labelled 'coefficient' can be regarded as the marginal influence of a particular variable upon the probability that a

Table 3.3. *The relationship between employment in 'complex' occupations, personal characteristics, job characteristics, and economic change*

Nature of influence	Males			Females		
	Coefficient	(t)	mean	Coefficient	(t)	mean
TIME-INVARIANT:						
White	.011	(.5)	.933	.130	(3.9)	.976
'O' levels	.112	(9.3)	.276	.177	(14.1)	.293
'A' levels	.058	(2.2)	.048	.110	(4.2)	.053
Low vocational quals.	.092	(8.9)	.326	.176	(14.7)	.233
High vocational quals.	.128	(7.6)	.095	.087	(4.3)	.076
Degree	.146	(4.6)	.030	.070	(1.6)	.016
TIME-VARYING:						
(a) descriptive of job:						
Industry sector						
Agriculture	-.207	(-6.6)	.028	-.534	(-5.4)	.002
Energy, water	.136	(5.6)	.043	-.021	(-.4)	.007
Minerals, metals	.149	(3.3)	.010	.185	(2.0)	.003
Motor vehicles, eng.	.079	(5.6)	.448	-.026	(-1.7)	.193
Other manufacturing	.071	(3.6)	.081	-.124	(-8.2)	.191
Construction	.088	(4.0)	.066	.323	(6.2)	.009
Distribution	.151	(8.3)	.112	.157	(11.0)	.184
Transport, comm.	.147	(5.7)	.038	.007	(.2)	.019

Insurance, banking	.227	(5.8)	.015	.233	(9.8)	.049
Public services	—		.143	—		.337
Industry not given	.076	(1.5)	.008	-0.19		.006
Workplace size						
Employed alone	—		.033	—		.042
2–24 persons	-.072	(-1.7)	.209	.021	(.6)	.341
25–99 persons	-.077	(-1.8)	.142	-.079	(-2.3)	.170
100+ persons	-.186	(-4.4)	.603	.074	(2.2)	.424
Other job characteristics						
Self-employed	.129	(5.3)	.053	.161	(5.1)	.027
Pay better than in previous job	.017	(1.8)	.610	-.004	(-.4)	.512
Part-time job	-.436	(-4.9)	.003	-.166	(-11.4)	.249
(b) descriptive of individual						
Unemployed at some time during year	-.158	(-5.4)	.026	-.101	(-2.9)	.021
Unemployed at some time in previous year	-.113	(-3.5)	.021	-.025	(-.6)	.016
Unemployed for majority of previous year	-.088	(-1.7)	.010	-.032	(-.6)	.009
Out of labour force for majority of previous year	-.078	(-1.3)	.005	-.011	(-.5)	.060
Cumulative years employed	-.006	(-2.1)	14.8	.005	(3.2)	11.1
Age	.021	(5.1)	30.1	.003	(.9)	29.9
Age squared	-.0002	(-3.4)	1,009	-.0001	(-2.1)	1,015
First child born in previous year	.018	(.6)	.029	-.038	(-.7)	.009
Second child born in previous year	-.020	(-.6)	.022	-.043	(-.6)	.006
Third or higher child born in previous year	-.058	(-1.6)	.016	-.090	(-1.4)	.007
Children aged 0–2 years in household	.001	(.1)	.173	-.051	(-2.1)	.062
Children aged 3–5 years in household	-.014	(-1.0)	.152	-.051	(-2.6)	.080

Table 3.3. *Cont.*

Nature of influence	Males			Females		
	Coefficient	(t)	mean	Coefficient	(t)	mean
Children aged 6–11 years in household	.013	(–1.0)	.198	–.069	(–4.6)	.196
Children aged 12 years or older in household	..	(.1)	.164	–.038	(–2.5)	.257
c) descriptive of national economic change						
Rate of inflation	..	(.3)	8.0	–.002	(–1.5)	7.9
Rate of unemployment	–.005	(–2.0)	5.1	–.006	(–2.5)	5.2
Rate of employment change	–.004	(–1.4)	.212	–.005	(–1.5)	.235
Time trend	.001	(.6)	71.2	.003	(2.8)	70.8
constant	.289	(3.4)		.303	(3.7)	
$\bar{R}^2$	.118			.227		
n	9,532			7,347		
F	32.1			53.6		
mean of dependent variable			.710			.689

Notes: A dash (—) indicates that the variable was the reference category.
Two dots (..) indicates a coefficient with a value less than .0005 in absolute magnitude.

Source: Social Change and Economic Life Initiative, Work Attitudes/Histories survey; Coventry locality, 1986.

person will spend each year of his or her employment history in a 'complex' job. For example, take the variable which indicates that a man was working in the motor vehicles/engineering sector of the economy. For each year that a man was observed working in this sector, the probability that he was also working in a 'complex' job is systematically decreased by approximately 8 per cent relative to the reference category, public services. The sign on the coefficient indicates whether the particular characteristic is associated with an increase (positive) or a decrease (negative) in the probability of being employed in a 'complex' job, the 't-value' indicates the statistical significance of these influences (t-values over 2.5 in absolute magnitude are indicative of highly significant relationships). The information on the sign and size of coefficient and its statistical significance should be compared with the mean value of the variable used to describe a particular characteristic, to gain an overall indication of the importance of the effect of a characteristic on the probability of observing a respondent in a 'complex' occupation.

Taking the analysis of men's occupational histories first, it can be seen that there are some powerful influences upon their employment in 'complex' occupations. First, qualifications have an obvious positive and marked influence. These influences are described as 'time-invariant' in that they do not vary over the working life of the individual. In other words, the possession of qualifications, particularly high-level vocational qualifications (such as professional accountancy qualifications) or a degree, makes it much more likely that a person will be employed in a 'complex' occupation in *every* year of his or her working life.

The remaining characteristics which are used to explore whether or not an individual is observed in a 'complex' occupation are all time-varying. That is, they vary through the working life of the individual. Some such influences are descriptive of the job in which the individual worked, some are descriptive of the individual (for example, previous work history, age) and some are characteristic of the particular period of time under consideration (for example, the prevailing rate of unemployment in the national economy). Looking first at the effect of industry sectors, it is apparent that the probability of observing an individual in the 'complex' occupational category clearly depends upon the industry in which a person was working in a particular year. This implies that the scope to engage in this type of work is, to some extent, demand-determined. That is, the type of occupation within which an individual works and the classification of the occupation as 'complex' work are determined by the opportunities to engage in such work in particular industries. From Table 3.3 it is evident that, for a man, employment in the motor vehicles and electrical engineering industries, which accounts for approximately 4,300 of the employment years in this sample, is associated with an 8 per cent increase in the probability that he will be working in a skilled occupation relative to men working in public services, after controlling for educational qualifications and many other influences. Insurance and banking and distribution are also sectors which improve the occupational position of men relative to public services, the reference category.

For men, there is a clear relationship between the individual experience of unemployment and the movement into occupations which are not classified as 'complex'. If individuals were unemployed at some time during the year for which their dominant economic status was employed, then there is a 16 per cent reduction in the probability that they have been classified to the 'complex' group of occupations. Unemployment in the previous year is associated with an 11 per cent reduction. Interestingly, it is not just the individual experience of unemployment that affects occupational status. A variable representing the national growth in joblessness, the economy-wide unemployment rate, is also included in this model. This variable, which is common to all respondents and varies through time only, is correlated with a decline in the proportion of respondents who are classified to 'complex' jobs. The coefficient on this variable implies that an increase of 10 percentage points in the national unemployment rate would be associated with a 5 per cent decline in the probability of having a job within the 'complex' category.

The result of this type of analysis when applied to information describing women's occupational work histories is similar to that for men in many respects; qualifications have the same positive effect upon whether or not a woman is working in a 'complex' occupational category. Sectoral influences are similar, particularly for the effect of working in insurance, banking and finance, and distribution. However, there are two areas where women's occupational histories deviate significantly from those of men. First, unemployment does not appear to have a strong depressing influence upon a women's occupational status. The effect is negative, as for men, but is much smaller and, for unemployment spells in the preceding year of each year of her work history, insignificant. On the other hand, the presence of children in the household has a systematic downward impact upon a woman's occupational status. The impact of children upon a woman's occupational history was analysed in two ways. First, the immediate impact of child-bearing was measured by creating a variable which takes on the value of unity only for the year immediately following the birth of a child. Three such variables were created, measuring the impact on occupational status of a first, second, or third or higher birth in the preceding year. For none of these variables was the coefficient statistically different from zero. In other words, short-run single-year effects from the birth of children on the occupational status of women are not found. Another set of variables relates to the presence in the household of children in various age groups. These effects are quite strong and are negative. These results indicate that it is not the experience of childbirth as such, but the presence of young children in the household which reduces the chances of observing a working woman in a 'complex' occupation by about 5–7 percentage points.

Other influences which are noteworthy are the impacts of employment size and part-time working. For both men and women, there is no systematic relationship between employment size and their occupational classification. For men employed in workplaces with 100 or more employees, a lower proportion are observed in 'complex' jobs. For women, the reverse is true. For part-time jobs, however, both men and women are less likely to be observed in jobs which are classified to the 'complex' group. This only represents a small proportion of all the male employment histories included in the analysis, but is a large and significant proportion of the female employment histories.

AN INTERNAL VIEW OF OCCUPATIONAL MOBILITY

Thus far, all of the evidence concerned with the impact of changes in occupations on the type of work people do has been couched in terms of an 'externally imposed' view of occupational structure. Occupations have been classified in terms of some external notion of the mix and complexity of their constituent tasks into 'complex' and 'simple'. This raises the issue of whether or not occupations can, or indeed should, be rated and classified on such a criterion. Consider, for example, the not unusual case of a woman, qualified as a nurse and having practised in such a job for ten years, returning to part-time paid employment as a cleaner following the birth of her second child. Using the externally imposed classification of jobs in 'complex' and 'simple' types, such as move would contribute to the aggregate picture of change in women's occupational structure through the child-bearing years that is so clearly evidenced in Figure 3.3. But does this represent 'deskilling' for the individual concerned? It could be argued that competing demands on her time arising from the domestic division of labour provide her with a complexity of paid/unpaid work arrangements which would be intolerable if she had not opted for an occupation such as cleaning.

This problem cannot be fully answered using the available data. However, this section examines the process of occupational mobility from the perspective of the individual. It thus anticipates some of the questions about the subjective aspect of skill examined in the second half of this volume, particularly in Chapters 6, 7, and 8. After giving a detailed account of all the jobs that they had ever held, each respondent was asked to reflect upon this historical account and to state which job, in their opinion, was their most skilled job. From this information it was possible to divide respondents into two groups; those who stated that their current, or most recent, job was the most skilled job in which they had ever worked, and those who referred to some earlier job. This section analyses the allocation of survey respondents to this dichotomous grouping.

Before moving on to discuss the more detailed analysis, Table 3.4 presents this information by age groups and for male and female respondents respectively. It can be seen that, for male respondents, there appears to be little variation by age. For females, the proportion who stated that they are currently in (or have recently been in) their most skilled job is considerably lower among the older age groups.

By using multivariate techniques, it is possible to control for a

TABLE 3.4. *Proportion of respondents who stated
that their current or most recent
occupation was their most skilled* (%)

Age group	Males	Females
20–29 years	52	54
30–39	48	38
40–49	40	34
50–59	47	31
All ages	49	39
base (= 100%)	473	540

Source: Social Change and Economic Life Initiative, Work
Attitudes/Histories survey, Coventry locality, 1986.

variety of effects which are likely to influence the probability that
respondents view their current job as their most skilled job. First,
there is a need to control for the different ages of respondents.
Younger respondents who have only had one job will, by
definition, be classified as working in the job which, in their opinion, was their most skilled. For older workers, particularly those
approaching retirement age, there may be a lifecycle influence in
that they choose to work in less demanding jobs as they
approach retirement. These competing influences suggest that the
age of the respondent should be entered into the model in a qua-
dratic form as a control variable.

Secondly, there is 'skill-distance' effect. Obviously, respondents
who are currently working in occupations which are generally
categorized as high in skill (for example, professional workers,
managers) have less 'opportunity' to describe their current occupations as lower in skill content than some previous occupation.
There must, therefore, be some broad control for current objective skill status to account for the greater opportunity that
respondents who are currently in low-skilled jobs have to
describe a previous job as higher in skill.

On the issue of deskilling, three processes are studied. First, if
respondents have ever had any experience of unemployment in

their work history, it could be argued that they are more likely to have moved into a job which they consider to be less skilled than some previous job. If this can be shown to be the case, it would link well with the findings shown in the previous section, that using an externally imposed and fairly crude categorization of jobs into 'complex' and 'simple', a personal experience of unemployment is correlated with a lowering of occupational status. Secondly, and more importantly, it seems reasonable to hypothesize that different industries will experience occupational change and deskilling at different rates and that this would depend upon the process of technical and organizational change taking place within each sector. Thus it seems plausible to expect that the probability that a respondent will state that their most skilled job is their current job will depend upon their current industry of employment. Finally, the influence of children was clearly shown to be an important factor in occupational terms.

Table 3.5 shows the results of analysis of the variable representing this subjective assessment of the relative skill content of a respondent's current job. As expected, for respondents who have been unemployed at some time in their working lives, there is a negative influence upon the probability that their current job is their most skilled. Surprisingly, there is no effect of the industry of employment. The most significant influences upon whether or not a female respondent is currently working in her most skilled job are the effects of family formation. As has been shown elsewhere, part-time working is predominantly related to family formation, in that this represents the method by which many women reconcile the competing demands upon their time to provide child care and family income.

SUMMARY

Continuing change in the structure of occupations is very much in evidence in Great Britain. These changes record the extent of organizational and technological influences upon the nature of work and are commonly referred to as part of the 'economic restructuring process'. This chapter reports upon an investigation of the extent to which these changes manifest themselves within the work history of individuals, seeking to distinguish between those who experience an increase in the complexity of their work from those who experience little change.

The study makes use of retrospective work and life history data collected from over 6,000 persons in six localities in England and Scotland. Retrospective data are open to misinterpretation if no account is taken of the work experience effect—the influences of job tenure and seniority on the nature of an individual's work. Simply measuring the extent to which an individual records his or her current work as more skilled than at some time in the past does not necessarily imply that he or she is a beneficiary of the growth of 'skilled' work, nor does it imply that there is any general tendency towards job enrichment. Indeed, it is feasible to envisage a situation in which all survey respondents reported that their work was 'more skilled' at the time of a survey than five years earlier, yet for the complexity and 'richness' of work to be in general decline. This situation could arise because of the general tendency for jobs to develop with the age and experience of the incumbent. The growth of specific job knowledge and the experience of a changing work environment makes the comparison of the skill level in a job now with the situation five years earlier such that the response of 'increasing skill' is most likely.

Two approaches to this problem are described in this chapter. The first approach uses the technique of external job classification to identify a set of occupations which are defined as 'simple' in terms of the nature of their constituent tasks. The net movement of different age groups of survey respondents into and out of such occupations over their working lives is observed. This technique indicates clearly the nature of the 'work experience' effect for males. Multivariate techniques were employed to examine for factors which are associated with the movement into or out of 'simple' jobs. Some interesting findings emerge from this investigation, notably the effect of unemployment, exerting an immediate and depressing influence on the general transition from 'simple' to 'complex' jobs. Sectoral influences are also marked. The transitions into or out of 'complex' jobs are often associated with changes in industry sector, a feature that has been well recognized in the broader studies of occupational change (Lindley and Wilson, 1988).

The general pattern of occupational change experienced by men can be summarized in graphical form, as shown in Figure

Table 3.5. *The relationship between subjective deskilling, personal characteristics, and current employment*

	Males		Females		All	
	Coefficient	(t)	Coefficient	(t)	Coefficient	(t)
Age	:	:	:	:	:	:
Age squared	:	:	:	:	:	:
Male	—		—		:	:
O levels	.215	(4.1)	:		.121	(2.2)
A levels	:		.195		:	(3.0)
Low vocational qualifications	:		:		:	:
High vocational qualifications	:		:		:	:
Degree	:		:		.181	(2.2)
Social Class of current employment:						
1	—		—		—	
2	:		:		:	
3(N)	:		:		:	
3(M)	:		:		:	

	(1)	(2)	(3)
4	−.223 (−3.3)	..	−.105 (−2.2)
5	−.302 (−2.4)	−.203 (−2.0)	(−.260) (−3.2)
Not known/not stated			
Respondent ever unemployed	..	..	−.100 (−2.7)
Respondent has had children	..	−.274 (−4.0)	−.125 (−2.8)
Currently working part-time	..	−.244 (−3.8)	−.280 (−5.2)
Industry of current employment (11 industry categories)	..	..	..
$\bar{R}^2$	.100	.222	.158
n	335	265	600
F	13.3	19.8	17.0

Notes: A dash denotes a variable which was excluded from the regression.
Two dots denote a variable which was originally included, failed a significance test (5%), and has been excluded from the re-estimated regression.

Source: Social Change and Economic Life Initiative, Work Attitudes/Histories survey, Coventry locality, 1986.

3.4. This shows, in a stylistic form, the impact of the 'work experience' effect and age on the proportion of three age groups in 'complex' jobs. The younger (x_2 and x_3) join the labour market with higher qualifications and with a higher proportion in complex jobs than their predecessors. All cohorts show an upward increase in the proportion working in complex jobs, but the fact that these profiles have been drawn with parallel lines indicates that, in this stylistic interpretation, gains from a general increase in 'complex' type jobs are captured simply by higher rates of entry of younger respondents into such jobs.

The situation for women appears to be quite different, particularly for women with children. The general pattern of better qualified younger respondents entering a higher proportion of complex jobs is observed as it was for men, but these gains all but disappear following a period of family formation. Stylistically, this effect can be represented as shown in Figure 3.5. As for men, successively higher proportions of the younger age-cohorts have been entering complex jobs, but the gains from such higher rates of entry are lost at or around the age of family formation. A major factor contributing to this increasing polarization of women's work is the low status of part-time jobs, often used on the main point of return to the labour market. What is of particular concern here is the fact that the occupational profiles in the post-family formation phase are so flat—there is little evidence that the effect is temporary. As a consequence,

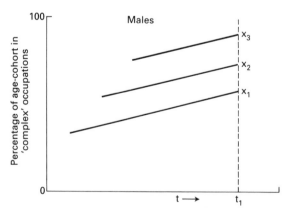

Figure 3.4. A stylized view of male occupational change

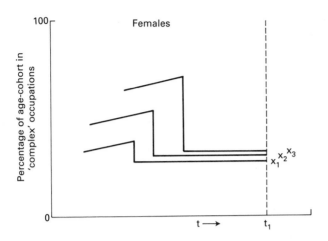

Figure 3.5. A stylized view of female occupational change

there is a growing disparity between the occupations in which women work prior to a period of family formation and those in which they work following the birth of their children.

A second view of the process of occupational change made use of a respondent's retrospective assessment of his or her most skilled job. Under the hypothesis that the work experience effect implies that a person's current job should *ceteris paribus*, be his or her most skilled job, the study investigates whether or not this is the case and attempts to identify significant events in the past history which correlate with whether or not a person's current job is his or her most skilled job. This investigation yields subjective confirmation to the crude but more objective evidence of downgrading of occupational status associated with family formation described in the first part of this chapter.

NOTES

An earlier version of this paper was prepared as part of the programme of research conducted within the Social Change and Economic Life Initiative (SCELI). Roger Penn, Jill Rubery, and

Michael Rose offered valuable comments upon this draft. Christine Jones gave valuable assistance with the computational work upon which the paper draws. Statistical analysis of the SCELI work and life history survey data was facilitated via the IDEAS software, developed in collaboration with Jon Barry, Brian Francis, and Richard Davies, Centre for Applied Statistics, University of Lancaster.

1. For a detailed account of the scale of these changes and their economic implications, see Bosworth and Wilson (1989).
2. For the reasons given by the Cambridge team in Ch. 7, some part-timers in this sort of work may set their expectations lower than full-timers, and Rose's analysis of job satisfaction and skill levels in Ch. 9 shows that in the Work Attitudes Histories sample, part-timers often expressed *higher* satisfaction with their jobs than full-timers in comparable work.
3. This is obviously a fairly crude distinction between the complexity of tasks in a job, but in the absence of more detailed information on the range and complexity of constituent tasks within an occupation, it probably represents a reasonable compromise between ease of classification and the purpose of classification. It is important to recognize that the 'simple' category represents those occupations which have only the most basic set of tasks. These do not usually require money-handling or the operation of machinery under the control of the operator. The resulting group of occupations is essentially the same as Classes VIIa and VIIb (Semi-skilled and unskilled manual and agricultural workers) in the Goldthorpe *schema* (Goldthorpe, 1987), with the exception that sales assistants and drivers are allocated to the 'complex' category of occupations.

4

Technical Change and Skilled Manual Work in Contemporary Rochdale

ROGER PENN

This chapter examines technical change and skilled manual work in the contemporary textile and engineering industries. It represents a contribution to the long-standing debate in sociology and social history about the significance of skilled manual workers in modern societies. Within social historical literature the skilled divide within the manual working class has been characterized by two quite distinct images: one of the 'labour aristocracy' and the other of the 'militant craftsman'. Nevertheless, as has been shown previously (Penn, 1985 and 1990*a*) social historians generally see technological change as the great destroyer of skilled manual work. Their disagreements tend to focus on the power of such craftworkers to curtail these processes in the short to medium term (Montgomery, 1976; Hinton, 1973; J. Scott, 1974; and Stein, 1978).

Most sociologists, on the other hand, see skilled manual workers as a continuing stratum within contemporary class structures. Dahrendorf (1959), Mackenzie (1973), Form (1973 and 1985), and Kern and Schumann (1987) all characterize the numbers of skilled workers as both substantial and increasing. Giddens (1973) and Goldthorpe *et al.* (1980), following Weber's (1968) earlier lead, represent them as an integral part of modern societies. Nevertheless, there is an alternative interpretation, popular amongst neo-Marxists, that regards skilled manual work as an archaic social form. The seminal account of manual work from such a perspective is Braverman's *Labor and Monopoly Capital*. More recent advocates of such a position include Elger (1982) and Armstrong (1988).

This chapter examines technical change and skilled work in the textile and engineering industries in Rochdale. Both industries have been central to the social historical and sociological debates outlined above. Engineering and textiles remain the two largest sectors of employment in manufacturing in contemporary Rochdale, accounting for over a half of all manufacturing employment. Consequently, the findings in this chapter represent a significant proportion of the overall contemporary relationship between technical change and skilled work in the town. These two industries were also examined in a previous research project which examined the historical development of skilled work in Rochdale (Penn, 1982a, 1983a, 1983b, 1983c, and 1985) and the present chapter can be seen as representing a continuation of that research. The chapter situates the research undertaken within the matrix of recent debates about the relationship of technical change and skilled work. Findings are then presented from a survey of textile and engineering plants in 1986 and an assessment of the various theories of developments in skilled work is provided in the light of these data. They therefore take the analysis of technical change and skill provided by Gallie in Chapter 2 a stage further by examining a specific local context in depth. They also set the scene for the comparison of skill changes in the two localities provided in Chapter 5.

STYLES OF CONTEMPORARY RESEARCH IN BRITAIN

There are two styles of research in contemporary Britain concerning the relationship of technical change and work organization. The first involves predominantly questionnaire surveys of technical change and employment conducted on various samples of firms. Examples would include the work of Daniel (1987), Cross (1985) and Northcott and Rogers (1984). These surveys have generally collected descriptive data; they have been generally a-theoretical and a-historical; and, as policy-driven research projects, they have been generally divorced from mainstream sociological inquiry. In particular, they are devoid of context and, at best, can only provide interesting pieces of information. Conspicuously, they fail to provide a model of the relationships between the elements examined—notably technological change, the division of labour, and the wider structural parameters of society. The other style of research, on the other hand, finds little difficulty in generalizing and can be seen in its purest form in the publications of the successive Labour Process Conferences that took place in Britain during the mid-1980s (Knights and Willmott, 1986*a* and 1986*b*). Unlike the previous tradition, much of the research reported in these books is cavalier in its treatment of data and often merely anecdotal. The aim of the present chapter is to forge a middle way between the Scylla of description and the Charybdis of abstraction by means of a theoretically grounded empirical analysis.

CONTEMPORARY THEORIES ABOUT TECHNICAL CHANGE AND THE DIVISION OF LABOUR IN CONTEMPORARY SOCIETIES

Three theories concerning the relationship between technical change and the division of labour have informed our research on skilled manual work at Lancaster University during the 1980s (Penn, 1990*a*, for an extended presentation of this research). The first theory was the 'skilling' thesis associated with human capital theory and post-industrialism. Its central argument was that advanced industrial societies required increasingly skilled workforces. Great importance was attached by writers like Fuchs (1968) and Bell (1974) to the emergence of electronics as a new force in production. Fuchs, for instance, argued that the evolution of new advanced technologies (particularly computers) required an increasingly educated labour force for their successful development and consequently that the workforces of advanced industrial societies were becoming more skilled.

The second model of secular trends in contemporary work was the Marxist theory of 'deskilling'. As was shown in the Introduction to this volume, the main text in this approach was Braverman's *Labor and Monopoly Capital* (1974). For Braverman, 'the logic' of capitalist production required the constant transformation of the techniques of producing. This involved increasing mechanization and automation and, as a corollary, the displacement of skills. The workforce became ever more degraded and deskilled. For Braverman the deskilling of labour was part of a generalized tendency for capitalist managements to use scientific knowledge to subdivide labour and increase their control over all parts of the profit-making process.

The third model of skilled work was the compensatory theory of skill. This was developed during the Skilled Worker Project at Lancaster University (Penn and Scattergood, 1985; Penn, 1990*a*). It can be outlined in terms of five propositions. First, it suggested that technical change generates processes of *both* enskilling and deskilling. This is due to a variety of factors that include the diverse nature of modern technological innovations, the relative size of the plants in which 'new technologies' are implemented, and the strategies of management and organized labour. Secondly, the compensatory theory suggested that across advanced capitalist societies these effects are *international*. This is partly due to the asymmetry between machine manufacture and machine utilization. Machine manufacture entails far greater inputs of skilled labour proportionately than machine utilization and there is an evident international concentration of machine manufacture between the advanced industrial economies. A further aspect of this international patterning to developments in skilled work involves the increasing internationalization of the major companies engaged in both machine manufacture and machine utilization. These twin processes suggested that research into the effects of technological change upon skilled work in the modern era should take an international frame of reference wherever possible.

The third proposition of the compensatory theory of skill suggested that technological changes tend to *deskill direct productive roles* but put an increased premium on a range of ancillary skilled tasks associated with the installation, maintenance, and programming of automated machinery. Fourthly, it was argued that technological change, therefore, tends to *advantage* certain occupational groups and *disadvantage* others. Finally, the theory concluded that technical change is affecting traditional forms of the division of labour and thus is posing *both threats and opportunities* for organized labour in advanced societies.

It is evident that there are fundamental disagreements between these various models about the dominant trajectory of skilled work in modern industrial societies. Nevertheless, there is a general agreement that technological change *is* a major factor in whatever outcomes are proffered by the respective models. Furthermore, all suggest that skilled work and skilled workers will form the basis of at least *some occupations at some period* in the development of modern productive systems. For Braverman, such work and such occupations were disappearing, whereas for human capital and post-industrial theorists they were expanding. The compensatory theory indicated that we need detailed, micro-level analyses of these phenomena in order to understand the nature of contemporary developments in skilled work. Such viewpoints largely determined the nature of the research questions and research design undertaken in Rochdale in 1986.

THE SURVEY OF TEXTILE AND ENGINEERING PLANTS IN ROCHDALE

The project reported in this chapter was undertaken as an 'Intensive Study' for the Social Change and Economic Life Research Initiative and involved an examination of technical change in the textile and engineering industries in Rochdale. Textiles and engineering had been the two dominant sectors of manufacturing industry in the town for over a century (Penn, 1985). They have also been interrelated historically, since the engineering industry began as a textile machinery manufacturing operation (see Penn, 1992, for further analysis of these historical relationships). By the mid-1980s engineering constituted the largest sector of manufacturing employment in Rochdale.

Initially our research involved the administration of a postal questionnaire to all textile and engineering establishments in Rochdale during the summer of 1986. This secured a response rate covering 40.9 per cent of establishments and approximately 50 per cent of employees in these two sectors. Most of our non-respondents were in very small establishments. Indeed, we secured data from 24 of the 30 plants employing more than 50 people in 1981 (Penn, Martin, and Scattergood, 1991). Nevertheless, almost half of the 71 responses came from establishments employing fewer than 25 people. We then selected firms from this overall data-set for further intensive research. This involved the collection of historical materials on the firm and a series of open-ended, semi-structured interviews with representatives of management and of the workforce at each establishment selected.

Profile of the Establishments Surveyed

We received completed postal questionnaires from 71 establishments. These included 22 textile plants, 20 establishments involved in machinery manufacture or toolmaking, and 23 in general engineering and springmaking. There were six further engineering plants that fitted none of these categories: these included founding (2), metal building materials and construction (2), hot-dip galvanizing (1), and maintenance services (1). The bulk of the general engineering plants were engaged either in sheet-metalwork (fabrication) or spring manufacture. Approximately one-third (22) establishments were subsidiaries of larger conglomerates, of which all but two were British-based companies.

The textile and engineering industries in Rochdale can be characterized by the following broad characteristics in 1986. There were a series of large, mainly British, companies owning plants in the town. These included T & N, Fothergill and Harvey (now Courtaulds), Renold, British Vita, Farrel Bridge, and the recently formed British Springs. Many of these companies owned a series of plants in the town, each of which generally employed between 50 and a few hundred workers. For instance, Fothergills, T & N, and Renold all had three plants in Rochdale and there were complex patterns of intra-dependence between each set (Penn and Scattergood, 1987). Furthermore, there were additional interrelationships between small local independently owned firms and these larger units (Penn, 1992). This was particularly noticeable in the engineering industry, where the machinery-makers routinely utilized local, small sheet-metalworking firms for fabrication work on a subcontracting basis. Rochdale had a wide array of textile and engineering plants and could be characterized as a competitive labour market, particularly for skilled manual labour (Penn, 1983b). Certainly, there was no one dominant employer in the locality or within either of the two industrial sectors under scrutiny. This had led to a situation where wages were generally higher in the larger establishments, but there was no *one* wage leader within the local labour market (Penn, Martin, and Davies, 1988; Penn and Dawkins, 1988).

TECHNICAL CHANGE IN THE ENGINEERING INDUSTRY

The Structure of Output

The type of work undertaken in the 49 Rochdale engineering plants in the sample reflected the pattern of production outlined earlier. Most firms (37) undertook either jobbing work or built machines or fabrications to the direct specification of their customers. This reflected the centrality of machine manufacture within engineering in Rochdale. The manufacture of a machine is quite unlike the production of pins or even automobiles. Output is rarely standardized and high-quality work is at a premium. Large inputs of skilled labour are required within a quite extensive division of labour (Penn, 1990*a*). Whilst the division of labour is less extensive in the small fabricating sheet-metal workshops, output is rarely standardized and again there is a premium on skilled labour. The picture is rather different in the spring-manufacturing subsector where springs are produced with large numbers of routine, semi-skilled, often female, labour in either continuous or large batch modes (26 firms were characterized by such a pattern of output). Some firms undertook both jobbing work and batch production or continuous production. In most cases these activities were performed within different sections of the same plant.

Computerization of Production

Computerization of production was not widespread in the engineering plants in our sample in 1986. Only six firms had Computer Aided Design (CAD), nine had Computer Numerically Controlled (CNC) machinery, three had computerized testing facilities, and seven had other automatic or semi-automatic machine controls. There were no robots reported in Rochdale! There was a pronounced tendency for such advanced technological systems to be installed in the machine-manufacturing establishments, as is revealed from Table 4.1. Nevertheless, such systems were not common in either sector of the Rochdale engineering industry and, of the nine firms that had installed CNC machinery, only two firms had other advanced microelectronic productive sub-systems.

TABLE 4.1. *Micro-electronically-based technologies installed in the Rochdale engineering industry by 1986*

	Machine manufacture	General engineering
CAD	4	2
CNC	6	3
Automatic/Semi-automatic machine controls	5	2
Computerized Testing	1	2
TOTAL number of firms	20	23

Overall, we witnessed a lumpiness of implementation and our subsequent intensive case-study interviews and observations revealed that such micro-electronically-based machines were merely 'islands' within a sea of more conventional equipment.

Maintenance of New Equipment

Almost all these microelectronic sub-systems had been introduced into plants employing 25 or more employees. All the automatic or semi-automatic machine controls were in such plants as well as seven out of the nine CNC machines and four of the six CAD systems. This is hardly surprising given the high cost of such equipment reported to us in our intensive interviews. Perhaps more surprising was the pattern of machine maintenance. Maintenance of CAD systems was 80 per cent by service contract and two-thirds of the maintenance of automatic and semi-automatic machine control systems was organized likewise. Only in the case of CNC machinery did 50 per cent of the establishments provide at least some of the maintenance, and even here only two of the nine establishments provided their own maintenance in its entirety. The main reason for this was one of cost. Most firms expressed a preference for 'in-house' maintenance but this was often seen as not an 'economic' proposition.

As can be seen from Table 4.2, there was a wide range of international sources for the microelectronic-based equipment installed in the Rochdale engineering industry. Half of the equipment came from Britain and, of the rest, most came from either

TABLE 4.2. *National origins of micro-electronically-based machinery in the Rochdale engineering industry*

	Britain	Other EC	Japan	USA	Other	Total
CAD	4	—	—	4	—	8
CNC	5	2	3	2	1	13
Automatic machine controls	2	1	—	—	3	6
Semi-automatic machine controls	8	—	1	2	2	13
Computerized testing	3	—	1	—	1	5
TOTAL number of firms	22	3	5	8	7	45

Note: Some systems came from more than one country.

the United States or non-EC Western European countries such as Switzerland, Spain, or Finland. Overall, it was also clear that much of the skilled work associated with the maintenance of modern equipment was not located in Rochdale but rather within specialist subcontracting firms based outside the locality. It was evident, furthermore, that much of the skilled work involved in the manufacture of such equipment was now located outside the British economy. This situation contains a certain irony, given the historic centrality of machine manufacture within Rochdale itself. In the past the Rochdale engineering industry was a centre both for the export of machinery and for the provision of sub-contracted machine maintenance activities. In recent years these roles have diminished and the Rochdale engineering industry has become a major recipient of such provision itself.

Changing Size of Plant and New Technology

It is evident from Table 4.3 that there was no clear relationship between the implementation of micro-technologies into produc-tion and the changing size of the workforce in the Rochdale engi-neering plants between 1980 and 1986.

TABLE 4.3. *The relationship between the implementation of micro-*
electronically-based machines and the changing size of the
workforce, 1980–1986

	Labour force size			
	Contracted	Constant	Expanded	Total
CAD	2	1	3	6
CNC	2	3	4	9
Automatic/semi-automatic machine controls	2	2	3	7
Computerized testing	1	0	2	3
TOTAL number of firms	7	6	12	25

Note: Constant = Expanded or Contracted by less than 10%.

Technical Change within Products

Of the 49 engineering plants surveyed, 13 reported that they incorporated microelectronics within the products that they manufactured. Of those who reported positively, almost all incorporated microelectronics within less than 25 per cent of their overall output. There was a significant difference between machine manufacturers and general engineering plants, with the former over twice as likely to report that their end-products incorporated microelectronics. None the less, the data confirmed an overall picture of a lack of pervasive computerization within engineering plants in Rochdale in 1986. However, 13 firms also reported plans to increase the incorporation of microelectronics within their output. There was no significant statistical relationship between such plans and either subsector of engineering, the size of the plant, or whether or not the firm was a subsidiary of a larger company. However, there was a highly significant relationship between plans to increase microelectronics within output *and* the use of microelectronics within production. This suggests strongly that further computerization is likely to be concentrated amongst the pre-existing small number of advanced engineering plants in the town.

It was evident that computerization of production was not widespread within the Rochdale engineering industry in 1986. Most of the advanced technological systems had been installed in machine-manufacturing plants but, even within these plants, computerization of production was not endemic. A high proportion of the maintenance of such equipment was obtained externally from machine suppliers, half of whom were based abroad. This either involved the use of maintenance workers based at British depots or at the overseas plants themselves. Finally, there was no apparent systematic relationship between the implementation of such micro-electronically-based machinery and changes in the overall size of the workforce between 1980 and 1986.

TECHNICAL CHANGE IN THE TEXTILE INDUSTRY

The Structure of Output

Rochdale has long been the centre for a diversified textile industry. It remains a site for both industrial and consumer textiles (Penn, 1985; Penn and Scattergood, 1987; and Penn, Martin, and Scattergood, 1991). Of the 22 establishments in our sample, one produced carpets, six manufactured consumer textiles, another six manufactured industrial textiles, and the remaining nine produced both consumer and industrial textiles. Only six firms reported that their output was significantly affected by changes in fashions. Half reported that they sold their output to a small number of firms and half to a large number. There was an even balance of fabrics manufactured. Six firms utilized cotton, six used man-made fibres, and eight made use of both. The remaining firm, the largest manufacturer in Rochdale (TBA Industrial Products, itself a part of T & N), used asbestos and man-made fibres. As we have shown elsewhere, historically industrial textiles have constituted a distinct sub-sector within textiles, with a more male, more full-time workforce than within consumer textiles (Penn and Scattergood, 1987). We have examined the distinct patterns within both sub-sectors of textiles in considerable detail elsewhere (Penn, Martin, and Scattergood, 1991) and therefore in this chapter the focus will be upon textiles as a whole in order to facilitate general comparisons with machine manufacture and general engineering plants.

Computerization of Production and Maintenance Provision

Only seven textile firms in Rochdale had introduced computerization into production by 1986. There was one Computer Aided Design and Manufacturing (CADAM) system and one computerized handling system, two automated inspection systems, and five automatic and five semi-automatic machine control systems. Most of the automatic equipment came from Switzerland (most frequently Sulzer-Roti machines) and only six of the total were from Britain. There were none from the USA, which reflected the collapse of the American textile machinery industry in Europe (see US Congress, Office of Technology Assessment, 1987). Most of the maintenance was undertaken by service contractors external to the plants in question. The level of apprentices was astoundingly low. In 1980 these 22 firms employed eight craft apprentices and eight technician apprentices out of workforces totalling 4,768. By 1986 there were six craft apprentices and three technician apprentices out of a reduced total of 3,273 employees in textiles. The lack of demand for newly skilled workers was also indicated by a general absence of reported skill shortages.

This compared significantly with engineering, where many of the plants reported shortages of skilled production operatives in 1986 and 1987.

Eleven textile firms had contracted, four had remained constant, and six had expanded in size between 1980 and 1986. We found no evidence to indicate any significant relationship between the few technological changes uncovered in textiles and changes in the size of the workforce. Overall, there was a far greater degree of technological change within the engineering sector than within the textile sector in Rochdale. Computerization of production was most likely in machine-manufacturing plants and least likely in textile plants. In both sectors most new machinery had come from abroad and was likely to have been maintained by firms external to the area.

TECHNOLOGICAL CHANGE AND SKILLED MANUAL WORKERS IN ROCHDALE

There were broadly two ways of examining trends in skilled manual work in Rochdale. The first involved an examination of trends in the numbers of such workers, whilst the second involved an assessment of the changing content of the work in which they were engaged. From our postal survey we were able to assess both facets of the problem. Our intensive case studies provided additional material on the changing content of skilled manual work. In our survey we asked engineering respondents to indicate the numbers of 'skilled manual workers' in 'production', in 'electrical or electronic maintenance', and in 'other maintenance'. We also enquired about 'semi-skilled machinists', 'other semi-skilled', and 'labourers and other unskilled'. Textile respondents were asked for the same information except for the question of 'semi-skilled machinists'. There is a clear and well-understood distinction between skilled and non-skilled manual workers in both industries (Penn, 1982*a* and 1985). Skilled manual workers comprise two distinct types. One type is apprenticed whereas the other involves accession to skilled status after a lengthy time in non-skilled work. In the latter case, skilled manual work stands at the apex of a career trajectory (Penn, 1990*a*, for an extensive discussion of these two forms). In engineering, skilled manual production and maintenance occupations are almost entirely apprenticed, whilst in textiles most maintenance workers are apprenticed but many skilled production workers are not. The minority of apprenticed skilled production workers in textiles generally undertake a rather shorter formal period of apprenticeship than in engineering, but this normally commences a few years after the initial entry into non-skilled textile employment.

Skilled Manual Workers as a Proportion of the Workforce

As is evident from Table 4.4, there was no clear relationship between the industrial sector of employment in Rochdale and the changing proportion of skilled workers in the workforces of the plants under scrutiny. There was a *marked* tendency for skilled workers to increase proportionately in machine-making plants, but no clear pattern within the two other sub-sectors of manufacturing examined. Overall the proportion of skilled workers in the workforce had remained more or less constant in 33 of the 56 plants from which we secured sufficient data to permit such comparisons. Nor was there any clear relationship between the changing proportion of skilled workers and the implementation of microelectronic technologies, as is revealed in Table 4.5.

Similarly, there was no significant relationship between the changing proportion of skilled workers and whether the labour force overall was contracting or expanding. Interestingly, there

TABLE 4.4. *The relationship between sector of employment and the changing proportion of skilled workers within the overall workforces in Rochdale, 1980–1986*

Proportion of Skilled Workers	Machine manufacture	General engineering	Textiles	Total
Decreasing	1	3	5	9
Constant	9	13	11	33
Increasing	5	5	4	14
TOTAL	15	21	20	56

Notes: 'Increasing' entails a proportionate rise of more than 10%.
'Decreasing' involves a proportionate fall of more than 10%.
The six 'other engineering' plants were excluded from this table.

TABLE 4.5. *The relationship between the implementation of micro-electronically-based machinery and the overall proportion of skilled workers in Rochdale, 1980–1986*

Proportion of skilled workers	New Technologies		
	Present	Absent	Total
Decreasing	2	8	10
Constant	13	21	34
Increasing	5	13	18
TOTAL	20	42	62

was also no significant relationship between the proportion of skilled workers and the recognition of trade unions within the plants (see Table 4.6), which suggested that union strategies of resistance to new technologies were of little importance within the processes uncovered.

TABLE 4.6. *The relationship between the changing proportion of skilled workers and recognition of trade unions within plants*

Proportion of unskilled workers	Trade union recognition		
	Yes	No	Total
Decreasing	4	6	10
Constant	20	14	34
Increasing	10	8	18
TOTAL	34	28	62

It was clear that the proportion of skilled workers in the Rochdale plants investigated had changed dramatically in a large minority of cases. In about one-quarter of the plants the proportion had risen by more than 10 per cent whilst it had fallen by such a proportion or more in another sixth of the plants. The 'skilling' process was most pronounced in the machine-manufacturing sector, whilst the 'deskilling' pattern was most common in the textile sector. Our case studies of specific firms threw further light upon the processes involved. In the machine-manufacturing sector, an already skill-intensive division of labour had become more skilled as the machines produced became more complex and accelerating competitive pressures put an increased premium on high-quality output. This had been achieved by an increasing reliance on skilled manual, mainly craft- or technician-apprenticed labour. Indeed, the Rochdale engineering employers had set up their own collective training facility in the town to co-ordinate 'off the job' apprenticeship training and, as Bragg (1987) demonstrated, these employers strongly supported apprentice training. Such results clearly revealed the sterility of Braverman's vision of a universal drive by capitalists to destroy craft skills in the modern epoch. Indeed, our evidence on the growth of maintenance subcontracting also suggested that Braverman-like arguments seriously misrepresented current developments in the relationship between computerization of production and skilled work.

Paradoxically, it was precisely the same drive towards improvements in the quality of production that had led to a reduction in the proportion of skilled manual workers in the textile industry. At F&H the underlying process was graphically illustrated. In order to maintain their position in the markets for engineered fabrics, F&H had been forced to invest in new Sulzer-Roti equipment during the early 1980s. The reason was essentially one of quality not price. The new machines could produce 250 per cent more than the previous equipment and consequently, whilst output had risen somewhat, employment of skilled machine operators had fallen. This had been accompanied by parallel reductions in machine maintenance personnel. It was not that the jobs themselves had been deskilled, rather than the number of skilled workers needed to operate and maintain such machines had fallen significantly as a result of such technological change.

THE REPRODUCTION OF A SKILLED WORKFORCE: THE CHANGING PATTERN OF APPRENTICESHIPS

Apprentice training involves investment in the next generation of skilled workers and is a major indicator of trends in skilled manual work. However, companies often engage apprentices with shorter-term considerations in mind, simply because they anticipate either an increasing or a continued need for skilled workers within their plants. Furthermore, as Francis and Penn show in Chapter 8, apprenticeships are also of considerable importance in the definitions of skill held by many employees. Since the late 1970s, there have been a large number of redundancies in the Rochdale area involving over 14,000 people between January 1980 and July 1987 (Carter, 1987), and this affected apprentice training in two ways. First, firms were able to recruit existing skilled labour from the ranks of the unemployed, and secondly, it was difficult morally and practically to make skilled workers redundant whilst simultaneously recruiting young people for apprentice training. Both of these factors were likely to have reduced apprentice recruitments. There was, therefore, a strong likelihood that there would have been a general decline in apprentice training in Rochdale within firms with declining workforces. It was also probable that this would have been modified by the presence or absence of trade unions within the plants in question.

Apprentice training did indeed fall sharply in Rochdale between 1980 and 1986. In engineering the annual intake at the Rochdale Training Association (which organized most apprenticeship training in engineering) fell from 90 in 1980 to 45 in 1986 (data supplied to the author by the RTA), whilst in textiles there had been an almost complete collapse of apprentice training. In the companies that replied to our questionnaires, we discovered that in 1980 there were 91 craft apprentices employed at 19 firms and 24 technician apprentices employed at 8 firms. By 1986 the number of craft apprentices had fallen to 52 employed at 17 firms. Of these craft apprentices, 12 were employed at one establishment, 5 each at two more and 3 each at four others. The number of technician apprentices had risen to 29. Seven of these were employed at one establishment and four each at three others. Clearly there had been a significant fall in overall craft apprentice training and a rise in technician apprenticeships. The latter reflected an overall increasing demand for skilled technicians, many of whom undertook activities traditionally performed by skilled craftsmen. However, as was indicated earlier, almost all these apprentices were employed in engineering plants (see Table 4.7).

There was no significant overall relationship between the changing proportion of apprentices and the specific industrial sec-

Roger Penn

TABLE 4.7. *Technician and craft apprentices in Rochdale.*

	1980	1986
Engineering		
Craft	83	46
Technician	16	26
Textiles		
Craft	8	6
Technician	8	3
Total	115	81

tor in Rochdale, as can be seen from Table 4.8. However, it is worth noting the complete absence of any increases in the textile industry where less than a fifth of firms actually trained apprentices at all (only four out of the 22 textile plants reported apprentices in 1986). Nor, rather surprisingly, was there any relationship between the implementation of microelectronic technologies and the changing ratio of apprentices to the workforce (Table 4.9). Likewise, there was no significant relationship between the changing size of the plant and apprenticeship patterns (Table 4.10).

TABLE 4.8. *The relationship between industrial sector and the changing proportion of apprentices in Rochdale, 1980–1986*

Proportion of apprentices	Textiles	Machine manufacture and toolmaking	General engineering	Total
Increasing	0	4	3	7
Constant	2	1	1	4
Decreasing	5	5	3	13
TOTAL	7	10	7	24

Note: The two 'other engineering' plants were excluded from this table.

However, there was an interesting relationship between whether the plant recognized trade unions and apprenticeship profiles (Table 4.11). It was evident that apprentices had increased overwhelmingly in firms where unions were not recog-

TABLE 4.9. *The relationship between the implementation of micro-electronically-based new technologies and the changing proportion of apprentices in Rochdale, 1980–1986*

Proportion of apprentices	Implementation of new technology		
	Present	Absent	Total
Increasing	3	5	8
Constant	3	1	4
Decreasing	6	8	14
TOTAL	12	14	26

nized and had fallen sharply in plants where they were recognized by management. Such results were consistent with the hypothesis that unions inhibited the number of apprenticeships in a period of high unemployment in favour of attempts to force employers to recruit existing unemployed skilled men from the dole queues.

There was an even more dramatic relationship between changing patterns of apprentice training and whether the firm was a subsidiary of a larger corporate unit, as is clear from Table 4.12.

TABLE 4.10 *The relationship between the changing size of plant and the changing proportion of apprentices in Rochdale, 1980–1986*

Proportion of apprentices	Size of plant			
	Contracted	Constant	Expanded	Total
Increasing	2	2	4	8
Constant	2	1	1	4
Decreasing	6	3	5	14
TOTAL	10	6	10	26

All the increases in apprentices had taken place in independent establishments with strong local links. It was clear that the firms where apprentices had increased were locally based engineering

TABLE 4.11. *The relationship between trade union recognition and the changing proportion of apprentices in Rochdale, 1980–1986*

Proportion of apprentices	Unions recognized	Unions not recognized	Total
Increasing	2	6	8
Constant	4	0	4
Decreasing	10	4	14
TOTAL	16	10	26

TABLE 4.12. *The relationship between whether a plant is a subsidiary of a larger corporate unit or is independent and the changing proportion of apprentices in Rochdale, 1980–1986*

Proportion of apprentices	Subsidiary	Independent	Total
Increasing	0	8	8
Constant	3	1	4
Decreasing	7	7	14
TOTAL	10	16	26

firms either in machine manufacture or sheet-metalworking where there had been an expanding need for skilled labour and which were not strongly organized by the AEU (Amalgamated Engineering Union), which was the main representative of engineering workers in the town at the time.

CONCLUSIONS

Our research on technical change and the division of labour in contemporary Rochdale focused upon the debate about skilled work and skilled workers. We have shown that there was considerable variation and heterogeneity within the two largest sectors of manufacturing industry in the town. The textile industry can be divided into two subsectors: consumer textiles and industrial textiles. Likewise the engineering industry can be separated into those firms engaged in machine manufacture and toolmaking and those engaged in sheet-metalworking or in springmaking. We have seen that 27 establishments across both sectors of manufacturing had experienced a growth in employment of more than 10 per cent between 1980 and 1986 whilst 27 had experienced a decline of more than 10 per cent. However, there was a marked difference in the relative buoyancy of employment within the two sectors: 21 engineering firms had expanded compared with 16 that had contracted. In textiles, only 6 had expanded and 11 had contracted.

Overall both our systematic survey research and our various case studies in Rochdale suggested a lumpiness to the development of microelectronic technologies in contemporary British industry. In Rochdale, at the time of the survey, such new technologies were concentrated in machine-manufacturing plants but even there the implementation of microelectronic technologies had been patchy. In both textiles and engineering, maintenance of such equipment was often performed by firms external to Rochdale which were parts of transnational conglomerate machine suppliers. There was no statistically significant relationship between the introduction of such new technologies and employment change. Indeed, there were as many examples of new technologies in firms where employment had been expanding as in those where it had fallen. Such results reveal the hazardous nature of case studies as a methodology for social scientific research in these areas. Only an integration of systematic inquiry *and* case studies can adequately grasp the dynamics of technical change and the division of labour.

The research also revealed that skilled workers were increasing as a proportion of the workforces of the machine manufacturers in Rochdale. This was despite a decline in overall employment in this sub-sector from 1,629 employees in 1980 to 1,203 in 1986. Such developments were unrelated to the implementation of microelectronic technologies. Likewise we discovered that skilled textile production workers were falling in numbers whilst there was little change in their overall job content. The findings on apprenticeships revealed that there had been a general fall in such training in Rochdale engineering and textile plants. However, technicians apprentice training had expanded whereas craft apprentice training had fallen sharply in the engineering industry. Skilled manual workers were, therefore, increasingly middle-aged in contemporary Rochdale. The voluntarist tradition of local apprentice training meant that there would be an emergent crisis in the supply of such skilled labour within a few years. Any significant reflation of the economy would simply accelerate the emergence of major and serious shortages in the supply of skilled manual labour in Rochdale.

What, then, of the theories outlined at the beginning of this chapter? There was little evidence to support Braverman's neo-Marxist image of a general deskilling of work in the contemporary era. Neither the evidence on the numbers of skilled workers nor on their job content provided more than marginal support for such a viewpoint. There was more evidence to support the skilling thesis, although there were sufficient counter-tendencies and counter-examples for it to be rejected as a global explanation. The compensatory theory of skill correctly identified many of the various ebbs and flows of changes in skilled work. In particular, it drew our attention to the international nature of the contemporary division of labour, especially in the area of machine maintenance. Much of the maintenance of modern equipment in contemporary Rochdale was undertaken on a sub-contracting basis by foreign suppliers of machinery. Studies of specific nation-states are clearly no longer entirely adequate for a satisfactory understanding of the processes involved in the relationships of technical change and skilled work. However, the compensatory theory overemphasized the likely deskilling of skilled production jobs. As the analysis indicated, the relationship between technological change and skill was crucially mediated by the extent of the market for the goods produced. The compensatory theory of skill also exaggerated the direct skilling of maintenance occupations *within* plants. In many cases such maintenance occupations were located externally to Rochdale in machine-supplying firms.

It was clear that skilled manual workers remained a significant stratum within the textile and engineering industries. This corroborated the sociological emphasis on the continuity of skilled workers within contemporary societies and provided no support for notions of their disappearance. Whilst skilled workers had not increased dramatically as a proportion of those employed within these two industries, they had certainly *not* disappeared. Technical changes had occurred in some of the plants surveyed but they had been incremental and not pandemic. These technical changes had not been associated with dramatic changes in the levels of skills or in the numbers of skilled manual workers in these two industries. There was a general picture of widespread but small increases in the proportions of skilled manual workers. This was particularly the case in machinery manufacture. The next chapter undertakes a broader examination of these issues in a wide range of establishments in Rochdale and Aberdeen.

5

Technical Change and the Division of Labour in Rochdale and Aberdeen

ROGER PENN, ANN GASTEEN, HILDA SCATTERGOOD, AND JOHN SEWEL

This chapter involves an examination of the effects of technical change upon the division of labour in Rochdale and Aberdeen during the 1980s. Its comparative analysis is based upon parallel data collected in the two localities by members of the Lancaster and Aberdeen teams. The chapter utilized data from the Policy Studies Institute telephone survey of establishments and from the follow-up survey of 74 establishments in the two localities. The chapter is designed to develop the literature on the relationship between technical change and the division of labour in two inter-related ways. First, the data permit a comparison of establishments within two localities whose economic fortunes could hardly have been more dissimilar during the 1980s. Aberdeen remained buoyant in the eye of the economic storm that struck Britain in the period after 1979. Rochdale, on the other hand, witnessed a threefold increase in the rate of unemployment between 1979 and 1982, and was subject to the fullest force of the Thatcherite economic maelstrom. This chapter examines various theories of the relationship between economic development and technical change in the light of the evidence about these quite different labour market and employment experiences in the 1980s. However, this was but one element in our comparative research strategy. Our data also permitted the matching of establishments in similar industrial sectors across the two localities. Such an approach enabled us to test hypotheses concerning the relative importance of specific industrial sectors in the determination of the relationship between technological change and the division of labour. In this sense, it also helps to clarify and enlarge upon the general findings on overall trends in skill put forward by Gallie in Chapter 2 and Elias in Chapter 3.

GENERAL LEVELS OF ECONOMIC ACTIVITY

Aberdeen and Rochdale experienced the economic vicissitudes of the 1980s in a dramatically different fashion. It is clear from Figure 5.1 that Aberdeen had been a relatively low-unemployment locality during the period since 1974 and especially so during the 1980s. Unemployment in Rochdale had followed quite a different trajectory. The rate trebled between 1979 and 1982 from 6 per cent to over 18 per cent. Unemployment remained at around 18 per cent from 1982 to 1986 and then began to fall somewhat. Rochdale can therefore be characterized as a locality particularly affected by high rates of unemployment during the 1980s. The reasons for these differing experiences of unemployment were complex. The major difference between the two localities centred on the impact of the oil industry upon employment in Aberdeen. Aberdeen had become a centre for the oil industry in the early 1970s. Most of the large oil companies had administrative centres in the city and there was a wide range of

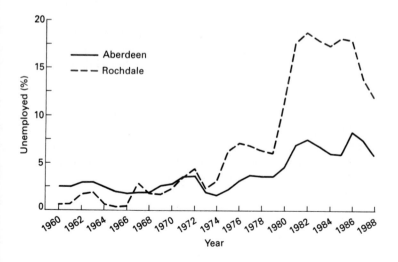

Figure 5.1 Unemployment 1960–1988 in Rochdale and Aberdeen

oil-related firms as well. The oil sector had acted as an engine of growth within the wider Aberdeen economy and insulated the city from the most severe effects of the national economic recession during the 1980s. By 1984 11.5 per cent of the Aberdeen workforce were employed in oil. This represented a location quotient of 4.0 when compared with the rest of Britain.

If Aberdeen had escaped many aspects of the recession as a result of the growth of a new industrial sector, Rochdale had suffered more than most as a result of the difficulties experienced by its traditional core manufacturing activities—textiles and engineering. As was seen in the previous chapter, these two manufacturing industries had long dominated employment in the town (Penn, 1985). Between 1980 and 1987 there were 4,702 redundancies in textiles and 2,422 in engineering (Carter, 1987). Employment fell dramatically in both sectors between 1970 and 1984—from 16,000 to 3,500 in textiles and from 4,900 to 4,100 in engineering (Haughton, 1985; Penn, 1989).

Clearly, Aberdeen and Rochdale formed an interesting comparison. They permitted the testing of the hypotheses that the state of the local labour market and, in particular, the rate of unemployment were critical variables in the determination of technological change and, by extension, of the power of management to combine such technological change with significant changes in the nature of the division of labour (Jones, 1982; Thompson, 1989). It also allowed examination of the radically different hypothesis propounded by Freeman (1988), amongst others, that there would be no significant locality variations since Britain is experiencing a technological climacteric of pandemic proportions in the contemporary era. It could well have been the case that technological change in the two localities had been similar both in its form and in terms of its effects on the division of labour, despite the differing levels of unemployment in the two localities. This chapter presents a systematic empirical analysis of these theoretical possibilities.

THEORIES OF TECHNICAL CHANGE AND THE DIVISION OF LABOUR

General Theories

As was seen in Chapter 4, there were three general theories concerning the relationship between technical change and the division of labour that informed our research. The first theory was the 'skilling' thesis associated with both human capital theory and post-industrialism. Such views have received a renewal of popularity amongst contemporary social scientists as a result of the emergence of theories of post-Fordism (Aglietta, 1979; Lipietz, 1983; Coriat, 1984) and of flexible specialization (Piore and Sabel, 1984; Katz and Sabel, 1985; Kochan, 1985). Writers in both traditions have argued that there is a generic structural change under way within advanced industrial economies involving a transition from a 'Fordist' mode of societal organization to a 'post-Fordist' one. Proponents of this thesis suggest that there is a general movement away from mass-consumption industries, based upon assembly-line techniques of production, employing semi-skilled operatives who perform highly specialized, routinized work under the aegis of scientific management, towards 'niche' markets, based upon batch production, employing multi-skilled workers who perform recombined or enlarged work under the umbrella of the new human resources style of management (Murray, 1985 and 1988, for two classic expositions; and Bagguley, 1989, for a trenchant critique). Further support for the notion of pervasive enskilling of the workforces of advanced societies has been provided by the authoritative summary of the literature on the effects of technical change upon clerical work by Lane (1988). She concluded that the balance of evidence clearly supported the conclusion that technical change had produced a skilling of clerical work in contemporary Britain.

The second model of secular trends in contemporary work was the Marxist theory of 'deskilling' associated with Braverman. This general model has also been very influential over the last 15 years. Crompton and Jones (1984) applied the same framework to argue that clerical labour has been deskilled by technical change. Noble (1984), Armstrong (1988), and Wilson and Buchanan (1988), amongst many, have argued that parallel outcomes were present within the sphere of contemporary manual work; and recently Martin (1988) has argued specifically that there has been a pervasive deskilling of machine maintenance work resulting from the advent of computerized diagnostic systems.

The third model of the relationship between technology and the division of labour was derived from the compensatory theory of skill outlined in the previous chapter. The research reported in this chapter presents a *revised* version of the theory (see Penn, 1990*a*, for the bases of the revisions). The *revised* compensatory theory of skill argued once more that technological change in the contemporary era was producing both enskilling and deskilling effects. In particular, research findings had already shown that machine maintenance skills had *increased* as the result of the insertion of microelectronic systems into production equipment.

The revised theory also argued that *some* production skills were increasing whilst *some* were decreasing and many other production skills remained more or less constant. These different outcomes were a function of the *specific form* of technological change. Critically, such differing outcomes were the result of whether the technological change involved either full automation or semi-automation. In the former case production skills are eliminated, whereas in the latter they are increased. The revised compensatory theory of skill suggested that contemporary technological change (much of which involves microelectronics) was producing increased machine-maintenance skills, increased production skills where technology is semi-automated, and decreased production skills where technology is fully automated. It also suggested that other production skills were generally unaffected by a wide range of small incremental changes.

Nevertheless, both versions of the compensatory theory of skill were devised explicitly to explain developments in *manual work*. In this chapter we propose a new element within the theory to explain recent developments within the office environment. We hypothesized that technological changes within the office would also produce a variety of effects upon levels of skill. We expected computerization of office functions to increase the skills of office machinery-maintenance workers. We also anticipated that the relationship of technical change and clerical and secretarial work would depend upon the specific form of the technology implemented. In situations where work could be subdivided and routinized by dedicated machines and specialized software, we would have expected an elimination of skills. In other situations, where versatile machines and complex software were utilized, we would have expected an enhancement of skills. We further hypothesized that the former scenario was most likely to apply in large offices, particularly within public administration and financial services' bureaucracies, since it was in these organizations that there were both the number of clerical workers and the financial pressures to promote such developments. We expected that the latter scenario would obtain in offices within manufacturing industry, which generally were relatively small and where the financial pressures to rationalize operations were generally less significant.

Specific Theories

None of the general theories outlined above could have provided, as they stood, a series of hypotheses about variations in the effects of technical change upon the division of labour in two localities over a relatively short period of time. These had to be constructed *ab initio*. It was clear from the earlier data on unemployment that Aberdeen had been economically more buoyant and therefore a significantly 'tighter' labour market than Rochdale during the 1980s. This could well have indicated that profits would have been higher in Aberdeen, with the result that investment in new equipment would have been significantly greater. It was also likely that training provision, often a marginal investment for employers, would have fallen less in Aberdeen than in Rochdale. If the skilling thesis was correct, then these twin processes should have produced a significantly greater expansion of skilled work during the 1980s in Aberdeen than in Rochdale. However, it was also likely that managements in Aberdeen would have been more constrained in terms of their capacity to alter working practices as new technologies were implemented, given the relative strength of unions and workgroups in the town over this period (Penn, 1985). On the other hand, it could have been the case that resistance was stronger in Rochdale, where employment prospects were bleaker during most of the 1980s. Furthermore, there were those who argued that Britain was in the throes of a technological revolution of such a pervasive nature that locality differences would be relatively insignificant (Freeman, 1988).[1] The results reported in this chapter tested both the various general theories of skilled work outlined above and the form of locality variations between Rochdale and Aberdeen.

GENERAL PARAMETERS OF TECHNICAL CHANGE IN ROCHDALE AND ABERDEEN

The data in this section were taken from a telephone survey of establishments in Aberdeen and Rochdale undertaken by the Policy Studies Institute in conjunction with the Aberdeen and Lancaster teams in the winter of 1987 (the Employer Baseline survey). There were 308 completed interviews for Aberdeen and 177 for Rochdale. The questionnaires were designed to provide basic information on a range of issues of interest to the teams. This 'baseline' information was also used as a basis for selecting 32 establishments for further intensive study in Rochdale and 42 in Aberdeen.[2] In this section we report the results of the telephone surveys in Aberdeen and Rochdale in respect of technical change and the division of labour.

The Introduction of New Equipment in Establishments, 1984–1986

It is clear from Table 5.1 that there was considerable similarity between Rochdale and Aberdeen as far as the introduction of new equipment between 1984 and 1986 was concerned. In general terms, larger establishments (employing more than 20 people) had introduced considerable new equipment over this relatively short period. In both localities, around 60 per cent of larger establishments had introduced new computer systems during the preceding two years and around one-third had introduced new equipment containing microelectronics. Far fewer smaller establishments had introduced new computer systems or microelectronics-based equipment. Larger establishments in Aberdeen had introduced relatively more word-processing equipment and relatively less new equipment containing no microelectronics. However, these differences disappeared when we controlled for manufacturing versus service-sector establishments. Overall, we

TABLE 5.1. *Introduction of new equipment in the preceding two years* (% Yes)

	Rochdale firms		Aberdeen firms	
	Large	Small	Large	Small
Word processing	32.0	16.4	46.5	13.2
New computer systems	59.8	23.6	60.4	25.3
New equipment or machinery (with microelectronics)	32.8	7.3	34.6	5.5
New equipment or machinery (without microelectronics)	47.5	16.4	38.7	13.2
N	122	55	217	91

Source: Employer Baseline survey.

concluded that there was little difference between Rochdale and Aberdeen in terms of the pattern of technological change between 1984 and 1986, but a large difference between larger and smaller establishments in both localities. These levels of technical innovation were remarkably high given the short duration covered by the questions.

Technological Change and Numbers Employed

As is evident from Table 5.2, few establishments reported that these technological changes had produced changes in the number of jobs over this two-year period. There was a slight tendency for larger establishments in Rochdale to report relatively more job increases than those in Aberdeen. Clerical work stood out in both localities as the area of highest relative job losses. Nevertheless, it is worth reiterating that most respondents indicated no significant change in numbers employed as a result of such changes.

Technological Change and Job Skills

However, Table 5.3 revealed that respondents at larger establishments were far more likely to report that technological change had produced higher levels in the skill of jobs over this two-year

TABLE 5.2. *Technological changes and changes in the number employed (larger establishments only)* (%)

	Rochdale jobs		Aberdeen jobs	
	More	Fewer	More	Fewer
Lower-skilled manual	4.9	7.4	1.8	3.2
Higher-skilled manual	7.4	4.9	3.2	3.7
Technicians	4.1	1.6	3.2	2.8
Professionals	4.1	0.0	3.7	1.4
Clerical	4.1	7.4	8.3	12.0
Administrative	8.2	4.1	2.8	3.2
Middle/senior management	1.6	0.8	1.8	0.0

Source: Employer Baseline survey.

period. In both Aberdeen and Rochdale the highest reported increases in job-skills (as Rose terms them in Chapters 9 and 10) were within clerical and administrative areas, where word processors and new computer systems predominated. There was also clear evidence of the enskilling of skilled manual jobs as perceived by our managerial respondents. These were particularly

TABLE 5.3. *Technological change and levels of skill for jobs (larger establishments only)* (%)

	Rochdale		Aberdeen	
	Increase	Decrease	Increase	Decrease
Lower-skilled manual	11.5	5.7	4.1	3.2
Higher-skilled manual	18.9	1.6	17.5	1.8
Technicians	7.4	0.0	12.0	0.5
Professionals	11.5	0.0	12.4	0.5
Clerical	22.1	0.8	30.9	1.8
Administrative	22.1	0.0	26.3	0.5
Middle/senior management	14.8	0.0	13.8	0.5

Source: Employer Baseline survey.

the result of the introduction of new microelectronic machinery. Overall there was no significant difference in responses from larger establishments between the two localities. This view of a general enskilling process particularly concentrated within clerical and administrative jobs was further supported by responses to a question concerning the need for further training as a result of such technological changes (see Table 5.4). Such a picture was further reinforced when respondents were asked to specify the areas of highest further training. In both Aberdeen and Rochdale, it was clerical and administrative areas that dominated the answers.

TABLE 5.4. *Technical change and further training needs in Rochdale and Aberdeen (larger establishments only (%)*

	Rochdale	Aberdeen
Lower-skilled manual	16.4	7.8
Higher-skilled manual	25.4	20.3
Technicians	10.7	15.7
Professionals	16.4	16.1
Clerical	36.1	40.6
Administrative	28.7	34.6
Middle/senior management	20.5	17.1
N	122	217

Source: Employer Baseline survey.

Summary

These data presented an initial general picture concerning the relationship of technological change and the division of labour in the two localities. In both Rochdale and Aberdeen there had been widespread technological change in the two years prior to the survey. Almost two-thirds of larger establishments in both localities reported new computer systems, most of which had been utilized in office environments. Around three-quarters of larger establishments had introduced new equipment or machinery (other than word processors and computer systems). In Rochdale these tended to include microelectronics relatively more often but this was due to a higher proportion of manufacturing plants amongst respondents to the telephone survey. In both localities smaller establishments were significantly less technologically dynamic.

In most cases these technological changes had not produced any significant impact on numbers employed. However, amongst those larger establishments that reported changes in numbers employed, there was a balance between reported job losses and reported job gains. Furthermore, there was no significant difference between the experience of such establishments in Rochdale and Aberdeen.

Again, in most cases, technological changes were not reported as having led to changes in levels of skill. However, where such changes were reported there was an overwhelming preponderance of respondents suggesting that skills were increasing, particularly in clerical and administrative areas. This was further supported by responses to questions about retraining. Once again there was no significant difference between Rochdale and Aberdeen in terms of responses to questions about these issues.

We were led to conclude from our analysis of these data that there was no significant difference between Rochdale and Aberdeen in terms of either technological change or the effects of such technological change upon the division of labour. However, we were aware that these data were based upon telephone questionnaires and that they were in a form that could not distinguish isolated technological change within establishments from pervasive internal technological dynamism. Nor were the data sufficiently detailed for us to provide a systematic assessment of the theories outlined earlier. Nevertheless, the results presented so far provided very little support for the deskilling thesis. Neither did they support any notion that the state of the local labour market is an important variable in the determination of these patterns. Our results suggested that *either* the skilling thesis *tout court* or the revised compensatory theory of skill best accounted for the patterns uncovered.

DETAILED PARAMETERS OF TECHNICAL CHANGE AND THE DIVISION OF LABOUR IN ROCHDALE AND ABERDEEN

A sample of establishments was drawn from the telephone surveys in Rochdale and Aberdeen for intensive analysis. 32 establishments were interviewed in Rochdale and 42 in Aberdeen. For the purpose of this analysis we excluded oil companies and oil-related firms from the Aberdeen data-set since these warranted a separate investigation. We have adequate data, therefore, from 21 establishments in Aberdeen and 32 in Rochdale. It is evident from Tables 5.7 and 5.8 that the Lancaster and Aberdeen researchers secured responses from a wide range of establishments across the broad spectrum of industrial sectors. There were 27 case studies within manufacturing, 10 in Aberdeen and 17 in Rochdale. These comprised 11 establishments in engineering (3 in Aberdeen and 8 in Rochdale), 8 establishments in textiles (2 in Aberdeen and 6 in Rochdale), and 8 in other sectors of manufacturing (3 in Aberdeen and 5 in Rochdale). There were 26 case studies within the service sector (11 in Aberdeen and 15 in Rochdale). These included 3 establishments in financial services, 4 in professional services, a matched comparison of British Telecom, 5 in education, 3 in transport and distribution, 4 in retailing, and 5 others in general public services. Each of these establishments was subject to intensive analysis centring upon the administration of a questionnaire containing a series of closed and open-ended questions. The questionnaires were completed by researchers from the two teams upon the basis of one or more interviews with managerial respondents. In addition, written materials were often provided subsequently by these respondents. These data were frequently supplemented by further telephone calls and site visits by team members.

Technical Change in Manufacturing Industries in Rochdale and Aberdeen since 1980 (see Table 5.5)

It was apparent that there had been widespread technical change, often involving both computerization of production and of clerical and administrative activities in most manufacturing plants

TABLE 5.5. *Technical change in manufacturing plants in*

	Engineering										
	Aberdeen			Rochdale							
	1	2	3	4	5	6	7	8	9	10	11
Technical change											
Production	✓	×	×	×	✓	✓	✓	✓	✓	✓	✓
Clerical/ administrative	✓	×	✓	✓	✓	✓	×	✓	✓	✓	✓
Computerization											
Production	✓	×	×	×	✓	×	✓	×	×	✓	✓
Clerical/ administrative	✓	×	✓	✓	✓	✓	×	✓	✓	✓	✓
Changes in production	CM	–	–	–	CNC CAD	–	CNC CAD CAM	NE	NE	Comp	CNC
Changes in clerical & administrative	WP	–	Comp	Comp	Comp	Comp	–	Comp	WP	Comp	Comp
Size	420	418	56	100	227	24	120	61	61	40	245
Independent	×	✓	×	✓	×	✓	×	×	✓	✓	×
Manual workers unionized	×	✓	✓	✓	✓	✓	✓	×	✓	✓	✓

Key: CM = Computer-aided manufacturing; WP = Word processors;
Comp = Computerization ; NE = New equipment;
QC = Computerized quality control; ✓ = Yes; × = No.

since 1980 (see Table 5.5). Technical change and computerization were more likely in the office than within production activities amongst the engineering plants. Almost all had introduced computerization of such activities as accounts, salaries, and correspondence during the 1980s. Such technological changes were pervasive throughout these offices. In engineering plants there had also been considerable technical change within production, often involving Computer Numerically Controlled machinery or Computer Aided Design-like systems. These changes were far less endemic than those within the office and were generally isolated within pockets of the engineering plants investigated. This corresponded to the findings of the Lancaster team's special study of technical change in the engineering industry analysed in the preceding chapter.

There was also considerable technological change within most textile plants. The three exceptions were not engaged in consumer

Rochdale and Aberdeen since 1980

Textiles								Other manufacturing							
Aberdeen		Rochdale						Aberdeen					Rochdale		
12	13	14	15	16	17	18	19	20	21	22	23	24	25	26	27
√	√	×	×	×	√	√	√	√	√	√	×	×	√	×	×
√	√	×	×	×	√	√	√	√	√	√	√	×	√	√	√
√	√	×	×	×	√	√	√	√	×	√	×	×	√	×	×
√	√	√	×	×	√	√	√	√	√	√	√	×	√	√	√
Comp	Comp	–	–	–	QC	QC Comp	Comp	Comp	NE	Comp	–	–	NE	–	–
Comp	Comp	Comp	–	–	Comp	Comp	Comp	Comp	Comp	Comp	Comp	–	Comp	Comp	Comp
551	640	90	100	47	200	310	1202	522	150	590	71	400	200	34	76
×	√	×	×	×	×	×	×	×	×	×	×	×	×	√	×
√	√	√	√	×	√	√	√	√	√	√	√	√	×	×	√

textiles but in specialist areas of industrial textiles (Penn, Martin, and Scattergood, 1991, for further discussion of this area of textile manufacture). Once again computerization of office activities was more pervasive than of production activities. Most examples of the latter involved the addition of semi-automated computer monitors designed to supply information about quality of output rather than highly automated textile machinery. Once again these findings were broadly similar to those reported in the previous chapter.

A similar picture was evident in the other plants in manufacturing. In all but one case there were extensive changes within their offices but less pervasive change in production. Indeed, the overall picture was very similar throughout manufacturing plants in Rochdale and Aberdeen in the 1980s. Most plants had witnessed wide-ranging computerization of office activities coupled with some degree of computerization of production. In the latter area, few firms had engaged in wholesale automation. This was supported by the view of the respondents themselves. In only two cases, a paper mill in Aberdeen and a textile plant in Rochdale, did respondents report that their plant was highly automated. There would appear to be no significant overall difference between Rochdale and Aberdeen in terms of these patterns. Nor was there any significant difference between larger and smaller establishments with the one exception that smaller plants tended to be less likely to have experienced computerization of production. Overall, therefore, these data were broadly similar to the general picture presented by the telephone survey reported in the previous section of this chapter and to the analysis presented in the preceding chapter.

Technical Change in Service-Sector Establishments in Rochdale and Aberdeen

The general pattern of technical change within service-sector establishments was very similar to that uncovered in manufactur-

TABLE 5.6. *Technical change in service-sector establishments in Rochdale and*

	Financial services			Professional services				BT		Education				
	A	A	R	A	R	R	R	A	R	A	A	R	R	R
	28	29	30	31	32	33	34	35	36	37	38	39	40	41
Technical change														
Point of provision	✓	✓	✓	×	×	×	×	✓	✓	×	×	×	×	✓
Clerical/ administrative	✓	✓	✓	×	×	✓	✓	✓	✓	✓	✓	✓	✓	✓
Computerization														
Point of provision	✓	✓	✓	×	×	×	×	✓	✓	×	×	×	×	✓
Clerical/ administrative	✓	✓	✓	×	×	✓	×	✓	✓	✓	✓	✓	✓	✓
Changes at point of provision	Comp	Comp	Comp	–	–	–	–	CD	CD	–	–	–	–	Com
Changes in clerical/ administrative	Comp	Comp	Comp	–	–	WP	ET	Comp	Comp	WP	WP	WP	WP	WP
Size	5	47	10	14	2	18	4	2688	318	2325	920	206	23	154
Independent	×	×	×	×	×	✓	✓	×	×	✓	✓	×	×	×
Manual workers unionized	N/A	N/A	N/A	N/A	N/A	N/A	N/A	✓	✓	✓	✓	✓	✓	✓

Key: Comp = Computerization; CD = Computer diagnostics; ET = Electric typewriter;
WP = Word processors; NE = New Equipment; EPOS = Electronic point of sale;
CT = Computerized timers; T = Yes; X = No;
N/A = Not applicable; A = Aberdeen; R = Rochdale

ing (see Table 5.6). Almost all service-sector establishments had experienced computerization of office functions. Many had seen the introduction of word processing and related computerized information systems. There were differences, however, between specific areas of services in terms of the degree of technical change at the point of service provision. Within financial services this was universal, as a result of the impact of computers upon tellers and cashiers in banks and building societies during the 1980s. On the other hand, professional services like those of accountants and solicitors had seen no technical changes at the point of service provision. There were no significant differences between British Telecom in the two localities, despite the far larger scale of operations in Aberdeen (see Penn, 1990*b*, for a detailed discussion of BT in Rochdale). The pattern in educational establishments was very similar to that in professional services. Offices in these establishments had all witnessed the advent of word processors but only one establishment—the only

Aberdeen since 1980

Transport & distribution			Retail				Other public services				
A	R	R	A	R	R	R	A	A	A	R	R
42	43	44	45	46	47	48	49	50	51	52	53
×	✓	×	✓	✓	✓	✓	×	✓	✓	✓	✓
✓	✓	✓	✓	✓	×	✓	×	✓	✓	✓	✓
×	✓	×	✓	✓	✓	×	×	✓	✓	×	✓
✓	✓	✓	✓	✓	×	✓	×	✓	✓	✓	✓
–	Comp	–	EPOS	EPOS	CT	Mixers	–	Comp	Comp	NE	Comp
Comp	Comp	Comp	Comp	Comp	–	WP	–	WP	WP	Comp	Comp
55	960	66	75	281	48	35	86	1010	12897	378	23
✓	×	✓	×	×	×	✓	✓	✓	✓	×	×
✓	✓	✓	✓	✓	×	×	N/A	N/A	✓	✓	N/A

secondary school—reported that computerization had affected their direct service provision.

The two larger retail outlets, one in Rochdale and the other in Aberdeen, had both witnessed the advent of EPOS (Electronic Point of Sale) technology in the 1980s and also the computerization of their office functions linking them with their head offices for ordering, salaries and stock-reporting. There was also wide-reaching computerization within the other public-service establishments.

Overall, we concluded that technological change had been widespread within service-sector establishments in both localities. There had been wholesale computerization of office functions, ranging from word processors in education and professional service establishments to integrated computerized systems in financial services and retailing. There had also been considerable

TABLE 5.7. *Changes in production and clerical/administrative and Aberdeen*

	Engineering										
	Aberdeen			Rochdale							
	1	2	3	4	5	6	7	8	9	10	11
Production changes											
Computerization	√	×	×	×	√	×	√	×	×	√	√
Numbers employed	×	N/A	N/A	N/A	×	N/A	×	N/A	N/A	×	−
Proportion full-timers	×	N/A	N/A	N/A	×	N/A	×	N/A	N/A	×	×
Pattern of hours worked	×	N/A	N/A	N/A	×	N/A	×	N/A	N/A	×	−
Flexibility of production	△	N/A	N/A	N/A	△	N/A	△	N/A	N/A	△	−
Flexibility of labour	△	N/A	N/A	N/A	△	N/A	△	N/A	N/A	×	×
Supervision	Less	N/A	N/A	N/A	×	N/A	Less	N/A	N/A	×	×
Clerical/Administrative changes											
Computerization	√	×	√	√	√	√	×	√	√	√	√
Numbers employed	▽	N/A	×	×	×	▽	N/A	×	△	×	×
Proportion full-timers	×	N/A	×	×	×	×	N/A	×	×	×	×
Pattern of hours worked	×	N/A	×	×	×	×	N/A	×	×	×	×
Flexibility of work	−	N/A	×	×	△	×	N/A	×	×	△	×
Flexibility of labour	−	N/A	×	×	△	×	N/A	×	×	×	×
Supervision	−	N/A	×	×	×	×	N/A	×	×	×	×

Key: √ = Yes; × = No; △ = Increased; ▽ = Decreased;
Ab. = Aberdeen; Roch. = Rochdale.

computerization of service provision in financial services and retailing but virtually no technical change in professional and educational services where the premium remained upon individual professional expertise with little direct technological input.

The Effects of Computerization upon Production and Clerical/Administrative Areas in Manufacturing Plants in Rochdale and Aberdeen (see Table 5.7)

Production

In most cases computerization was not reported as affecting numbers in employment. One Rochdale textile firm and both the Aberdeen textile mills reported that computerization of production had led to a fall in numbers employed. However, this had to be balanced by a reported increase at Rochdale's largest textile

areas in relation to technical change in manufacturing plants in Rochdale

Textiles								Other manufacturing							
Aberdeen		Rochdale						Aberdeen					Rochdale		
12	13	14	15	16	17	18	19	20	21	22	23	24	25	26	27
√	√	×	×	×	×	√	√	√	×	√	×	×	√	×	×
∇	∇	N/A	N/A	N/A	N/A	×	Δ	×	N/A	×	N/A	N/A	×	N/A	N/A
×	×	N/A	N/A	N/A	N/A	×	×	×	N/A	×	N/A	N/A	×	N/A	N/A
×	×	N/A	N/A	N/A	N/A	N/A	×	×	N/A	×	N/A	N/A	N/A	N/A	N/A
Δ	–	N/A	N/A	N/A	N/A	N/A	∇	Δ	N/A	Δ	N/A	N/A	N/A	N/A	N/A
Δ	Δ	N/A	N/A	N/A	N/A	Δ	×	Δ	N/A	Δ	N/A	N/A	Δ	N/A	N/A
×	Less	N/A	N/A	N/A	N/A	×	Less	Less	N/A	×	N/A	N/A	×	N/A	N/A
√	√	√	×	×	√	√	√	√	√	√	√	×	√	√	√
∇	∇	×	N/A	N/A	×	∇	×	×	∇	∇	×	N/A	×	×	×
×	×	×	N/A	N/A	×	×	×	×	×	×	×	N/A	N/A	×	×
×	×	×	N/A	N/A	×	×	×	×	×	×	×	N/A	×	×	×
–	–	×	N/A	N/A	×	Δ	×	–	Δ	×	×	N/A	×	Δ	×
–	–	×	N/A	N/A	×	×	×	–	Δ	×	Δ	N/A	×	×	×
–	–	×	N/A	N/A	×	×	×	–	Closer	×	×	N/A	×	×	×

plant. There were no reports of changes in the proportion of full-time employees as a result of these changes. Nevertheless, it is important to note that there were very few part-time employees within production in these plants during the 1980s (Penn, 1989; Censuses of Employment, 1981 and 1984). Such results corresponded closely to recent findings about the general demise of part-time employment in British manufacturing industry (Elias, 1989). Nor had computerization affected the pattern of hours worked within these manufacturing plants. There was an overwhelming opinion that computerization had increased flexibility of production and led to more flexibility amongst production employees. Half the establishments also reported that computerization had led to less tight supervision of such production employees.

Clerical/Administrative

Eight of the 22 manufacturing plants where there had been computerization of office functions reported changes in numbers employed as a direct result of such technological changes. Five (50 per cent) of the Aberdeen establishments reported a fall in numbers, whereas only three Rochdale plants reported any changes (two reported decreases and one reported an increase). There were no reports of changes in the proportion of full-time employees as a consequence of technological innovation. Interestingly, there were fewer reports of changes in flexibility of production or of labour in the area of clerical work.

Overall, computerization had been associated with little change whether in numbers employed, hours of work, or patterns of supervision in these manufacturing establishments. There was some evidence of technical change producing fewer employees in clerical and administrative areas of these plants and engendering more flexibility of production on the shop floor. There was little difference between Rochdale and Aberdeen, except that the numbers employed in clerical and administrative areas were far more likely to have fallen in Aberdeen as a result of computerization than in Rochdale. This was partly a function of the larger size of Aberdeen service-sector establishments when compared with those in Rochdale (see Table 5.6).

The Effects of Computerization upon Service Provision and Clerical/Administrative Areas in Service-Sector Establishments in Rochdale and Aberdeen (see Table 5.8)

Point of Provision

Most establishments reported that computerization had led to no changes in numbers employed at the point of service provision. Two establishments reported falls but two reported increases. The latter pair comprised the two branches of British Telecom. Almost all establishments likewise reported no changes in either the proportion of full-time employees or the pattern of hours worked as a result of computerization. All three financial services establishments reported increases in flexibility, as did both retail outlets and a large distribution centre for a retailing company. Few establishments reported significant changes in supervision. Overall most establishments reported little or no change associated with computerization of their service provision, with the exception of financial services and retailing organizations, where widespread computerization had increased the flexibility both of service provision and of their employees.

Clerical/Administrative Areas

Most service-sector establishments (21 out of 26) reported computerization of their office functions. Only three establishments reported effects upon numbers employed—all in a downward direction. There were no reports of effects upon changes in the pattern of hours worked nor on the proportion of full-timers employed (with one exception). However, ten establishments reported increased flexibility of work and eight reported increased flexibility of labour. There was only one reported change in the pattern of supervision.

Technical Change and Levels of Skill in Rochdale and Aberdeen

Manufacturing

We received responses from twenty-two establishments to questions concerning the relationship of technical change and changing levels of skill amongst employees (see Table 5.9). In eight of the nine establishments where there were no reports of computer-

TABLE 5.8. *Changes in direct service provision and clerical/administrative area Rochdale and Aberdeen*

	Financial services			Professional services				BT		Education				
	A	A	R	A	R	R	R	A	R	A	A	R	R	R
	28	29	30	31	32	33	34	35	36	37	38	39	40	41
Changes at point of provision														
Computerization	√	√	√	×	×	×	×	√	√	×	×	×	×	√
Numbers employed	▽	×	×	N/A	N/A	N/A	N/A	△	△	N/A	N/A	N/A	N/A	×
Proportion full-timers	×	×	×	N/A	N/A	N/A	N/A	×	×	N/A	N/A	N/A	N/A	×
Pattern of hours worked	×	×	√	N/A	N/A	N/A	N/A	×	×	N/A	N/A	N/A	N/A	×
Flexibility of provision	△	△	△	N/A	N/A	N/A	N/A	×	×	N/A	N/A	N/A	N/A	×
Flexibility of labour	△	×	△	N/A	N/A	N/A	N/A	×	×	N/A	N/A	N/A	N/A	×
Supervision	×	Less	×	N/A	N/A	N/A	N/A	×	×	N/A	N/A	N/A	N/A	×
Changes in clerical/administrative areas														
Computerization	√	√	√	×	×	√	×	√	√	√	√	√	√	√
Numbers employed	×	×	×	N/A	N/A	×	N/A	×	×	▽	×	×	×	×
Proportion full-timers	×	×	×	N/A	N/A	×	N/A	×	×	×	×	×	×	×
Pattern of hours worked	×	×	×	N/A	N/A	×	N/A	×	×	×	×	×	×	×
Flexibility of work	△	△	△	N/A	N/A	△	N/A	△	△	×	×	×	△	×
Flexibility of labour	△	×	△	N/A	N/A	△	N/A	△	△	×	×	×	△	×
Supervision	×	Less	×	N/A	N/A	×	N/A	×	×	×	×	×	×	×

Key: √ = Yes; × = No; △ = Increased; ▽ = Decreased.

ization on the shop floor, there was agreement that skills of production and maintenance workers had not changed significantly. The ninth such firm reported a general enskilling of production and maintenance workers. In the twelve establishments which provided data on the effects of computerization on the shop floor upon production and maintenance skills, eleven reported increasing levels of skills amongst maintenance craftworkers (the twelfth used contract maintenance workers). Eight establishments reported increasing skill levels amongst production craftworkers and only one (a large industrial textile manufacturer in Rochdale) reported decreases in skills amongst such workers. Four establishments reported increasing levels of skill amongst non-skilled workers but two, both large textile producers, reported decreasing levels of skill amongst non-skilled operatives. Twenty-two establishments reported computerization within their *in relation to technical change in service sector establishments in*

Transport & distribution			Retail				Other public services				
A	R	R	A	R	R	R	A	A	A	R	R
42	43	44	45	46	47	48	49	50	51	52	53
×	√	×	√	√	√	×	×	√	√	×	√
N/A	×	N/A	×	×	—	×	N/A	×	×	N/A	▽
N/A	×	N/A	×	×	—	×	N/A	×	×	N/A	▽
N/A	√	N/A	×	×	—	×	N/A	×	×	N/A	×
N/A	△	N/A	△	△	—	×	N/A	—	×	N/A	▽
N/A	△	N/A	×	△	—	×	N/A	△	▽	N/A	×
N/A	Less	N/A	×	×	—	×	N/A	Tighter	×	N/A	×
√	√	√	√	√	×	√	×	√	√	√	√
▽	×	×	×	×	N/A	×	N/A	×	×	×	▽
×	×	×	×	×	N/A	×	N/A	×	×	×	▽
×	×	×	×	×	N/A	×	N/A	×	×	×	×
△	×	×	△	△	N/A	×	N/A	×	×	×	△
△	×	×	×	△	N/A	×	N/A	△	▽	×	×
×	×	×	×	×	N/A	×	N/A	×	×	×	×

office activities. Of these, 50 per cent reported increasing levels of skill amongst clerical workers. There was only one reported incidence of falling clerical skills and this was at a food manufacturer in Aberdeen.

Services (see Table 5.10)

The data on the effects of computerization upon levels of service provision were affected by the form of the question. The researchers asked about skill levels of routine manual, skilled manual and clerical employees in these establishments in order to afford as close a comparison as possible with the 27 manufacturing establishments. However, in financial and professional services and within education and other general public services, all but one respondent stated that the question did not apply in relation to manual workers since the service was provided by

TABLE 5.9. *Technical change and levels of skill in*

	Engineering										
	Aberdeen			Rochdale							
	1	2	3	4	5	6	7	8	9	10	11
Computerization of production	√	×	×	×	√	×	√	×	×	√	√
Skill levels											
Unskilled	–	–	C	C	△	C	C	C	C	C	C
Semi-skilled	–	–	C	C	△	C	C	C	C	C	C
Production crafts	C	–	C	C	△	C	△	C	C	C	△
Maintenance crafts	△	–	C	C	△	N/A	△	C	C	N/A	△
Computerization of office	√	×	√	√	√	√	×	√	√	√	√
Skill levels											
Clerical	△	–	C	C	△	–	–	△	△	C	C

Key: √ = Yes;   × = No;   △ = Increased;   ▽ = Decreased;
        N/A = Not available;   Ab. = Aberdeen;   Roch. = Rochdale

professional or quasi-professional employees. British Telecom also, quite legitimately, only responded in relation to skilled maintenance activities. BT in both Aberdeen and Rochdale reported that computerization had increased the levels of skill amongst their skilled maintenance grades. These responses were corroborated by additional fieldwork at BT in Rochdale (Penn,

TABLE 5.10. *Technical change and levels of skill in*

	Financial services			Professional services				BT		Education	
	A	A	R	A	R	R	R	A	R	A	A
	28	29	30	31	32	33	34	35	36	37	38
Computerization of service provision	√	√	√	×	×	×	×	√	√	×	×
Skill levels											
Unskilled	N/A	N/A	N/A	N/A	N/A	N/A	N/A	–	–	–	N/A
Semi-skilled	N/A	N/A	N/A	N/A	N/A	N/A	N/A	–	–	–	N/A
Skilled production	N/A	N/A	N/A	N/A	N/A	N/A	N/A	–	–	–	N/A
Skilled maintenance	N/A	N/A	N/A	N/A	N/A	N/A	N/A	△	△	–	N/A
Computerization of the office	√	√	√	×	×	√	×	√	√	√	√
Skill levels											
Clerical	△	C	C	–	–	C	–	△	△	△	△

Key: √ = Yes;   × = No;   △ = Increased;   ▽ = Decreased;
        C = Constant;   N/A = Not available;   Ab. = Aberdeen;
        Roch. = Rochdale

manufacturing plants in Rochdale and Aberdeen

	Textiles							Other manufacturing							
Aberdeen		Rochdale						Aberdeen					Rochdale		
12	13	14	15	16	17	18	19	20	21	22	23	24	25	26	27
√	√	×	×	×	√	√	√	√	×	√	×	×	√	×	×
×	▽	–	C	C	C	△	C	–	△	–	–	–	–	C	C
×	▽	–	C	C	C	△	▽	–	△	–	–	–	△	C	C
×	△	–	C	C	△	△	▽	△	△	–	–	–	–	C	C
×	△	–	C	C	△	△	▽	△	△	–	–	–	△	C	C
√	√	√	×	×	√	√	√	√	√	√	√	×	√	√	√
△	△	△	–	–	△	–	–	–	–	▽	△	–	△	△	C

1990*b*). The other respondents reported that non-skilled manual skills were constant but that maintenance skills were increasing. We obtained richer data for the effects of technical change upon office skills in these service-sector establishments. Nine establishments reported increasing levels of clerical skills associated with computerization of the office and only one reported decreases.

service-sector establishments in Rochdale and Aberdeen

			Transport and Distribution			Retail				Other Public Services				
R	R	R	A	R	R	A	R	R	R	A	A	A	R	R
39	40	41	42	43	44	45	46	47	48	49	50	51	52	53
×	×	√	×	√	×	√	√	√	×	×	√	√	×	√
N/A	N/A	N/A	N/A	C	N/A	N/A	–	C	–	–	N/A	–	C	N/A
N/A	N/A	N/A	N/A	C	N/A	N/A	–	C	–	–	N/A	–	-	N/A
N/A	N/A	N/A	N/A	△	N/A	N/A	C	C	△	–	N/A	–	C	N/A
N/A	N/A	N/A	N/A	△	N/A	N/A	N/A	N/A	N/A	–	N/A	–	△	N/A
√	√	√	√	√	√	√	√	X	√	X	√	√	√	√
C	C	C	△	△	–	△	C	–	△	–	C	▽	–	C

CONCLUSIONS

The results from the 53 intensive case studies conducted in Rochdale and Aberdeen broadly confirmed the pattern identified in the larger sample of telephone interviews. In general terms, there had been considerable technical change in the plants examined, particularly in the area of office administrative functions. There was little difference between establishments in broadly matched industrial sectors in the two localities. The main area of systematic difference lay in the degree of perceived managerial discretion in terms of the execution of technical change rather than in terms of detailed outcomes within the division of labour. Such results confirmed the picture presented by Freeman (1988), amongst others, of a generic and pervasive set of technological changes under way in the contemporary period, associated with the advent of a new type of technology: microelectronics.

Nevertheless, whilst new microelectronic technologies were common in both Aberdeen and Rochdale, their effects upon the division of labour and, in particular, upon levels of skill amongst the workforce had been complex. There was little evidence to support the deskilling thesis associated with Braverman. There were very few examples of computerization being associated with a lowering of skills amongst workers in the establishments interviewed. There was greater support for the skilling thesis associated with human capital theory. However, whilst there was a strong positive association between computerization and increased levels of skills in many cases, such as outcome was by no means universal. There were *some* reports of deskilling in a few establishments.

Such conclusions raise an important methodological point, already emphasized in the introductory chapter to this volume: the limits of a purely case-study approach to debates about skilled jobs. It would have been possible to select (either deliberately or inadvertently) two or three examples to support each of the theories outlined earlier in this chapter.[3] Therein lies the danger of the kind of case-study approach that has predominated in recent debates about technological change and the division of labour and which has repeatedly been based upon research at one or two plants and/or firms. The wide range of empirical outcomes uncovered in the research reported here reveals the perils inherent in this tradition of inquiry.

The revised compensatory theory of skill also approximated much of the data. There was overwhelming support for its contention that maintenance skills were increasing as a result of computerization. There was no support for the claim made by Braverman (1974) and, more recently, by Martin (1988) that computerization was eliminating maintenance skills. It proved harder to provide an assessment of the proposition that there was a significant difference between automated and semi-automated environments in respect of the relationship between computerization and production skills. Only two plants reported that they were 'highly automated'. However, upon closer inspection, it was apparent that neither was automated in the sense specified by the theory. Neither approximated the levels of automation currently present, for example, within chemical plants or oil refineries. Both of the self-designated 'highly automated' plants in the sample reported increasing levels of skills amongst their production workers. Our data could not, therefore, either confirm or deny this aspect of the theory.

Nor did we uncover the asymmetries in skill change within clerical work that the revised compensatory theory suggested. Almost all offices that had been computerized reported increasing levels of skill for clerical workers. There was no significant difference between larger and smaller offices nor between public-sector and private-sector bureaucracies. Again, however, we do not consider our results to be definitive. Further research is required into these detailed aspects of contemporary computerization.

The overall picture, therefore, concerning computerization and the division of labour in contemporary Rochdale and Aberdeen was one of widespread skilling, particularly in the areas of machine maintenance and clerical work, combined with constant levels of skill in some clerical and some production areas. Furthermore, in two textile plants there was evidence of falling levels of skill amongst production workers. Our results should be seen, therefore, as broadly consistent with Gallie's findings presented earlier in this volume, but also as providing more detailed occupational refinements to his general conclusions about skill and the division of labour.

NOTES

1. The thesis that the present era is characterized by a secular change in technological systems has been advocated by amongst others, Mandel (1980) in his notion of 'long waves' and by Dosi (1984) in his notion of the 'materialization of a technological paradigm'.
2. Both the telephone questionnaire and the schedules used for the intensive follow-up case studies are available from either of the teams.
3. This methodological problem determined our method of presenting the data.

PART II
Subjective Dimensions of Skill

6

Management and Employee Perceptions of Skill

B. BURCHELL, J. ELLIOTT, J. RUBERY, AND
F. WILKINSON

This study is concerned with the evaluation of job content by employees and managers themselves. It therefore moves examination of skill towards its subjective dimensions, its links with work attitudes, and similar themes further developed in Chapters 7–10 of this volume. Jobs consist of a more or less complex array of tasks the characteristics of which are determined by the nature of the product or service, techniques of production, and ways by which production and labour are organized. The undertaking of different types of tasks requires of job holders varying combinations of a wide range of attributes, exercised at varying degrees of intensity. These include the ability to manipulate tools, machines, and materials; knowledge of products, processes, machines, organizations, and procedures; the capabilities of cultivating and maintaining social relationships; the acceptance of responsibility for property, output, standards, and people; physical strength; mental ability; tolerance of working conditions; the ability to organize, co-ordinate and exercise discretion in undertaking task requirements; and the exercising and acceptance of authority. Job content is determined by the task complexity of the job and the requirements of the tasks and it is the job content (and the intensity of effort) which determines the contribution made by the job holder to the production of goods and services.

Any attempt to evaluate job content encounters three basic problems: (i) the identification of the tasks involved in fulfilling the requirement of the job; (ii) the assessment of the attributes required of job incumbents and the intensity of their input in task performance; and (iii) the allotting of weights to the various elements of task requirements to reflect their relative importance in the construction of a measure of the overall value of job content. These difficulties arise because: (i) even the simplest of jobs are enmeshed in a complex social, technical, and market environment; (ii) the nature of tasks and the boundaries of jobs can be continuously modified by changes in the social, technical, and market environment and as a result of learning by doing within a given environment; (iii) it can be expected that there will be significant idiosyncratic elements in task content of jobs and in task performance; (iv) and there are no objective standards for measuring the relative importance of the different attributes required for task performance. The problem is further complicated by the fact that the relative worth of the different aspects of labour input are, to an important degree, socially determined. Moreover, the formal specification of job content is usually either unilaterally determined by management or fixed by bargaining. In both processes the formal job description is influenced by strategic considerations and, for the same reason, many of the details are left imprecise. Consequently, attempts to evaluate job content 'objectively' are fraught with difficulties which are to an important extent insurmountable.

This chapter reports the responses of managers and employees to a range of identical questions about the content of the employees' jobs. It is therefore based on different subjective perceptions of what jobs consist of from both sides of a hierarchical relationship which relates directly to the job in question. (This methodology may be contrasted with that used by Elias in Chapter 3, and by Francis and Penn in Chapter 8.) No attempt was made to evaluate independently the jobs studied because in our view that would in practice have imposed one more layer of subjectivity on the analysis for the reasons specified above. Moreover, our central interest is in the differences in the perceptions of employees and managers and the light these throw on the debate about work organization. However, the authors recognize that, although they addressed identical questions to employees and their managers, it is nevertheless possible that the wording of the questions may have been such as to be interpreted differently by the two parties. This is particularly so for questions about discretion and responsibility, which the managers may have interpreted in a broader context than did the employees. Problems may also arise from the aggregation of the data to form variables, constructed to make the analysis manageable, although tests have been carried out which supported the choice of the groupings used in the analysis.

The chapter first examines the deskilling debate and notes that the notion of skill, as generally understood within this controversy, encompasses only a subset of the components of job contents. It is also suggested that the direct evidence of the job incumbents has not been given sufficient weight in the deliberations. The second section and the appendices describe the survey and the construction of the variables. The third section summarizes the findings and the final section assesses the relative credibility of the employees' and managers' evaluation of the contents of jobs. The analysis reveals consistent similarities and differences in managers' and employees' perceptions of what jobs contain. In particular, managers see the incumbents of lower-rank jobs as exercising much less organizing skill and discretion than do the incumbents. It is our view that the differences revealed in managers' and employees' evaluation of job contents are of significant importance and need to be taken into account in the deskilling debate, policy discussions about the restructuring of work, and more generally in industrial relations.

THEORETICAL ISSUES

In the economic and sociological debate about the content of jobs the emphasis has been on the historical tendency towards progressive simplification resulting from increasing division of labour, managerial innovations, and changing technology. Adam Smith argued that a finer division of labour, by reducing the range of tasks in any job, increased productivity by saving the time which would have been lost if operators moved from stage to stage in the production process and by enhancing employee dexterity by increasing task specialization. Babbage suggested additional gains by observing that, as the training and pay for particular jobs was determined by its most skilled elements, savings could be made by separating out the skilled tasks from the mass of jobs and concentrating them in specialized occupations.

By these means both training and pay could be reduced and the employer would be able to adjust the attributes of its labour force more precisely to the task requirements of its system of production. Taylor built on the Babbage principle by advocating a three-stage process by which the task composition of work could be simplified. This involved (i) the disassociation of the organization of work from the skills of the employees by the acquisition by management of the knowledge traditionally possessed by skilled employees; (ii) the removal of all possible brainwork from the shop floor to the planning departments to separate the conception of work from its execution; and (iii) the use by management of the monopoly of knowledge to finely divide labour and to carefully plan and control every step in the labour process.

The second major factor identified as reducing the skill content of jobs is technical change. For Adam Smith the routinization of jobs by the division of labour created the opportunity for the development of machines which embodied the simplified tasks. The invention of machines to work metals and other materials and more precise methods of measurement have also been identified as important in removing the handicraft, know-how, and judgemental elements from craftwork and transforming craftworkers into machine setters-up and minders (Penn, 1982a). More generally the progressive division of labour and the incorporation of the skill element of work into machines is seen as part of a general historical process in which technology and work organization play a central but neutral role in the continuous expansion of the productivity of labour.

Marxists, by contrast, have identified technology, scientific management, and the division of labour as the main route by which capital's control of the labour process has been tightened. Marx (following Ure) recognized the potential of automatic machinery for breaking the skilled employees' control and replacing them by unskilled operatives (Lazonick, 1979). The centrality of such considerations for analysis of work organization has been reconfirmed by the labour process debate sparked off by Braverman (1974). From this emerges the proposition that the major consideration in choice of techniques and managerial systems is the extraction of surplus value rather than the enhancement of labour productivity (Bowles, 1985).

Discretion

Whatever the reasons for the historical development of labour organization there is a fairly broad census that work has been progressively degraded in two important ways. It is suggested that work has continuously lost its discretionary element as technology and managerial organization has progressively tightened the prescriptive limits to task performance. For the purpose of this discussion prescriptive limits can be defined as those set by management such that 'his subordinate will be in no doubt whatever when he has completed his task and completed it as instructed' whereas the discretionary element is such that 'his subordinate will have to use his own discretion in deciding when he has pursued the particular activity to the point where the result is likely to satisfy the requirement of his management' (Jacques, 1967: 77). This distinction is used by Fox (1974) as a starting-point from which to develop the notion of the 'low-discretion syndrome' which, he argues, typifies the mass of jobs and which can be contrasted with the 'high-discretion syndrome' which is the hallmark of a rather narrow range of high-level managerial and professional jobs.

The 'low-discretion syndrome' is characterized by five items which can be briefly summarized: (i) employees obey formal rules in carrying out their tasks; (ii) the co-ordination of employees' tasks is a managerial function; (iii) the employees perceive themselves as not being trusted and are closely supervised; (iv) technological and managerial constraints and monetary rewards are seen as more important than self-imposed standards for determining the pace of work and failure to meet standards results in punishment, more rules, tighter supervision, or some combination of these measures; and (v) any conflict between management and employees is handled on a group basis through bargaining processes. By contrast, the defining characteristics of high-discretion work patterns are: (i) a commitment to, and moral involvement in, the goals and values of a calling or organization; (ii) the recognition of the inappropriateness of close supervision; (iii) a problem-solving relationship between related work areas rather than standardized, externally imposed co-ordination; (iv) the recognition that punishment is inappropriate for the failure to effectively exercise high discretion because loyalty, support and goodwill are taken for granted and because, in the absence of clear-cut rights and wrongs, performance is a matter of fine judgement; (v) the resolution of disputes is a question of problem-solving rather than group bargaining. Between the small number of high-discretion jobs and the mass of those typified by low discretion, which are regarded by Fox as the opposite ends of a spectrum, lie such jobs as some craftworkers, technicians, clerical workers, lower professionals, and supervisory and administrative staff. These include such high-discretion elements as commitment to the organization but tend to be hedged in by the rules, controls, checks, monitoring devices, and possibly forms of discipline which characterize low-discretion roles.

Deskilling

The second way by which, it is argued, work has been degraded is by the progressive denuding of jobs of their skilled content and hence of any intrinsic worth. The central proposition of this thesis is that the process of deskilling has been both progressive and comprehensive and has embraced manual work in manufacturing and services and clerical, lower professional and administrative work in the white-collar area. This view has been criticized on several grounds. It has been argued that effective resistance by skilled employees has preserved their autonomy and obliged managers to adopt strategies which recognized this reality (Friedman, 1977). It has also been pointed out that the view that new technology invariably deskills is mistaken and that technical progress is one of both the destruction of old, and the creation of new skills (Wood, 1982).

But perhaps the most telling criticism of the deskilling thesis is the one-sided view of the nature of skill which is deployed. The vision of skill adopted by Braverman is that of the individualistic mechanic/artisan deploying a high level of 'complex objective competencies' (Beechey, 1982). Thus 'For the worker, the concept of skill is traditionally bound up with craft mastery—that is to say, the combination of knowledge of materials and processes with the practised manual dexterities required to carry on a specific branch of production' (Braverman, 1974: 443). Braverman also put stress on the social definition of skill when he argued that in the early days of the motorization of transport 'it might have made sense to characterize the former [horse-driving skills] as part of the common heritage and thus no skill at all, while [motor] driving, as a learned ability, would have been thought of as skilled' (1974: 430).[1] This would seem to define skill not by complex objective competencies but in terms of the degree of formality of its acquisition. This effectively rules out of the skill category the broad range of social, caring, household-organizing, tool-using, and other abilities acquired in the process of accession to the 'common heritage'. The narrowness of the definition of skill also, it is argued, leads to an overestimate of deskilling by downgrading important job elements. In this respect, attention has been drawn to the importance of social skills in group working; the degree of discretion retained by employees because of unpredictability in raw materials and production processes; the idiosyncracies of machines and work situations requiring specific skills; and the degree of unrecognized abilities—what has been called tacit skills (Manwaring and Wood, 1985)—required for a broad range of tasks.

Responsibility

In addition to the narrowness of its definition, there is a question of whether the concept of skill is a broad enough gauge, on its own, to be a reliable guide to differences in job content. In particular, many jobs carry a wide range of responsibilities which are not only, or even mainly, dependent on skill however defined. These include responsibilities for buildings and equipment, materials, valuables, and people which vary widely between jobs even on the same 'skill' level and which may increase as technology dependent on traditional skills is replaced by more complex automatic systems.[2] There can be no doubt that the burden of responsibility has an important bearing on the value of a job, a fact which is fully recognized in job evaluation. But how skill and responsibility compare in their contribution to the intrinsic quality of jobs is a question which cannot be settled on *a priori* grounds.

Workers' and Managers' Perspectives

A striking feature of the debate about the nature of skill and the broader question of job content is the absence of any substantial and systematically collected body of evidence on job content from those directly involved—the job holders. There is very important and detailed survey evidence which shows wide variations in the content of different jobs held by unqualified male manual employees (Blackburn and Mann, 1979), on different assembly lines (Wedderburn and Crompton, 1972) and between jobs with similar titles but in firms of different sizes (Craig *et al.*, 1982, 1985). In these studies the final judgement as to the nature and quality of job content rests with the researchers, although usually after consultation with employees, or their representatives, and with management. Moreover, when checks have been made using empirical evidence, it has been reported that employees' perception of job content has been in line with that of the researchers and/or managers (A. N. Turner and Lawrence, 1965; Hackman and Lawler, 1971). It might be concluded, therefore, that there is little is to be gained from a detailed survey of employees. But such a conclusion receives little support from the one major source of evidence of job holders' assessment of the content of their work which is to be found in their own oral and written testimonies (see, for example, Frazer, 1968 and 1969; Terkel, 1975). The job descriptions provided there by some assembly workers and others whose work is dominated by technology lends strong support to the deskilling thesis and many job holders reveal a significant degree of alienation from their jobs, especially from the way work is organized. However, the general impression from reading this literature is of wide variations in experiences and often a significant degree of ambiguity in the feelings and attitudes of particular employees towards their jobs.

A central purpose of the SCELI study was to systematically collect data from employees on their views of the contents of their jobs. Such information from the core Work Attitudes/ Histories survey has proved invaluable in the construction of broadly based indices of job content and the use of these in comparing the skill levels of jobs and the relationship between skill and pay (Horrell *et al.*, 1989, 1990). A second stage in the analysis is to contrast employees' perceptions of skill with those of their managers. Here the core surveys are of limited value because it is not possible to achieve from them a precise matching of employees' and managers' perceptions of what specified jobs require. Thus a special Related Study was undertaken by the

Cambridge team to explicitly address the issue of differing managers' and employees' perceptions.

JOB CONTENT AND SKILL; METHODS AND RESULTS

As a Related Study within the Social Change and Economic Life Initiative (SCELI) programme, the Cambridge team undertook a study of 23 Northampton employers which involved detailed interview surveys of a selection of employees employed in a representative range of occupations within the establishment. In addition management was asked a set of directly comparable questions about each of the occupations selected for the survey (see Appendix 6.1). These two data-sets thus provide us with a basis for comparing management's views of their employment system (as it relates to a specific occupation) with the perceptions of some of those employed in that occupation. The occupations were chosen to be representative of the range of occupations in the labour market, but the numbers interviewed in each occupation reflected the relative weight of the occupation within the establishment's employment structure. Thus we tried to select at least one occupation from the seven occupational classification system adopted by SCELI for the Employer Baseline survey,[3] provided that there was one such occupation within the establishment, but we chose to interview up to four employees in occupations which were relatively numerous and only one employee in occupations which were of minor importance in the employment structure. This procedure should result in the sample being more representative of the occupational bands in the labour market as a whole, as well as within the establishment, than if the same number were selected for each. In comparing management's and employees' responses, the management questionnaire for an occupation has been compared to each of the individual's within the occupation taken separately; that is, we have not assumed that we can construct an 'average employee' perspective but the management's questionnaire could be expected to apply to the average job holder, and thus to bear some relationship to the responses of individuals within the occupation.

Once the occupations were selected the employees to be interviewed were chosen, as far as possible on a random basis.

Nevertheless, the sample cannot be taken to be a representative sample of the Northampton labour market; the selection of employers aimed to achieve a reasonable proportion of the main types of industries (manufacturing, public and private services, etc.) and of large and small employers but, given these parameters, the main criterion by which they came to be included was the willingness of management to participate in the survey. There are some reasons for believing that this procedure has biased our sample towards the range of 'good employers' in Northampton, to those most concerned with their public image in the community. Not all the participating employers fitted this category but it was certainly the case that some of the employers providing the worst employment conditions refused to participate in this part of the initiative. In addition our sample of employees was clearly biased in favour of established employees, if only because selections were made from employee lists that were often several weeks out of date and the process of selection and interview was often spread over two or three months, so that completely new recruits would not be likely to appear in the sample. Thus we avoid the problem that some of a totally random sample of employees could be expected to give divergent answers to management simply because they had not yet acquired sufficient knowledge of the organization.

The interview schedule for employees came in two parts, one administered by an interviewer,[4] and a separate self-completion section usually given to the respondent ahead of the interview. The interviews were carried out at the employee's place of work and lasted 45 minutes on average; the self-completion section took approximately 20 minutes to complete. The purpose of the self-completion was simply to extend the range of questions that could be asked within the constraints of the budget and the time which managers considered reasonable for the employee interviews.

The survey comprised 270 employees of whom 246 answered both the self-completion and the main questionnaire, and had a questionnaire relating to their job completed by a manager. These 246 individuals were doing one of 148 different jobs, in one of the 23 firms where these interviews took place in the Northampton 'Travel-to-Work Area'.

The Northampton Travel-to-Work Area was typical of many

British local labour markets in 1987, when the survey data were collected. It had been going through a restructuring phase for some considerable period while its traditional footwear industry was in decline. Service industries were on the increase during this time; according to the 1984 and 1987 Censuses of Employment there had been an increase of 17 per cent overall in service-sector employment, but with increases of 39 per cent in the financial services and 17 and 21 per cent in *other services* and *transport and communication* respectively. Much of this increase was in part-time female employment, where there was a 26 per cent increase across all Standard Industrial Classification (SIC) divisions compared to an overall rate of increase in total employment of under 14 per cent.

The questionnaires included 28 questions concerning job content. Of these 13 asked about skills and abilities, 11 about different types of responsibilities, and 4 about the amount of discretion exercised by the job holder over various aspects of the job. This information was grouped and 9 job-content variables were constructed: discretion; responsibilities for people, resources, records/information, and output/standards; and clerical, social, organizational and physical skills.[5] The scaling of the relative importance of particular elements in the content of jobs varied between questions. For example, the respondents were asked whether their jobs required a lot, some, little, or none of each of the different types of responsibilities (which converted into a numerical scale of from 0 to 3), whilst they were required to record the degree of each skill or ability required on a continuous scale of 0 to 10, from 'not at all important' to 'absolutely essential'. The discretion variable was constructed from a range of questions designed to tap the different aspects of control, and this process created a numerical scale of from 0 to 14.[6]

It was possible to make detailed statistical comparisons between managers' and employees' perception on each of the nine measures of job content described above by using a repeated measures analysis of variance, with the seven job categories and the managers' versus employees' perspective as the independent variables.[7] Taking each of the nine job attributes separately, comparisons are made between the seven different job groups and the two perspectives, managers' and employees'. As well as testing for differences between the seven job classifications and between the two perspectives (managers' and employees'), the analysis of variance also tests for an interaction between these two effects; in other words, is the mismatch between managers' and employees' perception greater for some job classifications than for others?

The average points ratings given by employees and managers for each of the nine job-content measures for all jobs are given in Table 6.1. For this table the points ratings have been expressed as percentages of the highest possible point scores on each scale respectively.

Managers' perceptions of the importance of the different aspects of job content are presented in the second column of Table 6.1 and in the third column the indices of managers' perceptions are expressed as a percentage of employees' perceptions. If a job element registers less than 100 in column 3 of Table 6.1, this means that managers perceive this component to be of less importance than do the employees. This measure shows that overall employees and managers roughly agree on the degree of the different types of responsibilities carried by jobs (none of the differences were statistically significant) whilst for managers requirements of social skills are just significantly less statistically than those perceived by the job holders. (Managers also report that the amount of physical and social skills required to do the job are lower, but these differences are not statistically significant.) But the two most striking disagreements between managers and employees are found in the importance attributed to *organizational skills* and *discretion;* compared with employees, managers have significantly lower perceptions of the importance of these elements of job content.

The jobs were divided into seven categories: lower and higher grades of manual and of technical and professional employees, routine clericals, administrative and lower-management employees, and middle managers.[8] The rating of each job-content component can be expected to vary between these categories of jobs, so that the data in Table 6.1 will contain significant compositional effects. When employees' and managers' perceptions are aggregated, large inter-group differences in the relative importance of job elements are revealed. Repeated measures multivariate analysis of variance show these differences between the seven job groups to be very highly significant for eight of the nine

TABLE 6.1. *Employees' and managers' perceptions of job content: all jobs*

	Employees (% of max. points rating)	Managers (% of max. points rating)	Managers' perception as % of employees'
Skills			
Physical	49	46	94
Clerical	67	63	94
Social	77	70	91
Organizational	73	59	81
Responsibilities			
Resources	40	40	100
Records and information	38	39	103
People	48	48	100
Output/standards	55	56	102
Discretion	65	50	76

measures (the exception being responsibilities for resources, which was only just significant). These results are given in Table 6.2, where the combined managers' and employees' rating of each job is expressed as a percentage-ratio of the lower-skilled manual employees' scores. In all of the measures bar physical skill the middle managers were rated more highly than any of the other job groups. The lower-skilled employees were rated as having the least demanding jobs in terms of their clerical and organizational skills, their responsibilities for records and information, and output standards. The clerical workers tied for the last position on responsibilities for output standards, and had the lowest ratings for responsibilities for people and resources as well as the lowest levels of discretion in their jobs. Finally, whilst higher-skilled employees had the highest ratings for physical skills, they were the group for whom social skills were the least important. This last result can be explained by the fact that the lower-skilled manual category includes local authority and health service employees with caring responsibilities, and this helps explain the degree of importance claimed for social skills.

The features of the skill and responsibility measures within each job category which sit most uneasily with the deskilling hypothesis are the close similarities between the job contents of lower- and higher-skilled manual employees,[9] and the importance given to social and organizational skills and to discretion by employees in the lower-level job categories.

When we compare the degree of importance attached by managers and employees to the various aspects of job content within each job category, very clear differences emerge. The relative evaluation of the different elements of job content are shown in Table 6.3 in which again management's scores for each component are expressed as a percentage of those of employees. For physical and clerical skills the tendency was for managers to agree with the job holders about, or even give greater weights to, those skills which typify the jobs—that is, physical skills for manual employees—but to give less importance to the skills which did not—that is, physical skills for white-collar employees. Responsibilities for resources and for records and information were seen as more important by managers for technicians and lower professionals, administrators and lower management, and middle managers, but not, perhaps surprisingly, for technologists

TABLE 6.2. *Perceptions of job content by job category: average of employees' and managers' ratings as a percentage of ratings for lower-skilled production and service employees*

	Lower-skilled production and service workers	Higher-skilled production and service workers	Technicians and lower professionals	Technologist and higher professionals	Routine clericals	Administrative and lower management	Middle management	Sig[a]
Skills								
Physical	100	117	95	76	63	78	51	***
Clerical	100	127	127	190	178	183	192	***
Social	100	94	111	118	96	109	126	***
Organizational	100	113	163	172	111	154	196	***
Responsibilities								
Resources	100	121	129	97	96	104	172	*
Records and information	100	121	271	226	279	326	494	***
People	100	104	163	141	62	111	207	***
Output/standards	100	130	165	167	100	146	235	***
Discretion	100	115	151	172	95	147	194	***

[a] Statistical significance: *p < 0.05; ** p < 0.01; *** p < 0.001.

TABLE 6.3. *The relative valuation of job content: managers' ratings of job content as percentages of employees' rating of job content*

	Lower-skilled production and service workers	Higher-skilled production and service workers	Technicians and lower professionals	Technologist and higher professionals	Routine clericals	Administrative and lower management	Middle management
Skills							
Physical	100	103	119	72	72	84	86
Clerical	62	91	110	105	95	97	104
Social	82	85	99	106	91	94	107
Organizational	69	95	92	83	89	104	
Responsibilities							
Resources	89	98	102	89	86	108	117
Records and information	100	78	109	67	94	124	102
People	74	93	103	100	113	117	110
Output/standards	80	114	113	105	113	100	100
Discretion	55	73	91	89	59	82	102

and higher professional. Managers also showed a tendency to overrate white-collar workers' (and underrate manual workers') responsibility for people and to give all categories except the lowest manual more responsibility for output/standards than the job holders would want to claim.

Generally speaking, managers put a much lower valuation on social skills, organizational skills and discretion than did the incumbents for each job category except middle management. It can also be seen that the discrepancy between the managers' and employees' evaluation of job content is larger the lower the ranking of the job. There is a particularly sharp disagreement between lower-skilled production and service employees and their managers as to the importance of organizational skills and discretion in their jobs. (A further aspect of this will be examined in the following chapter.) This relative undervaluation is much less marked for technicians and lower professionals, or for technologists and higher professionals; and in the middle management job group, managers can be seen to have slightly higher perceptions of the importance of all job elements, except physical skills, when compared with the employees themselves. This interaction between the differences in managers' and employees' perceptions and job group is illustrated for the discretion component of job content in Figure 6.1, which clearly shows the greatest discrepancy occurs for routine clerical jobs and the lower-skilled production and service operatives' jobs (job groups 1 and 5). The multivariate analysis of variance showed this interaction effect to be significant for all of the job-content measures except in the case of responsibility for resources and responsibility for output.

The finding that managers tend to discount the amount of discretion exercised by employees in lower-skilled jobs is illustrated clearly by the conflicting accounts given by a manager and employees in ancillary jobs in the caring services in the public sector. Consider the following case as an illustration:

Three employees in an establishment provided a fairly coherent and consistent picture of the amount of discretion they are free to exercise in fulfilling the requirements of their job, with the leading hand reporting having slightly more than the other two, as we would expect. The description of discretion in the manager's questionnaire was, however, very different. According to their manager, who provided the matched questionnaire, the

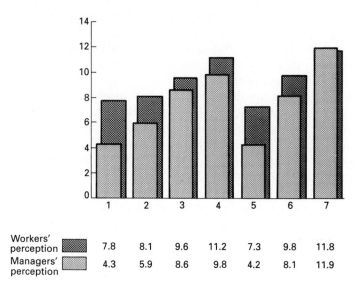

	1	2	3	4	5	6	7
Workers' perception	7.8	8.1	9.6	11.2	7.3	9.8	11.8
Managers' perception	4.3	5.9	8.6	9.8	4.2	8.1	11.9

Figure 6.1 Perceptions of job content: managers' and workers' perceptions of discretion by job type. See appendix 6.3 for description of job types

employees had hardly any choice over the way they did the job and were quite closely supervised, with the supervisor or boss determining how hard they worked. The manager's report also claimed that the job rarely involved setting targets and objectives or making non-routine decisions, although sometimes it did involve taking the initiative in reorganizing work. Thus out of a possible maximum of 14 on the discretion score the employees scored 11 (or more for the leading hand) but the management's view of the job resulted in a score of only 3. This is therefore a particularly clear example of the way in which management consider the scope for discretion in what is generally thought to be (and has been classified as) a lower-skilled job to be much more restricted than do the job holders themselves.

Bias and Error

So far all of the analyses and discussions in this chapter have centred on the question of agreement or disagreement between the aggregate scores of each of the job types. However, even when the *mean* job attribute score for managers and employees is identical, there is not necessarily good agreement on the relative position of each job within each of the seven job types. Put another way, so far the main consideration has been of bias, or the consistent tendency of managers to systematically underrate or overrate jobs compared to employees. A second, related, question is whether there is high or low consensus between managers and employees *within* each of the job categories.

This issue is best assessed by looking at the rank-order correlation of employees' and managers' scores on each of the nine attributes within each of the seven job categories. However, in order to simplify the resulting 63 correlations into a more easily digestible form, a technique called 'Median Polishing'[10] was used in order to give a summary correlation for each job category and a summary correlation for each job attribute. This allowed us to ask the following two questions: (i) Do managers show more agreement over job content with some groups of workers than others? And (ii) Do managers and employees show more agreement over some aspects of job content than others? The answer to both of these questions was *yes*.

The overall fit of the Median Polish model was a very modest 0.28 (or in other words, an R^2 of less than 0.08), showing that there was little agreement between managers and employees at the level of the individual job within each job category. However, there was more agreement within some job categories than within others; agreement was highest for middle managers, followed by lower managers, and least for the lower-skilled employees, followed (interestingly) by the higher professionals. It might be concluded from this that the more similar a job is to their own jobs, the more accurately managers can assess its content. For jobs very dissimilar to managers' jobs, they perform only a little better than they would by pure guesses based upon stereotypical notions of what a broad category of workers do.

There were also large and meaningful differences between the aggregate correlation coefficients for each of the nine job attributes. The highest agreement was found over the level of responsibility for people; this is not surprising, given that the level of supervisory responsibility within each job is usually stated very explicitly. At the other end of the spectrum the job attribute where there was least consensus was the level of discretion. This lends support to the assertion that the level of discretion in jobs is not only given less weight (as was demonstrated in the previous section) but also very poorly understood by managers.

SUMMARY AND FINAL COMMENTS

Judged by the perceptions of employees, the broad structuring of job content revealed by the survey evidence might have been predicted by reference to different types of work and to the hierarchical structuring of jobs. What was perhaps less predictable is the very close similarity between lower-skilled and higher-skilled manual employees in their perceptions of job content and importance given to social skills, organizational skills, and discretion by lower-skilled manual, higher-skilled manual, and routine clerical workers. The predictable structuring of job content is also clearly discernible in the perceptions of managers. But when compared with employees, managers tended to downgrade organizational skills, discretion, and to a lesser degree social skills and to upgrade certain types of responsibilities (for people and for output/standards). In other respects, managers' perceptions of job content were more in conformity with job stereotypes in that they placed less importance on the clerical skills of manual employees and on the physical skills of white-collar workers than did the holders of those types of jobs. Managers also perceived jobs to be significantly more hierarchically structured in terms of job content than did employees. This is especially so with respect to organizational skills and discretion but is also clearly observable for other job attributes.

It has to be emphasized that what is being reported here is an exercise in job self-evaluation by employees which necessarily involves a substantial subjective element. The extent to which such 'social constructs' diverge from objective measurements of job content (supposing such an exercise is ever possible[11]) cannot be assessed from the current data-set. Short-term, ahistorical laboratory experiments by social psychologists suggest that perceptions of jobs are coloured by 'social cues' picked up from supervisors and others and therefore the outcomes of these tests did not compare well with objective measures. However, field trials on experienced employees have found that their perceptions of job content more closely match that of expert evaluation (O'Brien, 1986).

The important contribution which O'Brien makes is to emphasize that objective features of a job are only one of a number of factors which combine to make up an employee's perception of his or her job; personal abilities and characteristics, job satisfaction, performance and motivation, and the information available to the employee interact in a complex way with objective features of the tasks which make up the job. However, it is important to notice that the 'subjectivity' is not randomly distributed but linked to broad categories which do embody some real differences in skills, however difficult it may be to find fully objective measures of them. The same is presumably also true for managers' perceptions of job attributes. If this is so in our case, it might usefully be asked from whom the survey respondents picked up their 'social cues' because the manual employees and routine clerical workers, who made up 50 per cent of the sample, were seriously at odds with their managers about the composition of their jobs.

The differences in managers' and employees' perceptions of job content is a central feature of the analysis requiring explanation. This difference is significantly greater in those aspects of the skills around which the deskilling debate has raged: organizational skills, discretion, and social skills. There seems little doubt that if the employees in the lower ranks of the job categories included in our survey and their managers became involved in the deskilling debate they would enter on opposite sides. It is also clear, on this evidence, that managers perceive many of the jobs they oversee as being typified by the 'low-discretion syndrome' to a greater extent than do employees who undertake those jobs. This difference might represent, it could be argued, an example of employees in lowly jobs talking up the content of that work to secure a greater degree of self-respect and/or social recognition (the 'rat-catcher' into 'rodent operative' syndrome[12]). But to carry this argument far we would have to suppose that self-importance was of greater significance to employees than to their managers because when the latter are asked to evaluate the social and organizational skills and discretion required of jobs subordinate to their own they are to an important degree evaluating the content of their own jobs.

The real issue would seem to be one of who knows most about the jobs and what conditions the responses of individuals to questions about matters about which they have incomplete information. Jacques (1967: esp. ch. 4) has argued that there are very few jobs without significant discretionary elements, the undertaking of which require organizational skills, however their limits are prescribed. This coupled with the growing volume of research findings indicating the importance of social and other unrecognized skills suggests that many of the relatively 'unskilled' jobs are much more complex and allow a greater degree of employee control than is allowed for by the deskilling hypothesis. This is not to argue that employees can readily change the objectives of their jobs, a constraint which applies at all levels of organizations, but that they exercise a significant degree of discretion fulfilling the requirements of their job. This being so it would appear unlikely that the managers would have the same degree of detailed knowledge of the job as the incumbent.

The psychological literature has demonstrated that individuals quite naturally make decisions based on instances that are most available to them. However, they fail to adjust sufficiently for the possible bias in this information and this may prejudice the use to which it is put (a phenomenon named the 'availability bias' by Tversky and Kahneman, 1973). Employees, being intimately familiar with the every-day nature of their jobs would probably base their judgements on the contents of their working time. The data that would be available for managers, however, is likely to be more abstracted and idealized job descriptions of the nature of the qualifications required of the job incumbents. The 'availability bias' is the term given to the bias in human inference that would lead managers to under-correct for the fact that their information sources are not representative. Furthermore, it might be argued that the less familiar a manager was with the precise inner workings of the labour process, the more they would have to use other sources of information which would in turn add to the level of bias. Managers might be more adept at assessing the job content of other managers but less so when it came to, for instance, manual jobs or those of routine clerical workers. This would explain the convergence between the employees' and managers' perception of job content the closer the job in question gets to that of the manager.

A closely related phenomenon to the 'availability bias' is the use of stereotypes in making judgements under uncertainty. While there is often a kernel of truth in social stereotypes, the stereotypes tend to exaggerate those differences. Thus relying on social categories rather than job content to make judgements about skill, responsibility, and discretion levels is likely to exaggerate differences between jobs.

One of the most common social stereotypes used to evaluate job content is the gender of the person employed in the job. Women's jobs are perceived as low-skilled, not because of an evaluation of job content but because the low pay and status of women employees is taken as an indicator of low skill and job content (Craig *et al.*, 1985). (Further aspects of this process will be examined in the chapter on gender and skill which follows this.) These views have been increasingly successfully challenged through claims made under the equal pay for work of equal value clause or through the implementation of new job evaluation schemes introduced under trade union pressure. Within banks secretaries have been admitted to be more skilled than messengers, and community care assistants to be more skilled than refuse collectors (*Industrial Relations Review and Report*, 1990). The 'undervaluation' of skill within the lower job categories found in this survey, particularly those in the service sector, thus fits with the emerging evidence of systematic undervaluation of skills in jobs traditionally carried out by women, a social stereotype which has been important in maintaining gender differences in pay.

Whatever the explanation for its existence, the 'perception gap' between managers and employees in the control elements of job content raises major issues for labour organization. If managers underestimate the degree to which the successful fulfilment of the requirements of jobs depends on the social skills, organizational skills, and discretion of the job holders, attempts to reorganize work may involve hidden costs. Our illustrative example was drawn from a public-sector service where the competitive bidding for contracts for ancillary services has led to the proliferation of work measurement schemes and an intensification of labour. If these exercises have led to an effective dilution of job content with the removal of areas of discretion and the scope to deploy organization and social skills by which employees effectively responded to the social and other requirements of patients, to emergencies, and to the uncertainties inherent in caring routines then any monetary savings may well have been swamped by a decline in the quality of service. An underestimation of the degree of control exercised by job holders might also lead managers to misjudge the degree of co-operation they will need from the workforce in introducing change and making the most effective use of new methods. In both these examples managers' stereotypical perception of work which emphasizes the paucity of job content and which receives strong support from academic accounts of the deskilling process stands as a major obstacle to the effective organization of labour and quite probably to the more effective motivation of employees.

NOTES

1. The relative status of these jobs were reversed Braverman argued, when motor transport became dominant.
2. Stieber (1959: ch. 8) in his study of the US steel industry wage structure showed the relationship between pay level, job status, and the degree of responsibility for throughput and value added.
3. Namely lower-skilled operatives, higher-skilled operatives, lower professionals, higher professionals, routine clerical, administrative and lower management, middle and upper management.
4. The interviewing was carried out by National Opinion Polls.
5. The form of the questions and the methods of constructing the variables are given in Appendix 6.1.
6. The points ratings for workers and managers are given in Appendix 6.2.
7. Available as part of the MANOVA command in the SPSSX package.
8. The procedure for allocating jobs to job categories is described in Appendix 6.3.
9. This is particularly marked for the evaluation by workers of the content of their jobs, especially organization skills and discretion (see Appendix 6.2).
10. The interested reader can find out more details of this exploratory data analysis technique in Marsh (1988).
11. We had at one point in the research contemplated our own evaluation of the jobs. We decided against this because of the difficulties

and costs involved but also because we realized that such an exercise would introduce one more layer of subjectivity into the study.
12. No slight is intended on the job of rat-catching which, as only a moment's reflection will reveal, involves considerable degrees of discretion and organizational and social skills.

APPENDIX 6.1

Measures of Job Content: Construction of Variables

Discretion

Four questions were asked reflecting on the discretion exercised. These questions and the scores (in parentheses) allotted to responses were:

How much choice do you have over the way in which you do your job?

A great deal of choice	(3)
Some choice	(2)
Hardly any choice	(1)
No choice	(0)

Which, if any of the following things are important in determining how hard you work in your job?

Machine or assembly line	(0)
Clients or customers	(1)
A supervisor or boss	(0)
Your fellow workers or colleagues	(1)
Your own discretion	(2)
Pay incentives	(1)
Reports and appraisals	(1)
None of these	(1)

How closely are you supervised in your job?

Very closely	(0)
Quite closely	(1)
Not very closely	(2)
Hardly ever	(3)

How often does your job require you to:

	most of the time	frequently	sometimes	rarely	never
determine targets or objectives	(2)	(2)	(1)	(0)	(0)
take the initative in reorganizing your work when necessary	(2)	(2)	(1)	(0)	(0)
make non-routine decisions?	(2)	(2)	(1)	(0)	(0)

The scores were then summed to give a discretion score.

Responsibility and Skills

There were 13 questions about skills and abilities on the questionnaire and 11 questions about responsibility. It was decided that rather than analysing each question separately, i.e. looking at 24 measures of job content, the questions should be grouped in some way to form indices of different aspects of job content. There are two ways of performing this grouping. One would be to simply read the questions and use some commonsense ideas to decide which should go together; the alternative method is to use factor analysis, a statistical technique used to identify a relatively small number of factors that can be used to represent the relationships among sets of many interrelated variables.

Having grouped the responsibility questions into four aspects of responsibility and the skill questions into four aspects of skill using commonsense methods, factor analysis (with an oblique rotation) was performed on the responsibility questions and then the skill questions to check the statistical validity of the groupings. The results of the factor analysis differed slightly depending on whether the self-reported data or management data was used, but the factors which emerged broadly agreed with our original commonsense groupings. The main difference was that with the skill questions only three factors emerged, one factor being an amalgamation of our 'social skills' and 'organizational skills'. It was decided that for the purposes of the analyses these two aspects of skill would be kept separate.

RESPONSIBILITIES: the questions, grouping and scores were:

For each of the following list of things that some people have responsibility for, please indicate how much responsibility you personally have for it at work.

a lot   some   little   none

Responsibility for people
Physical safety or health of others
Emotional or mental well-being of others
Education or training of others
Supervision of other people

Responsibility for resources
Buildings or equipment
Cash or other valuables

Responsibility for records/information
Confidential information
Financial records

Responsibility for output/standards
Output targets or deadlines
Quality standards
Official or professional standards

The respondents were asked to rate their responsibilities under the various headings on a fourfold scale: a lot, some, little, and none. These were given scores: a lot (3), some (2), little (1), none (0); to calculate the score for each main responsibility the scores were added and divided by the numbers of items under that heading.

SKILL: the questions, groupings, and scores were:

A person who does my job must be . . .

Clerical skills
Able to write clearly
Good with numbers

Social skills
Good at working in a team
Good at caring for others
Good at communicating

Organizational skills
Good at solving problems
Good at organizing others
Able to plan
Good at co-ordinating a range of tasks

Physical skills
Nimble fingered
Physically strong
Physically well coordinated
Good with machinery

All the above skills were scored by respondents on a scale from 0 to 10. To calculate scores for the main types of skills the scores were added together and then divided by the number of items under that heading.

TABLE 6.4. *Perception of job content: employees' and managers' scores*

		Highest possible score	Lower-skilled production and service workers	Higher-skilled production and service workers	Technicians and lower professionals	Technologist and higher professionals	Routine clericals	Administrative and lower management	Middle management	All grades
Skills										
Physical	E	10	5.3	6.2	4.6	4.7	3.9	4.5	2.9	4.9
	M		5.3	6.3	5.5	3.4	2.8	3.8	2.5	4.6
Clerical	E	10	5.2	5.7	7.0	7.8	7.6	7.8	7.9	6.7
	M		3.2	5.1	7.7	8.2	7.4	7.6	8.2	6.3
Social	E	10	7.7	7.1	7.8	8.0	7.0	7.9	8.5	7.7
	M		6.3	6.1	7.7	8.5	6.4	7.4	9.1	7.0
Organizational	E	10	6.3	6.5	8.1	8.7	5.9	7.9	9.3	7.3
	M		3.4	4.5	7.7	8.0	4.9	7.0	9.7	5.9
Responsibilities										
Resources	E	3	1.1	1.3	1.4	1.1	1.1	1.1	1.7	1.2
	M		1.0	1.3	1.4	1.0	1.0	1.2	2.0	1.2
Records and information	E	3	0.5	0.7	1.3	1.4	1.5	1.5	2.5	1.1
	M		0.5	0.6	1.4	0.9	1.4	1.8	2.6	1.2
People	E	3	1.4	1.3	2.0	1.7	0.7	1.3	2.4	1.4
	M		1.1	1.2	2.0	1.7	0.8	1.5	2.7	1.4
Output/ standards	E	3	1.4	1.5	1.9	2.0	1.1	1.8	2.9	1.6
	M		1.1	1.7	2.1	2.1	1.3	1.8	2.9	1.7
Discretion	E	14	7.8	8.1	9.6	11.2	7.3	9.8	11.7	9.1
	M		4.3	5.9	8.6	9.8	4.2	8.1	11.9	6.9

Note: E = employees; M = managers

APPENDIX 6.3

Categorization of jobs

For the purposes of the study a seven-way classification of jobs was developed as follows:

1. lower-skilled production and service operatives
2. higher-skilled production and service operatives
3. technician and lower professional
4. technologist and higher professional
5. routine clerical
6. administrative and lower management
7. middle and senior management

Each job in the survey was classified using information from the title of the job and the employee's brief description of his/her duties. When there was any doubt as to how to classify a job, the formal qualifications required to do the job were used as additional information.

A discriminant function analysis was carried out to discover how well employees could be assigned to these seven job categories using information from the questionnaires. When the 13 questions about skills and abilities, 11 questions about responsibilities, and 3 questions about discretion (from the employees questionnaire) were entered as independent variables 70% of women's and 68% of men's jobs were correctly classified. When the same questions were used but from the management 'jobs and skills' questionnaires, 90% of women's and 80% of men's jobs were correctly classified.

The employees who were incorrectly classified were identified and if both the self-reported discriminant function analysis prediction and the management discriminant function analysis prediction agreed that the employee should be in a particular job category the case was reconsidered. In all about 10 employees were reclassified in this way.

7

Gender and Skills

SARA HORRELL, JILL RUBERY, AND BRENDAN
BURCHELL

INTRODUCTION

Current debates over women's position in the labour market often centre on the question of how women's jobs compare in quality, job content, and skill requirements to those of men's. Are women segregated into jobs which make different types of demands on employees than those that men occupy? Can women's low pay be explained by their concentration in lower-skilled jobs than the average men's job, or is the problem one of low valuation of the skills used in women's jobs? Are there major differences by gender in job content or skills or are these differences more between full- and part-time jobs?

These questions cannot be answered without systematic investigation of the actual job content and skill requirements of the jobs occupied by men and women in the economy. Published data using occupational status for these job classifications will reflect the current labour-market status of jobs, while the agenda for women's labour-market research is to investigate whether this 'status' reflects job content and skill or the 'status' of women as employees. Most useful research in this area has up to now involved case-study techniques. One purpose of these studies has been to investigate whether women's jobs involve either attributes or skills not normally included in the assessment of jobs, or whether attributes usually associated with high skill are present in women's jobs but not recognized (see e.g. Armstrong, 1982; Coyle, 1982; Crompton and Jones, 1984; Craig et al., 1985). In practice both types of 'undervaluation' of women's jobs have been found; for example personal and caring skills are explicitly looked for by management in many female service jobs (Curran

1988; Craig *et al.*, 1985) but these requirements do not serve to enhance the status and pay of women's jobs. In other cases women's jobs involve responsibilities or manual skills which are not reflected in their status or grading; in some cases the responsibilities are shared by all women in the job category, so that responsibility pay is avoided and in others manual skills are more easily underestimated because of the use of informal instead of formal training systems.

This undervaluation does not arise by chance but relates to women's low status in the labour market: to use Armstrong's famous quote 'If it's only women it doesn't matter so much' (1982: 27). How jobs come to be recognized as requiring skills or involving responsibilities is a social and not a technically determined process (Rubery, 1978; Wood, 1982). If there are few pressures to reward women with higher pay or promotion, then there will also be limited pressure to examine the job content of women's jobs to legitimize a hierarchical structure. Women may find themselves concentrated in firms, industries, or even processes (Bettio, 1988) where the ability to pay is low because of low productivity. Many of these jobs will require high skill from the workers because of the use of less automated equipment but the pay will reflect the low productivity (Craig *et al.*, 1992: ch. 6), and as a consequence these jobs may become associated with low skill. In practice individuals find it difficult to compare jobs in terms of content or skill because of inadequate knowledge and the complexities of such a multi-dimensional comparison, so that the pay level of a job may be taken as itself a proxy for skill or job content.

Although we now have quite a good understanding of how and why 'undervaluation' may occur at a case-study level, we do not know how far these case studies can be generalized to all women's jobs, or indeed whether there is not a perverse danger of focusing too much on the valuation of women's jobs and not on their confinement to low-skilled employment. A more general study was required which would compare a representative sample of women's jobs to a representative sample of men's jobs but which would also build on the insights into the likely undervaluation of women's jobs from the case-study research. The Social Change and Economic Life Initiative presented such an opportunity. The sample for the Work Attitudes Histories survey in the

Northampton labour market of 1,000 individuals, including over 600 in employment, was used as a vehicle to explore gender difference in job content and skill of a random sample of adults aged 20 to 60. Questions were designed to look at jobs from a number of different dimensions, from the more conventional dimensions of education and training to the discretion allowed in a job, the actual job content, and the various technical and social attributes that are required for doing a job well. This range of questions reflects the various academic literatures and debates on skill from the human capital school, to the Braverman 'deskilling' hypothesis (1974) and the feminist critique of conventional job categorizations. By extending the range of dimensions of job content we hoped to avoid the problems of underestimating job content, although the problem of how to measure and compare different dimensions of jobs, common to all job evaluation exercises, still necessarily remains. The use of subjective responses from individuals to investigate job content raises certain problems as we have no other observations on job requirements against which to compare the individual responses.[1] (For a discussion of further aspects of the subjectivity of skill, which are relevant to this issue, see Chapter 6 above.) However, the collection of data direct from individual job holders also has significant advantages; it increases the likelihood that the data will reflect the actual job content and labour requirements, rather than those specified in job descriptions, and it reduces the likelihood that the data will simply reflect the actual position of the job in the pay hierarchy, as may be the case if similar information is collected from management representatives.

We first use the range of data available to build up a comparison of both the *level* of skill involved in men's and women's jobs and the *similarities and differences* in the components of men's and women's skill. This analysis of the various elements of skill is then used to construct an index of skill. This first section of the chapter treats the respondents' answers to the survey as data on which a comparison of actual job content can be made. In the second section we relax this assumption and use the data to explore the neglected issue of whether there are any systematic differences in the way men and women perceive and evaluate the skills and responsibilities involved in their jobs.

The Survey Sample

The survey sample which we have used for the analysis consisted of 365 men and 333 women aged between 20 and 60, and either in employment or self-employed at the time of the survey in the summer of 1986.[2] The analyses have been carried out with a weighted sample to adjust for problems of under- and over-representation in the survey sample; in particular to adjust for any biases arising from using the Kish grid system for selection of respondents, and for the over-representation of women in the sample. Within the weighted sample males account for 59% and females for 41% of those in employment. Within the male weighted sample, employees accounted for 85% and the self-employed for 15% but in the female weighted sample the proportions are 93.5% and 6.5% respectively. Only 4% of men in employment worked part-time (using self-definition of part-time work for employees and a cut-off point of 30 hours for the self-employed) compared to 44% of females in employment. Part-time men in employment have been omitted from many of the analyses, except when whole samples are used, on the grounds of small sample numbers and the likelihood that part-time working for men cannot be equated in a labour-market sense with part-time work for women. For most of the analyses we include both employees and the self-employed; however, one or two of the questions were not asked of the self-employed and we thus construct the skill index for employees only.

COMPARING MEN'S AND WOMEN'S JOBS: TOWARDS AN INDEX OF SKILL

To compare the skill level of men's and women's jobs requires the consideration of a wide range of factors to take into account both the different aspects of skill and job content and any differences in the nature of skills between men's and women's jobs. These factors are examined under three main headings; we start with the more conventional means of comparing skills, such as occupational scales and measures of training and qualifications. Secondly, we look in more detail at specific components of skill through questions designed to investigate the range of factors that might be important in doing a job well, and the range of responsibilities a job may involve. The third part looks at the degree of discretion or autonomy.[3] We conclude this section of the chapter by attempting to bring together this disaggregated analysis into an index of skill which takes into account all the different facets of skill that we have analysed.

Skill Levels of Jobs: Some Conventional Classifications

The usual starting-point for comparing the relative quality of jobs occupied by men and women is to turn to one or more of the now numerous occupational scales. The first section of Table 7.1 uses the Registrar-General's social class categories for 1980 to compare the distribution of male and female jobs for the whole sample, and also the distributions of male and female full-time workers and female part-time workers. These analyses reveal the widely known fact that there are significant differences in the distribution of male and female jobs by social class category; both men and women are concentrated in social class 3, but women are almost exclusively in the clerical category 3.1 and men in the skilled manual 3.2. Thus although in principle social class and occupational scales are hierarchically organized, in practice in the middle range jobs are classified by type (manual or non-manual) without any direct attempt at assessing which clerical jobs should be considered 'higher-quality' than which skilled manual jobs and vice versa. Thus it is necessary to look beyond these scales to determine relative job quality and skill. However, the distributions by social class already reveal some interesting points to note about the nature of gender differences in jobs. Apart from the already mentioned differences in concentration within social class 3, women are found to be over-represented in classes 4 and 5, the semi-skilled and unskilled manual classes, and under-represented in the professional classes 1 and 2, but further disaggregation reveals that it is only female part-time workers who are over-represented in classes 4 and 5 and under-represented in classes 1 and 2, with female full-timers being slightly more likely than male full-timers to be found in the higher classes and slightly less likely to be found in the lower classes.

The problem we have identified with occupational scales is that in practice no direct comparisons of different types of jobs are

TABLE 7.1. *Conventional classifications of skill, (employees and self-employed (%))*

	M	F	MFT	FFT	FPT[a]
Social class					
1. High professional	8	2	8	4	—
2. Lower professional	29	29	28	35	21
3.1 Clerical	10	37	10	37	37
3.2 Skilled manual	34	7	34	9	5
4. Semi-skilled manual	17	19	16	12	28
5. Unskilled	3	5	3	2	8
	100	100	100	100	100
Self-definition of skill					
See job as skilled	84	59	84	72	44
Do not see job as skilled	16	41	16	28	56
	100	100	100	100	100
Qualifications required for current job					
1. Further education or A levels + training	25	18	26	25	10
2. A levels or O levels + training	9	12	9	15	7
3. O levels *or* training	31	25	31	25	25
4. No qualifications	35	45	34	34	58
	100	100	100	100	100
Training for current jobs					
1. 2 years +	32	15	33	16	12
2. 6 months–2 years	9	11	10	16	5
3. 1–6 months	20	16	17	17	14
4. None	39	59	40	51	70
	100	100	100	100	100
Time taken to learn to do job well (employees only)					
1. 2 years +	31	13	33	17	9
2. 6 months–2 years	23	17	23	25	9
3. Up to 6 months	46	70	44	57	83
	100	100	100	100	100

Table 7.1. *Cont.*

	All	Full-timers	Women
Social class	G S	G S	FP S FP/S³
Skill	G	G	FP
Qualifications required	[G²]S	S	FP S
Training	G S	G⁴ S	[FP] S
Learning time	G S	G² S	FP S²

Analysis of variance[b]

[a] M and F used in all tables for all men and all women in employment, and MFT, FFT, FPT used for males in full-time jobs, females in full-time jobs; females in part-time jobs.

[b] G = gender, S = skill, FP = working time. Symbols are included if significant as 5% or less: significance is 1% unless otherwise indicated by superscript. Square brackets indicate a gender or working-time effect that was significant with a one-way analysis of variance but not in the two-way analysis of variance when 'skill' was controlled for. Significant interaction terms are shown by both symbols separated by /.

made. The remaining four variables shown in Table 7.1 do allow direct comparisons to be made. The first makes use of the respondents' own skill classification, that is, the response to a question in the survey 'Do you consider your current job to be skilled?' No less than 84% of men considered their current job to be skilled compared to only 59% of women. Further disaggregation again reveals that much of this gender difference is associated with women's concentration in part-time jobs. Comparing only the full-time workers shows a much smaller gender difference (84% to 72%) but only 44% of women in part-time jobs considered themselves to be in skilled jobs.

The final three variables are associated with the conventional means of comparing the skill levels of jobs, that is by comparing the 'investments in human capital' necessary to gain entry to the job or to learn to do the job well. Three aspects of training or learning are looked at. First the qualifications which the respondent considered would now be necessary for someone to get their kind of job (that is, distinct from both the respondent's own qualifications and from what was required when the respondent first got the job). The detailed responses to this question have been collapsed into four categories: a further-education qualification or a minimum combination of A levels plus some training; A levels or O levels plus some training; O levels or some training; no qualifications. The data show that men are significantly more likely to be employed in jobs with higher-qualification entry requirements than are women. However, dis-aggregation so that only men and women in full-time jobs are compared this time not only reduces the gender differential but actually reverses it so that women are significantly more likely to be employed in jobs with higher entry requirements. In practice almost all of the difference revolves around the middle two categories, with women much more likely to require A levels or O levels plus training, and men more likely to require only O levels or training (including here apprenticeships). Approximately one-third of both male and female full-timers require no qualifications for their jobs and approximately one-quarter of both groups require further education. These percentages compare to 58% of part-time jobs requiring no qualifications and 10% requiring further education.

Respondents were also asked whether they had received training for their current job and to estimate how long the training had lasted. This question on training was followed by a question of how long it had taken them after starting to do this type of work to learn to do it well (in this case only asked of employees, not the self-employed). The purpose of asking both about training and learning time was to try to ensure that the more informal types of training and learning by doing were included but, in practice, the pattern of responses to the two questions is remarkably similar, with significantly longer training and learning periods reported for men compared to women. This time when the data were disaggregated into full-time jobs and part-time jobs the difference between men and women's jobs, taking only full-timers, was reduced but remained significant in favour of men. However, the difference between the position for part-timers and that of full-timers, both male and female, is just as large as that for qualifications; 70% of part-timers said they had no training, and 83% said they had learnt to do their job well in under six months, compared to percentages for full-timers which varied from 40% to 51% for no training, and 44% to 57% for learning within six months.

One of the problems of analysing a whole set of variables associated with various aspects of skill for differences by gender and by working time is that it is not clear whether one is uncovering the same set of gender or working-time differences because of the correlations between the different variables or differences which either further amplify or modify the differences previously uncovered. To overcome this problem at least partially we have not only analysed the three samples (the whole sample of those in work, all in full-time jobs, and all women in work) using a one-way analysis of variance to test for gender differences in the first two samples and differences by working time among women,[4] but we have also used a two-way analysis of variance, to test for gender or working-time differences in responses after taking into account differences in the shares of 'skilled' jobs held by men and women or by full-timers and part-timers. The variable that we have used to control for the 'skill' of the job is the second variable analysed in Table 7.1, namely the perception by the respondents of whether their job was skilled. In fact, throughout the text we refer to jobs as 'skilled', using inverted commas, when these jobs are distinguished from 'unskilled' jobs simply on the basis of respondents' perceptions of their jobs as 'skilled'. The adequacy of this variable as an 'objective' control for skill will be returned to in the last section of this chapter. However, as the control variable may itself capture some sex bias in the sense that women and part-timers may be less likely to evaluate their job as skilled after controlling for job content and quality (see below), the use of this variable as a control factor in fact provides a very strong test of whether there are further gender and working-time differences, which exist over and above those accounted for in the response to the skill question.

The results of the two-way analyses of variance are presented in summary form at the bottom of Table 7.1.[5] The results from the one-way analyses testing for either a gender effect (for the whole sample or the sample of full-timers) or a working-time effect (for the sample of women) are only presented, and indicated in square brackets, whenever the gender or the working-time variable was not significant in the two-way analysis but was significant when 'skill' was not controlled for. These results show that for almost all the two-way analyses of variance gender and working time were significant even after controlling for 'skill'. 'Skill' was positively related to social class for both full- and part-time women workers, but the difference between the social class levels of 'skilled' and 'unskilled' part-time women's jobs was much greater than was the case for full-time women's jobs.[6] However, in general gender and working-time differences in job content do not seem to interact with the skill variable and are found to exist even after controlling for differences in shares of 'skilled' jobs.[7]

Components of Skill

So far we have been looking at a fairly standard range of variables which can be used as overall or global indicators of skill. An alternative approach, and one that is necessary in order to explore the issues associated with equal-value claims, is to look for diversity in the types or components of skill between men's and women's jobs. Indeed, if the types of skills and the ways in which those skills are acquired and used differ markedly between men's and women's jobs, then it is improbable that any fully satisfactory way of comparing levels of skills can be arrived at. Two batteries of questions were included in the team-specific part of the Northampton area work attitudes survey to explore the extent of diversity in men's and women's jobs. The first asked respondents to say how important they considered each of six factors to be in doing their job well. These factors included two which were related to specific experience or knowledge (lengthy experience of this type of work; having professional, scientific, technical, or business knowledge), one related to personal aptitude (having a particular knack or talent for this type of work), and three related to specific organizational knowledge or social skills (knowing your way round the organization; good relations with people at work; good contacts with clients or customers). The potential importance of social and organizational skills has been increasingly stressed in the literature on internal labour markets where the skills necessary to function in a collective labour process may be more important than simple technical skills (Manwaring, 1984). Moreover, personal and social skills may take on increasing importance with the sectoral shift towards service-based occupations (Curran, 1988) where good relations with clients become critical for commercial success, and analyses of skill which emphasize traditional manual and manufacturing-type skills may be underestimating the level of skills involved in the expanding job sectors.

The respondents' responses for each of these factors were scored from 1 (not important at all) to 5 (absolutely essential) and the average scores are shown in Table 7.2. There are significant differences in the distributions of responses for all six factors between men and women but the direction of the sex difference varied by factor. Women were more likely to stress the importance of good contacts with clients and customers and good relations with people at work, while men scored higher on the other four factors. However, analysis of responses for only full-time workers still revealed a strong gender difference in the importance attached to good relations at work and contacts with clients and customers, but the only factor where men continued to score significantly higher than women was on lengthy experience of this type of work. There was very little difference in mean scores attached to the remaining three factors: knowing your way round the organization; having a particular knack or talent; and, perhaps most surprisingly, having professional, scientific, technical, or business knowledge. The increased similarity between men and women which emerges when only full-timers are considered is matched by a widening divergence between part-timers and full-timers. However, the two factors which women were found to stress, relations at work and contacts with clients, did not fall into this pattern as there was virtually no difference in the average scores for women working full-time or part-time. These factors are thus clearly related to all types of women's jobs, whereas on the other four factors there is a much clearer difference between full- and part-time jobs than by gender *per se*. These results are also associated with differences in the proportion of 'skilled' jobs held by part-timers; 'skill' was associated with higher scores for all factors for the sample of women, and when the 'skill' variable is included in the analysis of variance, the part-time/full-time distinction is only significant for 'lengthy experience of this type of work' and for 'having a particular knack or talent'. The 'skill' variable is also significant for all factors for the whole sample, with the result that gender is not significant for having a knack or talent or having specialist knowledge. For full-timers the three factors already identified to have a gender effect remain significant by gender even when 'skill' is controlled for, while 'skill' is found to be significant for all factors except knowing your way round the organization and good relations at work.

TABLE 7.2 *Factors important in doing the job well, (employees and self-employed)*

	Mean scores[a]				
	M	F	MFT	FFT	FPT
1. Lengthy experience of this type of work	3.58	3.06	3.60	3.28	2.78
2. Knowing your way round the organization	3.40	3.14	3.41	3.31	2.93
3. Good relations with people at work	3.57	3.85	3.56	3.86	3.83
4. Good contacts with clients or customers	3.69	3.90	3.68	3.94	3.85
5. Having a particular knack or talent for this type of work	3.61	3.40	3.60	3.62	3.13
6. Having professional, scientific, technical or business knowledge	2.95	2.57	2.95	2.82	2.25
% saying essential or very important on:					
5 or 6 factors	25	20	26	25	13
3 or 4 factors	40	40	40	39	40
1 or 2 factors	28	32	28	31	33
0 factors	7	9	7	5	14

Analysis of variance[b]

	All	Full-timers	Women
1.	G S	G S	FP S
2.	G S		[FP] S
3.	GS^2	G	S
4.	G S	G S	S
5.	[G] S	S	FP S
6.	[G] S	S	[FP] S
no. of factors	[G^5] S	S	[FP] S

[a] Score 1 to 5; 5 = essential, 1 = not important at all.
[b] See note b to Table 7.1.

Gender and working time are thus clearly related to differences in importance rating for particular factors; but while gender is associated with differences in the factors emphasized by men and women (in particular women stress more social skills), working time is associated with part-timers having lower scores on most factors than full-timers. Introduction of the 'skill' variable tends to reduce the importance of the working-time distinction and also some gender effects (mainly those where men appeared to score higher before 'skill' was controlled for). Care must be taken with the interpretation of these findings because of possible differences in the propensities of men and women and full- and part-timers to consider their jobs to be skilled.

The purpose of including this question on different factors was essentially to explore diversity in types of skills. However, some jobs may involve a large number of these factors and for others only one or two may be relevant. The last section of Table 7.2 shows the percentage of respondents who considered that no less than 5 or 6 of the factors to be either absolutely essential or very important for their job, compared for example to the percentage who did not think any of the factors to be essential or even very important. Most respondents in practice fell into the middle two categories, identifying between one and four factors as very important for their job, with these categories accounting for between 68% and 73% of the sample for each group. The main difference in distributions is again between the female part-time workers and all full-timers, with part-timers being much more likely to consider none of the factors to be very important and much less likely to consider five or more to be very important. Two-way analysis of variance, however, reveals that much of this difference is again accounted for by the 'skill' variable, with the working-time variable losing significance once 'skill' is controlled for.

The second battery of questions which we included to tap diversity of skills was one relating to responsibilities in the job. The association of responsibility with concepts of skill or job status has been well established. Analyses of the restructuring of employment following automation and 'deskilling' of manual work have pointed to the way responsibilities, for output, value added, or quality, have been used to replace manual skill as a basis for job grading (Stieber, 1959; Bettio, 1988). Responsibility is also included as a key concept in most job-evaluation schemes, but the types of responsibility cited in a scheme do not necessarily reflect the full range of possibilities. Our concern was to try to identify all the types of responsibility that respondents felt their job involved, and not simply to concentrate on those normally included in a pay-grading scheme. In addition to the question in the core part of the questionnaire on whether their job involved supervisory responsibilities,[8] respondents in Northampton were also asked to say if their job involved each or any of the following responsibilities: for health or safety of others; for checking work; for machines, materials, or goods; for confidential information; for money; for maintaining output or services; and for meeting official or professional standards of quality or reliability. The first point to note in passing is the very high shares of respondents who consider their jobs to involve these responsibilities; with the exceptions of responsibility for money and responsibility for supervision, in each case over 50% of both men and women responded positively. Perhaps surprisingly the responsibility which attracted the highest response rate from both men and women (80% and 66% respectively) was that for meeting official or professional standards, possibly indicating a widespread feeling of responsibility for standards and quality (see Table 7.3).

The list of responsibilities was designed to include some types of responsibilities thought to be associated with female jobs and others more often associated with male jobs, alongside others where we had no particular preconceptions of the likely outcomes. As with the analysis of importance factors, however, differences in response are not found to be simply related to gender but also to relate to 'skill' and to working time. In fact the only responsibility which women were more likely to lay claim to was that for confidential information. Further disaggregation revealed that this was more a responsibility associated with female full-time jobs than with all female jobs. With the exception of confidential information and money, males were found to be significantly more likely than women to claim they had each of the other responsibilities, a result which also held true for comparisons of full-timers alone (except this time for responsibility for maintaining output or standards and responsibility for supervising others). However, controlling for 'skill' reduces the significance of gender, particularly when comparing full-timers, such that the only cases where men are found to be significantly

TABLE 7.3. *Responsibilities involved in the job, (employees and self-employed) (%)*

	M	F	MFT	FFT	FPT
Having responsibility for:					
1. Supervising others	48	31	48	43	15
2. Safety or health of others	69	53	69	51	54
3. Checking work	71	53	74	65	39
4. Machines, materials or goods	76	54	76	56	53
5. Confidential information	57	63	57	71	52
6. Money	44	48	44	47	49
7. Maintaining output or services	71	59	71	64	52
8. Meeting official or professional standards of quality and reliability	80	66	80	71	59
Considered their job involved:					
6–8 responsibilities	44	32	45	41	20
3–5 responsibilities	44	44	44	40	50
0–2 responsibilities	12	24	12	19	31

Analysis of variance

	All	Full-timers	Women
1.	G S	S	FP S
2.	[G] S^3	G S	
3.	G S	[G^5]S G/S^2	FP^2 S
4.	G	G	
5.	G S	G S	FP^5 S
6.	S	S	S
7.	G^2 S	S	[FP^3] S
8.	G^3 S	[G^2] S	S
no. of responsibilities	G S	S	[FP] S

Note: See notes a and b to Table 7.1

more likely to claim responsibilities after controlling for 'skill' are for the safety or health of others and for machines, materials, or goods. The skill variable is in fact found to be a significant factor for the whole sample and full-timers on all items except machines, materials, or goods. This last responsibility in fact seems to be generally related to male jobs irrespective of 'skill'. Women in part-time jobs are the least likely to say they have responsibility in six out of the eight cases, but there is only a significant difference for confidential information, checking work,[9] maintaining output, and, most marked of all, for supervising others. Only 15% of part-timers had this type of responsibility compared to over 40% for full-timers, and this low percentage compares with between 39% and 59% scores on all the other responsibility variables for part-timers. Taking the female sample alone, 'skill' is found to be significantly associated with claiming responsibility for all items except safety and health and machines, materials, or goods.

To summarize, then, the only responsibility clearly positively associated with the female gender is confidential information and this in turn is found only to be a characteristic of female full-time jobs. On most items, except responsibility for money which is only related to 'skill', males tend to score higher and part-timers lower, with female full-timers occupying a middle position. Part-timers are particularly unlikely to have responsibility for supervising others for checking work. However, these relationships are also closely related to 'skill' and the only item where men's higher score is not related to being in a 'skilled' job is responsibility for machines, materials, or goods.

The last section of Table 7.3 completes the analysis of this question by summarizing responses to all eight items. Men are significantly more likely to have responded positively to a large number of items, both for the whole sample and for full-timers only. Part-timers are much less likely to have responded positively to a large number of items and more likely to have said yes to two or fewer items. Again the number of responsibilities claimed is positively related to being in a 'skilled' job so that when 'skill' is controlled for gender is no longer found to be significant for full-timers, nor working time for the sample of women workers.

Discretion

The final aspect of jobs we explore as an indicator of skill is the degree of discretion or control that men and women feel they have over the way they do their work and the effort they put into their work; this accords with the Braverman (1974) notion of skill as the opportunity to exercise judgement and discretion within the job.

Three main questions were asked in the core survey which throw light on these issues. First, respondents were asked how much choice they felt they had over the way in which they did their job. Table 7.4 shows that there was very little difference in the responses to this question by men and women; 60% of men and 55% of women felt they had a great deal of choice and 8% of men and 12% of women felt they had no choice at all. The pattern of responses was even more similar when full-timers only were compared, and although the usual differences between full- and part-time women were revealed, these were of a much smaller magnitude than most of the other data we have been analysing, with 51% of part-timers still feeling they had a great deal of choice. 'Skill' was found to be more important than gender in determining the degree of choice; it was not found to be significant for the sample of women workers alone, but its inclusion in the two-way analysis of variance did serve to reduce the significance of the working-time variable.

The second question relating to autonomy specifically asked about the closeness of supervision. Women were significantly more likely to have close supervision than men but the differences were in practice quite small, with 73% of men and 68% of women saying either that they were not supervised at all or that they were not supervised at all closely. For once a higher percentage of women in part-time jobs fell into the unsupervised category (70% compared to 64% of women's full-time jobs); also the 'skill' variable was found not to be significant. There thus seems to be little evidence of a gender, a working-time, or a 'skill' factor in explaining the degree of supervision. The nature of the job and the actual possibilities for supervision may be in practice the critical variables which are not captured by the survey data.

The final question associated with the issue of autonomy and discretion asked respondents to say which factors were important in determining how hard they worked. These data thus enable us to explore the mechanisms of control, instead of the perceived level of choice or supervision. The most striking overall finding is that two-thirds of the sample considered that their own discretion was important in determining how hard they worked, and this

TABLE 7.4. *Scope for discretion or choice at work, (employees and self-employed) (%)*

	M	F	MFT	FFT	FPT
Amount of choice over the way that you do the job					
A great deal	60	55	60	59	51
Some	24	26	24	28	24
Hardly any	8	7	8	4	10
No choice at all	8	12	8	9	14
Closeness of supervision					
Not supervised at all	41	31	41	27	34
Not at all closely supervised	32	37	32	37	36
Quite closely supervised	20	24	20	25	22
Very closely supervised	8	9	8	10	8
Factors important in determining how hard you work					
1. Machine/assembly line	7	6	7	8	3
2. Clients/customers	32	47	31	47	45
3. Supervisor/boss	25	27	26	31	21
4. Fellow workers or colleagues	30	32	29	41	23
5. Own discretion	66	66	67	67	63
6. Pay incentives	29	7	28	9	5
7. Reports/appraisals	18	13	18	18	8

Analysis of variance

	All	Full-timers	Women
Choice	S	S	[FP⁵]
Supervision	[G]	G³	—
How hard you work:			
1.			
2.	G	G	
3.			
4.		G²	FP
5.			
6.	G	G	
7.	S²		FF²S⁴

Note: See notes a and b to Table 7.1.

proportion was remarkably similar for men and women, and for full- and part-timers. At the other extreme very few respondents considered that a machine or assembly line was important in determining how hard they worked. Only two factors were significantly related to gender: a much higher percentage of both full- and part-time women workers said that clients and customers were important in determining how hard they work than was the case for men. Conversely, pay incentives were much more frequently cited as a determinant of effort for men than for women. Women in full-time jobs were more likely to cite fellow workers and colleagues as important than were full-time men, but this did not appear as a general gender effect, as part-time women workers were the least likely to mention fellow workers or colleagues. The only factor to show a major difference between full- and part-timers was report and appraisal systems, but this difference may have arisen primarily because such systems were not used in part-time jobs. In practice all the gender effects we have identified are likely to be primarily related to the actual nature of the job and not necessarily to differences in the way women and men respond to constraints and incentives. Unfortunately, however, we have no data to check the proportions of men and women in jobs with pay incentives, or in jobs where there is direct customer contact. There is, however, indirect evidence to suggest that the system of control is not simply related to the status of the worker, but also to the intrinsic characteristics of the job. Unlike most of the other variables relating to job quality, the system of control was not related to whether or not the respondent perceived the job as 'skilled'. Clearly no attempt was made here to measure intensity of control or autonomy but nevertheless it is interesting that only reports and appraisals were significantly related to 'skill'.

All three variables relating to discretion and autonomy have failed to show very striking differences between the sexes, or between full- and part-time jobs. If discretion and autonomy are, as Braverman (1974) suggested, key indicators of skill, then either there is less difference between the skill level of men's and women's jobs than has been thought to be the case, or women do not perceive the constraints imposed upon them. An alternative explanation may be that discretion and autonomy are much more widespread characteristics of jobs than the deskilling debate would have us believe, and thus they are not the key distinguishing characteristics separating out the 'skilled' from the 'unskilled'. This supports Blackburn and Mann's (1979) finding that the degree of autonomy was an important variable within the 'unskilled' or non-qualified male labour market. It also appears to be the case that the deskilling debate has focused attention too much on the technological and supervisory control systems associated with manufacturing, and too little attention has been paid to the more social forms of control, arising for example from direct contact with customers, which are potentially just as constraining as machine control.

Constructing an Index of Skill

To summarize our findings across the spectrum of factors associated with skill that the data has allowed us to analyse, we have constructed an index of skill. We have included seven factors in the index for employees: for the first five factors we have allowed a maximum score of 2, but for the last two, which both relate to discretion, we have only allowed a maximum score of 1. The discretion variables have already been found not to have a strong discriminatory effect between either types of jobs or labour-supply categories. The maximum total score is thus 12. The details of the factor scores are as follows:

1. qualifications required: higher education, 2; some but below higher, 1;
2. length of training for current job; over 2 years, 2; 6 months to 2 years, 1;
3. length of time taken to learn to do job well; over 2 years, 2; 6 months to 2 years, 1;
4. importance attached to factors in doing job well; very important or essential on 5 or 6 factors, 2; on 3 or 4 factors, 1;
5. number of responsibilities in the job; 6 to 8 responsibilities, 2; 3 to 5 responsibilities, 1;
6. the degree of choice over how the job is done; a great deal of choice, 1;
7. how closely the job is supervised; not supervised or not at all closely supervised, 1.

The main variables that we have analysed in the preceding sections but which are not included here are the social class of the job and the perception of the job as 'skilled'. The purpose of constructing the skill index is to some extent to provide an alternative way of grading the job to that offered by social-class categories, so inclusion of a social-class score would be inappropriate. Similarly we are attempting to summarize the factors that may influence whether or not a job might be considered to be skilled and it thus appeared more appropriate to compare the skill index to the direct question on whether the respondent considered the job to be skilled than to include the latter in the construction of the index. Inclusion would have introduced an element of double counting, as is borne out by the almost 100% correlation between those in the top band of the skill index (see Table 7.6) and their perception of their job as 'skilled'. We also omitted the question on which factors determined how hard the

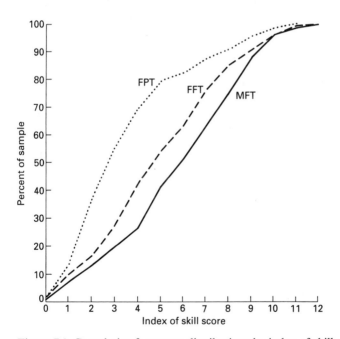

Figure 7.1 Cumulative frequency distributions by index of skill
FPT = females in part-time jobs; FFT/MFT = female/males in full time jobs

respondent worked, as these could not be readily converted to a hierarchical scale.

The cumulative frequency distributions of the skill index for male full-timers, female full-timers, and female part-timers (Figure 1) show clearly the pattern of divisions by skill implied by our analyses of the individual variables; male full-time jobs are distinctly less likely to fall into the lower-skill categories than female full-time jobs, thereby providing evidence of a gender effect in the distribution of skilled jobs, but by far the largest difference in the distributions is between part-time jobs and full-time jobs, with a distinct concentration of part-time jobs in the low-skilled categories, 69% of part-time jobs coming into the bottom third of the scale for the skill index. Table 7.5 summarizes these findings by showing the percentages of the distributions falling into three skill-index bands; low skill from 0 to 4 points; medium skill from 5 to 8 points, and high skill from 9 to 12 points. This banding helps to reveal the main differences between the groups: both the male and the female full-time jobs are concentrated in the medium-skill category, but women in full-time jobs are much more likely to fall into the low-skill category than men in full-time jobs (42% compared to 26%) and men are much more likely to be found in the high-skill category (25% compared to 15%). In contrast part-timers are very heavily concentrated in the low-skill category, although the share found in the high-skill category (9%) is not insignificant. The one-way analysis of vari-

TABLE 7.5. *Index of skill, (employees)* (%)

	M	F	MFT	FFT	FPT
Low (0–4)	27	55	26	42	69
Medium (5–8)	49	33	49	43	21
High (9–12)	24	12	25	15	9

Analysis of variance

	All	Full-timers	Women
Whole index	G S	[G] S	FP^5 S

Note: See notes a and b to Table 7.1.

ance showed a significant relationship between gender and the distribution across the skill index for the whole sample and for full-timers alone. Gender was no longer found to be significant for full-timers once the perception of the job as 'skilled' was entered into a two-way analysis of variance, but gender continued to be significant for the sample taken as a whole, indicating that for part-timers anyway the concentration in the lower-skill band was not fully explained by their responses to the 'skill' question. This finding is confirmed by the fact that both the working-time variable and the 'skill' variable were significantly related to the score on the skill index for the sample of women.

Perhaps more significant than the differences in the distribution of jobs between men and women full-timers is the extensive overlap in the distributions, so that 75% of male full-time jobs and 85% of female full-time jobs fall into the first two-thirds of the skill-index scale. Thus explanations of the low degree of overlap between male and female full-time workers' pay which stress women's concentration in lower-skilled jobs than men must be looked upon with scepticism (see Horrell *et al.*, 1989), although the argument for part-time work may be more sustainable, provided there is not a significant bias in the way part-timers perceive the demands of their job compared to full-timers.

Summary

Several points emerge fairly clearly from our analysis of the data on the skills involved in male and female jobs. The first is that there does seem to be a relatively systematic tendency for men to occupy more skilled jobs than women. The difference between the skill of men's and women's jobs declines if we compare only full-time jobs, but it is nevertheless apparent. The only factor on which women scored higher than men was the level of qualifications required to obtain the job; this is a very important indicator of the high quality of women's jobs but the weight of the evidence from all the other factors nevertheless suggests that men still have jobs with higher skill requirements. However, the more surprising aspect of this finding is the relative smallness of the differences in levels of skill between men's and women's full-time jobs, certainly in comparison to the much greater differences between full- and part-time jobs. It is in this major growth area of employment that the main differences in job quality and skill are occurring, thereby worsening the pattern of distribution of skilled jobs for women taken as a whole.

The second finding is that there are significant differences in the types of skill required in men's and women's jobs; in particular women tend to mention more social skills and social constraints, notably the role of direct contact with clients and customers, more frequently than do men. Too much of the debate on skills in the literature has concentrated on either the skills used by men or the skills used in manufacturing; there needs to be more research into the types of skills and the types of constraints found in women's jobs and in all service-sector jobs. A third related finding is the lack of a strong systematic link between other aspects of skill and the degree of discretion or autonomy in a job. Partly this finding arises from trying to make comparisons across the whole range of jobs, including manual and non-manual, service and manufacturing, and while there may be a link between levels of skill and autonomy in any particular organization or sector, differences in the nature of the job intervene to reduce the likelihood of finding such a relationship at the aggregate level. A further explanation may be that the reliance on workers' skill and discretion may be more pervasive than has been recognized because of the influence of the deskilling debate. In particular women may be used in low-grade or supposedly low-skill jobs in preference to men because they are considered to be more reliable in situations where even low-grade workers still have considerable discretion and autonomy.

This issue also brings us to the fourth finding, namely the relatively high scores from respondents on many of the questions about skill, suggesting that a large share of the employed population see their jobs as requiring a range of different and often quite demanding skills and responsibilities; the workforce as a whole does not appear convinced by either the deskilling argument or the argument that the qualities and attributes of the worker makes little difference to the productivity of the job in the lower-job grades. (This finding seems to complement the comments in Chapter 6 on the undervaluation of skills by managers.) However, for this survey we have no other independent evidence on job demands against which to compare the descriptions the respondents provided of their jobs, and thus the ques-

tion of the actual pervasiveness of skill and discretion requirements cannot be further explored. This question raises a related
issue, namely how individuals perceive and describe their jobs. So
far we have taken respondents' answers at face value as descriptions of jobs that can be aggregated and compared across individuals, and the relatively systematic patterns across a range of
variables that we have uncovered suggest that the data do reflect
differences in the quality of jobs. However, to the extent that
individuals, or indeed the sexes, differ in the way they perceive
and describe their jobs, we may need to modify or qualify the
above conclusions drawing on actual differences in jobs between
labour-force groups. It is to this issue of perceptions of skill by
men and women that we now turn.

PERCEPTIONS OF SKILL

From our initial analyses we already know that the overwhelming majority of men consider themselves to be in a 'skilled' job,
that a sizeable majority of women in full-time jobs consider their
jobs to be 'skilled', but that only 44% of women in part-time jobs
consider their jobs to be 'skilled'. We also know, from our analyses of variance, that many of the other job characteristics associated with skill are correlated with whether or not the respondent
considered themselves to be in a 'skilled' job. There is thus good
corroborating evidence to suggest that in answering the question
whether they considered their job to be 'skilled', the respondents
were using as their frame of reference the set of factors which
are generally recognized as contributing to skill (training,
qualifications, responsibilities, special skills or qualities, etc.). The
evidence of consistent responses across a range of diverse questions throughout a long questionnaire also provides support for
the view that the data can be taken to reveal genuine differences
in jobs between respondents. However, there may still be important differences in the significance that a particular individual or
type of worker will attach to a particular job characteristic.
These differences may be especially likely to occur if there is a
systematic tendency in the labour market for the skills and job
content of particular groups to be undervalued (that is, precisely
the phenomenon that we are engaged in investigating here) for

that undervaluation may even affect the employees' perception of their job.

These questions cannot be fully explored here but we have considered this question from one perspective, that is, by exploring whether there is any difference in the probability of men and women and full- and part-timers to describe their jobs as 'skilled', once one has controlled for other aspects of job content. The most general way of controlling for job content is to use our constructed index of skill. Table 7.6 shows that in the highest-skill bracket there is an almost perfect tendency for individuals from all labour-force groups to consider their job to be 'skilled', but in the medium- and lower-skill brackets women in part-time jobs are much less likely than full-timers to consider their jobs to be 'skilled'. It must be stressed that these results come about even after controlling for job content and are thus independent of the very high concentration of part-timers in the low-skilled bracket. No significant difference was found between male and female full-timers in their propensity to describe their jobs as 'skilled' after controlling for the index of skill. However, some gender differences between full-timers do appear in the rest of Table 7.6 where we have undertaken a similar analysis for the main variables used to construct the index of skill and for social class and

TABLE 7.6. *Perceptions of own job as skilled, controlling for index of skill, for component variables in the index of skill, and for social class, (employees and self-employed) (%)*

	MFT	FFT	FPT
Index of skill (IS) (employees only)			
Low skill	55	47	29
Medium skill	90	87	66
High skill	97	100	100
Qualifications required for the job (QR) Further education or A levels			
+ training	98	98	100
A levels or O levels			
+ training	97	84	68
O levels *or* training	86	77	59
No qualifications	69	55	25

	MFT	FFT	FPT
Training for current job (T)			
2 years +	97	100	100
6 months–2 years	97	88	83
1–6 months	82	78	43
None	71	55	31
Time taken to learn to do the job well (L) (employees only)			
2 years +	96	91	89
6 months–2 years	91	90	70
Up to 6 months	76	60	37
Importance of factors in doing job well (F)			
Essential or very important on:			
5 or 6 factors	95	89	79
3 or 4 factors	89	81	50
1 or 2 factors	74	46	33
0 factors	48	73	20
Number of responsibilities in job (R)			
6–8 responsibilities	90	87	75
3–5 responsibilities	83	75	39
0–2 responsibilities	61	35	31
Social class (SC)			
1. Higher professional	97	100	—
2. Lower professional	92	84	82
3.1 Clerical	88	61	47
3.2 Skilled manual	87	77	71
4. Semi-skilled manual	66	60	13
5. Unskilled manual	36	33	10

Analysis of variance

	Full-timers	Women
Index of skill IS	IS	FP IS
Qualifications required QR	G QR	FP QR
Training T	G T	FP T
Learning time L	G^4L	L
Importance of factors F	G F F/G	FP F
No. of responsibilities R	G R	FP R FP/R^4
Social class SC	G^2 SC	

Note: See notes a and b to Table 7.1.

occupational segregation. These all reveal a systematic tendency for part-timers to be much less likely to consider themselves to be 'skilled' after controlling for social class, qualifications required, training time, learning time (although not a significant difference), number of factors considered essential or important to do the job well, and number of responsibilities involved in the job. Thus part-timers appear to need to register a higher score on all of these factors than is the case for full-timers before they would consider their job to be 'skilled'.

Female full-timers were also significantly less likely to consider their job to be 'skilled' than male full-timers when controlling for each of the aspects of skill and social class. However, closer examination of the data reveals that much of this difference occurs in the lowest-skill bands. Thus women who have no qualifications, have received no training, are able to learn their job in six months, and have less than three responsibilities in their job are all much less likely to consider their job to be 'skilled' than men who gave the same responses, while the proportions who say their jobs are 'skilled' in the middle ranges of job content are much more similar between men and women. The data on importance of factors in doing the job well appear to contradict this trend, as a high percentage of women with no scores of essential or important consider their job to be 'skilled' but only eight full-time women fell into this category, so the high share only relates to six observations. Much of the difference in perceptions of 'skill' that thus emerges between men and women is more related to men's tendency to say they are in a 'skilled' job even when their job scores low points on any measure of job content. However, there is also a further significant and even more striking tendency for women in part-time jobs to do the opposite and maintain that their job is not 'skilled' even when scoring medium points on job content or quality. Only in the top parts of the job-content scales are part-time women as likely as full-time women to say that their job is 'skilled'. These findings of a tendency by women and part-timers to downgrade the skill level of their jobs may also apply to their assessments of other aspects of job content. For example women or part-timers may be less likely to recognize that they have responsibilities in a job or to stress the importance of various factors and qualities. If there is a systematic downward bias in the other aspects of job quality, then we would be underestimating the tendency for women and part-timers to downgrade their skill as each level of job content would represent a higher actual level of job content than was the case for men.

This evidence of differences in the tendency for men and women, and in particular women in part-time jobs, to describe their jobs as 'skilled', encouraged us to explore this issue further by asking in a follow-up survey, based on a subset of the original survey sample, not only whether they considered their job to be 'skilled' but also why they said that they thought their job was 'skilled' or not. (Francis and Penn, in the next chapter, report the results of asking a somewhat different question: what people meant by a 'skilled' job *in general*.) This follow-up survey sample only covered 184 of the original respondents. Using the same weighting as used for the main survey, this sample represented 168 respondents, of which 130 were in employment, and only 79 were in the same job. Comparisons of the responses of those who were still in the same job to the question whether they considered their job to be 'skilled' in the 1986 main survey with their responses to an identical question in the 1988 follow-up survey revealed that of the respondents who initially thought their job was 'skilled' 94% still considered their job to be 'skilled' two years later. However, only 5 of the 12 (42%) who had said they were not 'skilled' in the original survey and had remained in the same job still claimed to be 'unskilled' two years later. This upgrading of their perceptions of their jobs may be in part the result of completing extensive detailed surveys about their current job, which may have made them more conscious of what their job entailed. A further interesting methodological issue is revealed by the follow-up survey; although in principle the selection of respondents for the follow-up survey was random, in practice the achieved sample included a higher proportion of those who in the first survey had considered their job to be 'skilled'. Thus those in 'skilled' jobs appear to be more likely to be willing or available for reinterviewing. The consequence of this bias in selection was that in practice we only obtained a very limited number of responses to the question why they had said their job was not 'skilled' (20) compared to over 100 responses to why they said they thought their job as 'skilled'.[10] The responses to the question why they considered their job to be 'skilled' are analysed in Table 7.7.[11] The need for special training or qualifications was the most frequent response by both men and women. Men were, however, more likely to emphasize the nature of the job itself and any special expertise and knowledge required than were women. Other factors that were relatively frequently mentioned by women but not by men were the need for personal qualities such as patience and on-the-job experience. The differences between men and women in their responses were relatively small, but where differences can be detected they support the view that women emphasize social or personal skills and informal experience, and men, where they do not require special training, still tend to see the job they do as inherently skilled. This latter

TABLE 7.7. *Why respondents consider their jobs to be 'skilled' or not 'skilled'* (no. of responses: main reason only)

Job requirements	Males	Females in:	
		Full-time jobs	Part-time jobs
SKILLED			
Training, qualifications, or apprenticeship	19	8	6
Expertise, special knowledge	17	4	2
On-the-job experience	2	5	1
Personal attributes (e.g. patience)	1	4	1
Special abilities (not many can do it)	4	2	—
Job itself is skilled	18	6	3
Other	—	1	—
TOTAL	61	30	13
NOT SKILLED			
No training required	1	—	—
Anyone can do it	1	2	5
Job itself not skilled	2	—	6
Practice needed, not skill	1	—	—
Other	—	1	—
TOTAL	5	3	11

Source: Welfare survey 1988, carried out by PAS on behalf of the Cambridge SCELI team.

emphasis suggests that men tend to consider their own job as much more special and different from other jobs than do women, and could explain the tendency for men to consider their job to be 'skilled' even when scoring low on other aspects of job content as measured by the skill index.

The most frequent explanations of why both men and women considered their job not to be 'skilled' referred to the simple or repetitive nature of the job or to the fact that 'anyone can do it'. Some of the specific answers given, however, provide clues as to the reasons why women may tend to underestimate the skill level of their jobs. Some of their responses showed a tendency to downgrade the status or skill of a job because it was associated with female skills: 'anyone who knows how to sew could do it' or 'just working with old people is not a skilled job' or 'just a shop assistant'. One showed a clear tendency to equate skill with formal training only, and to discount qualities or attributes that may be acquired by other means: 'I suppose I haven't actually trained—more a caring job than a skill.' Others did not seem to count the training or experience they had acquired as important; 'anyone can do it with a bit of training' or 'it's the same job in any shop and a skill you acquire from experience'. Most telling of all was the simple reply: 'part-time only'. It may be the general association of part-time work with low-skill and casual work, an association found frequently in newspapers and in general discussions about employment, which could be the main reason for part-timers' undervaluation of the skill level of their job.

CONCLUSIONS

The first and perhaps most striking result of this comparison of the content and skill of men's and women's jobs is that the main cleavage in the quality or skill level of jobs is not between all male and all female jobs but between full-time and part-time jobs. The increasing share of part-time jobs in the economy will therefore be likely to depress further the average quality of women's jobs as measured in terms of job content and skill. In practice the growth of part-time work is likely to result in a polarization of skill levels within the female labour force, for at the same time more women are gaining access to professional and other high-quality jobs (Crompton and Sanderson, 1986). However, we show elsewhere (Horrell *et al.*, 1989) that these differences in skill and job content are not the main cause of the differences in pay between men and women; full-time women workers are also systematically lower-paid than men after adjusting for any differences in skill composition of jobs.

The second main result is that there is evidence to support the view that men's and women's jobs involve different skills or attributes and that women are particularly likely to stress the personal and social relationships which may be essential in service-type occupations. Here the difference is found to be more one of gender and not between full- and part-time jobs. It is thus essential for women to press for these types of attributes to be included more widely and given greater weight in job-evaluation schemes if 'female' job attributes are to be given similar weight to 'male' job attributes.

However, our results also suggest that perceptions of skills and job content are very much influenced by the current status attached to the job, so that rapid progress towards 'fairer' job evaluation of women's jobs may be unlikely. Part-timers were found to be particularly prone to undervalue the skill level of their job, which may be because they are reflecting the generally held attitude to part-time work as marginal employment. Perceptions of skill content are influenced not only by the status accorded the job by their employer and by society but also possibly by the centrality of wage work to the individual concerned. Men may attach a greater importance to their wage employment than women, leading to a tendency to see their job as skilled, while part-timers may see their jobs as more marginal to their lives and to their identity and thus be less concerned to see themselves as doing a skilled job. The influence of these two factors cannot be tested here, but the more important point for equal-opportunities policy is the importance of developing imaginative and diverse systems of measuring skill which aim to do more than reproduce the current grading and status of jobs, if there is to be any real progress towards the aim of equal pay for work of equal value.

NOTES

This chapter is based on data collected under the Social Change and Economic Life Initiative funded by the ESRC. The authors are indebted to all the other participants in SCELI who helped to develop the work attitudes questionnaire. We would particularly like to acknowledge the work of Carolyn Vogler, who managed the work attitudes survey from the centre, and the work of the other members of the Cambridge team both in developing the team-specific part of the questionnaire on which this paper draws and for their intellectual support in developing these areas of analysis. The work attitudes survey was conducted for the ESRC in summer 1986 by Public Attitudes Surveys Ltd.

1. In another part of the SCELI project the Cambridge team collected information from managers as well as employees on actual job content and skill. These data are also analysed in ch. 6.
2. This sample is large enough to make more systematic comparisons of different aspects of skill reported in men's and women's jobs than has been the norm in studies of women's employment which have relied either on case-study material or on the other inadequate national data sources.
3. Some of the questions were specific to the Cambridge team questionnaire and were therefore asked only of Northampton labour-market respondents, and not of respondents in the other five labour markets which participated in the work attitudes survey. These team-specific questions were designed to ask about different components of skill, including types of skills which might be expected to be associated with women's jobs even though these factors would not always be included in standard job evaluations. They therefore supplemented the questions on the more conventional aspects of skill asked about in the core survey.
4. As in almost all cases the differences between female full-timers and female part-timers were less pronounced than between male full-timers and female part-timers, it was not felt necessary to repeat the analysis of variance between male full-timers and female part-timers.
5. Analysis of variance was used throughout this chapter when testing for statistical significance of differences between groups of employees. In cases where, strictly speaking, the assumptions of analysis of variance were violated (e.g. skewed or dichotomous dependent variables) the results of these analyses were verified with non-parametric tests. For the sake of brevity and simplicity, these other analyses have not been presented here.
6. Indicated by the significant interaction term.

7. The only exceptions to this pattern were that there was no significant difference in training time between full- and part-time women workers if one controlled for 'skill', although working time was significant in the one-way analysis of variance. Also gender is only significantly associated with differences in the qualifications required for entry to jobs for the whole sample in the one-way analysis of variance. In this case the effect of comparing full-timers alone is not only to reduce the gender difference apparent in the aggregate distributions but to reverse it, so that women in full-time jobs on average require higher qualifications than men, although this difference is not statistically significant.

8. For employees this question was asked as part of a detailed battery of questions about their current job, whereas for the self-employed the only data came from the information collected in the work history schedule about their current job.

9. The existence of significant interaction term between 'skill' and working time should be noted; for part-timers it is much less likely that they would have responsibility for checking work if they were in an 'unskilled' job than is the case for full-timers.

10. These explanations as to why they said their job was 'skilled' or not 'skilled' refer only to the responses to that question in the 1988 survey. We include in Table 7.7 not only those who were still in the same job and still made the same response, but also those who had changed jobs or entered the labour market since 1986 and those who had changed their answer as to whether their job was 'skilled' between 1986 and 1988.

11. The survey question allowed for open-ended responses which were subsequently categorized for analysis.

8

Towards a Phenomenology of Skill

BRIAN FRANCIS AND ROGER PENN

INTRODUCTION

As we can see from the Introduction to this volume, there is considerable debate amongst social scientists about the concept of skill. Labour economists generally see skill as a property of an individual, made up of various combinations of education, training, and competence (Phillips and Taylor, 1980). Industrial sociologists, on the other hand, have normally regarded skill as an aspect of jobs themselves, derived from the imperatives of industrial and technological organization, without giving much attention to the relation between the skill of jobs and the skill of people (Braverman, 1974; Martin, 1988). This issue is examined further by Rose in the next chapter. Social historians have focused predominantly on the skilled divide within the manual working class and particularly on the role of apprenticed craftsmen in the development of trade unionism (Turner, 1962; More, 1980; and Penn, 1985). There is, therefore, no shared conception of skill amongst social scientists. The concept is both multi-valent and complex. The present chapter took this situation as its starting-point in an attempt to probe the phenomenology of skill.

As part of the ESRC's Social Change and Economic Life Initiative, respondents to the Work Attitudes/Histories questionnaire in Rochdale were asked a series of questions designed to assess *their own* notions of skill. In this chapter an examination of variations in response to the question 'What do you think is meant by the term "a skilled job"?' has been carried out. There were a range of responses that were coded initially into sixteen categories (see Appendix 8.1). However, most responses fell into five categories. The most frequent response (558 responses) involved the notion that a skilled job required training. In addition, a further 200 responses specifically mentioned the requirement for an apprenticeship or a trade. Consequently, over three-quarters of the respondents in Rochdale characterized a skilled job in terms of training in some form. The two other most popular responses were connected with whether the job required qualifications (232 responses) or high abilities (191 responses). The fifth most frequent response (117 responses) made reference to a job that required 'experience'. Some respondents only gave one criterion but many others mentioned two or more criteria in combination (see Table 8.1).

In the analysis that follows the Lancaster team examined the

TABLE 8.1. *Responses to the Question 'What is a Skilled Job?'*

	N
No answer	49
One response	938
Two responses	453
Three or more responses	107
TOTAL number of responses	1,547
Combinations	
Trade/Apprenticeship	65
Trade/Apprenticeship and Training	51
Training	241
Training and Qualifications	79
Training and High ability	43
Qualifications	51
Experience	25
High ability	62
Other combinations	321
Any Mention of a Factor	
Trade/Apprenticeship	200
Training	558
Qualifications	232
Experience	117
High ability	191
Other factors	249

factors that determined specific responses and those that determined the most popular combinations within the data-set.

CHARACTERISTICS OF THE ROCHDALE SAMPLE

The sample comprised 987 adults aged between 20 and 60 in the autumn of 1986. All respondents were from the Work Attitudes/Histories survey in Rochdale. Of these respondents 57% were female and 58.6% were aged between 20 and 39. Almost half were in full-time employment (47.1%) and another 14.7% in part-time employment; 12% were unemployed and another 3.2% were permanently off work sick. These figures were broadly similar to the official unemployment rate in Rochdale of 17.9% in the autumn of 1986 (*Employment Gazette*, October 1986). The self-employed accounted for 5.8% of the sample, with a further 16% identifying themselves as full-time home-makers.

The vast majority of the 79 respondents (8%) born outside the UK were immigrants from Pakistan, predominantly from Punjab and Kashmir. During their previous work histories 52.1% of respondents (513) had received some level of formal training. Of these, 179 (18.5% of the sample) had undergone some period of apprenticeship training. Almost all of this group were male.

Those respondents in employment ranged across a wide range of industrial sectors: 241 were employed in manufacturing, 201 in government and public services, and 223 in other service-sector locations. They were concentrated in a few key occupations groupings. There were 40 teachers, 34 nurses, 66 clerks, 36 shop assistants, and 34 cleaners. In our analysis we utilized both conventional class-aggregate measures and these more refined occupational groupings.

PRELIMINARY ANALYSIS

In our preliminary analysis we examined the relationship between a series of explanatory variables (see Appendix 8.2) and the question on what was understood by the term 'a skilled job'.

Apprenticeships

What were the characteristics of respondents who were more likely to mention 'apprenticeship' as a criterion of a skilled job? We found that older respondents, particularly males, were significantly more likely to mention this aspect of a skilled job (significance assessed at the 5% level throughout this chapter). Those with apprenticeship qualifications or City and Guilds certificates were far more likely to utilize this criterion. Manual workers, both the skilled and the non-skilled, were also significantly likelier to mention apprenticeships. Overall, apprenticeship was most likely to be seen as the basis of a skilled job amongst older, male, manual workers, particularly those with apprenticeship-like qualifications themselves. On the other hand, factors such as industrial sector and current economic activity status were not statistically significant factors.

Training

Training was more likely to be specified as the criterion by younger, female respondents employed in public-sector service industries, particularly those with higher-level qualifications (degrees, Higher National Certificate (HNC), or A levels). It was less likely to be mentioned by the older, male apprenticed workers described above. Given that apprenticeship is a specific and precise form of training, it is clear that for many respondents some form of training was the defining characteristic of a skilled job. Nevertheless, for a significant number of older, male, manual working-class respondents, apprenticeship was a powerful element in their perception of what was meant by the term 'a skilled job'.

Qualifications

Women were significantly more likely to mention qualifications as the criterion for a skilled job, particularly those in retail distribution. The non-skilled were also far more likely to specify qualifications as a criterion. Interestingly, it was people with lower-level qualifications themselves (such as those with CSE and O levels as their highest qualification) who emphasized this criterion when compared with those who were more highly qualified and those who reported no qualifications at all.

There was a massive difference between the younger and older members of the sample. Younger respondents (aged between 20 and 29) utilized qualifications more than twice as often as older respondents. There were also large occupational differences. Typists, shop assistants, warehousemen, and drivers were all far likelier to utilize this criterion than other occupational groups.

Of course, qualifications, training, and apprenticeships are strongly interconnected in the world of occupations. What is of interest here is the tendency for certain social groups to see a skilled job as constituted by qualifications rather than by training.

High Abilities

Men were significantly more likely to mention this criterion, particularly those who had received some formal training. High abilities were also mentioned far more often by those with higher qualifications (degrees or Higher National Diploma). Other factors were not statistically significant.

Experience

There were no statistically significant relationships between any of the variables examined and the likelihood of respondents specifying this as a criterion for a skilled job.

Combination of Criteria

In the analysis so far we have examined the social characteristics of respondents who stated any particular criterion, whether or not it was combined with other responses in a multi-response. The most popular combinations were those who mentioned both apprenticeships *and* training, qualifications *and* training, and high abilities *and* training. In this section we will provide an analysis of these responses.

Only Apprenticeship Mentioned (N = 30)

There was a very powerful relationship between this criterion being the only one mentioned and whether the respondent was male (twice as likely as females), a skilled manual worker (two and a half times more likely than the average) and had an apprenticeship qualification (four times more likely than average). Respondents aged between 50 and 60 years were far likelier to utilize this criterion solely (two and a half times as likely).

Only Training Mentioned (N = 139)

The only group who were far likelier to mention only training were teachers. In all other respects there was no large variation in the likelihood of this factor being mentioned *on its own*.

Only Qualifications Mentioned (N = 37)

Non-skilled manual workers, workers *without* any formal training, and workers who saw their current job as not skilled (particularly shop assistants) were far likelier to mention only qualifications. This is a very interesting result. Apprenticeships are very much the criterion used by older, skilled, time-served craftsmen. Qualifications are seen as the criterion of a skilled job by those who lack these qualifications themselves.

Only High Abilities Mentioned (N = 39)

This criterion was used far more often by men and by people who considered their *own* job as being skilled.

Training Combinations

There were *no* significant variations in answers that gave training and another criterion in combination. This was rather a surprising result. It suggested that the main variation was between the criteria themselves rather than any more complex pattern involving combinations of criteria. Consequently, our multivariate modelling of the data took the criteria themselves as the response variable rather than combinations of criteria.

Summary

Our preliminary analysis revealed that there were variations in perceptions of a skilled job. These variations were associated with certain explanatory variables. We found no significant ethnic effect and a scatter of factors associated with age, gender, qualifications, occupational group, and industrial sector. In Figure 8.1 we summarize the typical profile of respondents who were most likely to emphasize specific features of a skilled job.

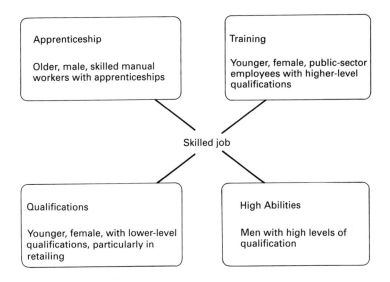

Figure 8.1 Perceptions of a skilled job

FURTHER STATISTICAL ANALYSIS OF THE DATA

So far, we have examined the responses to the perceptions of skill question purely in terms of cross-tabulations. This approach allowed us to gain an initial feel for the important explanatory variables, but it did not identify which individual characteristics were most related to skill attitudes. If, for example, gender, age, and job type show strong relationships with a particular skill perception within cross-tabulations, one or more of these variables might well be unassociated with the skill perception once the others are taken into account. For example, job type may prove to be unimportant once age and gender are taken into account, the significance of job type in the cross-tabulation being entirely due to differences in the age and gender proportions within each job type.

A more rigorous approach to the data involved the use of logistic regression analysis. This allowed us to model the probability of giving a particular response to the skill question as a function of a set of individual characteristics. Formally, we assume that the probability of individual *i* giving a particular response was p_i with a set of k individual characteristics or explanatory variables X_{i1}, X_{i2}, . . ., X_{ik}. The actual response Y_i of individual *i* to the question will either include the response of interest ($Y_i = 1$) or not ($Y_i = 0$). The logistic model assumed that:

- Y_i is distributed with a Bernoulli distribution with mean p_i

$$Y_i \sim \text{Bernoulli } (p_i)$$

- p_i is related through a function f(.) to a linear function of the explanatory variables

$$f(p_i) = \sum_{i=1}^{k} b_j x_{ij}$$

where the b_j are unknown parameters to be estimated.

- $f(p_i)$ is taken to be the logit function

$$f(p_i) = \log_e \left(\frac{p_i}{1 - p_i} \right)$$

For each of the five most common perceptions of skill, a binary logistic regression analysis was carried out on all those currently employed, using the statistical package GLIM™ (Payne *et al.*, 1987). It is important to note that one individual could potentially contribute up to four responses of skill perception and thus could contribute a non-zero response to more than one analysis. A set of explanatory variables was identified; and these are listed in Appendix 8.2. Using the standard GLIM convention, the categorical explanatory variables were entered into the analysis as a set of dummy (0,1) variables, or factors.

For each analysis of the five major responses considered here, two approaches were carried out. The first (method 1) took as a starting model all explanatory variables listed in Appendix 8.2 except for job type. The second (method 2) modified the starting model in the first analysis by replacing the social class and industrial-sector variables by the job-type classification. The job-type classification is therefore viewed here as an alternative representation of the social class and industrial-sector variables. The job types were constructed from the original occupational titles provided by respondents. These were then combined into the 18 categories listed in Appendix 8.2.

For each analysis and method, a backward elimination procedure was adopted, with the appropriate main effects model being fitted at the initial stage. At each subsequent stage, the least important variable was selected and removed from the model using the GLIM deviance (likelihood ratio statistic) as a criterion for comparing nested models (Aitkin *et al.*, 1989). The procedure was terminated when all remaining variables were significant. Where appropriate, categories of explanatory variables were collapsed to simplify the final model.

Skill Defined as Involving Trade or Apprenticeship

Using the first method, three variables contributed to the final model—gender, perception of current job as skilled, and level of qualifications achieved. All other variables were assessed not to be significant (change in deviance of 25.08 on 31 df; p = 0.40). Qualifications achieved could be further simplified into an indicator variable identifying those with higher academic qualifications (i.e. degrees, HNC, or A level). This gave a further reduction in deviance of 3.94 on 7 df (p = 0.79). Those having higher academic qualifications were less likely to mention apprenticeships than those not holding these qualifications. Males were more likely to mention apprenticeships than females, and those who perceived their current job to be skilled were less likely to mention apprenticeships.

The second method produced a simpler model, involving just two variables—job type and qualifications achieved, with all other variables, including gender and perception of current job as skilled, found to be unimportant (change in deviance of 18.28 on 15 df; p. = 0.25). Again, qualifications achieved could be simplified to an indicator variable identifying those with higher academic qualifications, giving a further deviance reduction of 3.449 on 7 df (p = 0.84). This model provided a better fit to the data than the first (though at the cost of more parameters), and is easier to interpret, with the gender and perception of current job effects being replaced by a single measure of current job type. The effect of qualifications was similar to the first method, with those having higher academic qualifications less likely to mention apprenticeships. The effect of job type showed substantial variation, with labourers, warehousemen, and managers being most likely, and teachers, typists, and artists being least likely to mention apprenticeships (see Figure 8.2).

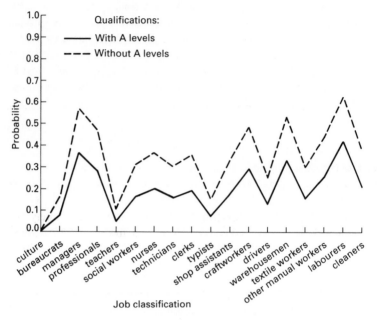

Figure 8.2 Fitted probabilities of defining skills as trade or
apprenticeship

Skill Defined as Requiring Training

A final model involving three variables—social class, highest
qualification, and economic activity—was produced by the first
method, with all other variables eliminated as unimportant
(change of deviance is 20.89 on 15 df; p = 0.14). As in the first
analysis, qualifications achieved could be further simplified into
an indicator variable identifying those with higher academic
qualifications (i.e. degrees, NHC, or A level). Similarly, economic
activity could be simplified into an indicator variable distinguishing full-time workers from part-time and self-employed workers,
and social class could be simplified into a three-category variable:
professional and managerial, skilled manual, and other classes.
The final model had a scaled deviance of 854.65 on 656 df, a
decrease of 11.33 on 11 df (p = 0.42). The model may be understood as follows: those of professional or managerial social class
have nearly double the odds, and skilled manual workers half the

odds of mentioning training compared to other social classes. Those employed full-time are more likely to mention training than part-time and self-employed workers. Finally, those with higher qualifications (A level or above) are more likely to mention training than those without higher qualifications.

The second method produced a model giving a better fit. Three variables were involved—gender, job type, and qualifications, giving a change in deviance of 15.5 on 14 df compared with the main effects model (p = 0.34). As in the first analysis, the qualification variable could be replaced by an indicator variable identifying those with higher qualifications from those without them. This gave a further small deviance reduction of 4.617 on 7 df (p = 0.71). The final model had a deviance of 835.64 on 641 df and can be summarized as follows: females were more likely to mention training than males and those with higher qualifications were more likely to mention training than those without. Most categories of job were similar in their response. Social workers and artists were far less likely to mention training compared with the reference group of clerks. Teachers, textile workers, and craft-workers were also less likely to mention training. Nurses, technicians, and labourers, on the other hand, were the most likely to mention training (see Figure 8.3).

Skill Defined as Requiring Qualifications

The first method produced a final model involving four variables—age, size of firm, social class, and gender, with all other variables found to be unimportant (change in deviance of 20.53 on 20 df; p = 0.43). The age variable could be further simplified into an indicator variable identifying those under 30 (change in deviance of 2.495 on 2 df; p = 0.29). The interpretation of the model is that unskilled manual workers and those working in large companies were less likely to mention qualifications, with young workers more likely than older workers and females more likely than males to mention qualifications.

The second method produced a final model which involved only three variables—age, job type and gender—which was rather more easily interpreted, although it provided a slightly poorer fit to the data (change in deviance of 20.53 on 20 df; p = 0.43). Again, the age variable could be simplified in the same way as

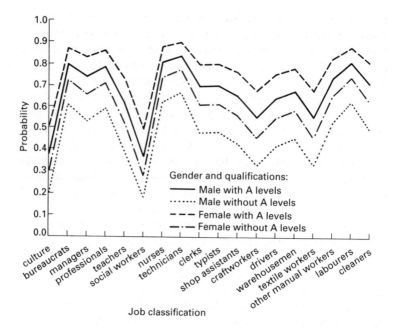

Figure 8.3 Fitted probabilities of defining skill as requiring training

the first method, giving a change of deviance of 1.228 on 2 df (p = 0.54). The effect of age and gender was similar to the first model. Drivers, warehousemen, and bureaucrats were identified as the most likely, and professionals and skilled manual workers as the least likely to mention qualifications (see Figure 8.4).

Skill Defined as Requiring Experience

There was no evidence that any of the explanatory variables were important in explaining this response. This was true both for the first (change in deviance 22.23 on 34 df; p = 0.94) and second (change in deviance of 24.44 on 40 df; p = 0.97) methods (see Figure 8.5).

Skill Defined as Requiring High Ability

Both the first and second methods produced a final model involving only two variables—gender and perception of current job,

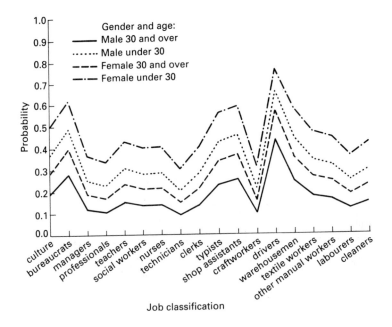

Figure 8.4 Fitted probabilities of defining skill as qualifications

with all other variables found to be unimportant (the first method gave a change in deviance of 21.00 on 32 df; (p = 0.93) and the second method gave a change in deviance of 35.35 on 38 df (p = 0.59)‡). The interpretation of the model is that males were more likely to mention high ability than females, and that those who perceived their current job to be skilled were more likely to mention high ability than those who do not have that view (see Figure 8.6).

Considering all the analyses together, it is clear that using job type rather than social class and industrial sector of employment provided a more consistent method of explaining variations in skill perception. For this reason, we will concentrate on the second method when interpreting the data further. For each perception of skill, we have presented the parameter estimates and standard errors of the final model (Table 8.2), and also presented a graph of the fitted probabilities of the final model plotted

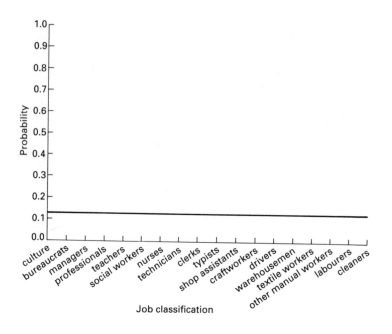

Figure 8.5 Fitted probabilities of defining skill as requiring experience

against job type (Figures 8.2–8.6). The use of job type in preference to social class and industrial sector of employment, however, does not mean that the first method is invalid; instead we view each method as giving an alternative representation of the same data, with the second method producing a clearer way of interpreting the data.

OCCUPATIONAL GROUPINGS

It was clear from our analysis in the preceding section that occupational groupings affected perceptions of a skilled job. Social workers, for example, were likely to emphasize high abilities and de-emphasize training. This could be a function of their own work situation. The differences amongst social workers in terms of both their competence and their effectiveness are probably perceived as a function of individual attributes and abilities

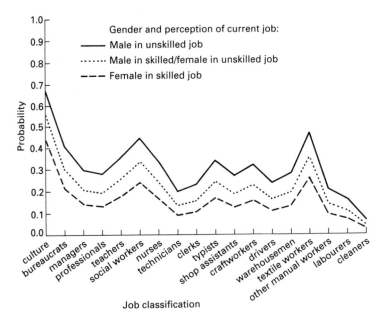

Figure 8.6 Fitted probabilities of defining skill as high ability

rather than as the result of training *per se*. Most social workers tend to feel that the core of their own job skills cannot be codified or learned through training courses. Likewise, drivers are likely to emphasize qualifications as the basis of a skilled job. In order to become an HGV driver, which is perceived by full-time drivers as the skilled area of driving, it is essential to possess the appropriate certificate. Without these it is not possible to be even considered as skilled within the community of full-time drivers. Artists and others in cultural occupations also emphasize high abilities and downgrade training. This corresponds to their own world of work. Artists regard their skills as inherently personal and tend not to see them as a function of training.

These separate, discrete analyses of skill perception were summarized into a single graphical picture by means of a simple correspondence analysis (Benzécri *et al.*, 1973; Greenacre, 1984) of the two-way table of occupational groups and skill perception. Simple correspondence analysis also provided information showing how

TABLE 8.2. *Parameter estimates and standard errors (in parentheses) of final logistic models for the given dependent variables*

	Trade or apprenticeship	Training	Qualifications	Experience	High ability
Intercept	-2.26 (0.43)	0.84 (0.34)	-1.82 (0.36)	-1.91 (0.12)	-1.20 (0.39)
JOB TYPE					
Art and culture	-4.94 (6.05)	-1.40 (0.92)	0.37 (0.91)	—	1.89 (0.85)
Bureaucrats	-1.06 (1.08)	0.53 (0.60)	0.88 (0.60)	—	0.82 (0.61)
Managers	0.87 (0.51)	0.21 (0.46)	-0.17 (0.55)	—	0.34 (0.54)
Professionals	0.48 (0.45)	0.46 (0.40)	-0.29 (0.48)	—	0.24 (0.47)
Teachers	-1.55 (1.08)	-0.36 (0.45)	0.11 (0.49)	—	0.60 (0.50)
Social workers	-0.21 (0.83)	-1.41 (0.57)	-0.01 (0.64)	—	0.98 (0.61)
Nurses	0.04 (0.56)	0.59 (0.48)	0.01 (0.49)	—	0.52 (0.53)
Technicians	-0.24 (1.12)	0.80 (0.85)	-0.44 (0.86)	—	-0.19 (0.87)
Clerks	0.0	0.0	0.0	—	0.0
Typists	-1.11 (0.81)	0.01 (0.46)	0.62 (0.48)	—	0.54 (0.56)
Shop assistants	-0.09 (0.56)	-0.19 (0.43)	0.76 (0.45)	—	0.20 (0.57)
Skilled manual workers	0.55 (0.45)	-0.62 (0.42)	-0.39 (0.51)	—	0.45 (0.49)
Drivers	-0.48 (0.83)	-0.26 (0.59)	1.57 (0.61)	—	0.03 (0.75)
Warehousemen	0.73 (0.50)	-0.09 (0.45)	0.69 (0.47)	—	0.24 (0.58)
Textile workers	-0.26 (0.59)	-0.63 (0.44)	0.27 (0.48)	—	1.07 (0.50)
Other manual workers	0.36 (0.40)	0.20 (0.34)	0.17 (0.37)	—	-0.14 (0.45)
Labourers	1.11 (0.60)	0.62 (0.59)	-0.18 (0.73)	—	-0.45 (0.85)
Cleaners	0.09 (0.54)	0.07 (0.44)	0.08 (0.50)	—	-1.46 (1.04)
Qualifications	0.84 (0.32)	-0.93 (0.24)	—	—	—
Age under 30			0.90 (0.20)		
Gender		0.54 (0.20)	0.53 (0.23)		-0.47 (0.24)
Perception of current job as skilled					-0.46 (0.22)

'close', in terms of occupational profile, the various skill perceptions were; and how close the occupations were in their skill-
perception profiles. We also included four 'passive' variables—
gender, qualifications (A levels or above, or not), age (under 30, 30
and over), and the respondents' perception of whether their current job was skilled (yes/no). These variables played no part in the
mathematical formation of the correspondence analysis, but were
superimposed on to the correspondence analysis plot.

Figure 8.7 shows the plot of the first two dimensions produced
by the correspondence analysis. These two dimensions accounted
for nearly 75% of the chi-squared variation in the table, and we
therefore restricted our interpretation to these two dimensions.

Interpretation of a correspondence-analysis diagram is complex.
It is often thought that points close together in the diagram indicate a positive association between the variables. However, this is
only partially true. Distances between different skill perceptions
(shown in bold type), and distances between different occupations
can be interpreted directly; so typists, shop assistants, and drivers
are similar in their perception of skill. However, though distances
between skill perceptions and occupations may not be interpreted

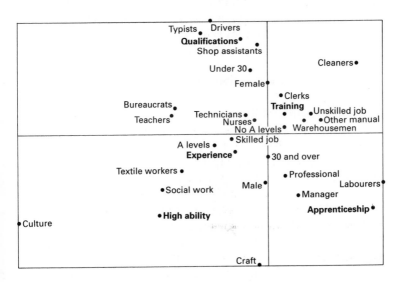

Figure 8.7 First two dimensions of correspondence analysis of
perceptions of skill

directly in this way, it is often useful to examine the quadrants in which skill perceptions and occupational groupings lie. Points in the same quadrant will usually be more related than points in different quadrants. The 'passive' variables such as age and gender were treated in the above interpretation as equivalent to occupational categories.

The correspondence-analysis plot both confirmed the previous analyses and also provided additional insights into the data. The occupational profiles of 'skill as qualifications' differed substantially from those of 'skill as high ability' and 'skill as apprenticeships'. The horizontal axis discriminated between cultural workers and social workers who (from the logistic regression modelling) think of skill as 'high ability' more than other groups, and cleaners and labourers, who do not. The vertical axis was also informative. It discriminated between typists, drivers, and shop assistants on the one hand, who were most likely to think of skill as involving qualifications, and craftworkers, labourers, managers, and professionals, who assessed a skilled job in terms of apprenticeships and ability. The passive variables gender and age can also be seen on this axis, which suggested that males and older respondents were more likely to think of skill in terms of apprenticeships and ability, whilst females and younger workers were more likely to think of skill in terms of qualifications.

CONCLUSIONS

It is apparent that skill means different things to different occupational groups. Statements such as 'improving the skills of the workforce' may, therefore, be threatening if employees interpret skill in terms of ability or experience. They may also react negatively if they perceive skill in terms of qualifications. Such results are critical for any efforts to improve the skill base of British industry. The discourse of skill has many chambers.

It is also evident that skill perceptions depend on age. However, it is not clear whether this is a cohort or an age effect. If it were the latter, this would suggest that individuals change their definition of skill during their lives, emphasizing qualifications in their early working life and emphasizing other skill factors in later life. However, this remains an open question.

It is clear that differing occupational groupings categorize skill in different ways. In this they are no different from social scientists. Our analysis has shown that these differences can be represented either in terms of the interaction of social class and industrial sector of employment, or in terms of a set of specific job groups. We believe that these job groups are easier to grasp cognitively and that there is a strong case for further research on the determinants of how different occupational groups perceive the spheres of work and employment.

APPENDIX 8.1

Responses to the question 'What do You Think is Meant by the Term "Skilled Job"?'

1. Involves a trade or an apprenticeship.
2. Requires training.
3. Requires qualifications.
4. Requires experience.
5. Requires high ability/competence/proficiency.
6. Can be done without supervision.
7. A difficult job.
8. Example of a specific job.
9. Not a job that anyone can do.
10. A job that is well paid.
11. A secure job.
12. A responsible job.
13. All jobs are skilled.
14. Involves intelligence.
15. Involves manual dexterity.
16. Other.

APPENDIX 8.2

Table 8.3. *Explanatory variables used in the preliminary cross-tabulations and in the logistic regression analyses*

Name of variable	Description of variable	Description of levels
FAGE	Age of respondent	1 = less than 30, 2 = 30 to 39, 3 = 40 to 49, 4 = 50 or more.
LC	Social class (Lancaster Collapsed Classification)	1 = proprietors and self-employed, 2 = professional, administrative and managerial, 3 = technical and supervisory, 4 = skilled manual, 5 = sales and routine services, 6 = non-skilled manual.
NATBUS	Nature of business	1 = primary, 2 = textiles, 3 = metalworking, 4 = other manufacturing and construction, 5 = transport and distribution, 6 = government and public services, 7 = other services.
SIZE	Size of company	1 = respondent only, 2 = 2-24 employees, 3 = 25-99 employees, 4 = 100-499 employees, 5 = 500 employees or more.
V97	Perception of current job as skilled?	1 = yes, 2 = no.

Variable	Description	Coding
HQUAL	Highest qualification achieved	1 = degree or equivalent, 2 = HNC/HND, 3 = A level or ONC, 4 = O level, 5 = City and Guilds, 6 = trade apprenticeship, 7 = CSE.
GENDER	Gender of individual	1 = male, 2 = female.
JTYPE	Job classification	1 = cultural jobs, 2 = bureaucrats, 3 = managers, 4 = professional, 5 = teachers, 6 = social workers, 7 = nurses, 8 = technicians, 9 = clerks, 10 = typists, 11 = shop assistants, 12 = craft workers, 13 = drivers, 14 = warehousemen, 15 = textile workers, 16 = other manual workers, 17 = labourers, 18 = cleaners.
ACTIV	Economic activity	1 = self-employed, 2 = employed part-time, 3 = employed full-time.
R6	Any periods of formal or organized training?	1 = yes, 2 = no.
R9	Any apprenticeships?	1 = yes, 2 = no.
ETHNIC	To which of these groups do you belong?	1 = English, Scottish, Welsh, N. Ireland or Irish Republic, 2 = other.

Job Satisfaction, Job Skills, and Personal Skills

MICHAEL ROSE

JOB-SKILL AND OWN-SKILL

Skill on the one hand and job satisfaction on the other are both well established subjects for research in the social sciences. But surprisingly, they have created largely separate streams of research. There has been relatively little research on exactly how skill and work attitudes such as job satisfaction interact. Nevertheless, most researchers into work behaviour would no doubt claim that they are closely associated.

The literature on attitudes to work, of which that on job satisfaction forms part, is massive. Social psychologists, in particular, have developed many methods of measuring work attitudes. Findings from social psychological research have often been applied in management education or training, or spread amongst personnel managers in the teaching of management reformers concerned with improving the quality of work as well as workplace efficiency. Some of these findings have also been used by sociologists of work concerned with workplace social relations or with the social distribution of economic and social values. It is widely accepted, then, that work attitudes are important for understanding the work behaviour of employees and workplace social relations, and even for grasping long-term trends in social relations and cultural values. O'Brien (1992, 1986) provides a review from a social psychological perspective sympathetic to sociology.

Yet the effect of varieties of skill or skill levels as such on work attitudes has never been examined in any real depth by social psychologists, and only occasionally, and in a somewhat restricted way, by sociologists of work (Blackburn and Mann, 1979). True enough, the once widespread debate on worker *orientations to work* (Goldthorpe *et al.*, 1969; Wedderburn and Crompton, 1972) attempted to define the work attitudes characteristic of certain occupations or specific work situations. True enough, these factors may represent skill levels indirectly. But, as with the earlier debate on worker alienation (Blauner, 1964), most studies dealt with a declining set of occupations and employees (male manual workers in manufacturing plants above all) and often used somewhat rough and ready measures of work attitudes, sometimes in a rather uncritical way. The revived debate of the 1970s on historical trends in manual workers' skill was, on the other hand, notable for the reluctance of those who accepted the thesis of a long-term reduction of skill (degradation) to examine its possible effect on employee attitudes ('consciousness').

There is an additional feature on the sociological material which should be noted. Sociologists of work, in examining skill, have never matched the methodological care shown by social psychologists in measuring job attitudes. On the contrary, they have often used simple indicators of skill which may not be fully comparable from one study to another. Occupational group, job title, and respondent ratings have all been used as proxy ('stand-in') measures of skill. A further problem, first discussed at length by Spenner (1983) in a review of sociological studies of trends in skill in the USA,[1] lies behind this use of single, non-comparable measures of skill.

Spenner pointed out that American analyses of changes in skill patterns often referred to the US Department of Labor's *Dictionary of Occupational Titles* (*DOT*), but that *DOT* embodies two logically distinct aspects, or modes, of skill. (So does the *Classification of Occupations and Dictionary of Occupational Titles* (*CODOT*), its British equivalent.) The first mode of skill has to do with the operations or responsibilities of a work role; the second mode refers to the skill type and level developed by individuals, and 'carried' by them from one job to another. In this second sense, then, skill approximates closely to the concept of *human capital* in the economic analysis of labour-market rewards and behaviour (Blaug, 1972). While this 'personal' skill may be enhanced by work experience, it is not a property of work processes themselves. Indeed, as Elias points out in his analysis in Chapter 3 of 'work-experience' effects on skill and its perception by individuals, the skill of jobs could, at least in theory, be in general decline while most individuals continued to experience a personal gain in skill. Many studies, Spenner went on to note, especially those influenced by the degradation of skills debate (Braverman, 1974), overlook this central ambiguity in the skill concept. As Chapter 1 points out (see the section 'Matching of Personal and Job Skills') there seem to have been only two significant attempts (Cockburn, 1983; Clark *et al.*, 1988) to confront it in actual field-studies in the British sociology of work. It is of particular importance to this and the next chapter.

SKILL-MATCHING IN
THE WORK ATTITUDES/HISTORIES SAMPLE

The Work Attitudes/Histories survey material produced by SCELI made it possible to handle this ambiguity in the concept of skill, thus avoiding, it is to be hoped, some of the pitfalls unrecognized by many of those contributors to the debate on skill who have relied upon just one or two indicators of skill. The core survey provided over a dozen skill measures besides collecting very full data on occupation.[2] (Additional data on skill and changes in skill were collected in three of the six localities covered in the 'core' surveys.[3]) These separate measures made it possible to estimate the skill level both of the work individuals were currently doing (*job-skill*) and that of their current personal skill attainment (*own-skill*).

Early analyses confirmed a relatively high degree of association between *all* available skill measures for the employee sample as a whole. This was to be expected, since most employees do hold jobs calling for skill at least roughly equivalent to the level of their personal skill. But a large minority of respondents in the Work Attitudes/Histories survey were thought to hold jobs where their high personal skill was not fully utilized; similarly, a large minority were also believed to have jobs for which they might lack comparable levels of training, work experience, or formal qualification.

After indicators as elements either of *job-skill* or of *own-skill* had been classified each set was converted into a composite measure. The procedure used also created a precise score for each type of skill for each respondent. When each set of scores was collapsed into seven equally sized bands, the extent of 'underutilization' and 'underqualification' could be estimated quickly, by examining the combination of rankings (1 to 7 for each aspect of skill). The resulting table has not been shown here because it is rather unwieldy. (It has 49 cells.) To give an idea of the extent of skill-matching in the employee sample more quickly, a score for skill difference is more useful. This was calculated simply by subtracting the skill rank of the job (1 to 7) from the skill rank (also 1 to 7) of the person. Cases where skill ranks were equal, or matched, produced a score of 0; where *job-skill* rank was higher than *own-skill* rank (an apparent situation of under-*qualification*) scores were negative (varying from –1 to –6); and where *job-skill* rank was lower than *own-skill* rank (under*utilization*) scores were positive (+1 to +6). The distribution of scores is shown in Table 9.1; as there were relatively few scores in the most extreme positions (above +5 or lower than –5), these cases are grouped with +4 or –4.

Table 9.1 shows the distribution of scores for skill difference on this nine-point scale. It is of broadly regular shape, but with slight skewing towards Overqualification. Only one in four employees were in approximately skill-matched jobs, though if the 'slightly' underqualified (–1) and the 'slightly' underutilized (+1) are included this shows that two-thirds were 'roughly' or approximately matched. But 35% of the sample seemed either to be 'seriously' underutilized or 'seriously' underqualified. Indeed there were several dozen striking imbalances or 'skill gaps'.

This nine-point scale, however, is in several ways unhelpful for examining the link between skill-matching and job satisfaction. One problem is that identical scores can be produced in very different ways, obscuring the varying levels at which matching or mismatching occurred. Using this measure, for example, matching can occur at seven levels, from very low *own-skill* combined with very low *job-skill* (1 and 1) to very high *own-skill* combined with very high *job-skill* (7 and 7). Similarly, a mismatch at +3 can be produced in four ways (from 7 and 4, to 4 and 1). As noted earlier, it would not be practical to discuss all 49 possible combinations in the full matrix of scores from which Table 9.1 was derived. Though it involves considerable simplification, a compromise was necessary to keep presentation manageable. In

	Frequency	%	Histogram
UNDERUTILIZED			
+4+	50	2	▪
+3	119	4	▬
+2	289	9	▬▬
+1	616	19	▬▬▬▬▬
MATCHED	826	26	▬▬▬▬▬▬▬
UNDERQUALIFIED			
−1	671	21	▬▬▬▬▬▬
−2	409	13	▬▬▬▬
−3	203	6	▬▬
−4+	55	2	▪

Note : The labels Underutilized, Matched, and Underqualified are explained in the section of Chapter 9 on 'Skill-Matching in the Work Attitudes/Histories Sample'. They refer to the overall degree of correspondence between the skill level of the job done by the respondent (job-skill) and his or her personal level of skill attainment (own-skill). The Underutilized were respondents whose skill attainment was higher than the skill level of the job they had at the time of the Work Attitudes/Histories survey: the Underqualified had skill attainment *below* the level of the skill of their present job; the Matched and skill attainment of approximately the same level as their current job. The degree of mismatching of skill attainment and skill of the job varies, sometimes sharply: and individuals can be matched at different levels. The table is based upon a classification of both skill attainment (own-skill) and skill level of current job (job-skill), with approximately equal bands scored 1 to 7 in each case. Scores shown result from subtracting the job-skill scores. The table shows that large minorities of respondents had a wide gap between their own-skill and job-skill, although the largest single group was of individuals matched at one of the seven levels. The 7-level banding is not used in other tables. (It'produces 49 subgroups.)

Source : Work Attitudes/Histories survey.

the earlier part of this chapter, then, tables will be shown in which scores for each of the composite skill variables have been grouped in just three bands (Low, Moderate, High), and then combined to show a smaller number of subgroups in broadly comparable skill situations (see Table 9.2).

Combining three levels of *job-skill* and *own-skill* results in just nine subgroups: three where the two types of skill are in the same band (the Matched); three where skill attainment was higher than the skill of the work done, that is where *own-skill* was higher than *job-skill* (the Underutilized); and three where *job-skill* was higher than *own-skill* (the Underqualified). Table 9.2 shows the resulting combinations.[4] Strictly speaking, the terms 'matched', 'underutilized', and 'underqualified' apply primarily to the data on skill that were available, with personal skill level acting as the point of reference. They should not be taken to imply judgements about skills shortages, the rationality of selection procedures, and similar questions for management which cannot be taken up here. Likewise, it is recognized that, in practice, other individual or workplace factors may sometimes have compensated for apparent skill 'deficits' or offset skill 'surpluses'. However, as will be seen shortly, the examination of job satisfaction suggests that the measures were adequate for their purpose. Finally, while the first part of the discussion will refer primarily to the nine subgroups, in later sections analysis will make use of the more precise (factored) scores for both *own-skill* and *job-skill*.

JOB SATISFACTION AMONGST SCELI EMPLOYEES

Some comment is also called for on the aspects of job satisfaction and the measures of job satisfaction that will be used. In industrial sociology, the most common approach to work satisfaction has been to distinguish between the *extrinsic* and the *instrinsic* factors in employees' jobs as a whole which create satisfaction or dissatisfaction. A whole school of management theory following Frederick Herzberg (1968) is also based on a contrast

TABLE 9.2. *Skills-matching and skills-mismatching: distribution of employees between main subgroups*

	Current job ('job-skill') score			Total
	Low	Medium	High	
Personal skill ('own-skill') score				
Low	Matched 668	Underqualified 348	Underqualified 33	1,049
Medium	Underutilized 235	Matched 788	Underqualified 327	1,350
High	Underutilized 15	Underutilized 381	Matched 436	832
TOTAL	918	1,517	796	3,231

Note: Table 9.2 uses a simpler, 3-level banding for each type of skill (High, Medium, and Low), to simplify analysis and presentation of the earlier part of the chapter. It shows approximate skill-matching at three levels, and some of the more extreme skill mismatches. See also note to Table 9.1 above.

Source: Work Attitudes/Histories survey.

between such job aspects. The first set of factors has to do with the 'instrumental' or 'economistic' aspects of a job; that is, with factors such as pay, promotion, and security. The second set relates to the more 'expressive' aspects of a job, such as its degree of interest, its challenge, and the discretion allowed in performing tasks and in meeting responsibilities. It has also been argued (Berg *et al.*, 1978) that the *authority* aspects of a job should be regarded as distinct from the first two, and that the degree of satisfaction with the experience of being supervised or managed, or with the competence of management in the workplace more broadly, may be particularly significant for overall job satisfaction. As will be shown, this claim is strongly borne out by the Work Attitudes/Histories findings.

The Work Attitudes/Histories data provide at least two measures for each of these three sets of job aspects. In the interview, currently employed respondents were asked to rate their satisfaction with eight separate aspects of their present post, and then to give an *overall* rating of their job satisfaction. An 11-point scale (0 to 10) was used for each of these ratings. This scale has also been collapsed into three bands (High, Moderate, Low) to simplify presentation of results in the first part of the chapter.

Responses were skewed towards the higher score-bands. This is a common, and unsurprising, finding in job-satisfaction studies. Employees are evidently more likely to stay longer in a job that they find relatively satisfying overall, or to seek another job if they are relatively dissatisfied. Even in times of high unemployment and lower job security, those employees who can do so seek to increase satisfaction (or reduce dissatisfaction) through changing jobs. It may also appear irrational, or to be a sign of humiliatingly low market capacity, to admit tolerating high dissatisfaction. Thus some dissatisfied employees may dissemble their true feelings to an outsider, resulting in skewing of results towards higher satisfaction.

While recognizing these difficulties, the Work Attitudes/Histories survey was not concerned so much with absolute levels of satisfaction as with relative ones, and their association with skill levels especially. But, partly to deal with the problem of possible bias in replies, the 'Low' band was set to cover the first six points of the scale (0–5) and thus represents a far greater range of options than the other categories. (These were: 6, 7, and 8 for

'Moderate', and 9 and 10 for 'High'.) To simplify presentation still further, many results for subgroups will be shown in the form of *balance of satisfaction*. This is a simple summary score produced by subtracting the percentage of Low scores in a given subgroup from its percentage of High scores.

It seems reasonable to expect that the *own-skill* and *job-skill* levels of individuals will affect their job satisfaction in very different ways. People will low *own-skill* have fewer opportunities to find challenging, better-paid work, and to resist offensively exercised supervision. It is reasonable for them to set their expectations as a whole at a lower level. Those with much higher skill attainment, on the other hand, may well have higher expectations and be more critical of their jobs as a whole. Overall, then, there may be a *negative* association between *own-skill* and satisfaction. Different general considerations should apply for *job-skill*. As the skill level of jobs increases, so do their *extrinsic* and *intrinsic* rewards; therefore *job-skill* should be positively associated with satisfaction because higher skilled work is better paid, more challenging, and less closely supervised.

Following this logic, imbalances of skill levels should affect job satisfaction in rather complex but still broadly predictable ways. It seems clear that underutilization and underqualification will act in quite different and generally opposed ways. People with jobs significantly higher in their skill level than their own training, qualifications, and experience (the underqualified) have *intrinsic* and *extrinsic* rewards that are higher than they might 'reasonably' expect; at the same time, their relatively lower personal skill may still limit their choice of jobs with other employers. The underqualified thus seem likely to have 'disproportionately' higher levels of satisfaction. For example, they should be generally more satisfied than people in similarly skilled jobs who have *own-skill* matching that of the job held. The underutilized, by contrast, who occupy posts below their skill potential, should be 'disproportionately' dissatisfied; even when their jobs actually are relatively highly skilled, they may be considered insufficiently challenging in terms of the employee's technical competence, or poorly rewarded in terms of his or her high stock of human capital.

Such 'skill effects' on job satisfaction may obviously be modified by many other factors, such as age and work experience, commitment to paid work as a whole, gender, the size of the workplace, experience of technical change, and public-sector versus private-sector employment. In a later section the effects of these influences will be examined, showing—perhaps surprisingly—that some of them operated less strongly than might be thought in the Work Attitudes/Histories sample. Some relatively simple associations between skill balances and satisfaction will be examined first.

PATTERNS OF JOB SATISFACTION

Levels of Job Satisfaction

Before considering the effects of skill matching, several findings about job satisfaction in the sample as a whole require brief comment. As noted earlier, response was 'bunched' in the higher ratings, suggesting that most respondents were relatively satisfied with most of the eight aspects of their jobs covered in the survey. All the same, very substantial minorities *did* express low satisfaction with at least some aspects of their jobs, while there was a general shift upwards for others. These differences in 'average' (in the sense of modal) levels of satisfaction have a clear pattern. Table 9.3 ranks each job aspect, and overall satisfaction, in terms of the *balance of satisfaction* (percentage in the 'High' score-band minus percentage 'Low' in the score-band, for the subgroup in question) in column 1. As column 2 shows, taking the simple percentages of High rankings produces a broadly similar result. Columns 3–5 show rankings in terms of the *intrinsic, extrinsic,* and *authority* classification of job aspects.

It is immediately clear that relative levels of job satisfaction differed greatly between specific job aspects, although there was still a positive balance of satisfaction for five of the eight specific aspects. Satisfaction with the *intrinsic* job aspect 'Using own initiative' came first by a large margin and was at a very high level (+45%). The second *intrinsic* factor ('Actual work') came in third place. The two aspects with the highest negative balances ('Total pay', 'Promotion opportunities') were both *extrinsic* aspects. On the other hand, balances for the two *authority* aspects differed sharply; while there was high satisfaction with 'Own relations with supervisor or manager', there was equally clear overall *dissatisfaction* with 'Ability and efficiency of the management'.

TABLE 9.3. *Differences in levels of job satisfaction between particular job aspects in the employee sample*

| | Balance | Proportion | Type of job aspect (rank) | | |
	(% High less % Low)	(% High)	Intrinsic	Extrinsic	Authority
Using initiative	+45	58	1		
Relations with supervisor/manager	+28	49			2
Actual work	+28	46	3		
Job security	+26	50		4	
Overall (self-rated)	+26	42			
Hours worked	+25	48		5	
Ability/efficiency of management	−11	28			6
Total pay	−17	24		7	
Promotion	−25	21		8	

Note: Respondents rated their satisfaction with each job aspect on an 11-point scale (0–10). To simplify analysis and presentation, these ratings were banded as follows: 0–5 = Low rating; 6–8 = Moderate rating; 9–10 = High rating. (Banding was not equal because of the bunching of ratings at the higher points: for further explanation and discussion, see text.) The scores in column 1 are for the '*balance of satisfaction*' produced by subtracting the percentage with Low ratings for the job aspect from the percentage with High ratings. These balances have been used to produce the ranking. (The two apparently 'tied' balances were produced by rounding; the exact balances varied slighly in each case, and Overall satisfaction has not been included in the ranking.) The introduction to the job satisfaction question-battery and instructions to the Interviewer ran as follows: 'I'm going to read out a list of various aspects of jobs, and after each one I'd like you to tell me, from this card, which number best describes how satisfied or dissatisfied you are with that particular aspect of your own present job'; (Instruction to Interviewer) 'Read out each item from list below and write in number chosen'. The card handed to the Respondent made it clear that he or she was to consider the full range of ratings, with 0 marking complete dissatisfaction and 10 more or less complete satisfaction. The order in which job aspects were rated and the full wording for each aspect were: Promotion prospects; the Total pay, including any overtime and bonuses; Relations with your supervisor or manager; your Job security; Being able to use your own initiative; the Ability and efficiency of management' the Actual work itself; the Hours you work. The Respondent was then asked: 'All things considered, how satisfied or dissatisfied are you with your present job overall, using the same 0–10 scale?'

Source: Work Attitudes/Histories survey.

The effects of the nine types of skill-matching on satisfaction also reflect these patterns, though exaggerating them in ways generally consistent with the arguments presented earlier. Results for each set of job aspects will be presented in turn in the remainder of this section.

Intrinsic Aspects

The very large balance of satisfaction with 'Using Own Initiative' in the Work Attitudes/Histories sample has already been noted in Chapter 1. (It is almost inexplicable in terms of theories of work degradation.) Table 9.4 shows that all subgroups also had posi-

TABLE 9.4. *Types of skill-matching and satisfaction with the intrinsic aspects of present job*

Skill situation of subgroup	Using own initiative (% High – % Low)	Actual work itself (% High – % Low)
Underutilized		
Low job-skill, Moderate own-skill	+14	—
Moderate job-skill, High own-skill	+31	+28
Low job-skill, High own-skill	+20	+7
Matched		
Low job-skill, Low own-skill	+30	+15
Moderate job-skill, Moderate own-skill	+48	+31
High job-skill, High own-skill	+64	+43
Underqualified		
Moderate job-skill, Low own-skill	+57	+31
High job-skill, Moderate own-skill	+67	+43
High job-skill, Low own-skill	+73	+33
Employee sample	+45	+28

Note: The scores are for the '*balance of satisfaction*' produced by subtracting the percentage of Low ratings for the job aspect from the percentage of High ratings. See also notes to Tables 9.1–3 for further explanation. Statistical significance (chi sq.) for this and following tables is not shown, but was >.0000 for all tables used to produce the balances shown in columns, with the exception of 'Total pay', where it was >.0001.

Source: Work Attitudes/Histories survey.

tive balances. But the size of the balance varied enormously—almost 30 percentage points either side of the sample balance of +45%. It does seem, from Table 9.4, that the Underutilized felt much more often that they lacked the opportunity to exercise the degree of autonomy or to take decisions for which they seemed to have training and qualifications, and that the Underqualified appreciated equally strongly their 'unusual' autonomy and 'exceptional' chances to take decisions.

For 'Actual Work Done', the differences are less striking. While the Underutilized with Moderate *own-skill* and Low *job-skill* had a zero balance (that is, the proportions for 'satisfied' and 'dissatisfied' were equal), those who had High *own-skill* and Moderate *job-skill* had the same balance as the sample. The Matched subgroups show the clearest patterns here, with the level of satisfaction rising with the skill level of the subgroup in a linear way. But the pattern for the Underqualified is also very different from that for 'Using Own Initiative'. Though the subgroup with the largest *own-skill* 'deficit' had the highest satisfaction with Using Initiative (73%), its balance for Actual Work Done (+33%) was not the highest. It should, however, be remembered that it was a small subgroup (33 cases)—and the 'greatly' Underutilized (15 cases) was even smaller. 'Work done' is a more encompassing (and perhaps vaguer) notion than 'Using initiative', and the small numbers may be a greater problem for reflecting (sometimes complex) tasks and responsibilities than in reflecting differences in autonomy, which may refer to just one aspect of this work. Even so, despite this 'aberration', when the two *intrinsic* aspects are considered together it appears that skill differences had the effects expected.

Extrinsic Aspects

Table 9.5 shows that skill-matching had a strong association with 'Promotion opportunities'. All subgroups had negative balances of satisfaction; but, irrespective of the type of matching, the 'balance of dissatisfaction' (as it can be considered here) fell with level of *job-skill*. The Underqualified were clearly the least dissatisfied overall and the Underutilized the most dissatisfied. For 'Total Pay', the effects seemed no less evident, with the Underqualified again the least dissatisfied and the Underutilized the most dissatisfied. Higher *job-skill* seems to have operated here

Table 9.5. *Types of skill-matching and satisfaction with the extrinsic aspects of present job*

Skill Situation of subgroup	Promotion (% High –% Low)	Total pay (% High –% Low)	Security (% High –% Low)	Hours worked (% High –% Low)
Underutilized				
Low job-skill, Moderate own-skill	–55	–26	+17	+8
Moderate job-skill, High own-skill	–50	–28	+15	+20
Low job-skill, High own-skill	–33	–33	+47	+7
Matched				
Low job-skill, Low own-skill	–60	–13	+22	+36
Moderate job-skill, Moderate own-skill	–36	–14	+28	+30
High job-skill, High own-skill	–27	–25	+27	+10
Underqualified				
Moderate job-skill, Low own-skill	–35	–8	+29	+37
High job-skill, Moderate own-skill	–25	–12	+36	+18
High job-skill, Low own-skill	–18	—	+42	+24
Employee sample	–38	–17	+26	+25

Note: The scores are for the '*balance of satisfaction*' produced by subtracting the percentage of Low ratings for the job aspect from the percentage of High ratings. See also notes to Table 9.1–3.

Source: Work Attitudes/Histories survey.

so as to push all scores downwards: having technically more challenging work may have increased dissatisfaction with pay 'disproportionately'. A similar pattern reappeared for 'Hours worked', though all subgroups had positive satisfaction balances; broadly speaking, the lower the level of *job-skill* the higher a subgroup's satisfaction with 'Hours'.

For 'Security', there is an at first somewhat puzzling pattern. Between the Matched subgroups there was little difference, with all having balances close to the sample balance. Amongst the Underqualified, however, all balances were above that of the sample as a whole, and rose with the level of *job-skill*. On the other hand, while two of the Underutilized subgroups had balances below that of the sample, the 'greatly' Underutilized (High *own-skill*, Low *job-skill*) had the highest balance (+47%) of any subgroup. Overlooking the possibility that this 'anomaly' reflects once more the small size of this subgroup, the result may be explained in several other ways. A number of the people concerned may have been well-qualified recruits undergoing a period of induction or familiarization requiring them to perform low-grade tasks before starting their 'real' job at a higher level in the firm. Alternatively, some of these employees may have accepted lower-skilled jobs precisely because they appeared more secure than jobs better matching their skills. It is also possible that some people in this subgroup were labour market re-entrants, returning to work after periods of unemployment or family formation; as Elias found (see Chapter 3), the Work History data show that many re-entrants had experienced some downgrading as a result of the break in their work careers. In all these situations, the 'surplus' of own-skill may have made the individuals concerned of exceptional value to the employer, and their posts genuinely more secure; alternatively, they may have believed this was the case.

For each major subgroup, there is usually a pattern that follows skill profiles. This is perhaps clearest for the Matched group as a whole. The Low skills Matched group had the least dissatisfaction with Pay but the most with Promotion opportunities; it had the highest satisfaction with Hours worked; and though it had least satisfaction with Security there was little to choose between the subgroups on this aspect. On the other hand, the High Matched subgroup had the least dissatisfaction with Promotion, but the most with Pay; it was very much less satisfied with Hours Worked than the employee sample as whole.

Apart from the problems noted, the main conclusion to be drawn from the table once again seems relatively clear. Higher *job-skill* increased satisfaction (or reduced dissatisfaction) with 'Security' and 'Promotion opportunities', but it had the contrary effects on 'Total Pay' and 'Hours Worked'. In all cases, however, there was evidence that a surplus of *own-skill* slightly reduced satisfaction, while a deficit increased it.

Authority Aspects

For 'Relations with own supervisor', the Underutilized were once again the least satisfied (though all sub-groups still had positive balances), and the Underqualified the most satisfied (see Table 9.6). There was little difference between the Matched subgroups—

TABLE 9.6. *Types of skill-matching and satisfaction with the authority aspects of present job*

Skill situation of subgroup	Relations with own supervisor/manager (% High –% Low)	Ability/Efficiency of the management (% High –% Low)
Underutilized		
Low job-skill, Moderate own-skill	+24	–19
Moderate job-skill, High own-skill	+7	–33
Low job-skill, High own-skill	+20	–13
Matched		
Low job-skill, Low own-skill	+32	–2
Moderate job-skill, Moderate own-skill	+28	–11
High job-skill, High own-skill	+30	–12
Underqualified		
Moderate job-skill, Low own-skill	+40	+6
High job-skill, Moderate own-skill	+31	–14
High job-skill, Low own-skill	+64	+27
Employee sample	+28	–11

Note: The scores are for the '*balance of satisfaction*' produced by subtracting the percentage of Low ratings for the job aspect from the percentage of High ratings. See also notes to Tables 9.1–3.

Source: Work Attitudes/Histories survey.

all three came close to the sample balance of +28%. The smallest balance of all (+7%) was amongst the Underutilized, and the highest (a massive +64%) amongst the Underqualified.

But dissatisfaction with the 'Ability of management' showed a more complex pattern. True enough, the highest negative balances by far were amongst the Underutilized, though once again the balance for the 'greatly' Underutilized (–13%) was unexpect-

edly 'favourable'. Two of the Underqualified subgroups, however, actually had positive balances; for the 'greatly' Underqualified it rose to +27%—almost 40 percentage points above the
sample balance. This might perhaps be expected of people who,
by definition, had been selected by the management of their
workplace for work roles in which their *formal* qualifications and
organized training seem very inadequate. On the other hand, the
Underqualified with Moderate *own-skill* and High *job-skill* had a
substantial, and negative balance (–14%).

It seems likely that higher *own-skill* may increase dissatisfaction
with management efficiency because people with more education
and/or higher technical or professional training may be more critical of authority, more aware of weaknesses and failures in management control systems, and more sensitive to their effects on
their own work roles. Likewise, frustration in a post much below
their skill attainments may have been expressed here. On the
other hand, people with high *job-skill*, many of whom are themselves supervisors or managers, may have better knowledge of the
problems which *their own* managers have to confront. This might
offset their readiness to adopt a critical view. The data are consistent with such an interpretation, though perhaps they are not
much more than that. Despite such obvious difficulties, however,
it does appear that balances of skill also produced some characteristic patterns in satisfaction with the *authority* aspects of a job.

General Job Satisfaction

The broad associations between skill-matching and satisfaction
suggested at the outset appear rather more clearly when general
job satisfaction is examined. Two measures for overall job satisfaction were available. The first was the respondent's own overall
assessment, on the 11-point rating scale, collapsed here into a
three-level measure with identical cutting-points to those used for
the specific aspects of job satisfaction. Column 1 of Table 9.7
shows the balance between High and Low percentages for each
subgroup. Here, the Matched subgroups all have balances only
just above the sample balance of +26%. The Underqualified
subgroups all have higher balances than any of the Matched and
the Underutilized subgroups. The Underutilized have the lowest
balances of all; for the 'greatly' Underutilized, the balance is

actually negative, despite the overall bias in the sample towards a large positive balance.

A second measure for general job satisfaction was created. It is a statistically composite measure computed from the original ('unbanded') respondent ratings for all specific job aspects, yielding precise scores for composite job satisfaction for each case. (The advantage of having such scores is that they permit the kind of multivariate analysis presented in a later section.) For Table 9.7, these scores have been banded so as to group just over 33% of all cases in each of the three bands (High, Moderate, Low). Column 2 shows the balance between percentages for High and Low in each subgroup. The results are far more pronounced than those produced using the Overall Satisfaction ratings. The Matched groups all have balances close to that for the whole sample, but the balances for the Underutilized are very much lower, and those for the Under-qualified very much higher.

This measure, which is certainly a more sensitive one statistically, confirms that skill-matching produces very distinct effects on job satisfaction as a whole. Though the results for the two small 'extreme' subgroups must again be treated somewhat cautiously, there can once more be no mistaking the broad way that skill-matching operates. However, it still leaves unclear the exact importance of each skill variable in relation to the other, or how far higher *own-skill* may modify the apparently strong effect of higher *job-skill*. Nor does it show how influential each mode of skill is in relation to other intervening workplace and individual variables. It is worth considering two such variables—Gender and Part-time work—separately, before presenting the more general model.

Intervening Variables: Gender and Part-Time Work

Several other chapters in this book (but especially those by Gallie, by Elias, and by Horrell *et al.*) show a close relationship between skill levels, gender, and full-time employment. Women's (measured) *job-skill* and *own-skill* levels are lower than men's, and the gap is particularly marked for women part-time workers. How far, then, does gender intervene in the association between still-matching and job attitudes? In answering this question, a further, more fundamental one needs to be confronted: is job sat-

TABLE 9.7. *Types of skill-matching and overall satisfaction with present job*

Skill situation of subgroup	Overall satisfaction rating (balance) (% High –% Low)	Composite satisfaction scores (balance) (% High –% Low)
Underutilized		
Low job-skill, Moderate own-skill	+7	–27
Moderate job-skill, High own-skill	+17	–15
Low job-skill, High own-skill	–13	–13
Matched		
Low job-skill, Low own-skill	+28	+1
Moderate job-skill, Moderate own-skill	+29	+5
High job-skill, High own-skill	+27	+4
Underqualified		
Moderate job-skill, Low own-skill	+35	+12
High job-skill, Moderate own-skill	+31	+13
High job-skill, Low own-skill	+36	+33
Employee sample	+26	+1

Note: The scores in column 1 are for the '*balance of satisfaction*' produced by subtracting the percentage of Low ratings for the job aspect from the percentage of High ratings. Those in column 2 were produced, in a similar way, by using an ordinal-level version of the composite job-satisfaction variable, divided into High scorers, Medium scorers, and Low scorers. Cutting-points for the bands were set to group scores in subgroups of approximately equal numbers of cases.

Source: Work Attitudes/Histories survey.

isfaction amongst some women affected by different expectations and demands from men's, as writers like Marsh (1991) and *a fortiori* Hakim (1991) have argued?

Table 9.8 confirms that gender and full-time employment are closely associated with types of skill-matching. Three features

TABLE 9.8. *Levels of skill-matching by sex and type of work contract* (%)

Skill situation of subgroup	Women		All Men	Sample
	Part-time	Full-time		
Underutilized				
Low job-skill, Moderate own-skill	8	9	6	7
Moderate job-skill, High own-skill	4	11	16	12
Low job-skill, High own-skill	1	—[b]	—[b]	1
Matched				
Low job-skill, Low own-skill	49	14	11	21
Moderate job-skill, Moderate own-skill	17	29	25	24
High job-skill, High own-skill	2	11	20	14
Underqualified				
Moderate job-skill, Low own-skill	14	12	9	11
High job-skill, Moderate own-skill	4	12	12	10
High job-skill, Low own-skill	1	1	1	1
Employee sample	23	28	49	100

[a] The male employee subgroup includes 20 part-timers. [b] These two subgroups both had 3 cases only.

Source: Work Attitudes/Histories survey.

stand out clearly. To begin with, part-timer women were dispro-portionately (49% of all) concentrated in the Low *job-skill* with Low *own-skill* subgroup, and only 2% came in the High Matched subgroup. In both the Underutilized and Underqualified cate-gories women part-timers were concentrated in the lowest-level subgroups. Secondly, the distributions for full-timer women and for all men are far less imbalanced, though there is a 'downward' bias which is clearest in the High Matched subgroup where men (20%) outnumber women full-timers (11%) by two to one. (Within each Matched subgroup the full-timer women also had lower *mean* skill scores than the men.) Thirdly, however, women (even part-timers) appear almost as often as men in the Under-qualified subgroups, and a little less often amongst the Under-utilized. On the measures used, then, gender *per se* affected overall skill position less than might have been expected. There was, in particular, no general concentration of women in the Underutilized categories.

It has been argued that positive satisfaction with most aspects of jobs in the Work Attitudes/Histories sample does seem primarily to reflect levels of *job-skill*, and may be somewhat offset by higher *own-skill*. It might therefore be expected that part-timer women, with their generally low *job-skill*, would account for a disproportionate number of Low satisfaction scores. In fact, the very reverse is true. Table 9.9 shows composite job satisfaction for all men employees, women full-timers, and women part-timers. The balance for men (–9%) is somewhat below the sample balance, while the balance for women full-timers (+3%) is just above it, and the balance for the women part-timers (+23%) far above it. It is tempting to suggest that their very low stock of *own-skill*, quite paradoxically, actually 'inflated' the job satisfaction scores of the part-timer women.

TABLE 9.9. *Banded composite scores for job satisfaction, by sex and type of work contract* (%)

	Women		All Men[a]	Sample
	Part-time	Full-time		
Low scorers	22	32	38	33
Moderate scorers	33	34	33	33
High scorers	45	35	29	34
Balance (% High –% Low)	+23	+3	–9	+1

[a] The male employee subgroup includes 20 part-timers. The table uses the ordinal-level version of the composite job-satisfaction variable. Cutting-points for the bands were set to group scores in approximately equal subgroups.

Source: Work Attitudes/Histories survey.

The broad effect of skill-matching in combination with both gender and type of labour-market participation is easier to show diagrammatically. Figure 9.1 plots the difference between *mean scores* for each of the (27) subgroups and the mean score for the sample as a whole on the composite satisfaction measure. Introducing the additional controls (sex, with women employees divided between full-timers and part-timers) produces one or two very small subgroups. None the less, a new pattern is evident:

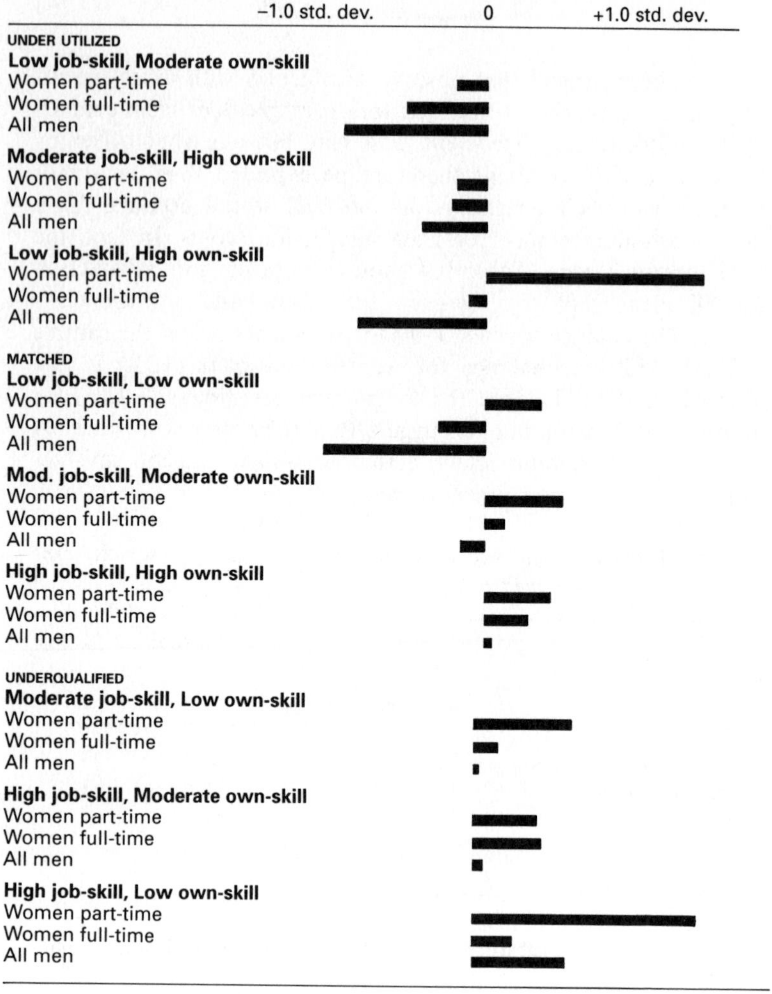

	−1.0 std. dev.	0	+1.0 std. dev.

UNDER UTILIZED
Low job-skill, Moderate own-skill
Women part-time
Women full-time
All men

Moderate job-skill, High own-skill
Women part-time
Women full-time
All men

Low job-skill, High own-skill
Women part-time
Women full-time
All men

MATCHED
Low job-skill, Low own-skill
Women part-time
Women full-time
All men

Mod. job-skill, Moderate own-skill
Women part-time
Women full-time
All men

High job-skill, High own-skill
Women part-time
Women full-time
All men

UNDERQUALIFIED
Moderate job-skill, Low own-skill
Women part-time
Women full-time
All men

High job-skill, Moderate own-skill
Women part-time
Women full-time
All men

High job-skill, Low own-skill
Women part-time
Women full-time
All men

[a]3 cases: [b]3 cases: [c]4 cases:

Note: The figure illustrates the degree of variation between sub-group mean scores for composite job satisfaction produced by the SPSSX Breakdown analysis. The mean score for the whole sample is zero and the bars indicate the relative 'distance' of a sub-group's mean score from this average, and whether it is lower or higher than the mean. (Bars stretching to the left indicate negative sub-group scores, bars to the right positive sub-group scores.) Actual scores for cases in any sub-group themselves fail either side of the mean of the sub-group concerned, in a more or less normal distribution. Sign. F for the scores was >,0000.

Source: Work attitudes/Histories survey.

Figure 9.1 Levels of skill-matching and mean scores for composite job satisfaction, by sex and type of work contract

(i) in all but one of the subgroups, the mean scores for men were lower than those for women; (ii) in all but one of the subgroups, full-timer women had a lower mean score than part-timer women. Overall, then, the new variables strongly confirm the underlying associations with skill-matching found earlier, but show relatively higher job satisfaction amongst part-timer women especially.

It would be too hasty to conclude that this finding shows that women as a whole, even part-timer women, have a much lower threshold of job satisfaction than men. There are broad differences in the work situations and labour-market positions of men and women employees. Further workplace, labour-market, and individual variables, such as technical change or years spent in employment, may intervene in a significant way. The effects of skill types themselves need to be more carefully examined, too, since in many of the subgroups women's average skill-scores are lower than those of the men in them. Over 30 other variables showing some significant statistical association with composite satisfaction were in fact distinguished in the early stages of analysis. The apparently strong effect of gender and part-time work on levels of job satisfaction will now be considered in relation to these variables, as well as to the two skill variables.

SKILL AND SATISFACTION: A GENERAL MODEL

To examine and control for the effects of each of these numerous possibly influential factors, multivariate analysis was undertaken using composite job satisfaction scores as the dependent variable. By its nature such treatment (or 'modelling') produces results that are harder to present in simple table or diagram form. (It can also introduce new difficulties in interpreting results.) Table 9.10 places what appear to be the essential findings in the first three columns, leaving more technical information (beta-weights and T-values) in columns 4 and 5.

Variables have been grouped into four sets: those of primary, secondary, and only marginal importance; and those which exerted no effect though they might have been expected to do so. Most of these 35 variables, as noted, had appeared to have some association with job-satisfaction scores, in the absence of other

TABLE 9.10. *Relative influence of the skill variables and other workplace and individual variables on scores for composite job satisfaction*

	Workplace variables	Individual variables	Direction	T-value	Beta
First-order influences					
Harmonious employer–employees relations	1			21.7	.289
Would change jobs if chance arose		2	Negative	18.4	.252
Own job more secure last 5 years	3			8.4	.111
Own pay considered fair		4		10.8	.137
Promotion chances best with current employer		5		7.1	.090
Second-order influences					
Skill of the current job high	6			9.8	.156
Part-timer employee		7		5.9	.075
Strong Expressive Work Ethic		8		5.9	.073
Increased promotion chances last 5 years		9		5.4	.071
Wide choice when took present job		10		5.8	.074
Recent organizational change cut staff	11		Negative	4.5	.059
Higher personal skill level		12	Negative	4.3	.067
Marginal influences					
Increased variety of tasks last 5 years	13			4.1	.052
Recent change in work organization	14		Negative	3.4	.044
Time in present part-time job		15		3.0	.050
Smaller workplace	16			3.3	.044

Variable				
Working for present employer helps promotion	17		3.3	.042
Woman employee		18	4.0	.061
Time in current full-time job		19	3.9	.060
Stronger economic individualism		20	2.7	.034
Skill of job done has increased last 5 years	21		2.1	.030
Do not enter the equation				
Private-sector workplace	*			
Recent introduction of computer equipment	*			
Recent introduction new machinery/equipment	*			
Training for job increased last 5 years	*			
Work effort increased last 5 years	*			
Supervision tighter last 5 years	*			
Pace of work faster last 5 years	*			
Responsibility increased last 5 years	*			
Higher current earnings		*		
Profession/managerial-level job		*		
Manual-level job		*		
Good chances better job next 2 years (anywhere)		*		
Easy to find a job as good as present one		*		
Secondary economic involvement		*		

Note: The table is based upon an Ordinary Least Squares (OLS) regression analysis. Adj. R^2 = .467.
Source: Work Attitudes/Histories survey.

controls. The significant influences have been ordered in terms of their statistical importance as controlling factors, which is usually close to their relative importance as individual explanatory factors in the model. (Technically speaking, this is the proportion of the variance in overall scores that they account for in a regression equation.) The 15 variables left out of the model cannot be listed in any order; they can all be regarded as equally non-significant. Those variables having a negative effect on satisfaction scores have been noted in the third column. Finally, the table separates the workplace influences (column 1) and the individual-level influences (column 2). Two essentially workplace factors which enter the equation (increase in variety of tasks, increase in level of skill) present a certain problem in that they may have had individual-level effects (particularly on *own-skill*), and are derived from personal judgements by respondents about the work situation. Thus, some ambiguity in them has to be accepted. (In fact, most variables relating to the experience of changing task structures, supervision, and effort did not enter the equation.)

The results as a whole need to be interpreted with care. Taking the workplace factors first, it hardly seems surprising that high general job satisfaction was 'created' essentially by working in a workplace considered to be 'harmonious', at a job whose security had increased while the labour market had declined, and was further enhanced by working in a smaller workplace at a job that increased promotion opportunities in general. Nor, turning to the most powerful individual-level factors, does it seem anything but predictable that job satisfaction was most closely associated with not wishing to change employers, considering one's present pay fair, and believing that one's own promotion changes are better with the current employer. It would have been astonishing if such factors had failed to prove important. In terms of the previous discussion, however, what seems more noteworthy is the *relative* influence of sex, the two skill variables, and part-time work.

Amongst workplace variables, the skill level of the current job was a second-order influence, but still the sixth most important of the 21 variables that had a significant effect, and the third most influential of the nine workplace variables. Indeed, all remaining workplace variables (apart from not having experienced recent work reorganization leading to staff cuts), had little effect. Perhaps the most surprising finding here was the relative unimportance of working in a smaller workplace. Larger workplaces can perhaps compensate for their social 'disadvantages of scale' by offering more promotion opportunities and better security. However, if 'harmonious workplace' is left out of the model, working in a smaller unit becomes more influential.

It also seems noteworthy that tighter supervision, actual earnings, and work intensification (increased work effort, pace of work faster over last five years) had no independent effect on job satisfaction.[5] Increased variety of work tasks over the last five years had a small positive influence, as did increased skill of job over last five years. As both might be considered ancillary aspects of personal skills, this influence is worth noting. Recent experience of some sorts of technical or organizational change—work reorganization personally affecting the respondent, or changes leading to redundancies or other staff cuts—did operate to diminish general satisfaction. On the other hand, workplace change involving new equipment, computers, or automation had no effect.

Amongst the individual variables, as noted, higher satisfaction was associated with several similarly 'obvious' factors, such as not wishing to change jobs, the sense of having been able to exercise choice when taking the present job, considering present pay fair, and having good prospects of promotion with the present employer. The length of time in the job currently held also operated in a marginally positive direction—but it may be worth noting that time in a *part-time* job was slightly more important as a controlling factor. Higher personal skill level was only the eighth most influential individual variable, and twelfth of the 21 variables that had significant effects. Nevertheless, it *did* exert an appreciable independent effect. More important, this was in a *negative* direction: for jobs of comparable skill, those people with higher training and qualifications *were* more likely to have lower scores for satisfaction with their current jobs than people with lower own-skill scores. This seems reasonable, in that such people may have higher career aims and expectations because they have more market power, and may thus be more likely to view their current job as a stage in an evolving career process. It is also consistent with the findings on the effect of skill-matching on satisfaction discussed earlier, with the Underqualified 'disproportionately' satisfied, and the Underutilized 'exceptionally' dissatisfied.

But, in the light of the earlier analysis and discussion, the most striking finding is that being a part-time employee emerged as the seventh most important controlling factor. Almost all part-timer employees in the Work Attitudes/Histories survey were women, outnumbering men part-timers in the sample by 40 to 1. Strictly speaking, by itself being a woman marginally increased satisfaction scores, but it came only in eighteenth place as a controlling factor. Moreover, although it seems probable that the very low— it was at times barely measurable—*own-skill* of the women part-timers may have operated in a few cases so as to inflate their satisfaction scores to 'artificially' high levels, the *own-skill* variable does not act as a substitute (or 'proxy') for the labour-market participation variable. In other words, according to this model it is *being a part-timer*, not having the lower *own-skill* of many part-timers, that is the more important influence. This greatly strengthens the view that while the job satisfaction of women full-time employees is indeed influenced by much the same factors as men's, that of women part-timers is influenced by quite distinct personal priorities and circumstances. (It should be possible to model some of the possibly important non-workplace factors involved, making use of the Household and Community survey data from SCELI.) But the criteria by which a job was evaluated do seem to have differed significantly amongst the women part-timers in the Work Attitudes/Histories survey, especially in comparison with the women full-timers, as well as with men.

At this point, some of the findings of Chapter 10 (on skill and the work ethic) can be anticipated. As will be shown there, an analysis of commitment to paid employment, reasons for having paid work, and labour-market ideology found three major, and distinct, aspects of work commitment. The strength of the first of these—an 'Expressive' Work Ethic—is associated closely with similar factors (*job-skill*, *own-skill*, and occupation being the strongest) to those affecting levels of job satisfaction, almost irrespective of sex.[6] Women part-timers, Chapter 10 shows, had an exceptionally low mean score for Expressive Work Ethic—not surprisingly, perhaps, given their very low overall skill levels and occupational position. Furthermore, another distinct work-commitment factor, Secondary Economic Involvement (implying the absence of strong, long-term involvement in paid employment) was associated overwhelmingly with part-time work.[7] Secondary economic involvement scores were included in the present analysis, but they had no effect. Apparently, these scores are so closely linked with part-time employment that they add little new information. Indeed, if the Part-timer variable is omitted from the regression, Secondary economic involvement becomes more influential. This seems to provide further support for the view that most women part-timers do indeed have distinct bases for evaluating their jobs, perhaps reflecting in turn their readiness to act as earners of a 'component' wage supplementing the earnings of a husband or male partner, and that generally their expectations of work are set very low—far lower even than the men or women full-timers who suffer from comparably large deficits of negotiable *own-skill*. How far they should be seen, following Hakim (1991), as 'grateful slaves' is perhaps more debatable and cannot be taken up here.

Scores for Expressive Work Ethic *did* exert an appreciable, and positive, independent effect; Expressive Work Ethic is the fifth most influential of the individual-level variables. People with strong commitment to paid work were also more likely to have higher job satisfaction. Almost by definition such people do not work part-time if they can work full-time, since Expressive Work Ethic is a composite measure reflecting such components as a career outlook on paid work, high esteem for paid work in its own right as well as in comparison to competing activities, and the propensity to regard work as a way of using personal skills and abilities to the full. Those people who *already* enjoy work providing such advantages may be better able to develop such a work orientation; in other words, an Expressive Work Ethic may in part reflect some of the favourable factors in a work situation that *also* create job satisfaction. All the same, general job satisfaction, as Chapter 10 will show, is only a very weak influence on Expressive Work Ethic. Any 'causal' link, therefore, seems more likely to run from work ethic to satisfaction: people having a strong Expressive Work Ethic may be better placed in labour-market terms to obtain jobs that are—in the employee's own scale of values, as well as in objective terms—more rewarding and challenging. At the same time, these employees may also be more highly motivated to find such jobs.

A third aspect of work commitment—an Economically Individualist personal labour-market ideology—also exerted a very marginal positive influence on general job satisfaction; to simplify, the strong supporters of 'go-getting', self-reliant labour-market values had slightly higher satisfaction scores. Some respondents (for example, Line managers) possessing a strong Expressive Work Ethic also had particularly high scores for Economic Individualism, while others (for example, Personnel or Computer managers) did not. It may be, then, that such respondents were less sensitive to disagreeable aspects of their work tasks or inadequacies in their rewards, and more tolerant of management authority, because of their view of the labour market as an arena for self-reliant struggle in which they should prove their own survival power. Those lacking this ideology, or holding less strong versions of it, may have been less tolerant of such disadvantages.

CONCLUSIONS

With regard to the main question taken up in this chapter, however, the multivariate analysis confirms that both the skill levels of jobs, and the skill attainments of individuals, are significant and *separate* influences on job satisfaction. However, while higher *job-skill* tends to increase job satisfaction, higher *own-skill* tends to depress it. Where *own-skill* and *job-skill* are seriously mismatched these effects will be more pronounced. The relation of these skill factors to other workplace and individual variables known to exert a significant influence on levels of satisfaction, as measured by a composite score based on self-ratings, seems in one sense straightforward.

However, before concluding it is necessary to sound a note of caution about this. The model shows a very high level of statistical fit. (Adjusted r^2 is almost .50.) Some survey researchers might regard this as suspiciously high for this type of data. Once again, it is important to take note of the problems that arise in analysing job-satisfaction levels in terms of the respondent's own reports of his or her organizational position and labour-market prospects. To come straight to the point, all the first-order influences produced by the multivariate analysis might also be regarded, at least in part, as *alternative* measures of overall job satisfaction rather than as 'determinants' of it.

In particular, employees enjoying exceptionally favourable or harmonious *individual* relations with their employer may exaggerate the harmony of the workplace as a whole and assess other aspects of their own jobs more favourably as a result. Likewise, people who have a *personal* sense of grievance and conflict with their employer may be more likely to generalize this personal experience to the relations between staff and employer as a whole. This may colour their judgements about many specific aspects of their jobs, and their evaluations of their own security, rewards, and promotion prospects, while making them keener to seek other work. No independent data about the level of conflict in the workplace was available to allow a check on this possibility. As a result, it is not known how far the 'Harmony versus conflict' variable in particular applied to real workplace circumstances. It might be, at least in part, individual and contingent.

Yet the second-order influences seem to be much less questionable on such grounds. With the possible exception of 'Increase in promotion chances', all are somewhat more 'objective'. Thus while the model may be less powerful overall for predicting levels of self-rated job satisfaction than it seems, this is not attributable to inadequacies in the two skill variables. *Own-skill* and *job-skill* may have a relatively still greater effect on job satisfaction than the model suggests. For example, their relative importance increases if 'suspect' variables are omitted, though the model then has less explanatory power in the formal sense. Again, although it is important to note possible weaknesses in the model, it is not thought to be seriously misleading. It is, after all, reasonable to assume that satisfaction *should* be strongly linked to objective features of the workplace and work situation, even if personal feelings may at times distort judgements about this environment. At the worst, the model probably overstates the influence of those workplace factors that *are* in reality the most significant. Further research is certainly needed to clarify these relationships, testing the influence of skills on job satisfaction in the light of more accurate measures. But this chapter seems to confirm the fundamental importance of skills for such subjective aspects of employment.

NOTES

1. As Spenner argued, it is important to make this distinction when examining long-run historical trends in skill. (See also Lee, 1982.) Some individual workers, and some occupational groups, experience work changes that result in tasks of lower skill than those for which they have training. The overall demand for skill may be growing throughout any given economy, and running well ahead of supply in some or many occupations, while other occupations or job types may be subject to severe losses of job-skill. Defining such scarcities is important to policy as well as understanding changes in society as a whole. For official classification practice see, e.g. US Department of Labor (1977); Central Statistical Office (1980), and Miller *et al.* (1980).

2. Measures regarded as job-skill indicators were: considers current work skilled; extent of discretion over work methods; qualifications *now required for recruitment* to the currently held job; has previously supervised other employees; supervises other employees at present; numbers of other employees supervised; how closely respondent is supervised; occupation (4-digit code); uses computerized equipment or information technology. Measures regarded as own-skill indicators were: any training for current type of work; length of training for current type of work; time taken to learn to do current work well; qualifications *actually held* by respondent; time spent as full-time student. Other available measures relevant to skill levels were: change in level of skill over five years; change in level of responsibility over five years; change in variety of tasks over five years; change in provision of training for own job over five years; source of training; necessity of qualifications (currently required) to do work competently. The measures chosen to create the composite skill measures are listed in the Appendix to this ch.

3. That is, in Northampton (Cambridge team), Rochdale (Lancaster team), and Swindon (Bath). The data collected in Northampton are discussed in full in the chapters by the Cambridge team in this volume. Besides including additional questions on skill change in their team-specific section of the Work Attitudes/Histories survey, Bath also carried out a Related Study involving five case studies of firms and 100 open-ended interviews with their employees. This provided the opportunity to replicate questions on skill change from the Work Attitudes/Histories survey, followed by probing questions.

4. The cases falling into each cell reflect the cutting-points used to convert the scores into (ordinal-level) categories. As noted in the text,

these cutting-points were identical for each set of factor scores. Choosing further cutting-points would have increased the number of both matched and unmatched categories, making presentation very much less manageable, though perhaps showing up more of the diversity in the skill position of sample members. The threefold division is adequate for the purposes of this chapter. For the multivariate analyses, which show the full effect of conditioning variables, the non-banded, interval-level versions of job-skill and own-skill variables were used, thus allowing fully for all individual mismatches in the sample.

5. A further remark might be added. The Work Attitudes/Histories data do not provide independent measures of work effectiveness. It is thus impossible to say whether the more satisfied employees were also more productive. They were not, however, better rewarded in terms of current earnings than those less satisfied whose workplace and individual circumstances were comparable (current earnings did not enter the equation) though they were very much more likely than others to consider their current pay to be fair. It seems questionable to assume that more satisfied employees, in any case, are more productive, and that they will be duly rewarded in money terms if they are more productive. The once influential Human Relations school of personnel management theory held the view that 'happy, well-integrated' workers are less demanding about money rewards because the social needs of employees are of prior importance to their economic ones. The data available are insufficient to explore such a claim properly, but the results of this chapter throw some doubt on it. Increases in productivity derive in considerable measure from high levels of personal skill. However, the Work Attitudes/Histories survey results seem to show that employees with high skill attainments may apply *more*, rather than less, demanding standards to extrinsic aspects of their jobs, and especially to their pay rewards, although they may well derive considerable satisfaction from performing tasks challenging their higher levels of training, education, and experience.

6. A strong Expressive Work Ethic is closely associated with Service-Class (Goldthorpe, 1987) employment, that is with having a professional or managerial-level occupation. The variable for Service-Class membership ('Professional or managerial occupation') did not enter the multivariate regression equation. But if Expressive Work Ethic is omitted, Service class does not replace it. This is perhaps surprising.

7. None the less, high levels of own-skill (in particular) and job-skill drastically cut scores for Secondary economic involvement amongst the small minority of women part-timers who had them. Again some women, especially those with high own-skill, who worked part-time

did have a strong Expressive Work Ethic. It seems probable that this minority of women did not work part-time from choice, but because of adverse domestic circumstances or some other constraint. Regrettably, the survey did not ask part-timers whether they would prefer to work full-time, or vice versa.

APPENDIX 9.1

Measuring Skill

The distinction between own-skill and job-skill is essentially a conceptual one. In particular, evidently, high levels of own-skill provide greater access to more highly skilled jobs; and people who perform skilled tasks increase their own competence, irrespective of their initial qualifications or training. When reliable measures for several aspects of skill are available for a large sample, as they were in the Work Attitudes/Histories survey, a high level of correlation between *all* measures should be expected.

This proved to be the case. Over a dozen variables which seemed directly applicable as skill measures inter-correlated very closely. A further half-dozen variables, which seemed indirectly relevant, showed moderate to high inter-correlation with the first set. Factor analysis of all these variables produced two or more factors, depending upon exactly which variables were included as items; but it proved difficult to interpret these new composite ('factored') variables. (For further discussion of factor analysis, see the Appendix to Chapter 10 and Norusis, 1985.)

One of them, however, was clearly linked to what might be termed prior qualification. Variables for time spent in formal education and paper qualifications were very closely associated with it (that is, 'loaded' heavily). This factor seems similar to the US Department of Labor's General Educational Development (GED) dimension of occupational skill; a second factor, though less clearly, seemed to approximate to the same organization's Specific Vocational Preparation (SVP), which has to do with the possession of 'hands-on' skills (US Department of Labor, 1977).

When a smaller number of variables were divided into two distinct sets, following the conceptual distinction between *job-skill* and *own-skill*, and factored separately they each produced a single, very distinct factor. The first set were: considering present job is skilled; being responsible for supervising other employees; the number of others supervised; the degree of choice over how to do the job; and the qualifications the employee considered were *necessary to obtain* his/her job at the present time. (The employee concerned quite often did not personally possess these qualifications.) The second set comprised: having some training for 'the type of work you do now'; the length of any training; the time taken 'after you first started doing this type of job to learn to do it well'; and the qualifications *actually held* by the employee.

Factor analysis calculates and allocates scores for each factor to each case used in the analysis, depending on the pattern of the individual's response to the relevant questions. (Missing data, as they were for this analysis, are usually replaced by a mean score for the variable in question.) Each employee in the Work Attitudes/Histories sample was thus 'scored' for the composite variables *job-skill* and *own-skill*. These versions of the variables had interval-level properties; that is, the scores of any two individuals could in theory be taken as providing an 'exact' measure of the 'real' difference between their levels of skill. (But a score does not purport to measure 'absolute' levels of skill.) It may be that the Work Attitudes/Histories data were insufficient to produce fully reliable interval-level scores. Fortunately, this was not necessary for the analysis carried out. It is believed that the scores produced are reasonable guides to real differences in levels of skill. (Their validity will be discussed further below.)

Interval-level variables are necessary for use in many multivariate analyses, but they are less helpful for purposes of exposition and description. For this purpose, simpler, ordinal forms of the variables were required. These were produced by grouping all scores falling within a specified range one of three bands—'High', 'Medium', and 'Low'. Once this had been done, it was easy to look at the overall ways the skill scores combined, and in particular how well skills were 'balanced' or 'matched', both overall and in given subgroups.

Leaving aside for a moment the question of whether the resulting composite variables actually did succeed in reflecting levels of *job-skill* and *own-skill*, they were at least relatively distinct. As can be seen from the analysis of matching in scores for *job-skill* and *own-skill* in Chapter 9, it seems apparent that the two composite variables are not duplicate measures but tap separate aspects of skill. In terms of them, almost half the sample had discrepant skill levels of a moderate or serious sort. Each variable also exerted a significant *independent* effect in the multiple regression equation for overall satisfaction. Again, there was a moderately high correlation between each skill score and gross earnings (in each case, $r^2 = .23$); but when scores are added together, the variance in earnings explained by this 'total skill' variable increased by 30% (to $r^2 = .31$). While the measures overlap, then, they are certainly not mere alternatives. Their own statistical association ($r^2 = .41$) is certainly high; but technically speaking, this still means that only two-fifths of the variance in scores for one can be explained in terms of change in scores for the other.

The question of validity—how far each composite variable actually does reflect the aspect of skill it is supposed to measure—can likewise be answered, at least in part, by pointing once again to the association between very different patterns of skill-mismatching and job satisfaction itself. Those employees whose personal skills seemed under used (and probably under-rewarded) would be expected to be far less satisfied than those who performed (and were rewarded for) work for which they lacked formal training, the most relevant experience, or paper qualifications. Employees in the subgroup whose 'surpluses' of *own-skill* were, relatively speaking, the highest were also by far the least satisfied with their opportunities to use initiative in their jobs (see Table 9.4), with their chances of promotion (Table 9.5), and with the ability and efficiency of their own managers (Table 9.6). The subgroup with the largest 'deficits' of *own-skill*, by contrast, had the highest levels of satisfaction (or the least dissatisfaction in the case of 'Promotion chances') with these job aspects. These findings are thoroughly consistent with the underlying logic of the conceptual distinction which the measures attempt to embody.

Their validity also seems high in terms of 'known groups'. Laboratory and experimental technicians, for example, often have extensive training and qualifications but relatively routine, unchallenging tasks; in terms of the ordinal versions of the skill variables, 74% of employees in this group had 'high' levels of *own-skill*, but only 50% had 'high' levels of *job-skill*. (No fewer than 50% of women laboratory technicians, on the measures used, had underutilized personal skill.) Again, many British managers are often thought to lack adequate or appropriate formal training for their responsibilities. In the employee sample, the proportion of managers in the 'high' group for *own-skill* was significantly lower than the proportion with 'high' *job-skill*. This was so for all managers, but also held true individually for the four main manager subgroups represented in the Work Attitudes/Histories sample: retail managers (–14%); general and line managers/supervisors (–22%); specialist/personnel/computer managers (–23%); and 'other managers' (–25%). Amongst shop assistants, 67% of men had matched 'medium' skill scores, but 49% of women part-timer shop assistants had matched 'low' scores. Significantly perhaps, male laboratory workers had the greatest degree of matching at 'high' (66%); part-timer women cleaners had the greatest matching (84%) at 'low'. On the intuitive level, these results also seem to point to considerable validity in these measures.

No doubt the measures could be improved, for example by taking into account work experience effects of the kind Elias describes in Chapter 3, and the social and tacit skills called for in much work done by women. Though not embodying such data, the measures correlate highly with those that do attempt to measure such aspects. In Chapter 7, the Cambridge team describe their special index of skill incorporating several additional indicators and omitting one or two others (such as defining one's current job as 'skilled'), for which data from the core survey were in fact available. This 'Cambridge index' of skill was used with the employee sub-sample (approximately 600 cases) for Northampton. An opportunity was taken to examine the association between scores on the Cambridge skill index for the Northampton employee sub-sample and its scores for *job-skill* and *own-skill* as measured here. The level of association with each one was high (for *job-skill*, $r^2 = .41$, and for *own-skill*, $r^2 = .50$), and suggest that many different combinations of indicators can produce a broadly acceptable all-purpose measure of skill.

As the Cambridge index of skill embodied several additional 'customized' indicators of the skills used at work, it should be a more accurate summary measure of these than the *job-skill* composite variable. However, it was not produced through factor analysis, but following a 'points system' which is explained in Chapter 7. This might affect results in some way. Interestingly, the Cambridge index correlated somewhat more closely with the *own-skill* composite variable. It may have been that people occupying higher-skilled jobs, as measured by the Cambridge indeed, were 'disproportionately' likely to have higher levels of training or qualification; in other words, its extra indicators might sometimes have acted as proxy measures of personal skill, or might have functioned as measures of 'credentialist' processes in selection for some jobs with special responsibilities.

If this was so, it would imply that 'real' skills mismatching in the Work Attitudes/Histories sample may have been less extensive than Chapter 9 concludes. There was no easy way of examining any of these possibilities with the data available when the comparison was undertaken. But any scaling down of 'measured' skills mismatching could only be of a minor kind, since the Cambridge index and the factored *own-skill* scores correlated only a little more closely than do the *job-skill* and *own-skill* scores themselves. Most 'deficits' and 'surpluses' of both personal skill and the skill of jobs would remain. As noted above, none of these measures purport to be highly calibrated measures of absolute differences in skills. The *own-skill* and *job-skill* variables aim merely to be accurate enough to bring out the effects of skill-matching on job attitudes discussed in this chapter, and their effect on work-commitment values examined in Chapter 10.

As the Cambridge team themselves conclude in Chapter 7, improvement of composite skill measures must perhaps pay more attention to the particular work tasks and responsibilities of given occupations; yet there may be theoretical and practical limits, as well as financial and operational ones, to attempts to produce better indices of skill that are intended to apply to the workforce as a whole. This is a persuasive argument. But, for a more restricted range of occupations, creation of more sensitive measures of both *own-skill* and *job-skill* should be both feasible and worthwhile.

10

Skill and Samuel Smiles: Changing the British Work Ethic

MICHAEL ROSE

THE WORK ETHIC PROBLEM

This chapter examines how skill and occupation affect the work ethic. The evidence presented suggests that the work ethic is not declining because of social change, as many observers have claimed, but rather that the strength of the work ethic reflects skill levels, and rises amongst groups that attain higher skill. It may therefore be possible to strengthen the work ethic by improving skills training amongst the less skilled. As in other chapters in this book the findings will be analysed in the light of previous research in the sociology of work and neighbouring fields of study. Previous research and debate on the work ethic, however, and the relevance of this research to skill issues, are perhaps less well known than the other problematics discussed in this book. Some of this earlier work will therefore be briefly examined in the first section of this chapter. (A full review can be found in Rose, 1988*a*.) The discussion will also refer to some problems and controversies in social and economic policy in the 1980s in Britain.

In its general or popular sense, the work ethic refers to a syndrome of attitudes and behaviour affecting the readiness to seek and hold paid employment, possibly in a 'go-getting', individualistic frame of mind. The term has other important meanings, but this is the main one. It is the meaning adopted by most researchers; it is also close to the next most common definition, paid work as a *central life interest* (Dubin, 1956; Meaning of Working [MOW] International Research Team, 1987). Commitment to paid work will be the meaning adopted here.

An explicit aim of government policy after 1979 was to produce a cultural change in Britain that revived commitment to

work and ambitious individual work behaviour. The policy
assumed that an appropriate structure of incentives would produce a *cultural* change. However, the findings presented below
suggest that a constraint on this programme was the type and
distribution of skill in the labour force, because work attitudes
and behaviour showing high commitment to employment may be
no less dependent upon skill levels and occupational factors than
they are upon incentives. (They also reflect opportunities, especially the relative availability of paid work itself, which cannot be
dealt with here.)

Previous research has not explored the relationship between
skill and the worth ethic in an explicit way. Indeed, much of the
large literature on the work ethic is concerned with vaguely con-
ceived social and cultural changes and has a moralizing or political tone.[1] It is thus of little use for social analysis except as
evidence about the role of economic ideologies in society.
Sociologists themselves have thought of the work ethic mainly in
relation to Max Weber's claim that capitalist growth reflected a
Protestant religious attitude to employment. Evidence is still produced to prove such a link. On the other hand, little previous
research has examined, in the light of strong empirical data, how
skill affects work attitudes or economic values. In this sense, the
chapter aims to open up a new problem area.

However, three types of previous contribution do need to be
mentioned. These were all concerned in one way or another with
commitment to work. Sometimes they came close to examining
the influence of skill in an explicit way. Alternatively, they looked
at the role of occupation in shaping employee work involvement.
Because occupation is closely related to skill levels and skill types
they too are relevant to this examination.

Work Group Studies

Numerous studies, many of them undertaken by social psychologists, have examined the commitment of workers to their
employer. In its earliest phase, this tradition adopted the Human
Relations view (Rose, 1988*b*: Part 3), which until the late 1950s
remained widespread, that employee commitment was produced
by skilful leadership techniques. The latter, it was claimed, could
build loyalty to a small workgroup, and a sense of 'belonging' in

the firm as a whole, thus reducing turnover and absenteeism, while boosting output ('performance'). Commitment to work was equated with commitment to the workgroup. In turn, this loyalty might be converted into commitment to the employer by skilful leadership or other personnel management techniques.

A more sophisticated version of the approach came to stress the importance of *challenge* in work tasks themselves as a source of commitment. The idea of challenge here includes many aspects of what has been called *job-skill* in Chapter 9. It was also recognized that challenge in work tasks was often subject to social control, not just by work designers, but by unions, or though direct competition between groups of workers. At this point, the social psychology of workgroups converged with industrial sociology in arguing that the technology and organization of the workplace were major influences on workers' attitudes and behaviour towards work (Argyris, 1959; Sayles, 1958; Woodward, 1958).

Gradually, the aim of shaping commitment through appropriate *styles of leadership* was replaced by the aim of systematically building challenge into work tasks. Social cohesion and high morale in a workgroup was to be increased by rebuilding skill— or at least, the degree of challenge—to counteract the effects of mass-production technology and the Fordist work-design mentality. Studies of coal-mining by the Tavistock Institute in Britain (Trist *et al.*, 1963) were a major influence here.

The Tavistock experiments with mining teams, which tried to restore some traditional skills to the experimental teams, became an inspiration for a series of movements amongst organization designers that reached a peak in the later 1970s. In the guise of Organization Design (OD) or Quality of Worklife (QWL) theory, this tradition became directly concerned with the work ethic, arguing that a fall-off in industrial discipline around 1970 amounted in large part to a rejection of Fordism. This Revolt against Work (Sheppard and Herrick, 1972), they asserted, showed a growth in expectations about the quality of work tasks rather than a loss of regard for paid work. Sociologists of work, it is apparent, were reaching similar conclusions. Issues of skill and occupation, however, were raised by them in a rather different way (Fox, 1974). Their critique of mass-production technology was far more direct. On occasion it made use of a radical political vocabulary.

Technology and Work Attitudes

By the mid-1950s, industrial sociologists in Britain especially (but also in the USA and France) had begun to argue that technology should be regarded as the overriding determinant of work attitudes. The transformation of traditional skills in the face of technological change—above all the onset of Fordism—was made a central explanation for an alleged long-term decline in workers' commitment. Building upon a remarkable early study by Chinoy (1955), the approach soon became focused upon the mass-production assembly line of the giant car plant. For industrial sociologists, this was the exemplar of fragmented work tasks and workers' *alienation*.

Exactly what alienation implies has never been agreed. In philosophy, it refers to a spiritual condition beyond the scope of social analysis in the strict sense.[2] Socially and psychologically, it implies a state of disaffection and demoralization created by working at mind-numbing unskilled tasks, in submission to the rigid discipline imposed by machinery, and in obedience to managers obsessed with output. The opposite of a state of alienation, in this perspective, is one of *freedom* (Blauner, 1964); freedom in the context of work can be achieved only if a worker's innate skills are used to the full. His or her commitment to work is conditional, at the very least, upon the abolition of Fordist factories and other production systems based on this model.

The landmark study of industrial workers in this period (Blauner, 1964) argued that worker commitment was subject to a kind of historical law of technological change. As automation gradually replaced fragmented and meaningless work, alienation would fall and commitment revive. Later studies showed that automated technologies, especially Blauner's example of oil-refining, did not necessarily produce the attitude changes he predicted (Gallie, 1978). Other critics were to point out that Blauner's analysis overlooked important sources of attitudes to work, such as family circumstances and economic calculation.

In developing the latter objections, writers like Goldthorpe and his associates (1969) stressed the importance of factors external to the workplace in shaping attitudes and behaviour at work; it is important to consider family situation and personal consumption patterns as influences on work commitment. However, these researchers made their point so forcefully as to divert attention—with one partial, but important exception (Wedderburn and Crompton, 1972)—for a time away from examination of the links between skill, occupation, and commitment. Only one extensive examination of how *orientations to work* (the term closest to work commitment or work involvement in the terminology used by Goldthorpe and his co-authors) may interact with skill was to be undertaken (Blackburn and Mann, 1979); and this study was restricted to male semi-skilled manual workers in one English town.

This tradition in industrial sociology, in Britain and France especially, had often focused on such worker groups, to the exclusion of other types of employees. It had also come to pay what now seems undue attention to the links between work and the political outlook and behaviour of male industrial workers (Mann, 1973; Touraine, 1955) at the very moment when this part of the working class was starting to shrink rapidly, and the working class itself began to account for less of the working population.

Examination of skill was for a time heavily affected by controversy over the *degradation hypothesis* (Braverman, 1974). The discussion gave rise to many heated assertions about trends in skill and workers' *consciousness*. But few of these were soundly based in research findings; the first British critique of 'Old Testament' degradation theory (Wood, 1982) concentrated on exposing the logical and historical weakness of the claim that skill was being eradicated by scientific management. It did not go on to explore the links between skill and work attitudes or workers' wider social and political consciousness.

This neglect was, historically speaking, paradoxical in at least two ways. First, between 1968 and 1973 developed Western countries had experienced a wave of industrial unrest energized at least in part by resistance to low-skilled work, which forced employers and governments not only to declare themselves in favour of improving the quality of working life (Rose, 1985: ch. 4 and 5) but to set up agencies to find alternatives to Fordism. Secondly, the first serious evidence began to accumulate that traditional class consciousness was following smokestack industry into the breaker's yard. Observers of this process (Inglehart, 1977; Bell, 1974; Touraine, 1971) were already claiming that a shift in the occupational structure towards a *post-industrial soci-ety* would be matched by correspondingly radical changes in eco-nomic values and associated political behaviour. Though heavily criticized from many points of view, these theories remain impor-tant points of reference for the issue of work commitment.

Post-industrial and Post-material Values

Paid work can be regarded as a core institution of capitalist industrialism, not simply because it became the main activity of daily life for most people as a market economy spread, but because paid employment also embodied and expressed some of the *central social values* of a market economy. Since an early study by Robert Dubin (1956), acceptance and approval of the *centrality of paid work* on the part of social actors has been one of the best-agreed sociological definitions of a work ethic (MOW International Team, 1987). It is not the only acceptable definition, perhaps, but no others can afford to overlook it.

From the late 1960s, many observers began to claim that employees in capitalist countries were losing previously strong commitment to paid work. There are two main versions of this *attenuation* hypothesis. The first, grounded in post-industrial the-ory properly speaking, sees such weakening as a permanent con-sequence of structural change. When factories are displaced by service industries, demand for a highly educated work force increases. Highly qualified technical and white-collar workers, it is said, will put more stress on non-economic or *post-materialist* rewards at work (Inglehart, 1977), especially on the *expressive* goal of *self-actualization* (broadly speaking, achieving one's potential as a human being). This can occur only when work allows individuals to use their innate abilities to the full, and they are less affected by traditional economic motivations.

In the stronger variants of the hypothesis, especially Daniel Bell's original (1976) forecast, the final result will be widespread rejection of the traditional work ethic, especially of its call for personal ambition and competitiveness at work: significantly, Bell talks of work losing a previously 'sacred' character as a *provision-ing* activity. But even those post-industrial writers who take a milder view (Yankelovitch *et al.*, 1983, 1985) consider that grow-ing *expressivism* amongst employees will create very different work orientations from the largely economistic ones prevailing in the factory age.

The second version of the attenuation hypothesis rejects the idea that the 'revolt against work' of the 1970s was caused by post-industrial values. In this analysis, lower work commitment resulted from cyclical economic factors and a phase of misgovernment in Western countries, rather than from long-term structural changes. In its more schematic variants, this analysis is hard to distinguish from New Right political doctrine and often aims to justify New Right policies (Gilder, 1982). Because of its influence on economic policy, above all in Britain in the 1980s, aspects of New Right thinking need to be noted here.

The New Right and Work Culture

There is no single New Right theory of economic behaviour. Rather than possessing such a unified theory its exponents have had a shared attitude and several agreed axioms. As applied to workers' attitudes and behaviour, its main contentions are that the long post-1945 economic boom, the growth of the welfare state, undisciplined trade-union power, and the extension of job-security rights temporarily and unnaturally lowered esteem for work and its rewards. A tight labour market, 'excessive' economic security, and an over-protective welfare state had destroyed *persistence* in the search for employment, undermined acceptance of workplace discipline, diminished respect for the *provider* role of wage-earners, creating a *psychology of entitlement* and a whole *culture of dependency* (Lawson, 1992; Seldon, 1990; Joseph, 1975).

New Right thinking not only accepts the post-industrial claim that an alteration in attitudes towards work had occurred during the post-war boom years: it actually takes this period as its starting-point. It is important to stress this. Quite unlike the post-industrial theorists, on the other hand, many of the New Right thinkers viewed work behaviour and values as the product of policy errors on the part of possibly well-intentioned but misguided consensus politicians, bureaucrats, and academics.

Desirable economic values could be restored by policy changes. The recommended strategy had two main trusts. For the better-off, or the more skilled, the incentive to work would be increased by cutting taxes on salaries and wages. For the poor, and the lower-skilled, labour-market pressures should be increased through reduction or removal of employment protection, higher unemployment (from withdrawing subsidies to ailing industries), lower unemployment benefit and tougher rules of entitlement, less welfare provision, less income support, etc. For all employees, policy should stimulate pursuit of self-interest and individual competition in the labour market and within firms. In time, it was argued, *respect for* paid work, and *self-reliance* in the labour market would revive. Self-actualization at work, furthermore, could now be regarded as another reward for individual striving, not as some kind of 'employee right'. Revival of the work ethic called for the ideological self-assurance needed to introduce these tough-minded policies, as well as the political means.

UNWRAPPING THE WORK ETHIC

The British governments of the 1980s set out to promote self-reliance, an *enterprise culture*, and strong labour-market individualism, by combining strong free-enterprise rhetoric with measures to boost the 'supply side' of labour. While the latter recognized that skills training had a role in economic revival, they seem to have taken no account of the effect of skill levels and types on work attitudes; indeed they seem to have underestimated the *technical* importance of training and education themselves. An increase in the size of the pool of available labour by itself does not lead automatically to an increase in the stock of skills. The development of work values relevant to the performance of the British economy may also depend on the stock and level of skill.

Results from the Work Attitudes/Histories survey throw direct light on these issues, as well as on some of the claims made in post-industrial theory. To anticipate, they show that expressive work values are probably spreading, but without necessarily reducing commitment to paid work and effective performance of work tasks; furthermore, they suggest that a strong work ethic need not imply strong support for individualist economic philosophies, or vice versa; finally, and most important of all for the theme of this volume, levels of skill seem to be powerful determinants of such attitudes. First, however, some technical points, and measures of the work ethic and skill, need discussing. (For a detailed explanation of the measures and scores used in this chapter, see Appendix 10.1.)

Three Aspects of Work Involvement

The work ethic refers most often to social values underpinning the readiness to seek and hold on to paid work, either as an employee or in self-employment. The term can also denote high commitment to work effort, and has been used in several other related ways. These meanings are logically distinct. For example, it is possible to have a high commitment to work effort (in domestic tasks, a hobby, voluntary or community service) without even being active in the labour market. Wanting to have a paid job does not mean the demands of work will be put before the competing claims of family life or recreation, though in practice high commitment to work of one sort is often associated with another.

This chapter, however, will overlook these complications and try to answer one main question: in what ways do skill and occupation affect the work ethic understood in its fundamental sense, as commitment to paid employment? In doing so it will examine three distinct aspects of work commitment: (i) general or *normative commitment* to paid work (the core of the work ethic); (ii) *rationale of employment* (reasons for having paid work); and (iii) *ideology of paid work*—more specifically, the degree to which *individualism* is seen as the most valid philosophy of the labour market.

Commitment to Paid Work

The Work Attitudes/Histories survey asked whether respondents would continue working if they were financially well enough off not to need paid work. The situation presented was somewhat hypothetical, but the question has provided the most widely accepted measure of commitment to paid work, and in one form or another has been asked regularly in many polls and surveys (Jowell and Witherspoon, 1984, 1985, 1986, 1987, 1988; Warr, 1982, 1985; for a review of such research see O'Brien, 1992). It is often referred to as the 'lottery' question, but the form used in the Work Attitudes/Histories survey did not ask respondents to imagine winning a lottery or inheriting a legacy. It is not thought that most respondents had any difficulty imagining such a situation when they were asked the question.

The 'lottery' question can be regarded as a guide to normative commitment to work; that is to say, as an indicator of how far the wish to have a job reflects social values and conventions rather than a response to financial incentives or economic insecurity. Some researchers treat it as a substitute (or 'proxy') measure for the work ethic as a whole (Hakim, 1991; Mann, 1986).

Table 10.1 shows 'support' for paid work at about two-thirds of all people in the Work Attitudes/Histories sample who were active in the labour market. (This is very similar to the level other surveys were showing for representative British samples in the 1980s.) Male employees were overall only a little more committed to work than women employees; the self-employed of both sexes were more highly committed than the employees; and the unemployed were the most highly committed of all according to this measure.

However, answers to the 'lottery' question may have been affected by other factors than normative commitment to employment. People who do not need a job may continue to work for many other reasons—ambition, habit, even from boredom. A second question, in the form of a statement that employed people enjoy more social esteem than unemployed people, deals with some of these objections. The 'esteem' statement was also endorsed by well over 60% of the active sample (see Table 10.1). The different levels of agreement for self-employed men and self-employed women suggest that the 'esteem' question did tap a complementary aspect of normative commitment.

A third aspect of commitment to paid work, the ability to think of one's current job as part of a career,[3] will not be examined at this stage. Results from this question, however, are very consistent with results for the 'lottery' and 'esteem' questions; and data produced by it were used to create the exact individual scores for the work ethic which become important in a later section of the chapter.

In much of the analysis presented here, the percentages of subgroups agreeing to the two questions will usually be taken *together*, in the form of a single summary score. To simplify, these scores show the percentage difference between the composite score for a subgroup and the mean composite score of the

TABLE 10.1 *Normative commitment to paid work in the major labour-market groups, all active subgroups* (%)

	Men				Women					Whole active sample
	Self-employed	Full-time employees	Part-time employees	Un-employed	Self-employed	Full-time employees	Part-time employees	Un-employed	Housewife returners	
Would continue to work even if did not need to	75	66	67	77	66	63	58	74	67	66
Employed people given more respect than unemployed (agreeing)	61	66	91	66	71	66	65	65	65	66
Score for Normative commitment to paid work	+5	0	+38	+16	+7	−5	−14	+9	0	0
N	247	1,770	21	455	116	1,007	796	285	477	5,178

Note: Full-time and part-time employees off sick in last seven days included. The table excludes: the permanently retired; the long-term sick; full-time students; full-time 'housewives' who said they did not wish to enter (or had no plans to re-enter) the labour market. The 'Housewife Returners' were women who said they did have such plans. (If they had actually been looking for work in the last month they were classified as 'Unemployed' even though not registered.)

The method for calculating *summary scores* for commitment to paid work in subgroups is explained briefly in the text of the chapter and in full in the Appendix 10.1 on Measures; the whole sample 'reference score' ($66 \times 66/100 = 44$) for this table is slightly higher than that ($64 \times 66/100 = 42$) for the employee sample. The exact questions were: (for Employees and the Self-Employed) 'If you were to get enough money to live as comfortably as you would like for the rest of your life, would you continue to work, not necessarily in your present job, or would you stop working?'; (for Unemployed and Non-Employed planning to return to work) 'If you were to get enough money to live as comfortably as you would like for the rest of your life, would you want to work somewhere or would you want to remain without a job?'; and 'I'm going to read out some differing views about *unemployment*, and I'd like you to tell me, from the card, how much you agree or disagree with each: "Employed people are given more respect than unemployed people".' The options were: Strongly agree; Agree; No strong opinions either way; Disagree; Strongly disagree.

Source: Work Attitudes/Histories survey.

employee sample as a whole. (For further explanation on scoring procedures see Appendix 10.1 on Measures.) This makes rapid comparison of groups far easier: for example, Table 10.1 quickly shows that overall normative commitment to employment amongst the unemployed of both sexes was higher than amongst the self-employed of both sexes. (Findings on the work commitment of the unemployed in SCELI are examined in Gallie, Marsh, and Vogler, 1984: ch. 4.)

Rationale of Paid Work

In practice, relatively few people of working age are faced with the choice of whether to work or not if they are to maintain an acceptable living standard. However, they usually can and do have more than one reason (or justification) for having a job; and some people are in the position to make trade-offs between income and other sorts of reward, while others would wish to do so if they could (Berg *et al.*, 1978: ch. 4). Nearly all employees can imagine such situations without any difficulty.

From a theoretical point of view, the *rationale* people put forward for working is important for two reasons. Firstly, as noted earlier, some sociologists of work (Goldthorpe *et al.*, 1969; Mann, 1973; Fox, 1974) have argued that capitalist industrialism promotes an instrumental or 'economistic' rationale of paid work amongst less-skilled workers. Secondly, the post-industrial theorists (Bell, 1976; Inglehart, 1977) argue that occupational change and new workplace milieux are creating different work values. Social psychologists like Daniel Yankelovitch and colleagues (1983, 1985) agree with Bell and have suggested that expressivism—the demand for a sense of self-actualization in work—is gradually spreading throughout the employed population of all advanced countries.

Reasons for working fell into four main types: (i) *provisioning* ('Working is the normal thing to do' and 'Need money for basic essentials'); (ii) *secondary economic* ('Money to buy extras' and 'To give a sense of independence'); (iii) *expressive* ('Enjoy working', 'Feel I'm doing something worthwhile' and 'Use my abilities to the full'); (iv) *social* ('For the company of other people', 'To get out of the house'). Main reasons and secondary reasons were combined for groups.[4]

The condensed data on work rationale are given in Table 10.2. It is immediately clear that reasons for working were predominantly economic or monetary in the sample as a whole: the weighted sample mean for a *provisioning* work rationale was 41%, and for a *secondary economic* rationale 27%. Overall, support for a *social* rationale (5%) was very low. (As noted earlier, it will be ignored in this chapter.) On the other hand, there was substantial minority support (25%) for an *expressive* rationale. Moreover, there are clear differences between the main employment categories in support for the main types of work rationale.

In considering the effect of skill level on work rationale it was soon found that the share of provisioning reasons tends to be fairly stable. (For all the currently employed it was around 38%.) What varies most sharply with skill level is the *relative importance of expressive versus secondary economic* reasons for working. Especially because of the importance of *expressivism* to the post-industrial theories of work values, discussion of *rationale* of paid work will be concerned above all with the balance of expressive reasons over secondary economic reasons. This balance will also be expressed in the form of a simple, summary score for expressivism in the first part of the chapter.[5] (The summary scores shown in the table are explained in Appendix 10.1 on Measures.)

Individualism and Paid Work

The work ethic may reflect personal morality or individual psychology (in extreme cases maybe, the pathological 'workaholism' that destroys health). Most social scientists also regard it as an aspect of patterned beliefs and perspectives, or ideologies, shared by social groups. For example, the work ethic is commonly regarded as an aspect of the protestant Ethic which may (Furnham, 1981)—or may not (Marshall, 1982)—have dynamized capitalist development as portrayed by Max Weber. How far Weber's examination of entrepreneurship can be extended to employee behaviour is not agreed. But the ideological themes of personal initiative, ambition, and rugged individualism came into the centre of social and political debates on paid work in Britain in the 1980s. It is worth asking what links there may be between beliefs in such ideas and skill and occupation.

Table 10.2. *Support for four rationales of paid work in the major labour-market groups, derived from combined and weighted reasons for working (%)*

	Men				Women					Whole active sample
	Self-employed	Full-time employees	Part-time employees	Un-employed	Self-employed	Full-time employees	Part-time employees	Un-employed	Housewife returners	
Provisioning	51	55	43	42	27	38	23	33	23	41
Secondary Economic	18	20	27	27	33	31	43	32	42	27
Expressive	29	26	28	25	34	27	21	25	21	26
Social	2	1	3	4	7	7	14	10	14	6
Balance of expressive reasons	+61	+30	+4	-7	+3	-13	-51	-22	-50	-4
N	248	1,786	21	457	118	1,026	802	272	480	3,612

Note: The categories used are explained in detail in the text. They were produced from collapsing 10 possible reasons for working. Scores are for subgroups as a whole, with weighting for first and second choices. The method of grouping reasons for working and calculation of scores is explained in Appendix 10.1 on measures.

Source: Work Attitudes/Histories survey.

Two questions tapping economic individualism in philosophies of paid work were particularly relevant. One refers to the efficacy of individual *persistence* in the search for paid work. Respondents were asked how far they agreed that out-of-work people 'can always find another job if they really want one'. A belief in such persistence is not, of course, necessarily associated with a strong personal work ethic. It is easy to see that some people who themselves have a somewhat *weak* work ethic, and indeed avoid work if they can, may none the less strongly endorse individualist labour-market beliefs; believing that one can always find a work, if one really wants to work, is obviously not the same as actually wanting to work, or admiring those people who do. By the same token, people who themselves have strong commitment to paid work may believe that such persistence, although perhaps laudable, may be of little use if work is scarce or one lacks the skills in demand.

A second question tackled the issue of *dependency* and the work ethic head-on by asking whether respondents agreed or not that 'the welfare state reduces the will to work'. Once again, group percentages for each question will be combined in the first part of the chapter, with the composite score showing the percentage variation from the sample mean.

Table 10.3 shows that individualist work ideology was most strongly supported by the self-employed of both sexes, and least strongly by the unemployed of both sexes. As the self-employed are by definition people who do constantly seek work independently, it is perhaps not surprising that those in the survey were more likely to endorse the efficacy of self-reliance in the labour market, and to be readier to say that the welfare state lowers individual motivation to find work. (Perhaps it is worth asking why more self-employed people *did not* endorse these statements.) Unemployed people suffer a predicament that will predispose them to give very different responses. (Again, why did not more of the unemployed reject statements that are prejudicial to them?)

The only clue in Table 10.3 to how skill may affect acceptance of individualist ideology lies in the column for women part-timers. These employees were no more likely to say that unemployed people can always find work, but very much more likely to agree that the welfare state cuts the will to work. Of the active groups, part-timer women also had the lowest average skill levels.

Table 10.3. *Support for economic individualism (self-reliance ideology) in the major labour-market groups* (%)

	Men				Women					Whole active sample
	Self-employed	Full-time employees	Part-time employees	Un-employed	Self-employed	Full-time employees	Part-time employees	Un-employed	Housewife returners	
People can always get another job if they really want one	59	41	43	25	52	43	40	28	41	42
The welfare state reduces the will to work	66	51	40	32	64	49	60	45	51	52
Score for economic individualism	+86	0	−19	−62	+60	0	+14	−40	0	+21
N	242	1,762	20	449	115	1,004	783	282	475	5,136

Note: Scores are for the groups as a whole. The method of calculating the summary scores is explained in Appendix 10.1 on measures: the 'reference score' for the whole active sample varies slightly from that for the employee sample. The exact questions were: 'I'm going to read out some differing views about *unemployment*, and I'd like you to tell me, from the card, how much you agree or disagree with each: "People can always get another job if they really want one"', with the options. Strongly agree; Agree; No strong opinion either way; Disagree; Strongly disagree; and 'I'd like to get your opinion about the system of taxes, services, and benefits that's commonly known as the welfare state. Do you agree or disagree with, or have no strong opinions about, the following statements: "The welfare state . . . reduces the will to work"'.

Source: Work Attitudes/Histories survey.

Amongst those agreeing with the 'persistence' and 'dependency' statements, there was greater support for right-wing ideas underlying government policy, and less support for collective action in the workplace, especially in the form of trade unionism. Skill was a powerful independent determinant of support for individualist work ideology: but it *operated in a generally negative way.* (This finding will be examined further in due course.)

SKILL TYPES AND THE WORK ETHIC

Chapter 9 argued that it is often desirable to distinguish between the skill of jobs (*job-skill*) and the skill developed by individuals (*own-skill*). When examining work attitudes, it is essential. Levels of each one, it was shown, can affect job satisfaction in quite different ways. (Chapter 9 shows that the degree of skills-matching seems particularly important.) Are there similar effects on the work ethic? There are, but it is not easy to present them briefly. To begin with, then, some of the indicators of each aspect of skill will be examined in turn and separately. This allows comparison with other studies using just one of these indicators, as well as making the findings easier to digest.

Self-Defined Skill

Currently employed people were asked to say whether they considered their present work to be skilled or not. Two-thirds said it was. Table 10.4 shows that people who considered their work to be skilled had slightly higher normative commitment to work— their score is 10% higher than for employees as a whole. But those who thought their work was not skilled had a very low score: it was 18% below the employee mean. Those claiming to be skilled had a clearly higher balance (+32%) of expressive reasons over secondary economic reasons for working. The non-skilled even more clearly lacked an expressive work rationale: their score was highly negative, falling to −59% of secondary economic reasons. The association with individualistic labour-market ideology was negative for those with skilled work and positive for the non-skilled, although the scale of the deviation is barely significant in each case. However, it does point to a pattern that recurs more clearly once skill is better defined.

TABLE 10.4. *Effect of seeing one's job as skilled on support for the main aspects of the work ethic* (%)

	Says current job is skilled	Current job not skilled
Normative commitment		
Would continue to work	67	56
Employed people given more respect	69	60
SCORE	+10	–18
Rationale of paid work		
Provisioning	43	39
Secondary Economic	22	37
Expressive	29	15
SCORE	+32	–59
Individualist ideology		
People can always get another job if need one	41	41
Welfare state reduces will to work	51	54
SCORE	–2	+4
N	2,318	1,125

Source: Work Attitudes/Histories survey.

Ratings of job-skill by respondents such as this one attempt to imply a definition of skill in terms of the technical features of the work done; and the proportion claiming skill certainly rises in line with occupational level. But they do rely on an individual's own judgement, and some replies certainly reflect *ad hoc* gradings, long-standing conventions, or a negotiated order in firms and local labour markets. Such *social definitions of skill* (Sadler, 1970; Blackburn and Mann, 1979; Lee, 1982) are especially likely to reflect gender factors in lower-grade work; the Cambridge team provide further evidence of this for the Work Attitudes/ Histories sample in Chapter 7. (Later it will be shown that once skill levels are properly controlled gender became only a very weak influence on the 'core' work ethic.) Indicators of control in the work process avoid some of these problems.

Skill as Control in the Work Process

As pointed out in the opening section, the sociological theories both of alienation in work (Blauner, 1964) and of skill degradation (Thompson, 1983, 1990) define skill largely in terms of the degree of control exercised by workers within the technical limits of the work process and the chain of authority of the workplace. The Work Attitudes/Histories survey had separate measures for four particular aspects of control: (i) the *pace and effort* of work; (ii) the degree of control over *methods of working*; (iii) any *supervision of other people* involved in the work process; and (iv) the *closeness of supervision* of the employee's own work.

For critics of early industrialism such as Marx machinery brought about worker alienation through the loss of craft skill and its deadening effects on the mind: the machine controlled the worker, rather than the reverse. The scientific management movement (Rose, 1988*b*) of the early twentieth century, under the leadership of F. W. Taylor, aimed to deskill many engineering jobs after subjecting them to strict time-and-motion study and close supervision. Soon after, the Fordist factory (Littler, 1985; Friedman, 1977) turned the mass-production assembly line, with its repetitive, semi-skilled work, into the model of labour in the industrial age.

Walker and Guest (1952), Blauner (1964), and the Luton team (Goldthorpe *et al.*, 1969) considered assembly-line work and repetitive machine-minding either as the immediate source of anti-work attitudes or as an environment likely to reinforce highly instrumental work orientations and kill off expectations of expressive rewards from work. For Alan Fox (1974), machine-paced work was to exemplify poor *trust relations* between management and employees, in which it was assumed workers neither had nor could develop commitment to work.

The Work Attitudes/Histories survey data bear out much in these portrayals (see Table 10.5). Those respondents who said their work effort was closely affected by an assembly line or a machine had a low score for normative commitment to work and a strikingly low score for expressivism: over four-fifths of their reasons for working were economically instrumental. They scored just above the mean for individualism.

The data in Table 10.5 understate the continuing alienation

TABLE 10.5. *Effect of degree of control in the work process on support for the main aspects of the work ethic* (%)

	Assembly line or machine affects own work effort	Great deal of choice over doing work	Supervises other people directly
Normative commitment			
Would continue to work	57	66	69
Employed people given more respect	63	67	70
SCORE	−15	+5	+15
Rationale of paid work			
Provisioning	57	43	46
Secondary Economic	25	23	19
Expressive	14	29	32
SCORE	−44	+26	+68
Individualist ideology			
People can always get another job if need one	41	42	41
Welfare state reduces will to work	56	52	51
SCORE	+8	+2	−2
N	257	1,911	1,252

Source: Work Attitudes/Histories survey.

and instrumentalism of machine-paced workers: the question probably worked so as to include in this subgroup some employees (including managers and technicians) whose jobs were closely affected by assembly lines, but who did not work on them personally. In fact, an overall majority (61%) of the 257 respondents in the group still saw their jobs as skilled. However, the question caused widespread difficulty; almost one in ten people in this subgroup were unable to say with certainty whether they looked on their work as skilled or not skilled, and this was much above the sample average for 'don't know' responses to the question.

Among those whose effort was directly paced by machines or

assembly lines and who *did not* see their work as skilled, fewer than half would have preferred to stay in paid work. The overall score for commitment in this group is 26% lower than the employee mean score. Again, the score for expressivism in this non-skilled *and* machine-paced category is amongst the very lowest (–76%) for any subgroup, while almost nine out of ten of the reasons given for working were economistic. If this group exemplifies lack of control and deprivation of intrinsic meaning in work, it also confirms some of the main findings of the *technological implications* school of industrial sociology.

Indeed, like the machine-minders in Blauner's study (1964), the alienation of this group even seems associated with strong endorsement of economic individualism. Although the score for labour-market individualism for all those affected by assembly lines was barely (+5%) above average, for those who also saw themselves as having non-skilled work it jumped to +30%.

However, only 257 (7%) of the employee sample were affected directly by a machine or an assembly line. None of the other workplace features examined in the Work Attitudes/Histories survey is quite so specific about technological factors impinging on the act of working. Questions dealt with a number of other influences on work effort—incentive payments, a supervisor, or workmates. But these are all organizational or social, not technological. Moreover, these factors were much less likely to be experienced as narrowly constraining in the same way as machinery—or rather, as *traditional* kinds of production machinery.

The qualification is an essential one. As Duncan Gallie points out in Chapter 2, use of *computerized or automated equipment* was not associated with lower skill. Computer/automated equipment was perceived, much more often than not, as adding to work discretion provided it remained under the control of the operator. Analysis for this chapter showed that use of such equipment is *positively* associated with other skill measures, and very significantly so in statistical terms. Those who said they used such equipment had higher than average levels of normative commitment to paid work, a modest but positive balance of expressive reasons for working, and a slightly lower than average score for individualistic ideology.

But how did the degree of autonomy and discretion (for example, in the choice of methods) affect commitment? The overwhelming majority of all employees claimed that they had at least some discretion over how hard they worked in their jobs. A large minority of those that lacked discretion over *how hard* they worked still said they had substantial control over their *methods* of working. (Over 50% of the employee sample said they had a 'great deal' of choice over the way they did their present jobs.)

Table 10.5 shows that the pattern of work involvement for the 'high-discretion' group was less strong than for those who said their work was skilled. But those lacking any control over how they did their jobs certainly had very low commitment to work and very rarely gave expressive reasons for working. Yet this indicator does not distinguish between different aspects of work methods; and people do not like to admit they lack any control over their work and may be ready to find at least one area which offers choice.

This difficulty remains when the context of control at work is other people, but in a much less serious form. Supervision of other people requires specific, mainly social skills. Being a supervisor had very strong effects on normative commitment to work (the score is 15% above the mean) and on expressiveness (+68%). The first two effects also increased with the number of subordinates, suggesting that social skills are important for understanding the work ethic. On the other hand, being a supervisor had no significant effect on scores for labour-market individualism.

Supervision is an incomplete measure of the social skill required in a job. As the Cambridge team show in Chapter 6, it is important to recognize that considerable social skill may be needed in far more jobs than employers, work designers, or social scientists may recognize. All supervisors must exercise social skills; but lack of subordinates does not show that social skill is not required in a job. Some employees, like sales representatives, health visitors, or telephone service engineers, work alone in the sense of having no colleagues around them; but their dealings with customers or clients all require social skills of a high order. Finally, all jobs are supervised: even top managers are accountable for their actions. But those jobs that are more closely supervised are also more likely to be lower-skilled.

Qualifications Needed for the Job

A final measure of skill called for in a job was the type and number of qualifications the employer would now require from someone doing the respondent's currently held job. A requirement for *any* qualification, however minor, it should be noted, had a pronounced effect on the work ethic variables. Where no qualifications were required, commitment to work veered in the opposite direction.

Table 10.6 shows a gap of 34% in the scores for people with posts requiring no qualifications and those requiring three or more. There is an even wider gap in scores for expressive work rationale. Although provisioning was mentioned equally often by them, those saying their job needed several qualifications expressive reasons for working outweighed secondary economic reasons by 70%. For those in jobs now calling for *no* qualifications, the position is almost the reverse. For labour-market individualism, those having 'no-qualifications' jobs scored well above the sample mean (+29%), while those in jobs requiring several qualifications scored well below it (–20%).

Though job-skill affected individualism less than it affected normative commitment or expressivism, it still did have an effect on the ideological aspect of the work ethic. One of the most interesting features of Table 10.6, however, is that the level of *academic* qualifications required affected the work ethic scores more strongly than the level of *technical* qualifications. True enough, the effect on commitment and expressiveness was strong where jobs called for *high-level* technical requirements. Need for a Higher National Diploma (HND) or for a Higher National Certificate (HNC) produced a large jump in scores even compared with the intermediate technical certificates (OND/ONC). However, there was no similar effect on individualist ideology; scores for jobs requiring HNC are close to the employee sample mean.

Where a job required a mainly academic qualification, there were far sharper changes in levels of normative commitment. These higher scores were produced largely by much greater endorsement for the 'esteem' statement by people in jobs now calling for high academic qualifications (A level or higher), though the particularly high endorsement for the 'lottery' state-

TABLE 10.6. *Effect of qualifications now required to do current job on support for the main aspects of the work ethic* (%)

	Technical/professional qualifications			Level of academic qualifications			Number of qualifications NOW required	
	Trade apprent.	ONC OND	HNC HND	O Level	A Level	Univ Degree	Three or more	None at all
Normative commitment to paid work								
Would continue to work	65	68	69	69	72	75	72	61
Employed people given more respect	63	69	72	70	80	81	71	60
SCORE	−2	+12	+19	+14	+38	+45	+22	−12
Rationale of work								
Provisioning	57	56	48	42	41	41	40	41
Secondary Economic	19	17	17	23	20	13	20	35
Expressive	23	26	33	32	36	44	34	15
SCORE	+21	+53	+94	+39	+80	+238	+70	−57
Individualist ideology								
People can always get another job if they need one	42	43	44	40	35	32	38	46
Welfare state reduces the will to work	51	46	50	50	44	41	46	59
SCORE	0	−7	+3	−6	−28	−38	−18	+27
No. times mentioned	253	114	205	619	270	341	1,014	1,362

ment by those in jobs now requiring a university-level degree or certificate is worth noting.

And having a job now needing high academic qualifications had a spectacular effect on work rationale. Table 10.6 shows that, for those in jobs now requiring a degree, expressive reasons actually overtook provisioning reasons for working, and were given almost two and a half times more often than secondary economic reasons. Similarly, jobs requiring higher *academic* qualifications were associated with levels of labour-market individualism well below average; scores for respondents with posts now needing a university degree or diploma were almost 40% below the employee mean. They stand in sharp contrast with jobs requiring higher *vocational* qualifications.

It bears repeating at this point that a large minority of respondents in 'selective' jobs *did not personally possess* all, or even any, of the qualifications they mentioned as now necessary to obtain their current job. Indeed, as Chapter 9 shows, there was considerable mismatching of qualifications required for a job and qualifications possessed, resulting either in 'underutilization' or in 'underqualification' of employees in terms of their own skill attainments. It is therefore important to consider the separate effects of levels of personal skill on the work ethic scores.

Skills Possessed by Individuals

Four measures of the skill level or technical competence of individuals (own-skill) will be briefly examined here: (i) *having training* for the currently held job: (ii) the length of the *training period* for this work; (iii) the length of the *period of learning/improving*, in post, before doing the work competently; and (iv) the technical, vocational, and academic *qualifications actually held* by the employee.

Chapter 9 on skill and job satisfaction showed that these variables tap different or additional aspects of skill and can vary independently from the skill of a job currently held. One important result is skill mismatching. Two out of five employees in the Work Attitudes/Histories sample suffered varying degrees of mismatch between the level of competence they possessed as *individuals* and the level of skill they were called upon to reach in their jobs. Many mismatches were not large, and for some purposes it may make little difference if the distinction is overlooked. It will be shown, however, that they may be important for understanding commitment to work. The own-skill variables will be thought of largely as measures of personal competence and of labour-market power: that is, as measures of *human capital* (Blaug, 1972). After examining their independent effect, the interaction of own-skill with job-skill in influencing the work ethic are easier to appreciate.

At first sight, Table 10.7 seems merely to repeat the picture showing how job-skill variables affect the work ethic. For example, levels of association with normative work commitment, expressiveness, and individualism, for most subgroups, were rather similar to those for people who saw their jobs as skilled. Yet only 48% of employees had training for their present job, as opposed to the 65% who considered it to be skilled. Some employees no doubt had other kinds of training or work experience that was a good substitute for job-specific training. After making such allowances, a minority of employees remained who had 'skilled' work that apparently required no training, partly reflecting the effects of social definitions of job-skill.

All three aspects of the work ethic changed in line not only with the length of the training period but also with the respondent's estimate of how long it had taken to learn to do their present work well. (Those who were still learning were asked to estimate how long it would take them to acquire this competence.) As with formal training, time taken to learn to do the job well was usually short; many respondents estimated it at less than a month. As the learning and improving period lengthened, commitment to work increased, expressive reasons for working replaced secondary economic or social ones, and endorsement for individualist ideology fell.

SKILL IN A GENERAL MODEL

For the sample as a whole, then, the separate measures of own-skill produced comparable results to using those for job-skill: that is, for each aspect of skill position, higher skill was associated with similar changes in the work ethic. But, at the level of *individuals*, neither the measures, nor the job-skill and own-skill

TABLE 10.7. *Effect of training, work-learning experience, and qualifications actually held on support for the main aspects of the work ethic* (%)

	Has some training for for current	Training period was 1 year/longer	Time taken learning to do job 1 year/longer	Qualifications actually held equals 3 or more	Employee sample
Normative commitment to paid work					
Would continue to work	67	69	68	76	64
Employed people given more respect	69	72	71	74	66
SCORE	+10	+19	+14	+33	0
Rationale of paid work					
Provisioning	45	46	47	38	39
Secondary Economic	22	19	19	21	27
Expressive	30	33	32	36	24
SCORE	+36	+74	+68	+71	-11
Individualist ideology					
People can always get another job if they need one	41	40	39	36	42
Welfare state reduces the will to work	50	49	50	44	52
SCORE	-4	-8	-9	-26	0
N	1,723	941	1,158	1,653	3,643

Source: Work Attitudes/Histories survey.

they reflect, are fully interchangeable. Chapter 9 showed that about 40% of employees in the sample had unmatched or poorly matched job-skill and own-skill, with the level of matching affecting job satisfaction. It is therefore important to consider how far each type of skill independently affects the work ethic.

In the examination of skill and job satisfaction in Chapter 9, it was shown how two composite variables were created from the separate job-skill and own-skill indicators. Once again, it is possible to estimate the separate effect of each aspect of skill position by a more complex statistical treatment, using scores for each of these composite skill variables banded into High, Medium, and Low categories. Table 10.8 shows each one producing very similar associations *with normative commitment* to work, on the one hand, and with having an *expressive* rationale of paid work on the other. Yet the associations with *individualist ideology* are rather less similar for the two measures, and they have some curious features. For example, people with medium job-skill scores had higher overall scores for Individualism than those with low job-skill; on the other hand, people with low own-skill had a high overall score for Individualism.

These associations take no account of intervening variables such as sex, age, size of workplace, employment sector, job satisfaction, an so on. It was possible to control for such variables, and many others, after producing composite scores for the work-commitment variables. At this stage, it was found that the composite work-ethic variables differed in an important respect. Factor analysis showed that, at the individual level, having expressive reasons for working *and* high commitment to paid work were very closely associated. They lie at the core of what seems to be a very distinct composite work-ethic variable. This finding in itself throws doubt on those post-industrial theories of work which regard expressivism as a threat to commitment because it supposedly runs counter to employment as a central life value.

The first composite variable, then, was 'normative-expressive work commitment', but it will be termed simply 'work ethic' here. A second factor was closely associated with views on the efficacy of *persistence* in the search of the unemployed for paid work, and the risks of *dependency* resulting from a developed welfare state. This second factor will once again be called

TABLE 10.8. *Effect of composite variables for job-skill and own-skill on support for the main aspects of the work ethic* (%)

	Score for job-skill			Score for own-skill		
	High	Medium	Low	High	Medium	Low
Normative commitment to paid work						
Would continue to work if didn't need to	73	64	54	70	64	57
Employed people given more respect	74	66	62	74	67	59
SCORE	+26	-2	-22	+21	0	-22
Rationale of paid work						
Provisioning	44	44	41	46	44	40
Secondary Economic	19	28	43	18	28	42
Expressive	35	25	13	35	26	14
SCORE	+84	-11	-70	+94	-7	-67
Individualist ideology						
People can always get another job if they need one	36	45	41	37	43	43
Welfare state reduces will to work	47	53	55	47	50	58
SCORE	-23	+9	+3	-20	-2	+14

Source: Work Attitudes/Histories survey.

(labour-market) Individualism. The third composite variable (or factor) that also seemed readily interpretable was associated with a low involvement in paid work, and with having secondary economic or social reasons for seeking work. (This *secondary economic* factor will not be examined in detail here; the ways in which the separate variables 'loaded' on to each factor is examined in Appendix 10.1.)

To summarize: factoring confirmed that the three separate aspects of the work ethic defined earlier in this chapter were related closely at the individual level, in ways that bear out the earlier analysis based on table percentages, but allow it to be clarified. To simplify, the new composite scores had technical features (they are *interval-level* measures[6]) which made it a fairly straightforward task to estimate the relative influence of both aspects of skill position on the work ethic, while controlling for the possible effect of a number of other, intervening variables.

The multivariate analysis used for examining skill and the work ethic controlled for almost 30 independent variables. These variables were known to have some correlation with work ethic scores, in the absence of any other controls. However, almost half did not appear in the regression equation because an apparent initial effect disappeared when all variables were simultaneously controlled. Similarly, some of the variables that did appear in the equation were found to have far less effect than expected. Most influence was exerted by a half-dozen key variables. The results are presented in a simplified, diagrammatic form in Figure 10.1.

Expressive Work Ethic

The single most influential variable was having a professional or managerial-level job. People in such jobs normally possess a long-term, strategic view of paid work, which has developed either upon their obtaining promotion to their higher-level posts, or which they had thanks to self-selection into professional training for a known career even before starting work. Several other variables reflecting the advantaged position of people in the labour market (wishing to change jobs, having higher jobs-market confidence) also appear in the model. Yet both aspects of skill exerted a strong, independent, and additional influence: they

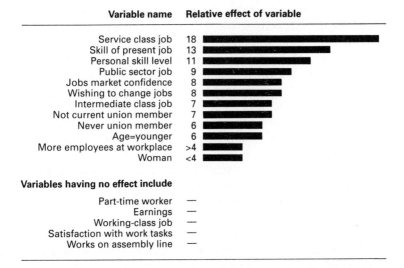

Variable name		Relative effect of variable
Service class job	18	
Skill of present job	13	
Personal skill level	11	
Public sector job	9	
Jobs market confidence	8	
Wishing to change jobs	8	
Intermediate class job	7	
Not current union member	7	
Never union member	6	
Age=younger	6	
More employees at workplace	>4	
Woman	<4	

Variables having no effect include

Part-time worker	—
Earnings	—
Working-class job	—
Satisfaction with work tasks	—
Works on assembly line	—

Note: OLS multiple regression; adjusted r^2=.200; dependent variable, factor scores for Expressive Work Ethic; estimated effects based on beta-weights; 12 other 'no-effect' variables not shown.

Source: Work Attitudes/Histories survey.

Figure 10.1 Relative influence of skill and other major independent variables on the composite scores for the Expressive Work Ethic variable produced by factor analysis

were second and third in importance. High levels of job-skill or of own-skill, it can be argued, actually do increase the market capacity of individuals. It thus does not seem surprising that those individuals who had job mobility had a high commitment to employment and a strategic view of it. It should be noted, however, that having a professional/managerial-level job did not, as it were, automatically 'guarantee' a strong work ethic but simply made it very much more likely.

The model also shows that the effects of skill variables were, in this case, additive; that is, each skill variable made a distinct and separate contribution of a positive kind to the work ethic score. This means that the effect of skill-matching worked in quite different ways than in the case of job-satisfaction, where 'surpluses' or 'deficits' of own-skill had strongly contrasting effects. According to this model, for example, a combination *either* of very high own-skill with very low job-skill, *or* of very low own-skill with very high job-skill would have somewhat similar effects on total scores. Yet the model also provides further evidence that the skill variables were separate—not alternative—measures, each tapping quite distinct aspects of skill. If they had been alternative measures, one or the other of them would not have appeared in the equation; if one had been omitted, important information would have been ignored.

Several other variables should briefly be noted. First, having a public-sector job was a strong influence but is not easy to fit into a general explanation based on the theme of jobs-market confidence. At the time of the fieldwork, public-sector employment was becoming less secure, and its ethos was already subject to fierce attack. The variable seems to confirm that some public-sector employment (for example, in teaching, social services, and health-care) does continue to require, and secure, a strong vocational commitment. The finding that 'non-unionism' (Not current union member, Never union member) also increased work-ethic scores is not inconsistent with this. Employees in the private sector (two-thirds of the sample) were less likely to be unionized in any case; it is possible that those who were non-unionists may also have felt higher market confidence. Larger workplaces had a slight positive effect. But age had a slight negative one; in other words, younger people were slightly *more* likely to have higher work-ethic scores than comparably situated older workers.

But the most striking 'low influence' variable was sex: being a man slightly increased scores, being a woman slightly reduced them. According to this model, then, there *is* a difference in commitment to paid work attributable to gender alone. Yet the effect of the variable is almost trivial—technically speaking it accounts for at most 3–4% of the variance in work-ethic scores. Again, it is possible that some variables have been omitted from the model (such as those relating to domestic situation) which would have reduced the 'gender effect' still further, or removed the variable from the model.

Another variable that failed to enter the model was Part-time employee. In the Work Attitudes/Histories sample, this variable was almost equivalent to 'Woman part-timer'. (Only 1% of part-timers were men.) It was shown in Chapter 9 that having part-time work appears to have a distinct, relatively strong, and positive influence on job satisfaction. (A possible explanation of this is that such employees had both different and lower expectations of work.) But part-time work had no independent effect on work-ethic scores. This is at first somewhat surprising. Women part-timers, it should be noted, often had high scores for secondary work involvement, which in some ways may be regarded as the inverse of the work ethic as defined here. However, as the discussion of the findings on skill and job satisfaction pointed out, women part-timers suffer quite disproportionate deficits of own-skill and job-skill; in fact, half the part-timer cases in the Work Attitudes/Histories sample had low scores for *both* aspects of skill.

The observations of the Cambridge team in Chapter 7, on the evaluation of unrecognized skills amongst those people who have low-graded tasks, should be noted once again at this point. The everyday social, domestic, or other tacit skills used in much part-time work are largely overlooked by the skill measures used here. However, the fact must be faced that these skills *are* usually 'overlooked' in the rewards and social recognition of such work. The skill measures may show the low level of what might be called 'negotiable' skill among such employees in a somewhat brutal way; but they are not misleading in terms of the recognition and evaluation—in the everyday world as in the labour market itself—of the tacit skills these employees possessed. The model suggests, however, that when women *did have* the same levels of negotiable skill as men they had as strong a work ethic, irrespective of whether they worked full-time or part-time.

Labour-Market Individualism

Regression analysis of the scores for individualism showed that they were affected most strongly by political loyalty. Conservative voting was by a very wide margin the most important influence on individualism scores. Labour voting was negatively associated with them, though far less strongly. So was commitment to trade unionism. Such a link with the political correlates of individualism and collectivism was perhaps to be expected.

However, own-skill and job-skill once again appeared among the six most important influences, in third and sixth place. Yet, in this case, their effects were very different: *each had a small but significant tendency to pull scores downwards*. In other words, a higher level of either variety of skill had the overall effect of reducing scores for individualist ideology. Once again, own-skill exerted the stronger influence. Other, individual factors (high overall job satisfaction, good job mobility prospects) seem to have counted for much more than workplace factors (Working mainly with men). Above all, gender had a rather clear effect, as did being a part-time worker. Full-time women employees were more likely to have slightly higher scores than men; sex, therefore, appeared as an independently important influence. So too, in this case, did having a higher score for Secondary Economic work commitment. Women, especially part-timers, were more likely to have high scores for this type of commitment; those who *did not* have them, however—even those who were part-timers— were less liable to endorse individualist ideology. Variables not entering the equation included—surprisingly perhaps—private-sector employment, number of employees at the workplace, age, and earnings.

Overall Effects of Skill Factors

One of the most important findings is that job-skill and own-skill exerted, in each case, strong independent effects. For the work ethic, these effects were positive: *higher scores for either of the two aspects of skill increased the score for work ethic.* But for individualism the effect of the variables was negative; *higher scores for either of the two aspects of skill reduced scores for individualism*; however, the effect of the skill variables was less strong in this case.

There are several possible explanations for these quite different effects of the skill variables on different aspects of work commitment. People who have more skilled ('better') jobs, or who have higher levels of training, have more to gain from continuing in employment and can perhaps take a more generous view of the labour-market insecurity suffered by those less advantaged than themselves. Those with skill advantages may be more likely to value expressive rewards partly because they gain them more often in doing their own work, and partly because their higher levels of education and training have encouraged such attitudes. Being more likely to have a strategic or career perspective on their own work history, they may also project such expectations on to people with less employment security.

Furthermore, people with challenging work are also more likely to gain higher prestige and self-esteem from being employed. This may help to account for such people agreeing more often with the statement that employed people enjoy more respect. Many of them, perhaps, themselves enjoyed such esteem. Amongst some of the more skilled this attitude may, none the less, have been offset by strong opinions about 'welfare scroungers'; as noted earlier, many higher-skilled employees rejected the statement that employed people gain more respect than the unemployed. But the statement was rejected most often by those employees who themselves had lower skill, and in particular many part-time women employees. This is hardly surprising. These employees had work graded as very low-skilled, and, as Chapter 7 shows, its real elements of skill might be discounted because they were deemed to be 'natural', everyday domestic or social attainments. It is the normal experience of such employees that the jobs they have do *not* generally bring much respect.

The main conclusions of the foregoing section raise two further questions. To begin with, must it be concluded, somewhat paradoxically and perhaps implausibly, that a strong work ethic is more often than not *incompatible* with strong individualism? Secondly, is either set of work values likely to change substantially in coming years? Brief answers to each question can be put forward after looking at the way occupation affects the relation between the work ethic and individualism.

OCCUPATIONAL CHANGE AND WORK ETHIC

Data for selected occupational groups was examined in order to answer the two questions with which the previous section closed. The multivariate analysis showed that having professional/ managerial work had a strong effect on the work-ethic scores, but hardly any on scores for individualism. It is necessary to examine this occupational variable more closely. The Work

Attitudes/Histories survey provided detailed (four-digit) occupational classification of currently held jobs. It was therefore possible to distinguish, in particular, between various types of
managerial occupation. However, the 18 occupational groups
were chosen to reflect all levels of the occupational structure.

It is easiest to begin by using the simplified method of presenting data adopted in the earlier part of the chapter; that is, in
terms of analytically defined aspects of work commitment—the
'simple' work ethic (commitment to paid work), expressiveness,
and individualism. (It will be shown later that using factor scores
produces very similar results.)

Table 10.9 shows the skill position and work commitment for
the 18 targeted occupational groups together accounting for half
(1,760) the Work Attitudes/Histories employee sample. The data
have been simplified to help presentation. The columns for the
three aspects of work commitment once again show the proportional variation of summary scores for each group from the sample mean scores. Columns for the skill variables show the
proportions of each group in the 'High' skill bands of the composite skill variables.

The occupational groups have been banded in the 1987 version
of the three-class Goldthorpe scheme.[7] All but one of the skill
and work-commitment levels shown in Table 10.9 were closely
associated with class position. For example, all the service-class
groups have high levels both of job-skill and own-skill; in all but
one case, they had 'simple' work ethic scores above average; and
in every case they had large positive scores for the balance of
expressive reasons for working. In the intermediate-class groups
there was a sharp decline in the proportions in the High skill
bands. Yet the work commitment scores of the Intermediate-class
groups were less clearly patterned. Sales representatives, for
example, seemed to fall closer to the managerial groups in the
service class than to other intermediate-class groups in their work
values. The working-class groups stood out for the very small
proportions appearing in the 'High' skill categories. (It should,
however, be noted that these occupations under-represent more
skilled males in the building, transport, and vehicle trades.) The
assemblers apart, their scores for 'simple' work ethic were low
compared even with the intermediate-class groups; and their
scores for the balance of Expressive Work Ethic were lower still.

Table 10.3. *Levels of skill and support for the main aspects of the work ethic in selected occupational groups (%)*

	Job-skill high	Own-skill high	Normative commitment	Expressiveness	Individualism
Service class					
Staff managers	67	44	+43	+264	−31
Foremen/h.supvsrs	72	79	−19	+42	+70
Managers, other	53	28	+2	+54	+79
Retail managers	33	19	+24	+26	+88
Teachers	57	63	+52	+68	−63
Lab technicians	50	74	+21	+81	−40
Welfare workers	23	40	+45	+56	−22
Nurses[a]	34	52	+19	+74	−8
Intermediate class					
Sales reps	19	22	+29	+32	+28
Typists	33	14	−5	−289	−4
Clerks	22	14	−5	−23	−8
Office mach ops	18	16	+26	−46	+47
Working class					
Shop assistants	1	1	−7	−63	+5
Domestic staff	1	4	−21	−49	−4
Warehouse staff	3	4	−7	−43	−22
Catering	1	0	−19	−53	−4
Caretakers	0	1	−24	−84	−4
Assemblers	4	0	+17	−72	+10

[a] Includes one-third of nurses classified as intermediate-class.

Source: Work Attitudes/Histories survey.

The more or less straightforward distribution of work commitment in terms of Goldthorpe (1987) class group is broken by the scores for individualism. These show a quite remarkable pattern. Instead of growing larger—or smaller—at higher levels of class, scores for individualism grew *more varied*. The widest difference in scores between working-class groups was only 32 points; for intermediate-class groups it was 75 points; but amongst the service-class groups it was no less than 151, ranging from the highly non-individualist teachers (−63) to the highly individualist retail managers (+88).

One possible reason for the occupational difference—the gender composition of some of these groups—can be largely discounted. As was noted earlier, the multivariate analysis of individual scores showed that sex *per se* had only a marginal influence on normative-expressive involvement in work; yet women had rather higher scores for individualism. These associations can now be specified more closely. Two of the targeted service-class occupational groups (teachers, laboratory technicians) had an evenly balanced sex ratio; others had either a disproportionate number of men (line managers) or women (welfare workers, nurses). It was, in fact, in the heavily male-dominated management occupations that scores for individualism were highest of all.

Table 10.9 shows that support for the work ethic and endorsement of individualism can vary independently, with occupational group as a key intervening variable. This is still more apparent if the variation is plotted on a graph. Figure 10.2 shows the 'mean position' for each of the service-class groups and five of the remaining groups. The vertical axis shows the group's mean score for (factored) work-ethic scores, and the horizontal axis the mean score for (factored) individualism scores. (In each case, the sample mean is 0, shown by the intersection of the axes.) All the service-class groups except foremen, forewomen, and higher supervisors had positive mean scores for work ethic. But they divided more evenly for individualism. Differences in actual occupation, then, not simply in occupational level, as well as skill level, seem to provide a key to explaining combinations of the work ethic-scores and the individualism scores.

Several explanations for the difference in individualism scores can be suggested though not followed up here. One might be in

Figure 10.2 Combination of mean scores for Expressive Work Ethic and for Economic individualism in selected occupational groups

terms of private-versus public-sector employment. Most teachers, welfare workers, and nurses—the 'least individualist' groups of all on the measures used—were public-sector employees. Does public-sector work have an indirect socializing effect on employment values, reducing support for individualist ideology? Or does it shape political outlook directly, as some New Right commentators argue? A problem here is that the multivariate analyses showed that public-sector employment itself had, overall, no effect on scores for individualism. (It did have a mild, but positive, effect on factored worth-ethic scores.)

An alternative explanation is that self-selection into some of these occupations, following longer formal education and per-

haps lengthy vocational training, reinforced values hostile to individualism as an ideology which were already held by recruits,
possibly as a result of political socialization in the family, and
that led them to choose their occupation in the first place. This
seems a more plausible explanation and can be linked to another
apparent motive for choosing a career in one of the 'low-individ-
ualism' occupations. All of the latter seem directly or indirectly
concerned with providing high-level personal, professional, or
caring services. This seems to hold, to some extent, even for the
(largely private-sector) specialist manager group, since its largest
subgroup includes personnel and industrial relations managers.

Again, none of the 'high-individualism' groups were concerned
with providing personal professional services. Moreover, the context of their work seems much more directly related to market
forces and signals, despite growing pressures of this kind every-
where in Britain in the 1980s. The line manager groups were also
made up largely of employees in the private sector, and thus
more likely to work in organizations where promotion to management posts in the first place, and subsequent moves upwards,
may be made on the basis of an individualistic, 'go-getting'
employment record or self-reliant psychological attributes considered relevant to the managerial role.

It may thus be significant—and is certainly worth noting—that
in two of the three high-individualism management groups own-
skill levels were lower than job-skill levels. The analysis of
Chapter 9 showed that 'under-qualification' is associated with
much higher than average job satisfaction. Some managers with a
deficit of own-skill had, perhaps, overcome what may have been
a serious handicap to promotion. It seems reasonable to suggest
that strong beliefs in individual striving and competition in the
jobs market may have helped to motivate these managers, or, in
some cases, brought them to the attention of their own superiors.
Here, too, processes of self-selection, socialization, and co-opta-
tion may help explain some of the influence of occupation as an
intervening variable.

At this point the second issue raised at the beginning of the
section—the implications of the Work Attitudes/Histories
findings for the overall trend in work values—can be taken up.
The main movement in occupation structure, in Britain as in
other advanced countries, is towards an increase in service-class

employment and a contraction in the male industrial/manual working class, above all in the semi-skilled workforce in manufacturing. There has been a continuing modest rise in some intermediate-class occupations, and a fairly rapid increase in routine 'personal-service' and low-grade manual occupations.

All such employee groups were well represented in the targeted occupations examined in this section. The service-class groups seem particularly good instances of growing 'people-handling' and 'information-handling' occupations. The working-class occupations—shop assistants (this group includes stackers and check-out staff), domestic staff (mainly cleaners), warehouse workers, catering-trade workers, and caretakers (including maintenance staff)—are equally good representatives of the expanding working-class occupations.

It has been shown that a strong work ethic, as defined in the Work Attitudes/Histories survey, was closely linked to higher skill, and to managerial and professional occupations. It mattered little whether the work ethic was measured by the simpler percentage-scores method or by the precise scores derived from factor analysis. In both cases the picture was almost identical. The service-class groups, with the partial exceptions already noted, are characterized by an often very strong work ethic. Their continued expansion signals a *strengthening* rather than a weakening of the work ethic. One other important change is in the position of better-qualified women employees. The growing skill attainment of these women, and the (slow but steady) growth in readiness to recruit them into more demanding jobs, or to promote them, through the 'glass ceiling', into positions of greater authority, should operate to reinforce their already strong commitment to paid work. For this reason alone it seems reasonable to predict that the normative-expressive component of the work ethic will strengthen considerably in the service-class occupations.

The working-class groups, with one partial exception, all had very low scores for the work ethic. The Work Attitudes/Histories survey suggests that the expansion of these groups may create an offsetting trend. These occupations for the most part offer low-skilled tasks to poorly trained employees. True enough, the skill levels of these workers may have been rising overall during the 1980s; yet, as Gallie in Chapter 2 shows, these increases were proportionately far lower than for groups higher in the occupational structure. In effect, something of a skills polarization seems to have been occurring, if the SCELI employee sample is a good guide. Absolute levels of skill may have been rising at every level, but they were apparently rising faster at the already most highly skilled levels. Furthermore, it is hard to see how many low-grade manual tasks could be rapidly upgraded to provide more challenge, or how the people who perform them could be more rapidly enskilled, without a more ambitious training effort and more adequate work-design resources. As explained in the closing section of the Introduction to this volume, in the Work Attitudes/Histories survey, the groups already most disadvantaged in skill also saw the least increase in their training provision. A possible conclusion is that the trend towards more sharply contrasted skill positions might be accompanied by a comparable widening in the gaps in values and attitudes relating to work.

Since individualism is less closely related to skill levels than is the work ethic, it is riskier to forecast changes to it. It may be that the privatization of large parts of the public sector, or the replacement of a public-sector *service culture* by a private-sector *enterprise culture* in those workplaces not yet privatized, will produce an alteration of values amongst their employees. This was surely one of the expectations behind the programme. The data are an inadequate basis for discussing the likelihood of this outcome; but, given their limitations, they provide little evidence that such a 'cultural revolution' was occurring at the time, or would do so over the short term. A large majority of Work Attitudes/Histories employees, for example, supported higher public expenditure on the health and other social services. In this sense, a form of collectivism was still strong in the employee sample, with the enterprise culture remaining, perhaps, a political shibboleth. Opinion polls and other surveys about these issues throughout the 1980s (Jowell and Witherspoon, 1984, 1985, 1986, 1987) point in much the same way.

IN CONCLUSION

The more general conclusions to which this chapter leads are clear. The survey findings indicate that the work ethic is not declining in Britain, thanks either to the onset of post-industrialism or to the long-term effects of a 'welfare-spoiled' post-1945 period of economic growth and consensus politics. On the contrary, the findings of the Work Attitudes/Histories survey suggest that in many respects the work ethic is strong at most occupational levels, and that the growth of service-class jobs and the higher employment participation of women could produce an overall strengthening of the work ethic. At the same time, this trend might be offset by the growth of those lower-skilled personal service and similar occupations, where the quality of skills training and development still typically ranges from the indifferent to the abysmal.

Campaigns to strengthen the work ethic by political means such as strong endorsement by the government for individualist labour-market philosophies in the 1980s seem to have had little impact on personal work values by the time of the survey. They may indeed have had little more practical effect in workplaces than to encourage people who already believed in strong economic individualism to echo the official message more confidently. Perhaps, too, some people who had no strong personal belief in the message were readier to follow political fashions in those years and endorse it verbally, if at times half-ironically.

It therefore remains to be seen whether the profound changes in economic values perceived by the more sanguine observers of a British economic miracle in the later 1980s (Lawson, 1992) were any more solidly based than the economic achievement itself proved to be. The present writer knows of no serious evidence for the widespread, permanent conversion of the British labour force to an enterprise culture, in the sense originally intended.

In any case, as this chapter has shown, individualist labour-market ideologies appear to have no direct and necessary connections with a strong worth ethic. Those who have such values *may* also be more highly committed to employment and also work hard in their jobs; just as probably, they may not. Any policy conclusion therefore seems clear: support for individualism will *not*, by itself, strengthen the work ethic; on the other hand, support for the improvement of skills, especially through training and qualification, might well produce this result.

NOTES

1. For a review see Rose (1988*a*).
2. The concept of alienation was often used in an over-general way by some critics of assembly-line work. Chinoy (1955) was the first to show that it was possible to retain a great deal to the concept's philosophical meaning when analysing the work actual situation and work involvement of employees.
3. The question was: 'Do you see yourself as having a career?' Approximately half the employee sample said they looked on their work as a career; for men employees the figures were 61% for women full-timers, 56%; for women part-timers, 24% for all self-employed, 68%.
4. Respondents were asked to choose a main reason and a second reason for having a paid job from a list of 10 possibilities. As noted in the text, the 10 reasons were reduced into a set of four: Provisioning; Secondary Economic; Expressive; and Social. The *weighted percentage* score for a subgroup gave extra weight to first-choice answers, counting subgroup percentages for *both* answers. For a given subgroup, each of the four sets of reasons was calculated as follows: percentage first choice *multiplied by* 2, *plus* percentage second choice, *divided by* 3. For further explanation and examples see Appendix 10.1 on Measures.
5. The balance for 'expressiveness' was computed as follows: subgroup weighted percentage for Expressive reasons *minus* group's weighted percentage Secondary Economic reasons, *divided by* subgroup weighted Expressive percentage *plus* subgroup weighted Secondary Economic percentage. For further explanation and examples see Appendix 10.1 on Measures.
6. An advantage of having an interval-level score is that it allows creation of better ordinal-level measures and multivariate analysis such as multiple regression. The scores derived from factor analysis are automatically converted into a standardized form in SPSSX; that is, they are equally spread either side of 0, with the range of 1 standard deviation set between +1 and –1. This means that 67% of all cases have values within this range. For further discussion see Norusis (1985).
7. Since 1987, the Goldthorpe scheme has classified *personal-service workers*, such as retail workers in particular, as working-class, not intermediate-class (Goldthorpe, 1987). Though Goldthorpe did not base his revision primarily in terms of the skill levels of such workers, the SCELI data on skill show that the change was amply justified in terms of either own-skill or job-skill. On the bases of the skill mea-

sures, there also appears to be a case for 'promoting' at least some sales representatives and similar staff from the intermediate into the service class. In the Work Attitudes/Histories sample, their levels of skill were close to those of retail managers, and the great majority (78%) considered their work as a career, a level which is characteristic of service-class groups in the Work Attitudes/Histories sample.

APPENDIX 10.1 MEASURES OF WORK VALUES

Differences in Work Commitment between Subgroups

The analysis in the first section of the chapter is based upon subgroups (male employees, female employees, respondents who said their job was skilled, etc.). Results for subgroups have been tabled with independent variables (the subgroups) in the columns and dependent variables (for example, the percentage of the subgroup's members saying they would continue working even if they did not need to) in the rows. Thus percentage responses in the subgroups, for each indicator separately, can be inspected. The indicators are set out in three groups, with a summary score for each group. This layout is explained in more detail below.

The indicators, with their summary scores, were grouped in three categories (*normative commitment* to paid work; personal *rationale* for paid work; and *individualist ideology* with regard to the labour market) which were deemed to correspond broadly with major aspects of the work ethic as defined in social science research or political debate. As explained in the main text, two indicators were used for *normative commitment* and two for *individualist ideology*. For *rationale* of paid work, the indicators were ten possible reasons for having paid work, which themselves had to be grouped first.

For each of these three aspects of the work ethic, *summary scores* were computed to simplify comparison between subgroups. These scores represent the *percentage difference* from a reference score, which was the score for the whole sample. The 'whole sample' was usually that of all currently employed people. In Tables 10.1–3, however, the sample is all economically active people interviewed for the Work Attitudes/Histories survey; this included all subgroups but home-makers ('housewives') who said they had no plans to enter or to return to the labour market, the fully retired, and the permanently sick. Some small subgroups—the temporarily sick, full-time students, and people on government training schemes—are not shown in these tables though they were included in calculations for the 'currently active' sample. (In fact, the results hardly vary if these groups are omitted.)

Commitment to Paid Work

The first step in producing this score was to create a *reference score*, applying to the whole sample. This can be regarded as a rough and ready index figure for the employee sample which *combined* the two percentage figures for each indicator (i.e. endorsements of the statements 'Would continue working . . .', and 'Employed people gain more respect'). This was done simply by: (i) multiplying the two percentages together, and (ii) dividing this product by 100. An index figure for a subgroup was then computed in the same way. The degree of 'deviation' of this figure from the sample reference score was then arrived at by (iii) subtracting the *sample reference score* from the subgroup index figure; and (iv) dividing the balance by the *sample reference score*. The resulting difference, expressed as a percentage, is the *subgroup score*.

This can be illustrated by reference to Table 10.10, which shows the percentages for those currently employed people who said their jobs were skilled, for those employees who said their jobs were *not* skilled, and for the whole employee sample. The *sample reference score* is: (64

TABLE 10.10. *Method for computing index figures and scores for normative commitment to paid work in subgroups* (%)

	Subgroup saying 'Job IS skilled'	Subgroup saying 'Job NOT skilled'	Employee sample
Indicators of normative commitment to paid work			
Would continue to work	67	60	64
Employed people given more respect	69	60	66
Index figure	46	34	42
Subgroup SCORE	+10	−19	0

Note: The exact questions were (for Employees and the Self-Employed): 'If you were to get enough money to live as comfortably as you would like for the rest of your life, would you continue to work, not necessarily in your present job, or would you stop working?'; (for Unemployed and Non-Employed planning to return to work): 'If you were to get enough money to live as comfortably as you would like for the rest of your life, would you want to work somewhere or would you want to remain without a job?'; and 'I'm going to read out some differing views about *unemployment*, and I'd like you to tell me, from the card, how much you agree or disagree with each . . . "Employed people are given more respect than unemployed people".' The options were: Strongly agree; Agree; No strong opinions either way; Disagree; Strongly disagree.

Source: Work Attitudes/Histories survey.

×66)/100 = 42. The subgroup index figure for those saying their jobs were skilled is: (67 × 69)/100 = 46, a difference of +4 from the sample. In percentage terms, the *subgroup score* is: [(46 – 42)/42] × 100 = +10%. (All percentages were rounded up and down.) Similarly, the index figure for the 'Says job not skilled' subgroup is: (56 × 60)/100 = 34; and its *subgroup score* is [(34 – 42)/42] × 100 = –19%.

TABLE 10.11. *Method for computing index figures and scores for economic individualism (self-reliance ideology) in subgroups, illustrated by favourability to trade unions* (%)

	Favourable to unions	NOT favourable to unions	Employee sample
Indicators of individualist ideology			
Unemployed can always find a job	27	52	42
Welfare state cuts the will to work	39	66	52
Index figure	11	34	22
Subgroup SCORE	–50	+55	0

Note: The exact questions for indicating individualism were: 'I'm going to read out some differing views about *unemployment*, and I'd like you to tell me, from the card, how much you agree or disagree with each . . . "People can always get another job if they really want one",' with the options: Strongly agree; Agree; No strong opinions either way; Disagree; Strongly disagree; and 'I'd like to get your opinion about the system of taxes, services, and benefits that's commonly known as the welfare state. Do you agree or disagree with, or have no strong opinions about, the following statements? "The welfare state . . . reduces the will to work".' The question on favourability to trade unions was: 'From this card, how favourable are you to trade unions?', (on the card) 'Very favourable', 'Quite favourable', 'No strong feelings either way', 'Not very favourable', 'Not at all favourable'.

Source: Work Attitudes/Histories survey.

Individualist Ideology

Subgroups scores for this aspect of work values were produced in a similar way. Table 10.11 shows the results for two subgroups, those employees who said they were 'Favourable to trade-unions', and those who said they were 'Unfavourable' to them. (A strong association between attitudes towards trade unions and endorsement for individualism was to be expected.) In this case, it should be noted, the sample reference score is lower: $[42 \times 52)/100] = 22$. The index figure for the 'Favourable to unions' subgroup is $[(27 \times 39)/100] = -11$; for the 'Unfavourable to unions' subgroup the index figure is $[(52 \times 66)]/100 = +34$. The *subgroup score* for the 'Favourable' subgroup is thus: $[(11 - 22)/22] \times 100 = 50\%$; and for the 'Unfavourable' sub-groups $[(34 - 22)/22] \times 100 = 55\%$.

Rationale of Paid Work

As noted earlier, the sub-group data for rationale of paid work were treated differently. For theoretical reasons, explained in the text, the main concern was with the relative frequencies of: (i) *Expressive* reasons for working; and (ii) *Secondary Economic* reasons for working. The data on reasons for working were also complex in their 'raw' form and had to be simplified considerably to permit manageable treatment, even before computing any summary score for rationale of paid work. In the Work Attitudes/Histories survey, interviewees had been asked to choose a *main reason* for having a paid job from a list of ten options (if the choice 'None of these reasons' is included), and were then asked to choose a *second reason* from the same list. In effect, then, each interviewee can be seen as ranking the reasons offered to them as of first importance, second importance, and third importance (with eight separate options tying in third place). More precise information about rationale of paid work would have been obtained by explicitly asking respondents for their third (and even their fourth) most important reason for having a paid job. Regrettably, time pressures in the interview did not allow this. But the data available still provided an acceptable level of detail for the purposes of the analysis carried out here.

From inspection, it can be seen that some of the reasons have thematic similarities. In fact, they can be grouped into four broad categories in terms of their underlying logic (i) *Provisioning* ('Need money for essentials', 'Working is the normal thing to do'); (ii) *Secondary Economic* ('To earn money to buy extras', 'To give me a sense of independence'); (iii) *Expressive* ('To use my abilities to the full', 'To feel I'm doing something worth while', '[I] enjoy working'); and (iv) *Social and Other* ('For the company of other people', 'To get out of the house', 'None of these reasons'). Statistical analysis (see below under 'Work Ethic Factors') showed that this grouping had considerable validity from an empirical viewpoint, as well as logically.

It was decided to omit the *Social/Other* category from the analysis of subgroups because the two 'social' reasons accounted for only 6% of all reasons given, and in many subgroups rather less than this. It is, however, worth noting that endorsement of 'social' reasons tended to 'echo' the frequencies for Secondary Economic reasons, though at a lower level; that is to say, subgroups that had frequencies for Secondary Economic reasons higher than that of the employee sample also had frequencies for Social/Other reasons higher than the sample. (In computing scores for *individuals* rather than for subgroups, the Social/Other reasons *were* included in the analysis.)

Any subgroup had a first-choice frequency *and* a second-choice frequency for each of the three sets of reason retained in the subgroup analysis. To have examined all of these frequencies separately would also have been impractical in this chapter. The simplest way to reduce this detail would be to combine the percentage for first choice of one of the four sets of reasons with the percentage for second choice of it, then divide by two. But this would give no weight to the relative importance of a first-choice reason to respondents in any subgroup. A simple method of weighting first-choice frequencies was necessary.

It was decided that the percentage of first-choice reasons should be given double weight, added to second-choice percentage, and the sum divided by 3. The results of this (relatively cautious) weighting procedure are illustrated in Table 10.12. This table deliberately uses *dummy data* in order to bring out the effect of weighting more clearly. Table 10.12 likewise includes 'results' for Social/Other reasons, though these are not examined in detail in the chapter; and it shows percentage figures for the 'implied third choice' for each type of rationale, providing a further reminder of the importance of provisioning reasons as a whole, and the unimportance of social reasons.)

The unweighted mean results show, correctly, that Provisioning reasons were the most important group by far. But it suggests that Secondary Economic and Expressive reasons were of equal importance; and it exaggerates the importance of Social/Other reasons, which were given by only 3% as first choices though six times as often as second choices. The weighted results, on the other hand, do show the greater frequency of Expressive reasons, as opposed to Secondary Economic reasons, as first choices. They also give a combined percentage for provisioning reasons that seems to summarize the data rather better than the unweighted mean.

The summary score used in discussing the Rationale of Paid Work in subgroups is a *balance of expressive reasons*. Table 10.13 illustrates how this balance was calculated, using for illustration six subgroups produced by breaking the employee sample down by sex and level of formal qualification. (Both these variables have important effects on the readiness to choose Expressive reasons as opposed to Secondary economic reasons for working.) Table 10.13 shows the combined (weighted) percentages for Provisioning, Secondary Economic, and Expressive reasons for working in the six subgroups. Lack of qualifications in a subgroup

TABLE 10.12. *Effect of weighting reasons for having paid work in subgroups; illustrated by dummy data* (%)

	1st choice	2nd choice	3rd choice	Simple mean	Weighted mean
Grouped reasons for having a paid job					
Provisioning	50	30	20	40	43
Secondary Economic	12	38	50	25	21
Expressive	35	15	50	25	28
Social and other	3	17	80	10	8

Note: The exact questions asked were: 'Here are some reasons for wanting a paid job. At the moment, which *one* would come closest to your own *main* reason?' (After first reason given): 'And which would be your *second* most important reason?' The options were in each case: 'Working is the normal thing to do'; 'Need money for basic essentials such as food, rent, and mortgage'; 'To earn money to buy extras'; 'For the company of other people'; '[I] enjoy working'; 'To use my abilities to the full'; 'To feel I'm doing something worth while'; 'To give me a sense of independence'; 'To get out of the house'; 'None of these [reasons]'. There was also a 'Don't know' option for each.

Source: Work Attitudes/Histories survey.

TABLE 10.13. *Method for calculating scores for expressive work rationale in subgroups, illustrated by reference to qualifications actually held* (%)

	Qualifications					
	All men		Women full-timers		All full-time employees	
	High	No	High	No	High	No
Provisioning	59	67	41	49	49	52
Secondary Economic	8	11	18	33	15	28
Expressive	27	11	35	9	30	9
Difference (% of Expressive reasons less % of Secondary Economic reasons)	+17	0	+17	−22	+15	−19
BALANCE of Expressive reasons	+212	0	+94	−72	+100	−67

Note: The four types of rationale of paid work were created by combining the first-choice and second-choice reasons for working (see Note to Table 10.12 for list of options); they are explained in the accompanying text.

Source: Work Attitudes/Histories survey.

increases the proportions giving Provisioning and Secondary Economic reasons, while reducing the proportion giving Expressive reasons. It is clear, though, that the *relative* changes in the proportions for Secondary Economic and for Expressive reasons are far greater than those for Provisioning. This is most apparent for the two subgroups where the sexes are combined. (In fact, scores for provisioning amongst women have been slightly 'inflated' by leaving out part-timers, who chose provisioning reasons less often than the full-timer women.)

The relation between proportions choosing Secondary Economic and Expressive reasons in a subgroup can be expressed most simply as the arithmetic difference between them, as shown in Table 10.12. But this would, in many cases, understate the relative importance of Expressive reasons among all reasons *other than* Provisioning reasons. For example, the simple difference for Highly qualified men (+17%) is exactly the same as for Highly qualified women full-timers (+17%); yet the men chose Expressive reasons over three times as often as Secondary Economic reasons (27 versus 8), while the women chose them only twice as often (35 versus 18). This problem is avoided if this relative frequency is shown as a percentage figure. The percentage is calculated by dividing the proportion for Secondary Economic reasons by the difference. Thus, for the men with High qualifications, the percentage balance is [(17/8) × 100] = +212%; for the women it is [(17/18) × 100] = +94%.

It might be noted that all scores for subgroups, and especially this last one, were computed in such a way as to highlight those differences between subgroups most relevant to the discussion. They are not intended to show, and cannot be taken as showing, 'absolute' differences between subgroups; yet they do give some valid idea of the scale of differences. Some form of reduction was necessary in any case in order to discuss the prevalence of different rationales of paid work in subgroups.

Work Commitment at the Individual Level

At the subgroup stage of analysis, combinations of responses at the *individual* level remain unclear though subgroup results suggest they must be systematic. The second half of the chapter, however, required an examination of these associations, and the production of appropriate measures for the different aspects of work commitment. It was then possible to show the association, at the individual level, of these variables with a range of workplace and individual characteristics, examining in particular the effect of different skill levels.

Factor analysis was used to produce composite variables for this purpose, as it was for producing the composite skill variables used in this and Chapter 9 (See the Appendix to Chapter 9 on 'Measuring Skill'). The following discussion does not assume specialist knowledge of this technique. (For a general description of the factor analysis provided in SPSSX see Norusis, 1985.)

Factor analysis examines all associations between a set of variables already thought to be related on logical, theoretical, or empirical grounds, searching for one or more 'factors' apparently underlying them. If the variables are *all* more or less closely interrelated, factor analysis shows how closely any single variable is associated with (or in technical terms, 'loads' on) this underlying factor. Factoring also creates a new variable representing the factor, computing 'unique factor scores' for each case in the analysis. These factor scores are points on an *interval-level* scale, allowing their use in other advanced analyses. Alternatively, they can be converted into an *ordinal-level* variable by setting suitable cutting-points, typically for the 'High', 'Medium', or 'Low' scoring cases. (The choice of cutting-points can be to some extent a matter of convenience.)

Often, however, factoring indicates that there is more than one underlying factor—thus sometimes upsetting earlier expectations. Where more than one factor is found, new variables (factors), each with its own set of 'unique factor scores', can be generated. The factoring process is usually carried out in order to maximize the distinction between factors and reflect this difference in scores.

The variables used in the factoring of work commitment were those used to examine subgroups, and one further one (viewing one's work as a career). The main initial difficulty was, once again, how to handle 'reasons for having paid work'. Several solutions were attempted, each producing broadly comparable results when used in factoring. The method chosen finally was to group reasons into the four categories outlined earlier (Provisioning, Secondary economic, Expressive, and Social/Other). A score for each one was computed for each case in the sample, as follows: reason chosen first = 2; reason chosen second = 1; reason not chosen = 0. The range of scores for each set of reasons was thus 0–3. (0 = reason not chosen either first or second; 1 = reason chosen second only; 2 = reason chosen first only; 3 = reason chosen first *and* second.)

All individuals scored zero for at least two of the four 'grouped reasons for working' variables—and an appreciable number, having chosen first and second reasons from the same group, scored zero for three of them. (The group of reasons with most zero scores was Social/Other.) This no doubt affected the results of the factoring results, but the extent of any distortion was regarded as acceptable.

Factoring the nine work-values variables produced four factors. The results of a factor analysis have to be 'interpreted'. A shorthand way of understanding this is as a problem in giving the factor a name that conveys the apparent meaning in an intelligible and adequate way. The main guide in doing so is the way in which the separate variables (or 'items') associate with ('load' on) the factor; some may do so either in a clear positive way, others in a clear negative way, and some hardly at all.

The first factor had very strong positive loadings for Expressive reasons for working, and moderately strong loadings for always wanting a paid job and seeing work as a career. On the other hand it had moderately strong negative loading for Secondary Economic reasons for working and a clearly negative (though not very strong) loading for Provisioning reasons for working. For 'Unemployed people can always find a job', for 'The welfare state reduces the will to work', for 'Employed people gain more respect', and for having secondary economic reasons for working, the loadings were close to neutral. Clearly, this factor seems to be related to close involvement in paid work linked to self-expression in work and a career outlook. These themes seem close to the idea of normative commitment to work embodying a long-term challenge to skills and abilities: it was seen as approximating to the work ethic as a central life-interest as well as to high commitment to paid work; as pointed out in the text, having an Expressive rationale of work forms an integral part of it.

The second factor had high positive loading on Secondary Economic reasons for working, moderate negative loading on seeing work as a career, and extremely heavy negative loading on having Provisioning reasons for working. The people with high personal scores for this factor were above all women part-time employees with very low levels of formal education, training, and qualification with low-skilled jobs. Women employees with higher levels of *own-skill* and *job-skill* who worked full-time, and most men employees, had very low individual scores for this factor.

The third factor was associated with very high positive loadings for endorsing the view that unemployed people can always find a job if they really want to, and the view that the welfare state cuts the will to work. Though wishing always to have paid work loaded positively on this factor, it did so rather weakly. On the other hand, there was a moderate to strong *negative* loading for the view that employed people gain more respect. In other words, a high score for this factor was associated to an appreciable extent with the view that having a paid job *does not* gain respect.

Further analysis, and enquiries of a more qualitative kind, suggest that a possible interpretation would be that such individuals take the view that paid work *ought* to bring social esteem, but that in fact it often does not. Two further findings are worth mentioning here. Firstly, members of certain occupations (many managers on the other hand, members of very low-skilled occupations on the other) endorsed the 'low respect' view more frequently. Secondly, women with full-time work, irrespective of occupation, tended to endorse the view that the employed *do* gain more respect, while women with part-time work tended to endorse the contrary view. As noted in discussion of the effect of skill on this Economic Individualism factor, multivariate analysis did show small negative associations with both skill variables. However, it was most closely associated with political values (and thus very probably with political socialization).

The fourth factor was rather more difficult to interpret, since it lacked heavy loading on any items, of either a positive or a negative kind. Since it was the weakest in the statistical sense also, it is not discussed in the chapter. However, a more extensive factor analysis of work values was undertaken, for a smaller sample, using additional items relating to commitment to work and work effort. These were drawn from 'team-specific' questions asked of the 1,015 respondents in Swindon. This analysis generated additional factors, but the three described above remained distinct and amongst the easiest to interpret.

With the full Work Attitudes/Histories sample, it was possible to undertake the factoring including all the major labour-market groups (even those 'home-makers' who intended to return to paid work), or to restrict it to employees only (or even to *full-time* employees only). Changes in the sample used for factoring—provided it included full-time employees—had no effect on the main pattern that emerged and relatively little on loadings for the individual items. More technically speaking, the method of rotation used to produce the factors and factor scores used here was Varimax, which aims to maximize distinctions between factors; but using different methods of rotation produced very similar results.

METHODOLOGICAL APPENDIX

The Social Change and Economic Life Initiative

DUNCAN GALLIE

---

1. INTRODUCTION

The Social Change and Economic Life Initiative (SCELI) focused on six local labour markets—Aberdeen, Coventry, Kirkcaldy, Northampton, Rochdale, and Swindon. These were selected to provide contrasting patterns of recent and past economic change. In particular, three of the localities—Coventry, Kirkcaldy, and Rochdale—had relatively high levels of unemployment in the early and mid-1980s, while the other three had experienced relatively low levels of unemployment.

In each locality, four surveys were carried out designed to provide a high level of comparability between localities: the Work Attitudes/ Histories Survey, the Household and Community Survey, the Baseline Employers Survey, and the 30 Establishment Survey. The interview schedules for these surveys were constructed collectively by representatives of the different teams involved in the research programme. In addition a range of studies was carried out that were specific to particular localities. These were concerned to explore in greater depth a number of themes covered in the comparative surveys.

A distinctive feature of the research programme was that it was designed to provide for the possibility of linkage between the different surveys. The pivotal survey (and the first to be conducted) was the Work Attitudes/Histories Survey. This provided the sampling frame for the Household and Community Survey and for the Employers Baseline Survey. The Baseline Survey in turn provided the listings from which organizations were selected for the 30 Establishment Survey.

The field-work for the Work Attitudes/Histories Survey and for the Household and Community Survey was carried out by Public Attitudes Surveys Research Ltd. The Baseline Employers Survey was a telephone survey conducted by Survey and Fieldwork International (SFI). The interviews for the 30 Establishment Survey were carried out by members of the research teams.

TABLE A.1. *The Work Attitudes/Histories Survey 1986: achieved sample*

	Aberdeen	Coventry	Kirkcaldy	Northampton	Rochdale	Swindon	TOTAL
Eligible addresses	1,345	1,312	1,279	1,400	1,350	1,321	8,007
Achieved sample							
Main sample	997	990	1,011	957	987	955	5,897
Booster sample	48	23	—	65	18	60	214
Total interviewed	1,045	1,013	1,011	1,022	1,005	1,015	6,111
Response rate (%)	78	77	79	73	74	77	76

2. THE WORK ATTITUDES/HISTORIES SURVEY

This survey was concerned primarily with people's past work careers, their current experience of employment or unemployment, attitudes to trade unionism, work motivation, broader socio-political values, and the financial position of the household.

Two pilot studies were carried out in the preparation of the Work Attitudes/Histories Survey, testing questionnaire items, the placing of the work history schedule, interview length, and the contact procedure. The main field-work was conducted between June and November 1986. The objective was to secure an achieved sample of 1,000 in each of the six localities. As can be seen in Table A.1, the target was marginally exceeded, providing an overall sample of 6,111.

The sampling areas were defined in terms of the Department of Employment's 1984 Travel to Work areas (TTWA), with the exception of Aberdeen. In Aberdeen, where the TTWA was particularly extensive and included some very sparsely populated areas, the Daily Urban System area was used to provide greater comparability with the other locations.

A random sample was drawn of the non-institutionalized population aged 20–60. The electoral register was used to provide the initial selection of addresses, with probabilities proportional to the number of registered electors at each address. A half open-interval technique was also employed, leading to the identification of a small number of non-registered addresses in each locality. Doorstep enumeration of 20- to 60-year-olds was undertaken at each address followed by a random selection using the Kish procedure of one 20- to 60-year-old at each eligible address.

To provide sufficient numbers for analysis, it was stipulated that there should be a minimum of 150 unemployed respondents in each locality. A booster sample of the unemployed was drawn in the localities where this figure was not achieved through the initial sample. The booster sample was based on a separate random sample of addresses, with a higher sampling fraction in the wards with the highest levels of unemployment. As with the main sample, addresses were selected from the electoral register. But, for the selection of individuals, only the unemployed were eligible for inclusion. This booster sample was implemented in five of the six localities, producing a total of 214 respondents. Response rates for the combined main and booster sample were approximately 75 per cent in each of the localities, ranging from 73 per cent in Northampton to 79 per cent in Kirkcaldy (see Table A.1).

Where appropriate, weights have been used to take account of the booster sample, using the estimates of the proportion of unemployed available from the initial sample. There are also weights to provide a Kish adjustment for household size and to correct for an over-representation of women in the achieved sample (3,415 women compared with 2,696 men). The sex weight assumes equal numbers of men and women in the relevant population, as is shown to be almost exactly the case by examination of census data.

The interview consisted of two major sections. The first was a life and work history schedule in which information was collected about various aspects of the individuals' labour market, family, and residential history over the entire period since they had first left full-time education. Information about family and residential history was collected on a year grid basis. Information about labour market history—including spells of unemployment and economic inactivity—was collected on a sequential start-to-finish date-of-event basis. In the case of 'employment events' further information was collected about *inter alia* the nature of the job, the employer, hours of work, number of employees, gender segregation, and trade union membership. The second part of the interview schedule was a conventional attitudinal schedule, with a core of common questions combined with separate subschedules designed specifically for employees, for the self-employed, and for the unemployed and economically inactive.

While the greater part of the questions in the schedules provides direct comparability between localities, some scope was given for teams to introduce questions that would be asked only in their own locality (or in a subset of localities). This usually involved teams introducing a broader range of questions for investigating one or more of the themes covered in the common questions.

3. THE HOUSEHOLD AND COMMUNITY SURVEY

In 1987 a follow-up survey was carried out involving approximately one-third of the respondents to the 1986 Work Attitudes/Histories Survey. This focused primarily on household strategies, the domestic division of labour, leisure activities, sociability, the use of welfare provision, and attitudes to the welfare state. The survey was conducted in each of the localities, with the field-work lasting between March and July. The survey produced an achieved sample of 1,816 respondents, of whom 1,218 were living in partnerships and 588 were living on their own. Where applicable a range of questions was asked of partners as well as of the original respondents.

The sampling lists for the survey were generated from computer listings of respondents to the Work Attitudes/Histories Survey who had agreed to being reinterviewed. To ensure that a sufficiently large number of the unemployed respondents from the Work Attitudes/Histories Survey were reinterviewed, it was decided to specify that, in each locality, approximately 75 of the households in the follow-up survey would be from households where the respondent was unemployed at the time of the Work Attitudes/Histories Survey. For sampling, the lists were stratified into four groups, separating the unemployed from others and people who were single from those with partners. The sampling interval was the same for those of different partnership status, but different sampling intervals were used for the unemployed and for others to obtain the target numbers of people who had been unemployed at the time of the first survey.

In the event, 87 per cent of respondents (ranging from 84.8 per cent in Coventry to 89.7 per cent in Aberdeen) had indicated that they were willing to co-operate in a further phase of the research. Since the sampling areas were once more defined in terms of local labour markets, there was a further attrition of the original eligible sample due to people leaving the area (between 7 per cent and 9 per cent, depending on the locality). Response rates (for those that had agreed to be reinterviewed and were still in the area) were 75 per cent or better in each locality, ranging from 75 per cent in Rochdale and Northampton to 77 per cent in Kirkcaldy. The structure of the achieved sample is given in Table A.2. It should be noted that the table describes respondents with respect to their characteristics at the time of the Work Attitudes/Histories Survey, 1986, since this was the relevant factor for the sampling strategy. The economic and partnership status of a number of respondents had changed by the time of the second interview. For instance, while 1,223 of these respondents were classified as having had partners in 1986, the number with partners at the time of interview in 1987 was 1,218.

The questionnaire for this survey consisted of three sections: an interview schedule including questions of both respondents and partners, a respondent's self-completion, and a partner's self-completion. There was a shorter separate schedule for single people. The questionnaires included an update of the life and work histories of the original respondent and a full work history was collected for partners interviewed. The self-completion for respondents and partners was used at different points in the interview to collect independent responses from partners where it was thought that issues might be sensitive or that there was a danger of contamination of responses. The respondents and their partners filled in the relevant sections of the self-completion in the presence of the interviewer, but without reference to each other. The great majority of questions were common to all localities, but, again, a limited number of locality specific questions were allowed.

The *Time Budget Survey*. The data available through the Household and Community Survey interview was extended through a linked time

TABLE A.2. *The Household and Community Survey 1987: achieved sample by characteristics at time of Work Attitudes/Histories Survey*

	Aberdeen	Coventry	Kirkcaldy	Northampton	Rochdale	Swindon	TOTAL
Total issued	390	400	399	404	402	394	2,389
Achieved sample							
Employed/non-active with partner in 1986	153	162	167	163	155	175	975
Employed/non-active, single in 1986	68	54	62	60	68	48	360
Unemployed with partner in 1986	42	42	40	40	45	39	248
Unemployed, single in 1986	41	44	40	38	32	38	233
Total interviewed	304	302	309	301	300	300	1,816
Response rate (%)	78	76	77	75	75	76	76

budget survey. This project was directed by Jonathan Gershuny of the University of Oxford. The final five minutes of the Household and Community Survey were devoted to introducing the time budget diaries to the individual or couple present. The diaries were designed to cover a full week starting from the day following the household interview. They required natural-language descriptions of the diarist's sequences of activities to be kept on a fifteen-minute grid, for the whole week, together with any secondary (i.e. simultaneous) activities and a record of geographical location and whether or not others were present during the activities carried out. Interviewers left behind addressed, reply-paid envelopes for return of the diaries at the end of the diary week.

Forty-four per cent of those eligible (802 of the original 1,816 respondents and 533 of their 1,218 partners) completed usable diaries for the whole week. This low rate of response, though not unexpected from a postal survey, raises the issue of the extent of non-response biases. In anticipation of this problem, a number of questionnaire items were included in the original Household and Community Survey interviews which were intended to 'shadow' or parallel evidence from the diaries (i.e. questions about the frequency of participation in leisure activities and about the distribution of responsibilities for domestic work). An analysis of the two sources of data showed that the distribution of frequencies of the questionnaire responses of those who failed to complete diaries was very similar to the distribution of questionnaire responses for those who did keep diaries. From this we may infer an absence of bias at least with respect to estimates of these leisure and unpaid work activities (for a fuller account, see Gershuny 1990).

4. THE EMPLOYER SURVEYS

The implementation of the Baseline Employers Survey, which was a telephone survey, was the responsibility of Michael White of the Policy Studies Institute. The schedule was drawn up in collaboration with a working party of representatives from the different teams involved in the SCELI programme.

The survey involved a sample of establishments. The major part of the sample was drawn from information provided from the Work Attitudes/Histories Survey about people's employers. Each of the 1,000 individuals interviewed in each locality was asked, if currently employed, to provide the name and address of the employer and the address of the place of work. The sample was confined to establishments located within the travel-to-work areas that formed the basis of the research programme. Approximately 12 per cent of establishments initially listed

TABLE A.3. *The Baseline Employer Survey*

	Aberdeen	Coventry	Kirkcaldy	Northampton	Rochdale	Swindon	TOTAL
Sample from survey	345	280	229	287	233	273	1,647
Booster sample	52	54	32	51	55	39	283
Out of area	1	30	16	27	11	4	89
Eligible	396	304	245	311	277	308	1,841
Interviews	308	203	174	209	177	240	1,311
Response rate (%)	77.7	66.7	71.0	67.2	63.9	77.9	71.2

could not be included in the sample because of insufficient information or closures. The sample covers all types of employer and both the public and the private sectors.

This method of generating a sample differs from a straight random sample drawn from a frame of all establishments. The latter would have resulted in a very large number of small establishments being included, while there was considerable theoretical interest in medium-sized and large establishments as key actors in the local labour market. The method used in SCELI weights the probability of an establishment's being included by its size: the greater the number of employees at an establishment, the greater its chance of having one or more of its employees included in the sample of individuals (and hence itself being selected).

The above method is closely related to sampling with probability proportional to size (p.p.s.); however, there are generally too few medium-sized and large establishments to generate a true p.p.s. sample. To increase the numbers of these medium-sized and large establishments, an additional sample of private sector employers with fifty or more employees was drawn from market research agency lists, supplemented by information from the research teams. The booster consisted of all identifiable establishments in this size range not accounted for by the basic sampling method. The sampling method, then, was designed to be as comprehensive as possible for medium-sized and larger employers. In practice, 70 per cent to 85 per cent of the sample by different localities were provided through the listings from the Work Attitudes/Histories data, while only 15 per cent to 30 per cent were from the booster sample. The structure of the achieved sample is presented in Table A.3. The sample so generated under-represents smaller, and over-represents larger, establishments, but provides adequate numbers in all size groups. It is also approximately representative of employment in each area, but it is possible to use weighting to achieve an even more precise representation of local employment. This was carried out using tables of employment by size group of establishment within industry group within each local labour market, from the 1984 Census of Employment (by courtesy of the Statistics Division, Department of Employment).

There were five stages of piloting over the summer of 1986, particularly concerned to develop the most effective contact procedure. The main field-work period was from October 1986 to February 1987. The overall response rate was 71 per cent, ranging from 64 per cent in Rochdale to 78 per cent in Aberdeen and Swindon.

The interview schedules focused particularly upon occupational structure, the distribution of jobs by gender, the introduction of new technologies, the use of workers with non-standard employment contracts, relations with trade unions, and product market position. Different questionnaires were used for large and small organizations, with fewer questions being asked of small organizations. There were also minor variations in the schedules for public and private organizations, and for different industries. The four industry subschedules were: (1) manufacturing, wholesale, haulage, extractive, agriculture; (2) retail/hotel, catering/personal, and other consumer services; (3) banks, financial and business services, and (4) construction. These were designed to provide functionally equivalent questions with respect to product market position for different types of organization.

In each locality, there were follow-up interviews in at least thirty establishments—the 30 Establishment Survey—designed in particular to explore the motivation behind particular types of employer policy. While steps were taken to ensure that cases were included across a range of different industries, the composition of the follow-up sample was not a random one, but reflected team research interests. In contrast to the other surveys, the data from this survey should not be assumed to be generalizable to the localities.

5. THE RELATED STUDIES

Finally, most teams also undertook at least one smaller-scale further enquiry in their localities, each being designed exclusively by the team itself and funded separately from the three main surveys. These Related Studies sometimes built upon previous fieldwork a team had undertaken in its locality, and upon the resulting network of research contacts. Adopting for the most part documentary, case-study, or open-ended interviewing techniques of enquiry, the Related Studies dealt with special issues ranging from local socio-economic history to present-day industrial relations trends.

In one sense, then, the Related Studies can be thought of as freestanding research projects. At the same time, however, in interpreting the findings from a related study, a team could take advantage of the extensive contextual data provided by the main surveys. What is more, thanks to their use of methodologies permitting enquiry in depth and over time, the Related Studies could throw more light on many of the quantitative (and at times somewhat summary) findings of the main surveys. Several Related Studies were of particular value in validating and extending core-survey findings.

BIBLIOGRAPHY

AGLIETTA, M. (1979), *A Theory of Capitalist Regulation*, London: New Left Books.

AITKIN, M., ANDERSON, D., FRANCIS, B., and HINDE, J. (1989), *Statistical Modelling in Glim*, Oxford: Clarendon Press.

ARGYRIS, C. (1959), 'Understanding human behaviour in organizations', in Haire, M. (ed.), *Modern Organization Theory*, New York: Wiley.

ARMSTRONG, P. (1982), 'If it's only women's work it doesn't matter so much', in West (1982*a*).

—— (1988), 'Labour and monopoly capital', in Hyman, R., and Streeck, W. (eds.), *New Technology and Industrial Relations*, Oxford: Blackwell.

ATKINSON, A. J. (1984), 'Emerging U.K. work patterns', in *Flexible Manning: The Way Ahead*, University of Sussex Institute for Manpower Studies, Report 88, Falmer, Sussex.

—— (1985*a*). 'Flexibility: Planning for an uncertain future', *Manpower Policy and Practice*, 1: 26–9.

—— (1985*b*), 'The changing corporation', in Clutterbuck, D. (ed.), *New Patterns of Work*, Aldershot, Hants: Gower Press.

—— (1988), 'Recent changes in the internal labour market structure of the UK', in Buitelaar, W. (ed.), *Technology and Work: Labour Studies in England, Germany and the Netherlands*, Aldershot, Hants: Avebury.

BAGGULEY, P. (1989), 'Post-Fordism: A critical analysis', University of Lancaster, Department of Sociology (mimeo).

BECKER, G. S. (1964), *Human Capital*, New York: National Bureau of Economic Research.

BEECHEY, V. (1982), 'The sexual division of labour and the labour process: A critical assessment of Braverman', in Wood (1982*a*).

BELL, D. (1974), *The Coming of Post-Industrial Society*, London: Heinemann.

—— (1976), *The Cultural Contradictions of Capitalism*, London: Heinemann.

BENZÉCRI, J.-P. *et al.* (1973), *Analyse des données*, vols. i and ii, Paris: Dunod.

BERG, I. (1970), *Education for Jobs: The Great Training Robbery*, New York: Praeger.

—— FREEDMAN, M., and FREEMAN, M., (1978), *Managers and Work Reform*, New York: Free Press.

BERGER, S., and PIORE, M. (1981), *Dualism and Discontinuity*, Cambridge: Cambridge University Press.

BETTIO, F. (1988), *The Sexual Division of Labour: The Italian Case*, Oxford: Clarendon Press.

BLACKBURN, R. M., and MANN, M. (1979), *The Working Class in the Labour Market*, Cambridge: Cambridge University Press.

BLAUG, M. (1972), *The Economics of Education*, Harmondsworth, Middl.: Penguin.

BLAUNER, R. (1964), *Alienation and Freedom: The Factory Worker and his Industry*, Chicago: University of Chicago Press.

BOSWORTH, D. L., and WILSON, R. A. (1989), *The British Productivity Miracle*, Coventry: University of Warwick Institute for Employment Research.

BOWLES, S. (1985), 'The production process in a competitive economy: Walrassian, neo-Hobbesian and Marxian models', *American Economic Review*, 75/1: 16–36.

BRAGG, C. (1987), 'The development of apprentice training in the contemporary Rochdale engineering industry' MA dissertation, University of Lancaster (Dept. of Sociology).

BRAVERMAN, H. (1974), *Labour and Monopoly Capital*, New York: Monthly Review Press.

BURAWOY, M. (1979), *Manufacturing Consent*, Chicago: University of Chicago Press.

CAMPBELL, A., and WARNER, M. (1988), 'Workplace relations, skills training and technological change at plant level', *Relations Industrielles*, 43: 115–30.

CARTER, R. (1987), *Rochdale Employer Network: First Quarterly Report*, Rochdale, Lancs.: Rochdale Training Association.

CENTRAL STATISTICAL OFFICE (1980), *Standard Industrial Classification*, 1980 revn., London: HMSO.

CHINOY, E. (1955), *Automobile Workers and the American Dream*, New York: Doubleday.

CLARK, J., MCLOUGHLIN, I., ROSE, H., and KING, R. (1988), *The Process of Technological Change: New Technology and Social Change in the Workplace*, Cambridge: Cambridge University Press.

COCKBURN, C. (1983), *Brothers: Male Dominance and Technical Change*, London: Pluto Press.

CORIAT, B. (1984), *La Robotique*, Paris: Éditions de la Découverte.

COYLE, A. (1982), 'Sex and skill in the organisation of the clothing industry', in West (1982*a*).

CRAIG, C., GARNSEY, E., and RUBERY, J. (1985), *Payment Structures and*

Smaller Firms: Women's Employment in Segmented Labour Markets, Research Paper 48, London: Department of Employment.

—— RUBERY, J., TARLING, R., and WILKINSON, F. (1982), *Labour Market Structure: Worker Organisation and Low Pay*, Cambridge: Cambridge University Press.

CROMPTON, R., and JONES, G. (1984), *White-Collar Proletariat*, London: Macmillan.

—— and SANDERSON, K. (1986), 'Credentials and careers: Some implications of the increase in professional qualifications among women', *Sociology*, 20/1: 25–42.

CROSS, M. (1985), *Towards the Flexible Craftsman*, London: Technical Change Centre.

CURRAN, M. (1988), 'Gender and recruitment: People and places in the labour market', *Work, Employment and Society*, 2/3: 335–51.

DAHRENDORF, R. (1959), *Class and Class Conflict in Industrial Society*, London: Routledge.

DANIEL, W. W. (1987), *Workplace Industrial Relations and Technical Change*, London: Pinter.

DEX, S. (1988), 'Gender and the labour market', in Gallie (1988*a*).

DOERINGER, P., and PIORE, M. J. (1971), *Internal Labor Markets and Manpower Analysis*, Lexington, Mass.: D. C. Heath.

DOSI, G. (1984), *Technical Change and Industrial Transformation*, London: Macmillan.

DUBIN, R. (1956), 'Industrial workers' worlds: A study of the "central life interest" of industrial workers', *Social Problems*, 3: 131–42.

—— (1958), *The World of Work*, Englewood Cliffs, NJ: Prentice-Hall.

EDWARDS, R.C. (1979), *Contested Terrain: The Transformation of the Workforce in the Twentieth Century*, New York: Basic Books.

—— REICH, M., and GORDON, D. M. (1975), *Internal Labour Markets and Manpower Analysis*, Lexington, Mass.: D. C. Heath.

ELIAS, P. (1988), 'Occupational mobility, family formation and part-time work', in Hunt, A. (ed.), *Women in Paid Work: Issues of Equality*, London: Macmillan.

—— (1989) 'A study of trends in part-time employment, 1971–86', University of Warwick Institute for Employment Studies.

ELGER, A. (1982), 'Braverman, capital accumulation and deskilling', in Wood (1982).

—— (1990), 'Technical innovation and work reorganisation in British manufacturing in the 1980s: Continuity, intensification or transformation', *Work, Employment and Society*, 4.2 (Special Supplement): 67–101.

Employment Gazette (1986), London: HMSO, Oct.

ETZIONI, A. (1975), *A Comparative Analysis of Complex Organizations*, 2nd edn., New York: Free Press.

FORM, W. (1973), 'The internal stratification of the working class', *American Sociological Review*, 38/6: 697–711.

—— (1985), *Divided We Stand: Working-Class Stratification in America*, Urbana: University of Illinois Press.

FOX, A. (1974), *Beyond Contract: Work, Power and Trust Relations*, London: Faber.

FRAZER, R. (ed.) (1968–9), *Work*, vols. i and ii, Harmondsworth, Mddx.: Penguin.

FREEMAN, C. (1988), 'Evolution, technology and institutions: A wider framework for economic analysis', in Dosi, G., Freeman, C., Nelson, R., Silverderg, G., and Soete, L. (eds.), *Technical Change and Economic Theory*, London: Pinter.

FRIEDMAN, A. (1977), *Industry and Labour*, London: Macmillan.

FUCHS, V. (1968), *The Service Economy*, New York: Basic Books.

FURNHAM, A. (1981), 'The Protestant work ethic and attitudes towards unemployment', *Journal of Occupational Psychology*, 55/2: 277–85.

GALLIE, D. (1978), *In Search of the New Working Class: Automation and Social Integration in the Capitalist Enterprise*, Cambridge: Cambridge University Press.

—— (ed.) (1988a), *Employment in Britain*, Oxford: Blackwell.

—— (1988b), *The Social Change and Economic Life Initiative: An Overview*, ESRC–SCELI Working Paper 1, Oxford: Nuffield College.

—— MARSH, C., and VOGLER, C. (eds.) (1984), *Social Change and the Experience of Unemployment*, Oxford: Oxford University Press.

—— —— —— (1994) *Social Change and the Experience of Unemployment*, Oxford: Oxford University Press.

—— PENN, R., and ROSE, M. (forthcoming): *Trade Unionism in Recession*, Oxford: Oxford University Press.

GERSHUNY, J. I. (1990), 'International comparisons of time use surveys: Methods and opportunities', in Schweizer, R. von, Ehling, E., and Schafer, D. (eds.), *Zeitbudgeterhebungen*, Stuttgart: Metzer-Poeschel.

GIDDENS, A. (1973), *The Class Structure of the Advanced Societies*, London: Hutchinson.

GILDER, G. (1982), *Wealth and Poverty*, London: Buchan & Enright.

GILMOUR, I. (1992), *Dancing with Dogma*, New York: Simon & Schuster.

GIORDANO, L. (1988), 'Beyond Taylorism: Computerisation and QWL Programmes in the Production Process', in Knights and Willmott (1987).

GOLDTHORPE, J. H. (1980), *Social Mobility and Class Structure in Modern Britain*, Oxford: Clarendon Press.

—— (1987), *Social Mobility and Class Structure in Modern Britain*, 2nd edn. Oxford: Clarendon Press.

GOLDTHORPE, J. H. LOCKWOOD, D., BECHHOFER, F., and PLATT, J. (1969), *The Affluent Worker: Industrial Attitudes and Behaviour*, Cambridge: Cambridge University Press.

GREENACRE, M. (1984), *Theory and Applications of Correspondence Analysis*, New York: Academic Press.

HACKMAN, J. R., and LAWLER, E. E. (1971), 'Employee reactions to job characteristics', *Journal of Applied Psychology*, 55/3: 259–86.

HAKIM, C. (1991), 'Grateful slaves and self-made women: Fact and fantasy in women's work orientations', *European Sociological Review*, 7/2: 101–21.

HARTMAN, G., NICHOLAS, I. J., SORGE, A., and WARNER, M. (1984), 'Consequences of CNC Technology: A study of British and West German manufacturing firms', in Warner (1984).

HAUGHTON, G. (1985), 'The dynamic of the Rochdale labour market', University of Lancaster, Department of Sociology, Working Paper 3.

HERZBERG, F. (1968), *Work and the Nature of Man*, St Albans: Staples Press.

HILL, S. (1981), *Competition and Control at Work*, London: Heinemann.

HINTON, J. (1973), *The First Shop-Stewards Movement*, London: Allen & Unwin.

HORRELL, S., RUBERY, J., and BURCHELL, B. (1989), 'Unequal jobs or unequal pay', *Industrial Relations Journal*, 20/3: 176–91.

—— —— —— (1990), 'Gender and skills', *Work, Employment and Society*, 4/2: 189–216. (Reprinted as Chapter 7 of this book.)

HULIN, C. L., and BLOOD, M. R. (1968), 'Job enlargement, individual differences, and worker responses', *Psychological Bulletin*, 69/1: 44–55.

Industrial Relations Review and Report (1990), 'Job evaluation and equal value: recent developments', 10 Jan., 455: 11–14.

INGLEHART, R. (1977), *The Silent Revolution: Changing Values and Political Styles amongst Western Publics*, Princeton, NJ: Princeton University Press.

JACQUES, E. (1967), *Equitable Payment*, London: Heinemann.

JONES, B. (1982), 'Destruction or redistribution of engineering skills? The case of numerical control', in Wood (1982).

—— and WOOD, S. (1984), 'Qualifications tacites, division du travail et nouvelles technologies', *Sociologie du Travail*, 24/4: 207–21.

JOSEPH, K. (1975), *Reversing the Trend: A Critical Appraisal of Conservatives Economic and Social Policies*, London and Chichester: Rose (with J. Sumption).

JOWELL, R., and WITHERSPOON, S. (eds.) (1984) *British Social Attitudes*, Aldershot, Hants: Gower.

—— —— (eds.) (1985) *British Social Attitudes*, Aldershot, Hants: Gower.

—— —— (eds.) (1986) *British Social Attitudes*, Aldershot, Hants: Gower.

—— —— (eds.) (1987) *British Social Attitudes*, Aldershot, Hants: Gower.

—— —— (eds.) (1988) *British Social Attitudes*, Aldershot, Hants: Gower.

KALLEBERG, A. L., and BERG, I. (1987), *Work and Industry: Structures, Markets and Processes*, London: Plenum Press.

KATZ, H., and SABEL, C. (1985), 'Industrial relations and industrial adjustment in the car industry', *Industrial Relations*, 24/3: 415–30.

KELLY, M. (1989), 'Alternative forms of work organisation under programmable automation', in Wood (1989).

KERN, H., and SCHUMANN, M. (1987), 'Limits of the division of labour', *Economic and Industrial Democracy*, 8/2: 151–70.

KERR, C., DUNLOP, J. T., HARBISON, F., and MYERS, C. A. (1960), *Industrialism and Industrial Man*, Cambridge, Mass.: Harvard University Press.

KNIGHTS, D., and WILLMOTT, H. (eds.) (1986a), *Gender and the Labour Process*, Aldershot, Hants: Gower.

—— —— (eds.) (1986b), *Managing the Labour Process*, Aldershot, Hants: Gower.

—— —— (eds.) (1987), *New Technology and the Labour Process*, London: Macmillan.

—— —— (eds.) (1990), *Labour Process Theory*, London: Macmillan.

—— —— and COLLINSON, D. (1985), *Job Redesign: Critical Perspectives on the Labour Process*, Aldershot, Hants: Gower.

KOCHAN, T. (ed.) (1985), *Challenges and Choices Facing American Labor*, Cambridge, Mass.: MIT Press.

LANE, C. (1988), 'New technology and clerical work', in Gallie (1988a).

LAWSON, N. (1992), *The View from No. 11*, London: Bantam Press.

LAZONICK, W. (1979), 'Industrial relations and technical change: The case of the self-acting mule', *Cambridge Journal of Economics*, 13/3: 231–62.

LEE, D. (1981), 'Skill, craft and class: A theoretical critique and critical case', *Sociology*, 15/1: 56–78.

—— (1982), 'Beyond deskilling: Skill, craft and class', in Wood (1982).

—— (1989), 'The transformation of work and the transformation of training in Britain', in Wood (1989).

LINDLEY, R. M., and WILSON, R. A. (1988), *Review of the Economy and Employment*, Coventry: University of Warwick Institute for Employment Research.

LIPIETZ, A. (1983), *L'Envoi inflationniste*, Paris: Maspero.

LITTLER, C. (1985), 'Taylorism, Fordism and job design', in Knights, Willmott, and Collinson (1985).

MACKENZIE, G. (1973), *The Aristocracy of Labour: The Position of*

Skilled Craftsmen in the American Class Structure, Cambridge: Cambridge University Press.

MANDEL, E. (1980), *Long Waves of Capitalist Development*, Cambridge: Cambridge University Press.

MANN, M. (1973), *Consciousness and Action amongst the Western Working Class*, London: Macmillan.

—— (1986), 'Work and the work ethic', in Jowell and Witherspoon (1986).

MANWARING, T. (1984), 'The extended internal labour market', *Cambridge Journal of Economics*, 8/2: 61–8.

—— and WOOD, S. (1985), 'The ghost in the labour process', in Knights, Willmott, and Collinson (1985).

MARSH, C. (1988), *Exploring Data*, Cambridge: Polity Press.

—— (1991) *Hours of Work of Women and Men in Britain*, Equal Opportunities Research Series Report, London: HMSO.

MARSHALL, G. (1982), *In Search of the Spirit of Capitalism*, London: Hutchinson.

—— NEWBY, H., ROSE, D., and VOGLER, C. (1988), *Social Class in Modern Britain*, London: Hutchinson.

MARTIN, R. (1988), 'Technological change and manual work', in Gallie (1988*a*).

MASSEY, D. (1984), *Spatial Divisions of Labour: Social Structures and the Geography of Production*, London: Macmillan.

MEANING OF WORKING INTERNATIONAL RESEARCH TEAM (MOW) (1987), *The Meaning of Working*, London: Academic Press.

MILLER, A. R., TREIMAN, D. J., CAIN, P. S., and ROOS, P. A. (1980), *Work, Jobs and Occupations: A Critical Review of the Dictionary of Occupational Titles*, Washington, DC: National Academy Press.

MONTGOMERY, D. (1976), 'Workers' control of machine production in the nineteenth century', *Labor History*, Fall.

MORE, C. (1980), *Skill and the English Working Class*, London: Croom Helm.

MURRAY, R. (1985), 'Benetton Britain: The New Economic Order', *Marxism Today*, Nov.: 28–32.

—— (1988), 'Life after Henry (Ford)', *Marxism Today*, Oct.: 8–13.

NICHOLS, W. A. T., and ARMSTRONG, P. (1976), *Workers Divided*, Glasgow: Fontana.

NOBLE, D. (1984), *The Forces of Production*, New York: Alfred Knopf.

NORTHCOTT, J., and ROGERS, P. (1984), *Micro-Electronics in British Industry: The Pattern of Change*, London: Policy Studies Institute.

NORUSIS, M. J. (1985), *SPSSX Advanced Statistics Guide*, New York: McGraw-Hill.

O'BRIEN, G. E. (1986), *Psychology of Work and Unemployment*, Chichester: Wiley.

—— (1992), 'Changing meanings of work', in Hartley, J. F., and Stephenson, G. M. (eds.), *Employment Relations*, Oxford: Blackwell.

OFFICE OF POPULATION CENSUSES AND SURVEYS [OPCS] (1980), *Classification of Occupations*, London: HMSO.

PAYNE, C. *et al.* (1987), *The GLIM 3.77 System*, Oxford: Numerical Algorithms Group.

PENN, R. D. (1982*a*), 'Skilled workers in the labour process', in Wood (1982).

—— (1982*b*), 'The Contested Terrain: A critique of Edwards' theory of working-class fractions and politics', in Day, G. (ed.), *Diversity and Decomposition in the Labour Market*, Aldershot, Hants: Gower.

—— (1983*a*), 'Trade union organisation and skill in the cotton and engineering industries in Britain, 1850–1960', *Social History*, 8/1: 37–53.

—— (1983*b*), 'Theories of skill and class structure', *Sociological Review*, 31/1: 22–36.

—— (1983*c*), 'The course of wage differential between skilled and non-skilled manual workers in Britain between 1856 and 1964', *British Journal of Industrial Relations*, 21/1: 69–90.

—— (1985), *Skilled Workers in the Class Structure*, Cambridge: Cambridge University Press.

—— (1988), 'Unemployment in six localities between 1923 and 1988', University of Lancaster, Department of Sociology, Social Change and Economic Life Initiative Working Paper 57.

—— (1989), 'Changing patterns of employment in Rochdale, 1981–1984', University of Lancaster, Department of Sociology, SCELI Working Paper 51.

—— (1990*a*), *Class, Power and Technology: Skilled Workers in Britain and America*, Cambridge: Polity.

—— (1990*b*), 'Skilled work at British Telecom', *New Technology, Work and Employment*, 5/2: 135–44.

—— (1992), 'Contemporary relationships between firms in a classic industrial locality: Evidence from the Social Change and Economic Life Initiative', *Work, Employment and Society*, 6/2: 209–27.

—— and DAWKINS, D. (1988), 'The development of skilled earnings differentials in the British Engineering Industry between 1962 and 1984', University of Lancaster, Department of Sociology, Social Change and Economic Life Initiative Working Paper 34.

—— and SCATTERGOOD, H. (1985), 'Deskilling or enskilling? An empirical investigation of recent theories of the labour process', *British Journal of Sociology*, 36/4: 611–30.

—— —— (1987), 'Corporate strategy and textile employment', University of Lancaster, Department of Sociology, Social Change and Economic Life Initiative Working Paper 12.

PENN, R. D. and SCATTERGOOD, H. (1991), 'Gender relations, technology and employment change in the contemporary textile industry', *Sociology*, 25/4: 569–87.

PHILLIPS, A., and TAYLOR, B. (1980), 'Sex and skill: Notes towards a feminist economics', *Feminist Review*, 6: 79–88.

PIORE, M., and SABEL, C. F. (1984), *The Second Industrial Divide: Possibilities for Prosperity*, New York: Basic Books.

POLLERT, A. (1988), 'The flexible firm: Fixation or fact?', *Work, Employment and Society*, 2/3: 281–316.

ROSE, M. (1985), *Reworking the Work Ethic: Economic Values in Socio-Cultural Politics*, London: Batsford Academic.

—— (1988a), 'Attachment to work and social values', in Gallie (1988a).

——(1988b), *Industrial Behaviour: Research and Control*, Harmondsworth, Mddx.: Penguin.

ROUTH, G. (1987), *Occupations of the People of Great Britain*, London: Macmillan.

RUBERY, J. (1978), 'Structured labour markets, worker organisation and low pay', *Cambridge Journal of Economics*, 2/1: 17–36.

—— and WILKINSON, F. (eds.) (1994), *Employer Strategy and the Labour Market*, Oxford: Oxford University Press.

RUNCIMAN, W. G. (1990), 'How many classes are there in British society?', *Sociology*, 24/4: 377–96.

SADLER, J. (1970), 'Sociological aspects of skill', *British Journal of Industrial Relations*, 1/1: 22–31.

SAYLES, L. R. (1958), *The Behavior of Industrial Work Groups: Prediction and Control*, New York: Wiley.

SCOTT, A. MACEWEN (ed.) (1994), *Gender Segregation and Social Change: Men and Women in Changing Labour Markets*, Oxford: Oxford University Press.

SCOTT, J. (1974), *The Glassworkers of Carmaux*, Cambridge: Cambridge University Press.

SELDON, A. (1990), *Capitalism*, Oxford: Blackwell.

SENKER, P., SWORDS-ISHERWOOD, N., BRADY, T., and HUGGETT, C. (1981), *Maintenance Skills in the Engineering Industry: The Influence of Technological Change*, London: Engineering Industry Training Board.

SHEPPARD, H. L., and HERRICK, N. Q. (1972), *Where Have All the Robots Gone? Workers' Dissatisfaction in the 1970s*, New York: Free Press.

SORGE, A., and WARNER, M. (1986), *Comparative Factory Organization*, Aldershot, Hants: Gower.

SPENNER, K. I. (1983), 'Deciphering Prometheus: Temporal change in the skill level of work', *American Sociological Review*, 48: 824–37.

STEIN, M. B. (1978), 'The meaning of skill: The case of the French engine-drivers, 1837–1917', *Politics and Society*, 8/3–4: 399–428.

STIEBER, J. (1959), *The Steel Industry Wage Structure*, Cambridge, Mass.: Harvard University Press.

STURDY, A. J. (1990), 'Clerical consent: An analysis of social relations in insurance work', Ph.D. thesis, UMIST, Manchester (Manchester School of Management).

—— KNIGHTS, D., and WILLMOTT, H. (1992), *Skill and Consent*, London: Routledge.

TERKEL, S. (1975), *Working*, London: Wildwood House.

THOMPSON, P. (1983), *The Nature of Work*, London: Macmillan.

—— (1989), *The Nature of Work*, 2nd edn., London, Macmillan.

TOURAINE, A. (1955) *La Conscience ouvrière*, Paris: Seuil.

—— (1971), *The Post-Industrial Society*, New York: Random House.

TRIST, E. L. (1981), *The Evolution of Socio-Technical Systems*, Toronto: Ministry of Labour.

—— HIGGIN, G. W., MURRAY, H., and POLLOCK, A. B. (1963), *Organizational Choice*, London: Tavistock.

TURNER, A. N., and LAWRENCE, P. R. (1965), *Industrial Jobs and the Workers*, Cambridge, Mass.: Harvard University Press.

TURNER, H. A. (1962), *Trade Union Growth, Structure and Policy*, London: Allen & Unwin.

TVERSKY, A., and KHANEMAN, D. (1973), 'Availability', *Cognitive Psychology*, 5/2: 207–32.

US CONGRESS, OFFICE OF TECHNOLOGY ASSESSMENT (1987), *The US Textile and Apparel Industry*, Washington, DC: US Government Printing Office, OTA-TET-332.

US DEPARTMENT OF LABOR (1949, rev. 1967 and 1977), *Dictionary of Occupational Titles*, Washington, DC: US Government Printing Office.

WAINWRIGHT, J., and FRANCIS, A. (1984), *Office Automation: Organisation and the Nature of Work*, Aldershot, Hants: Gower.

WALBY, S. (1986), *Patriarchy at Work*, Cambridge: Polity Press.

WALKER, C. R., and GUEST, R. (1952), *The Man on the Assembly-Line*, Cambridge, Mass.: Harvard University Press.

WARNER, M. (1984), *Microprocessors, Manpower and Society*, Aldershot, Hants: Gower.

WARR, P. (1982), 'A national study of non-financial employment commitment', *Journal of Occupational Psychology*, 55: 11–121.

—— (1985), 'Twelve questions about unemployment and health', in Roberts, B., Gallie, D., and Finnegan, R. (eds.), *New Approaches to Economic Life,* Manchester: Manchester University Press.

WEBER, M. (1968), *Economy and Society*, vols. i–iii, ed. G. Roth and C. Wittich, New York: Bedminster Press.

WEBSTER, J. (1986), 'Word processing and the secretarial labour process', in Allen, S., Purcell, K., Waton, S. and Wood, S. (eds.), *The Changing Experience of Employment*, London: Macmillan.

WEDDERBURN, D., and CROMPTON, R. (1972), *Workers' Attitudes and Technology*, Cambridge: Cambridge University Press.

WEST, J. (ed.) (1982*a*), *Work, Women and the Labour Market*, London: Routledge.

—— (1982*b*), 'New technology and women's office work' in West (1982*a*).

—— (1990), 'Gender and the labour process: A reassessment', in Knights and Willmott (1990).

WILKINSON, F. (1981), *The Dynamics of Labour Market Segmentation*, London: Academic Press.

WILSON, F. (1988), 'Computer numerical control and constraints', in Knights and Willmott (1987).

—— and BUCHANAN, D. (1988), 'The effect of new technology in the engineering industry: Cases of control and constraint', *Work, Employment and Society*, 2/3: 366–80.

WILSON, R. A. (1989), *Review of the Economy and Employment, 1988–89*, i, Coventry: University of Warwick Institute for Employment Research.

—— (1990), *Review of the Economy and Employment, 1990*, Coventry: University of Warwick Institute for Employment Research.

WOOD, S. (ed.) (1982), *The Degradation of Work? Skill, Deskilling and the Labour Process*, London: Hutchinson.

—— (ed.) (1989), *The Transformation of Work*, London: Unwin Hyman.

WOODWARD, J. (1958), *Management and Technology*, London: HMSO.

YANKELOVITCH, D., NOELLE-NEUMANN, E., and SHANKS, M. (1983), *Work and Human Values: An International Report on Jobs in the 1980s and 1990s*, New York: Aspen Institute for Humanistic Studies.

—— ZETTERBERG, H., STRUMPEL, B., and SHANKS, M. (1985), *A World at Work*, New York: Octagon Books.

ZIMBALAST, A. (ed.) (1979) *Case Studies on the Labor Process*, London: Monthly Review Press.

INDEX

Aberdeen:
  automation in 143–9
  locality 43, 130–2
  SCELI team 14, 130, 140
  travel to work area 33 n.
ability:
  criterion of skill 224, 227–8, 234–5,
    240
  own managers' 252–3
  required in job 159
actor (social):
  approach to skill 15–31
  definition of skilled job 20–2, 222–41
  perception of skills 98–100
AEU, see Amalgamated Engineering
  Union
Affluent Worker study 7, 284–5
affluent workers 27
age, most skilled job and 98–100
Aglietta, M. 133
Aitken, M. 231
A-level qualifications 195–6, 231, 303–4
alienation in work 166, 225, 284, 299
Amalgmated Engineering Union 126
  for job content 169–70
  gender effect 197
  skill index in 210–11
  working-time and 205
  use by Cambridge team 221
ANOVA, see 'Analysis of variance'
apprenticeship 118, 122–6
  criterion of skill 224, 226–7, 231,
    240
Argyris, C. 283
Armstrong, Peter 3, 107, 133, 189
assembly line work 26
Atkinson, A. J. 77
attributes (job holders') 159–60
authority aspect of job 249, 257–9
automation 109
  effects on skill 134
  impact of 77

in Aberdeen locality 143–9
in Rochdale locality 143–9
skill and 62–4
autonomy (at work), see 'discretion'
'availability' bias 180

Babbage, C. 161, 162
Bagguley, P. 133
balance of job satisfaction 251–5
bargained skill 34 n.
Baseline Employers survey 336, 342–5
Bath team 274
Beechey, V. 164
Bell, D. 27, 56, 109, 285–6, 292
Benzecri, J.-P. 237
Berg, I. 22, 24, 250, 292
Berger, S. x, 43
Bettio, F. 190, 201
Blackburn, R. M. 166, 208, 224, 285,
  298
Blaug, M. 245, 306
Blauner, Robert 13, 41, 77, 225, 283,
  299, 301
Blood, M. R. 27
Bosworth, D. L. 106
Bowles, S. 162
Bragg, C. 122
Braverman, Harry 1, 3, 13–14, 41, 56,
  62, 107–9, 111, 122, 154–5, 162,
  164–5, 191, 205, 207, 223, 246, 285
  see also degradation; deskilling
British Journal of Sociology vii
British Springs company 112
British Telecom plc 141, 145, 149, 152
British Vita company 112
Buchanan, D. 134
Burawoy, M. 15
Burchell, B. 15, 16, 18, 73

CAD, see computer aided design
CADAM, see computer aided design
  and manufacture

Cambridge team 9, 17, 15–16, 21–3, 106, 274–9, 298, 302, 313
  see also Northampton: index of skill 279–80; related study for SCELI 166–7
careers 24, 28, 290, 320, 323, 333
career mobility (skill in) 55
Carter, R. 123, 132
case-studies of skill 345
  Aberdeen 154–5
  limitations 62, 127, 154–5, 190
  Rochdale 119–22
catering sector 77
Census of Employment 148
  for 1984 169, 344
  for 1987 169
central life-interest 28, 281
  see also careers
challenge in job-tasks 282
child-care provision 28
children's effect on job-choice 89–97
Chinoy, Eli 284
Clark, Jon, (and colleagues) 1, 11, 24, 34 n., 62, 246
Classification of Occupations and Dictionary of Occupational Titles (CODOT) 79, 83, 245
class scheme (Goldthrope) 44
  see also social class
clerical workers 44, 315–18
clients (contact with) 199
CNC, *see* computer numeric control
Cockburn, C. 1, 3, 24, 34 n., 246
cohort analysis 86–7
commitment to work, *see* work ethic
compensation theory 13–14, 110–11, 128, 134
  revised 140, 155
'complex' occupations 10, 78–9, 82–5
components of skill 183–8, 198–204
computer:
  in British Telecom 151–2
  equipment 301
  impact on employee skills 62–4
  occupations 80
  in office 134–5, 143–9, 155
  technical change and 109
  women and 68–9
  work attitudes and 301
Computer Aided Design (CAD) 113–14, 142
Computer Numeric Conrol (CNC) 113–14, 142

Computer Aided Design and Manufacturing (CADAM) 118
control:
  over work 2, 299
  strategies 42
  system and skill 207
  see also management
core versus peripheral activities 77
Courtaulds Textiles, plc 112
Coriat, B. 133
Coventry locality 43, 63, 91–2
Coyle, A. 189
craft:
  criterion of skill 47
  debate on 107
  model of skill 164
  occupations (declining) 80
  see also skill
craftsmen (militant) 107
Craig, Christine 3, 166, 181, 189–90
credentialism 22, 279
Crompton, Rosemary 1, 41, 133, 166, 189, 219, 224, 285
Cross, M. 108
culture of dependency 35 n., 287–8
Curran, M. 189, 198

Dahrendorf, R. 107
Daniel, W. W. 62, 65, 108
data on skill 4–5, 276–80
Davies, R. 106, 112
Dawkins, D. 112
degradation of skill 54
  hypothesis 1–2, 6, 163, 285
  see also deskilling
Department of Employment 344
dependency culture 35 n., 287–9
deskilling:
  debate 1, 56–8, 285–7
  elements of 164–5
  hypotheses 83, 133, 140, 191
  in textile industry 121
  job control and 160–7
  limits to 154, 212
  possibly overstated 212
  resistance to 164
  specialization and 161–2
  subjective views 99–100
  the 'internal' view 98
  thesis disconfirmed 154–5
  work control and 208
  see also Braverman
Dex, S. 66

Dictionary of Occupational Titles (DOT) (United States) 245
discretion in work 16, 163–4, 204–8, 254–5
  different views 170
  disparate estimates of 177–8
  managers' view 175–6
dissonance in skill perceptions 175–7
division of labour:
  main changes 1–3, 79–81, 110
  marxist theory and 162
  technical change and 130
distribution of skills 41
Doehringer, P. 43
domestic skills 21
  see also tacit skills
Dosi, G. 156 n.
downward social mobility 51–7
Dubin, R. 28, 281, 285

Economic and Social Research council v, 1
economic calculation 29
economic individualism 29, 272, 294–5, 313–22
Edwards, R. 43
effort and skill 36 n.
electronic point of sales (EPOS) technology 146
Elger, T. 33 n., 35 n., 107
Elias, P. 9, 18, 20, 23, 75, 78, 87, 131, 148, 160, 245, 257, 260, 278
Elliott, Jane 15, 16
employee attitudes (ambiguity in) 166, 242–8, 272–4
Employer Baseline survey 167, 342–5
employer strategies 32 n.
Employers' 30 Establishment survey 342–5
engineering:
  crafts 13
  enskilling in 121
  industry trends 6, 107–8
  Rochdale and 111–17
enskilling 110, 133
enterprise culture 35 n., 288, 322
EPOS, *see* electronic point of sales
equal value rules 181
esteem for paid work 290–1
ethnicity of Rochdale sample 225, 228
Etzioni, A. 27
Evaluation of jobs 159–60
'experience effects', 78–101

experience criterion of skill 224, 234, 240
'external' view of occupational change 78–9
expressive work ethic 270–3, 285
expressive rationale of working 293
extrinsic job factors 26
extrinsic job satisfaction 249, 255–7

factor analysis 276–80, 308
family formation (ocupation and) 88–97
Farrel Bridge company 112
females (in 'complex' jobs) 83–8
  see also women
'feminized' workplaces 69
findings of research:
  consistency 7
  limits 8–9
flexibility debate 1, 4, 35 n., 148–9
Fordism 2, 27, 283–4, 299
Form, W. 107
Fox, A. 163–4, 283, 292, 299
fragmented work strikes 27
Francis, B. 20, 21, 22, 48, 62, 78, 106, 123
Frazer, R. 166
Freeman, C. 132, 136, 154
Friedman, A. 164, 299
Fuchs, V. 109
Furnham, A. 293

Gallie, D. 5, 8, 9, 18, 23, 65, 108, 131, 260, 284, 292, 301, 321
Garnsey, E. 3
gender:
  job satisfaction and 260–5
  segregation in labour market 32 n., 189–92
  skill and 18–20, 65–73, 100–4, 189–209, 260–5
  occupational change and 83–5
  see also women
'General Educational Development' dimension 276
general job satisfaction 259–60
Gershuny, J. 342
Giddens, Anthony 107
Gilmour, Sir Ian 27
Giordano, L. 65
GLIM software 230–1
Goldthorpe, J. H. 7, 27, 44, 107, 224, 275, 284, 292, 299

Goldthorpe class schema 44, 51, 316–22
'grateful slaves' 26, 271
Greenacre, M. 237
Guest, R. 299

Hackman, J. R. 166
Hakin, C. 26, 260, 271, 289
Hartman, G. 65
Haughton, G. 132
HCS, *see* Household and Community survey
Herrick, N. Q. 27, 283
Herzberg, F. 249
high discretion job profile 163–4
Higher National Certificate 303
Hinton, J. 107
HNC, *see* Higher National Certificate
Horrell, Sara 18, 73, 166, 211, 220, 260
hours worked (satisfaction with) 256
Household and Community survey v, 270, 336, 339–42
hotel industry 77
Hulin, C. L. 27
human capital theory 29, 109, 154, 245
Human Relations in Industry movement 275
Human Resources Management theories 133

IDEAS software 106
ideologies of paid work 293–97
income, impact on demand for skills 77
index of skill 192–8, 208–11
Industrial Relations Review and Report 181
information (for job defnition) 16
information (on skill used) 17
information technologies 770
see also computer; automation
Inglehart, R. 285–6, 292
instrumentalism 299–300
internal labour market debate 198
international skill changes 110
intrinsic job factors 24
intrinsic job satisfaction 249, 254–5

Jacques, E. 163, 180
Jacques, M. 35 n.
jobbing work 113
job categories in feminist critique 191

job content:
  determining 160
  problem evaluating 159–60
  relative importance of parts 170–2
  scales of 169
  status effects 189
job losses 137, 140
job satisfaction 24–6
  bias problem 250–1
  gender and 260–5
  general model of skill and 265–72
  individual variables 265–72
  job security and 256
  overall 259–60
  part-timers' 26, 260–5
  in SCELI sample 252–60
  sociological work on 244
  types 249–50
  work ethic and 270–3
  workplace variables 265–72
Job-skill 22, 24, 138, 283
  defined 246
  effect on job satisfaction 251, 265–72
  part-timers' 260–5
  status and 189
  work ethic and 297–305
job segregation (by gender) 189–92
job stereotyping 181
Jones, Bryn 1, 13, 22, 65, 132
Jones, G. 41, 133, 189
Joseph, Sir Keith 287
Jowell, R. 289, 322

Kahneman, D. 180
Kallenberg, A. L. 24
Kelly, J. 65
Kern, H. 107
Kerr, C. (and colleagues) 41
King, R. 34 n.
Kirkaldy locality 43, 44, 62
Kish grid sampling 192, 338
Knights, David (and colleagues) 1, 3, 15, 109
Kochan, T. 133

Labor and Monopoly Capital 107, 109
labour aristocracy 107
labour economics, skill in 223
Labour Process Conference 109
labour process debate 15, 162
labour market ideology 27–9
Lancaster team 11–14, 20–3, 107–29, 130–55, 142, 224–43, 274

Lane, C. 62, 133
Lawler, E. E. 166
Lawrence, P. R. 166
Lawson, Nigel (Lord) 35 n., 287, 322
Lazonick, W. 162
learning time, *see* training
Lee, D. 31, 298
Liepietz, A. 133
life and work histories 339
life-cycle:
    effect on job skill 99
    mobility over 87–8
Lindley, R. M. 101
Littler, C. 299
logic of capitalism 109–11
logistic regression analysis 229–31
'lottery question' 289–90
low discretion syndrome 163, 179
Luton 'affluent worker' team 299
    see also Goldthorpe, J. H.

machinery manufacturing 113
Mackenzie, G. 107
McLoughlin, I. 34 n.
maintenance of equipment 114–16
male breadwinner role 28
male (in 'complex' jobs) 83–8
management:
    appropriation of skill 162
    authoritarian 41
    choice in technical change 154
    employee satisfaction with 252–9
    of human resources 133
    perceptions of skill 15–18
    reformers 27
    strategies 17
    unfamiliarity with jobs 180
    work ethic in 30, 310–11
Mann, M. 166, 208, 224, 285, 289,
    292, 298
manufacturing:
    decline of 80, 83
    of machines 113
    skill increases in 59
    of springs 113
Manwaring, T. 165, 198
market environment of job 160
Marsh, C. 182, 260, 292
Marshall, G. 44, 293
Martin, C. 111, 112, 117, 143
Martin, R. 62, 134, 155, 223
Marx, K. 162, 299
Marx 299

Marxist theory:
    deskilling in 109
    of division of labour 162
Mass production 2
    see also Fordism
Meaning of Working enquiry 281, 285
measurement:
    of job content 159–60
    of job satisfaction 260
    of longitudinal change in skill 78
    of skill 47–8, 160–1, 276–80
    of work values 325–35
Median Polish method 177–9
method, in Northampton related study
    167–8
microelectronics 116, 154
    in Aberdeen 136–7
    in Rochdale 136–7
    training for 124–8
    see also computer
militant craftsman theories 107
Miller, A. R. 274
misclassification of occupations 80
mismatching of skill 23, 246–9
modeling:
    actor definitions of skill 232–6
    skill and job satisfaction 265–72
Montgomery, D. 107
moral involvement in work
    see work ethic
More, C. 223
'most skilled job' judgements 79
MOW, *see* Meaning of Working
    enquiry
Murray, R. 133

nature of post-industrial work 77
neo-marxist view of skill 107–8, 128
neo-Weberian account of skill 107–8
New Right and work 287–8, 319
Noble, D. 133
non-manual occupations (growth) 41
non-skilled workers 51
normative work commitment 29,
    289–92
    see also Work Ethic
Northampton 16, 43, 202, 274
    team specific studies in 161–222
    labour market 168
    travel to work area 168–9
    see also Cambridge team
Northcott, J. 108
Norusis, M. J. 276

'objectivity' in job evaluation 160
O'Brien, G. 27, 179, 244, 289
occupations:
  classification of 44
  compensation theory and 110
  economic individualism and 29
  gender segregation by 66
  problems with scales of 193–6
  structure in Rochdale sample 225
  targeted 22, 236–41
  work ethic and 315–22
OD, *see* Organizational Design movement
office automation 42, 143–9, 155
  see also microelectronics
office-work skills 134–5
official standards (and skill) 202
oil industry 131–2, 284
O-level qualifications 48–9, 68, 195–6
ONC, *see* Ordinary National Certificate
on-job experience 72
operationalizing 'skill' 161
optimist scenario 41, 45, 75
Ordinary National Certificate
Organizational Design (OD) movement 283
organizing ability 16, 170, 172–5, 198–204
orientations to work 26–7, 285
'overqualification' 62, 247–52
Own-skill 22, 24
  defined 246
  effect on job satisfaction 251
  in a general model 265–72
  part-timers' 260–5
  work ethic and 305–6

part time work 15, 18–19
  concentration of 193–6
  job satisfaction and 260–5
  'marginality' of 220
  pay in 166
  skill change and 72–4
  self-rated skill of 216
  work ethic and 26, 28, 312–13
pay:
  incentives 207
  satisfaction with 255–7
  of women 189–92
Payne, C. 230
Penn, Roger 5, 13, 20, 21, 22, 48, 107,

108, 110, 111, 112, 117, 119, 123, 132, 135, 143, 145, 148, 160, 162, 223
perception of jobs 160–1, 166, 181
persistence in labour market 287–8
personal skill, *see* own-skill
pessimist scenario (for skill) 45, 56, 75
peripheral employment 4
Phillips, A. 3, 223
Piore, Michael 3, 133
polarization of skills 42, 56, 75, 322
Policy Studies Institute (PSI) 344
policy and labour market 281–2
Pollert, A. 1
'polyvalence' (task versatility) 3
postal survey in Rochdale 111, 119
post-fordism 133
post-industrialism 27, 109, 286, 323
post-material values and work 286–7
Prandy classification scheme 44
primary labour market 42–3
professional standards 202
professionals' work ethic 310–11
promotion opportunities 255–7
Protestantism and work 282, 293
provisioning rationale of work 285, 293
PSI; *see* Policy Studies Institute
'psychology of entitlement' 287–8
Public Attitude Surveys Ltd. vii, 336

qualifications 21
  criterion of skill 224, 226–7, 231, 233–4, 240
  level of women's 211
  need for 195–6
  public service employees' 62
  work attitudes and 303–4
Quality Working Life (QWL) movement 27, 283, 285
questionnaires in skill debate 108
question reliability 160–1
QWL, *see* Quality Working Life movement

rationale of paid work 292–3
Registrar General 44, 45
  see also social class
regression techniques 229–31
re-interviewing of respondents 217
Related Studies (in SCELI) 4
relations with supervision 257–9
Renold company 112
reproduction of skill 122–6

research styles, contrasted 108
resistance to deskilling 107, 164
response-rates in SCELI surveys 338,
  340, 344
responsibility 201–4
  automation and 65
  of current job 48–9
  for handling resources 16, 165–7
retest of questions 19, 160–1
'revolt against work' movement 283
robots 113
  see also computer, microelectronics
Rochdale related study 12–14
Rochdale 43, 274
  apprenticeship in 118
  automation in 63, 143–9
  case-studies in 119–22
  declining engineering industry 116
  employment patterns 108
  microelectronics in 117
  postal survey 111, 119
  sample 20
  skill status in 119–20
  skilled workers in 119–22
  subcontracting in 112
  team-specific questions for 223
  textile industry 117–19
  trade unions 32 n.
  training in 122–6
Rochdale Training Association 123
'rodent operative syndrome' 17, 179
Rogers, P. 108
Rose, Michael 5, 17, 22, 24, 26, 34 n.,
  106, 138, 223, 281, 282, 285, 324 n.
Routh, G. 44
Rubery, Jill 5, 15, 16, 18, 73

Sabel, C. F. 3, 133, 298
'Samuel Smiles' work values 27
Sanderson, K. 219
Sayles, R. L. 34 n., 123, 283
scales:
  job content 169
  occupational 193
Scattergood, Hilda 13, 110, 111, 112,
  117, 143
Schumann, H. 107
Scientific Management movement 17,
  41, 299
scientific knowledge 109–10
scores:
  for skill perceptions 183–7
  skill matching 247–9

work ethic 308–10
Scott, A. 5
Scott, J. 107
screening processes 22
secondary economic work rationale
  26, 27–3, 293
secondary labour market 42–3
Seldon, A. 287
self-help values 27–9
self-actualization and skill 285–6, 292–3
self-defined skill 297–8
self-reliance in labour market 288
Senker, P. 13
service class 44–5, 57, 59, 315–23
service culture 322
sex, *see* gender
Sheppard, H. L. 27, 283
SIC, *see* Standard Industrial
  Classification
'simple' occupations 78–9, 82–5
skill:
  ability criterion of 224, 227, 234–5,
    240
  apprenticeship and 224, 226–7, 231,
    240
  assembly line and 207
  'Cambridge' index of 192–8, 208–11
  career break and 10
  caring 189–90
  case-studies 6
  class and 47
  comparisons 192–8
  compensation theory 11–14
  components 191–2, 198–204
  control elements in 299
  craftsman model 164
  decreases 50–1
  deficits in manufacturing 59
  discretionary 204–8
  distributions 50
  effect of automation and computers 8
  experience and 224, 227, 234, 240
  gender debate and 1
  in handling clients 199
  hours worked and 219–20
  increases 50–1
  individualism and 313–14
  job satisfaction and 265–72
  labour economics and 223
  levels 193–8
  measurement problems 244–6
  modeling actor definitions 232–6
  neo-marxist interpretation 128

skill (*cont.*):
  new jobs 8
  official standards 202, 276
  operational limits to 161
  organizational 198–204
  pay and 166, 189–92, 207
  perceptions 8, 15–23, 213–20, 235–9
  polarization 10, 41–76, 322
  professional standards and 202
  qualifications and 224–7, 231, 233–4, 240, 303–4
  responsibility and 201–4
  social cues of 178–9
  socially defined 190, 298
  social 198–204
  sociological approach to 223
  status, defining 119–20
  stereotyping of 178–80
  subjective aspects 98–100
  system of control and 207
  in targeted occupations 236–9, 241
  of task 34 n.
  technical change and 149–53
  training and 224, 227, 322
  trust and 299
  under-rating of 216–19
  versatility ('polyvalence') 3
  women's 189–222, 212–13, 261–2
  work ethic and 297–306
  work experience effects 88–100, 245–6
  see also deskilling; social skills; tacit skill
'skill-distance' effects 99–100
skill enquiries in SCELI research (structure) 6
Skilled Worker Project (Lancaster University) 110
skilled workers 'survival' 128
skilling 109, 133
  see also enskilling
Smith, Adam 3, 161, 162
social class:
  fathers 49–50
  Goldthorpe 316–22
  Registrar General's 83, 193
social definition of skill 190
social environment of job 160
social history, technical change and 107
social psychology of work attitudes 282–3
social skills 16, 198–204, 298
  growing importance 180–1
  in low-skill jobs 172–5

social cues for 178–9
  work ethic and 302
  see also tacit skill
Sorge, A. 13
Southampton studies of skill 34 n.
  see also Clark, Jon
specialization and deskilling 161–2
Specific Vocational Preparation (US Department of Labor) 276
Spenner, K. I. 24, 225–6, 274
Standard Industrial Classification (SIC) 169
Stein, M. B. 107
stereotyped skills 178–9
Stieber, J. 182, 201
Sturdy, A. J. 15
styles of management 283
subcontracting 112
subjectivity:
  in definitions of skill 19
  in experience skill 51–4
  in perception of jobs 160
  in questionnaire responses 191
supervision, change in 149
  see also management
surveys of skill trends (limitations) 11
Swindon 43, 274
  team-specific questions in 36 n.
  trade unions 32 n.
  travel to work area 33 n.

tacit skills 11, 21, 28, 73, 165, 279, 313
T&N plc 112
targeted occupational groups 29, 236–9, 241, 315–22
Tavistock Institute of Human Relations 283
Taylor, F. W. 3, 41, 162, 223, 299
TBA Industrial Products company 118
team-specific questions 33–4 n., 183–6, 223
technical basis of skill 21–2, 213–19, 226–36
technical change 62–5
  division of labour and 130
  measure of occupational change 80
  polarization following 75
  skill in 149–53
  social history and 107
  theories of 109–11
  training and 139
technological implications approach to skill 301

technology, work attitudes and 284–6
technical environment of jobs 160
telephone survey of employers 136, 342–5
Terkel, Studs 166
textile industry 107–8, 117–19
Thatcher government policies 27, 287–8, 322–3
theories of skill change:
  enskilling 133
  human capital 29, 109, 154, 245
  human resources management 133
  post-Fordist 133
  post-industrial 286–7
  skills compensation 110–11, 155
  technical change 133–6
  trust relations (Fox) 163–4
  see also deskilling
Thompson, Paul 1, 132, 299
time-budgets survey 340–2
Touraine, Alain 285–6
Trade Unionism in Recession 32 n.
training 21, 122–6
  as criterion of skill 224, 227
  effort 322
  present job 196
  provision 30, 36–7 n.
  for technical change 139
  times 196
  versus 'experience effects' 78–9
Travel to work areas 33 n., 168–9, 338
Trist, E. L. 27, 283
trust relations at work 163, 299
Turner, A. N. 166, 223
Turner 223
Tversky, A. 180

under-qualification for jobs 24, 246–9
under-utilization of skills 24, 246–9
underrating of skill 189–90, 216–19
unemployment 96–7, 131–5
Ure, A. 162
US Department of Labor 274, 276
using initiative in job 252–3

validity of skill measures 277–8
Vogler, C. 221, 292

Wainwright, J. 62
Walby, S. 3
Walker, C. R. 299
Warner, Malcolm 1, 13
Warr, Peter 289
Weber, Max 107, 282, 293

Webster, J. 62
Wedderburn, D. 166, 224, 285
welfare state 295–6
West, J. 1, 62
White, Michael 342
Wilkinson, Frank 1, 5, 15, 16
Willmott, Hugh 3, 15, 109
Wilson, F. 62, 101, 133
Wilson, R. A. 77
Witherspoon, S. 289, 322
Women in Employment survey 87–8
women:
  in 'complex' jobs 83–8
  downward job mobility 98
  jobs skill elements 198–204
  part-timers seen as 'grateful slaves' 26, 271
  pay inequality 189–92
  polarization of work and 104
  previous research on skills 1–3
  in professional and technical jobs 85
  skill deficits amongst 66
  storng work ethic of 320–3
  work histories of 87–8
  work satisfaction of 260–5
Wood, S. 1, 22, 62, 164, 165, 283, 285
Woodward, J. 283
Work Attitudes/Histories survey 4–7, 32–6 n., 246, 288–97, 336–9
Work, Employment and Society vii
'workaholism' 36 n., 293
work:
  as 'central life interest' 281
  commitment 27–28
  effectiveness 275
  effort 30–1, 35–6 n.
  environment of 82–3
  experience effects 78–9, 245, 278
  job satisfaction and 254
  technology and attitudes towards 284–6
work ethic 27–30, 281–335
  job satisfaction and 270–3
  main aspects 288–97
  modeling skill and 308–15
  post-material values and 286–7
work histories from SCELI (Elias' use) 9–10
workplace size effect 97, 265–70

Yankelovitch, D. 285, 292

Zimbalast, A. 1